## Early Praise for
# Freedom from Mid-East Oil

### Deepak Chopra, President of the Alliance for a New Humanity

"We owe Jerry Brown, Rinaldo Brutoco, and James Cusumano a huge debt for writing *Freedom from Mid-East Oil*. If we follow the very practical ideas in this book, we can quickly move beyond our oil addiction which poses a great threat to the world in the 21st century. However, this book goes beyond that. Oil addiction, global warming, ecological devastation, social injustice, extreme ecological disparities, racial poverty, war and terrorism, and Hurricane Katrina, are all interdependent and linked to each other. The practical steps offered in this book could literally save our world."

### Amory B. Lovins, Chairman and Chief Scientist of Rocky Mountain Institute and World Business Academy Fellow

"This stimulating synthesis provides a roadmap for solving the oil and climate problems simultaneously. The World Business Academy's Prometheus Plan in *Freedom from Mid-East Oil* exemplifies the business leadership necessary to begin the profitable transition beyond oil."

### Hazel Henderson, author, *ETHICAL MARKETS: Growing the Green Economy*

"I welcome *Freedom from Mid-East Oil* as a practical way to boost U.S. security and help grow our green economy—all based on existing technologies. Instead of continuing to fund terrorism by relying on Middle East oil, we can invest in all the viable, homegrown U.S. sources: solar, wind, efficient biofuels, geothermal, ocean energy and proven efficiency technologies. The bargain of the century! This Plan can help create millions of new jobs in the "sustainability sectors" of our economy, and boost our exports as well."

**Robert D. Wagner, Jr., Veteran senior banker to the oil and gas businesses of Texas and former President of The Petroleum Club of Houston.**

*"Freedom from Mid-East Oil,* by Jerry Brown, Rinaldo Brutoco, and James Cusumano of the World Business Academy, is the kind of rigorous analysis of our energy future that is desperately needed in the dialogue about initiatives and options that is beginning to consume our American energy consciousness. Bravo to the authors for devoting the time and energy to do this critical work in such a painstaking fashion.

"The rapid run-up in energy costs of the last three years, and the impact of scenes like New Orleans in early September 2005, in conjunction with the political upheaval in the Middle East since 9/11, has had the effect of moving the realities of our energy society and its impact on the earth into mainstream consciousness. Petroleum, as a primary energy source, has served us well for almost 150 years, but, as a non-renewable resource, its use in the staggering proportions of today cannot continue. And the effect of burning hydrocarbons in the proportions we are doing today is clearly having a devastating impact on the ecosystem that sustains human life. As these realities have emerged into full consciousness, the question has clearly evolved into one of, 'how do we get to the point where our use of hydrocarbons is reduced to sustainable levels, giving us the time to develop more eco-friendly, longer-term energy sources?'

"Messrs. Brown, Brutoco, and Cusumano provide an excellent possible road-map through the forest of how. This is exactly the kind of analysis that we, the American people and our leadership, need to begin the work to move to a new energy world. The Native American saying that, 'we don't inherit the earth from our ancestors, we borrow it from our children,' highlights the importance of this work. The vision beyond hydrocarbons that this work provides is a valuable gift to all of our children."

**David Cole, Chairman & President,
Maui Land & Pineapple Company**

"A concise and realistic plan for escaping the forces of remote tyranny by celebrating our American know-how and indomitable spirit. *Freedom from Mid-East Oil* both informs and inspires action."

**Robert B. Tucker, Author of *Driving Growth through Innovation*, and President, The Innovation Resource Consulting Group**

"*Freedom from Mid-East Oil* offers a well-documented, credible, pragmatic set of policy solutions to end America's dependence on Middle Eastern oil, but goes further. It shows you how to 'do well as you do good' by taking advantage of the dawning Age of Renewables. I heartily recommend this book to executives and entrepreneurs who seek to understand the vastness of the changes taking place, and to first movers in shaping the future."

# FREEDOM FROM

Jerry B. Brown, Ph.D.   Rinaldo S. Brutoco, J.D.   James A. Cusumano, Ph.D.

**www.worldbusiness.org**

Printed in Canada.

Library of Congress Cataloging-in-Publication Data

Jerry B. Brown, Ph.D., Rinaldo S. Brutoco, J.D., James A. Cusumano, Ph.D.
   Freedom from mid-east oil
      p. cm.
   Includes bibliographical references and index.
   ISBN: 978-0-9794052-3-5 (hardcover)
   ISBN: 978-0-9794052-2-8 (softcover)
   1. Energy    2. Business    3. Environment
   HD 9502-9502.5

                                                      2007929760

This book was printed on recycled paper that is 100% post-consumer content, Processed Chlorine-Free, and Forest Stewardship Council-certified.

ANCIENT FOREST
FRIENDLY

# CONTENTS

# ACKNOWLEDGMENTS

A book of this scope, depth and breadth could never be undertaken by any intrepid individual or group of individuals without standing on the much greater body of work of many brilliant pioneers in the environmental community, from Rachel Carson with her seminal work, *Silent Spring* in 1962, up to the present day. These holistic thinkers began the process of identifying a new way of living with the earth rather than dominating it. Their collective awareness and advocacy rejected humanity's historical belief that nature is here to be exploited, which set the stage for our current realization that we have only one Home Planet—and we must at all costs nurture it back to health.

Above all, we dedicate this book to the thousands of researchers, scientists, and visionary business leaders, past and present. Over the past three decades they have reprised the role of Paul Revere to warn America of its looming energy and climate crises. We are deeply indebted to them for their foresight and persistence. We are pleased to see that their time has come and their message has been received.

In dealing with such a broad range of topics—from oil to economics, from geopolitics to global warming—the authors have had the privilege of drawing on the insights of several groups of experts working since early 2004 in varied ways as the Energy Task Force of the World Business Academy. We especially want to acknowledge the contributions of two members of the Academy's Energy Task Force, Nathan Glasgow of the Rocky Mountain Institute, and Robert D. Wagner, Jr., former president of the Petroleum

Club of Houston. We have also been privileged to draw on the advice and writings of several world-renowned Academy fellows: Amory Lovins, founder of the Rocky Mountain Institute and one of the planet's foremost energy efficiency experts; Lester Brown, president of the Earth Policy Institute and the "guru of the global environmental movement"; and Hazel Henderson, founder of Ethical Marketplace and an internationally-acclaimed economist and futurist.

While it is customary to thank individuals, we want to especially acknowledge dedicated public-interest organizations, national commissions, and think tanks, whose impressive analyses of energy and climate issues created the conceptual framework and provided core data upon which this book is based. Foremost among these organizations are: the Natural Resources Defense Council and its seminal reports on *Securing America* (vehicle efficiency) and *Growing Energy* (biofuels); the Rocky Mountain Institute and its groundbreaking study *Winning the Oil Endgame*, which describes a viable path to an oil-free society; the Worldwatch Institute, through its *American Energy* report on the renewable path to energy security and *Biofuels for Transportation* report on the emerging global biofuels market; and the Earth Policy Institute and its brilliant *Plan B 2.0, Rescuing a Planet Under Stress and a Civilization in Trouble*. Other groups whose work inspired and informed this book include: American Council for an Energy Free Economy, Apollo Alliance, The Arlington Institute, Electric Power Research Institute, Institute for the Analysis of Global Security, National Commission on Energy Policy, Union of Concerned Scientists, and the U.S. Energy Information Administration

While all authors are in debt to their editors, this book literally owes its life to the editorial and coordinating skills of the fourth member of the principal writing team, Madeleine Austin, the Academy's Director of Research and Policy Development. A special debt of appreciation also goes to David Zweig, senior editor of the World Business Academy, who helped shape a wide-ranging manuscript in its earliest incarnation. The manuscript also benefited tremendously from the keen insights of Katherine Thomas, Chief Operating Officer of the Academy, who also provided scores of hours of manuscript proofreading and managed the production of the book.

Our special thanks go to Jeffery Burton, Brandy Espinola, Chris Funk, and Philip Santa-Maria, students at Florida International University in Miami, who conducted voluminous background research on key topics. Elliot D. Brown, a physics graduate student at FIU, provided research and drafting suggestions for the hydrogen chapter. Lalla Brutoco co-created the concept and directed the execution of the graphic design for the cover, with skillful technical asistance from David Reeser.

Our special thanks to Academy Fellow James B. Channon, a pioneer of the corporate visioning process and for the last five years, the leader of Project Earthrise, the Academy's 100-year vision project from which the Energy Task Force emerged. He is a continuous inspiration and a constant friend.

And finally, our deepest expression of appreciation goes to our World Business Academy "family" of Directors, Members, Fellows and subscribers who have been a constant source of support and motivation for twenty years. As is the case with our "blood relatives" without whose steady patience and support this book could never have been initiated or finished, our Academy "relatives" have never failed to challenge us to achieve extraordinary scholarship as we live our Academy mission: to educate, inspire, and transform business leaders to take responsibility for the world. Thank you, one and all.

# PROLOGUE:
# THE MYTH OF PROMETHEUS

*By Robert D. Wagner, Jr.*

Prometheus was one of the Olympian gods of ancient Greece. He was a cousin of Zeus, the head of the Olympian pantheon. In the stories of Prometheus written down by Hesiod, Homer, and others of that time, he was known as the creator and protector of humankind. Prometheus was at odds with Zeus in this respect, for Zeus had little regard for human beings. Prometheus stole fire from the gods and gave it to humanity to help humans survive and evolve. This angered Zeus so much that he had Prometheus chained to a rock in the Caucasus Mountains. Each day a divine eagle would tear out his liver and each night it would grow back. This happened for many generations until Heracles, a son of Zeus, killed the eagle and freed Prometheus. The feat added to Heracles' fame and these exploits pleased Zeus so much that he allowed Prometheus to remain free and take up residence with the gods on Olympus.

Prometheus' name means forethought in ancient Greek. He was known as the most clever, wise, and steadfast of the gods, with the capacity to see the future, a trait that Zeus did not possess. His strength of character, his wisdom and capacity of forethought, and his general disdain for Zeus's indiscriminate use of power upon occasion put him at serious odds with Zeus within the pantheon. As an epic figure in both the ancient and modern literature, Prometheus has always been portrayed as a steadfast advocate for humanity and as an opponent of the abuse of power.

To punish mankind for the offenses of Prometheus, Zeus ordered Hephaestus to mingle all things good and bad and put them in an ornate box. He blended a sample of all these substances into the form of a woman and brought her life, sending her to marry the brother of Prometheus. Prometheus had warned his brother Epimetheus not to accept gifts from the gods, but Epimetheus (meaning "afterthought") paid no heed, married Pandora, and opened her dowry box. Despair and suffering poured from the box and afflicted mankind throughout eternity.

The mythologies of the ancient world were developed within all cultures over many centuries, mostly by the constant oral retelling of stories. Their general intent was to provide humankind with a means to understand and to accept the mysteries of existence and the diverse personalities both of gods and men. The amazing thing about them is that, as in the stories of Prometheus, they can present wonderfully imaginative ways to see the everyday world, even in our modern times.

Humanity now stands at the pinnacle of the Hydrocarbon Age, in which energy is developed by burning the elements of life, hydrocarbons. This Age first began with the discovery of fire by a proto-human species approximately 500,000 years ago. In mythic terms, it is the energy given to us by Prometheus. Hydrocarbons powered all the advances of the Industrial Age. However, our hydro-carbons of choice—from wood to plant and animal products to coal and, eventually, to oil and gas—are wreaking devastation on the ecosystem. Moreover, their dwindling supply makes this form of energy increasingly less viable. Similarly, the absence of forethought brought not only the good, but more pointedly, the disastrous contents of Pandora's box to humankind. In effect, the collective species is approaching a crisis point not unlike the time before the discovery of fire, when our survival required a form of energy to provide light and heat.

In many ways, the central god of our collective psyche today is science. With incentives aligned and resources properly aggregated, it can provide the solutions to virtually any problem confronting the human species. But we need the vision of Prometheus to give us the insight to develop new forms of energy today. Such development will be not without controversy; established science will scoff at attempts to innovate. Developers of new energy forms may be vilified, much as Prometheus was persecuted by Zeus for his efforts on our behalf. But, like Prometheus, the compelling nature of the need will allow the new innovators to prevail. In time, their vision and resolute determination will prevail over the myopic view of traditional beliefs.

# PART I

# OUR GLOBAL
# ECONOMY AT RISK

# 1

## The Choice Is Ours

*"[The Iraq War and Middle East conflicts are] far more than a war against terrorism. And I think it will last probably at least as long as the Cold War did, which was 45 years. This is really the first war the United States government has ever fought in which we pay for both sides. This is not a good plan. We need to stop paying for their side. And one very important way to do that is to recognize that oil in particular has some very specific problems . . . ."*

—James R. Woolsey, former director,
Central Intelligence Agency

**Can the U.S. achieve energy independence from the Persian Gulf in 10 years?** *Yes.*

- With the Prometheus Plan, the U.S. can replace Middle Eastern oil by 2015.

- Without energy independence, the U.S. faces recession, possible depression, and decline as a world power.

- Oil is our number one national security, environmental, and economic issue.

- Businesses and the states must lead the way in addressing the energy and climate change crisis, because the federal government has not.

## A TITANIC MISCALCULATION

We are experiencing the initial phase of the first major oil shock of the 21st century. Its shock waves will soon reverberate throughout the global economy.

To avert both economic and environmental disaster, the world must immediately pursue a radical solution to the energy crisis. In making such a drastic departure from a badly broken system, we must seek an emergency exit that is as safe as possible, knowing full well that everyone who jumps into a lifeboat is still at risk.

Remember the *Titanic?* The great ocean liner departed Southampton, England, in 1912, as headlines proclaimed it "the biggest moving man-made object ever built" and "the ship that could not be sunk." This struck some observers, in hindsight, as *hubris,* the Greek word for excessive pride and arrogance. *Hubris* is usually followed by suffering and punishment.

The *Titanic,* because of gross miscalculation caused by arrogance, was not designed with enough lifeboats to save all its passengers. Those passengers who made it to the lifeboats were the fortunate survivors. All the others perished.

For decades, the American public, acting out of *hubris,* has been living under the delusion that the fossil-fuel energy system that has been powering the planet for the past 100 years—a blink of an eye in the geologic history of the planet—was somehow inexhaustible.

Since the first oil crisis of 1973, America has been sold this false belief by extremely powerful Arab sheikhs and oil executives, who were aided by domestic politicians eager for massive financial contributions and other favors while parroting this self-destructive nonsense.

As a result, this colossal and complex planetary energy system was left vulnerable to a fossil fuel system that has created an energy and climate change crisis—and we have perilously too few lifeboats. The "lifeboats" which would save our society are the renewable energy systems we could profitably build today, using existing technology. Regrettably, without enough lifeboats, not everyone will survive. Even more unfortunate, because of global climate change, we now know that the fossil fuel iceberg has already struck and the floodwaters are pouring in. We are out of time.

The impetus for this book can be stated simply as follows: the carbon-based, climate-changing, planetary fossil-fuel system will, like the *Titanic*, sink beneath the waves of history much more quickly than most thoughtful observers ever imagined possible.

To understand the danger, one must grasp the current levels of the two greenhouse gases other than water vapor that contribute the most to heating our planet—carbon dioxide ($CO_2$) and methane. Levels of $CO_2$ are higher than any time in the last 750,000 years. Levels of methane, 20-60 times more destructive than $CO_2$, are higher than any time in the last 650,000 years. When frozen permafrost melts, it releases potentially disastrous levels of methane and $CO_2$. More permafrost has already melted than at any time in the last 100,000 years, and Siberia is warming faster than any other place on earth. The gases released by melting permafrost accelerate global warming in a dangerous spiral. The planet is in trouble, and the problem is greenhouse gas emissions from fossil fuels.

**It is, therefore, imperative that we rapidly commercialize renewable energy systems and extend them around the planet, so that we do not have to perish in the energy and climate change crisis that has already begun. Those few who truly understand the current situation will do their utmost to see that the world stops using fossil fuels *now*, so we can survive the epochal, slow-motion catastrophe that is unfolding.**

Hopefully, it is not too late to avoid "sinking." We still have choices. Individually or collectively, it would be *hubris* for us to fail to seize them and *act*. It is clear we *must act now to halt global warming*. We must act now to reconstruct our economic system to base it on renewable energy rather than increasingly costly and scarce fossil fuels that can be secured only with great geopolitical risk.

In every major transition in the history of humanity, losers greatly outnumbered winners. Whether they were blinded by their vested interest in the prior regime or by their lack of information, the losers stayed behind. They failed to act before the critical hour.

The winners anticipated the changes, made the necessary plans, and took the necessary action.

A radical shift is coming. It will transform the way we generate, store, distribute, and use energy. It will permanently alter the planetary fuel system as we rapidly make the transition from oil and commercialize technologies that will harness the abundant and sustainable renewables that can power our future.

The winners will be those individuals and companies who conscientiously seek out and act upon the most up-to-date information in two critical areas: the *speed* at which the present petroleum-based, fossil-fuel system is exhausting itself, and the steps necessary to *identify and implement* the energy-efficient and climate-compatible renewable technologies that are available today to replace that system.

This book contains a national Prometheus Plan that will allow America to achieve freedom from Persian Gulf oil in 10 years or less by eliminating the need for all imports of Middle Eastern oil.[1]

This book can help you become a winner—a survivor in the coming energy transformation. It will help you understand where "the lifeboats" are and how to get to them.

This book can help you and your company navigate the turbulence whipped up by $100/barrel oil—the price paid in 2006 by one power plant in Hawaii, for example.

This book can help America, and ultimately other nations as well, survive the looming energy crisis.

This book explains what we can do as a civilization if we are willing to provide enough "lifeboats" for every passenger on Spaceship Earth.

Most of us can be "winners" or survivors in this planetary energy transformation. But we must start *now.* There is no time to waste. The good news is that with existing technology and reasonable investments, we can begin by eliminating all dependence on Middle Eastern oil within 10 years. And we can do so in a manner that mitigates the emerging challenges of climate change.

## A Nation of Petroholics

We have become a nation of "petroholics" hooked on liquid black speed—the methamphetamine of energy—much of which is supplied by Middle Eastern potentates who deal in oil and, sometimes, terrorism. If we do not move quickly to end our addiction, a future historian reflecting back from 2015 will see that rapidly escalating oil prices between 2005 and 2010 were an economic tsunami that triggered a recession and possibly a depression of an unprecedented scale, even when compared to the Great Depression of the 1930s.

Looking back from the future, a historian will be able to identify the business winners and losers in the new age of energy scarcity, which began in 2005 with the end of cheap oil.

Toyota, with a current market capitalization of $200 billion and the seller of well over one million advanced gas-electric hybrid cars annually, will be seen as a winner. Ford and GM, with market capitalizations that have dropped to $15.4 billion and $12.5 billion, respectively, will probably be seen as losers who missed out on the global auto-efficiency revolution and only belatedly exhibited an interest in "going green." DaimlerChrysler will be praised for its wisdom in mid-2006 when it elected to build fuel-efficient engines, ethanol-capable cars, and a hybrid SUV—and for the $2 billion it invested in converting its American domestic car fleet from petroleum. However, the company will be criticized for not making those changes in its vehicle production fast enough to avoid its financial distress and break-up in 2007.

The historian looking backwards from 2015 will note that all of the domestic airlines in the U.S. wishfully premised their business plans and sometimes their bankruptcy strategies on oil costing less than $60/barrel when oil prices had already risen to the mid-$60s. United Airlines' bankruptcy exit plan is a case in point.

That future historian would also look back in wonderment at how many companies, acutely dependent on energy prices, failed to rethink their energy strategies as oil hit $78/barrel in 2006, dipped for a few months to the low $60s, and rose to over $78/barrel in July 2007.

Given the entire U.S. economy's vulnerability to oil prices, every one of its sectors—not just its transportation sector—and every American business and citizen will pay dearly when skyrocketing demand from China and India sends oil prices above $100/barrel. It will be clear to future observers that the business survivors of the "great energy shakeout" saw something that the non-survivors did not see at the time or were too rigid to accept. That "something" was accurate information about the inevitable energy transformation looming at the end of a century-long run of cheap fossil fuel in the form of oil.[2]

## THIS IS AN ENERGY WAR

This book begins with the facts that every informed citizen and business leader should know. But unlike the recent wave of doomsday forecasts about the end of oil and civilization, it moves rapidly to explore the technologies and strategies available *today* that can create a new, sustainable, and abundant energy economy for the 21st century.

**It is well known that the world runs on oil and that the era of cheap oil is over forever. It is also well known that oil is the fundamental national security, environmental, economic, and equity issue of our time.**

For the U.S., the most important domestic and foreign policy challenge is achieving energy efficiency and independence from Middle Eastern oil—and ultimately *all* imported oil. More than the War in Iraq and the War on Terrorism (which are inherently intertwined with our oil dependence), oil dependence is the defining threat to this nation in the new century, much as the Cold War was in the latter half of the 1900s.

The 20th century was roiled by nationalism, popular revolts, and communist revolutions waged under the banner of competing ideologies. The 21st century will be roiled by conflicts over energy and resources under the guise of clashing religions.[3] The battle has already begun: 9/11 was the "shot heard round the world."

> *"The world is changing before our eyes—dramatically, inevitably and irreversibly. The change we are seeing is affecting more people, and more profoundly, than any that human beings have ever witnessed. I am not referring to a war or terrorist incident, a stock market crash, or global warming, but to a more fundamental reality that is driving terrorism, war, economic swings, climate change, and more: the discovery and exhaustion of fossil energy resources."*
>
> — RICHARD HEINBERG, *THE PARTY'S OVER*, 2003

Given the projected global supply-demand curves for energy, the next 10 years will be critical, bringing growth or recession, energy abundance or energy poverty, a sustainable future or the aftershocks of climatic catastrophe worse than the 2004 tsunami. Acting individually and collectively, you and I get to choose which it will be. Literally, we get to choose. But to choose wisely, we must know what our choices are. We must know what is possible.

In his highly acclaimed book, *The End of Oil*, business and environmental writer Paul Roberts gives us a rare peek behind the scenes of a high-level, closed-door U.S. intelligence community conference convened in 2002, "The Geopolitics of Energy in 2015," which explored four future global energy scenarios.[4]

The first two scenarios pointed to optimistic, even rosy outcomes, in which aggressive environmental policies and a series of technology breakthroughs "cut oil demand so significantly that by 2020, the world is using 13 million barrels a day less than most baseline forecasts." The second two pessimistic scenarios, both premised on the lack of any aggressive policies to make the dramatic shift to renewables, predicted a collapse of Western civilization as we know it.

One of the two pessimistic scenarios explored the impact of a "peak" in conventional oil production sometime between 2010 and 2015, after which declining output in the North Sea, Alaska, Iran, and Venezuela pushed the global economy into recession. The other pessimistic scenario, "A Darker Middle East," was much grimmer. It assumed the War in Iraq had backfired and led to fundamentalist Islamic regimes replacing friendly governments in Saudi Arabia, Kuwait, and other Arab members of the Organization of Petroleum Exporting Countries (OPEC).[5] New nationalist governments cut oil production by 20% for three years and 10% thereafter. This long-term supply disruption set the stage for the "end of the modern energy economy based on cheap oil." Oil prices soared beyond the world economy's ability to adjust, creating catastrophic effects on all modern, energy-intensive societies.

Ironically, with 2007 oil prices already having reached $78/barrel, the most surprising outcome of this four-scenario exercise by the intelligence community was not the relatively modest increases in oil prices that were found to be sufficient to trigger a recession and depression. Rather, it was that all of the "experts"—among our best and brightest—found the two pessimistic scenarios to be more probable than the optimistic ones.

Even more ominous was the outright complacent negativity of some of the participants. Roberts observed, "In today's political climate, the idea of an energy future created proactively, by thoughtful policy or a technological breakthrough, struck some as highly unlikely." We simply do not believe that such pessimism is warranted about Americans, a people long known for their resourcefulness, political will, and capacity to profit from technological innovations.

Even Abu Dhabi, the capital of the United Arab Emirates, the fourth largest OPEC oil producer and home to about 10% of the world's known reserves, has launched an ambitious effort to become a world leader in commercializing renewable energy technologies, including wind, solar, and hydrogen. Abu Dhabi has paired with the Massachusetts Institute of Technology to bring this plan to reality. An MIT representative said, "This is the first oil-producing state that has . . . agreed with the concept that oil may not be the only source of energy in the future. That is a significant realization."[6]

Surely the U.S. is as astute as Abu Dhabi, as capable of seeing what needs to be done and doing it. Now.

## IT IS A CHOICE

As they say in Alcoholics Anonymous, "Your best thinking got you here." In other words, "thinking within an old paradigm nearly killed you." The best thinking of our oil-addicted experts leads to a bleak future. They are suffering from a lack of imagination, ingenuity, and, most of all, information. They are excellent candidates for "Petroholics Anonymous."

Other experts see it differently. Our research reveals that, contrary to the gloomy prognoses expressed above and echoed daily in the media, every credible, recent energy futures study concludes that it is indeed possible to cut at least half of U.S. oil imports from the Middle East (or their equivalents) within the next 10 years. These independent studies, which we discuss in Chapter 8, were conducted by the Rocky Mountain Institute, the Earth Policy Institute, the Natural Resources Defense Council, the Union of Concerned Scientists, the Institute for the Analysis of Global Security, Apollo Alliance, and the bipartisan National Commission on Energy Policy.

Moreover, even these estimates of future oil savings, made by knowledgeable research groups, are too conservative. **By following the Prometheus Plan, America can *completely* eliminate its reliance on oil imports from the Middle East within 10 years.**

This strategic plan for making the transition from fossil fuels to renewables grew out of the work of the Energy Task Force of the World Business Academy. The 10-year Prometheus Plan and our plan for the following years both take into account the reality of continued terrorism for the foreseeable future, but a sudden cataclysmic event that brought widespread devastation, such as a successful terrorist plane attack on a nuclear facility, would necessarily change our predictions and timeframe.

The noted British futurist H.G. Wells remarked, "Human history becomes more and more a race between education and catastrophe." Nowhere is this truer than in the bad news/good news energy story.

The bad news is that after failing over the past three decades to achieve energy independence, this is our *last chance* to manage an orderly and peaceful shift to a sustainable energy future that creates the preconditions for global peace and prosperity. If we continue to postpone difficult choices, we face a more violent and anarchic future.

The good news is that the technologies needed to dramatically reduce U.S. oil consumption are available *now* and more plentifully than they were 30 years ago—the last time the U.S. took energy efficiency seriously. The even better news is that these technologies are now profitable.

## High Noon in the Desert

Our modern world runs on oil. It is the life blood of civilization and the motor of progress. This black elixir supplies 40% of global energy and 90% of all transportation fuels.

So the specter of $100 per barrel oil as the "new price reality" is cause for grave concern. This is especially true when the new world of $100 oil is forecast not by oil-conspiracy bloggers, eco-alarmists, or doomsday prophets, but rather by energy analysts from the prestigious Wall Street investment banking firm of Goldman Sachs. In February 2006, Goldman Sachs warned that the cost of a barrel of oil could top $100 in the near future. "Oil markets may have entered the early stages of what we have referred to as a 'super spike' period," Goldman analyst Arjun Murti noted. Only a few months later, in May 2006, *Newsweek* reporter Karen Miller observed, "Now predicting $100 oil has become respectable. Just look at the futures market, where call options on $100 barrels—a novelty when the first one appeared last year—have become commonplace."

Certainly, oil prices have spiked sharply in the past. But those increases were directly attributable to geopolitical disruptions of the market. For example, as Figure 1 shows, OPEC dramatically raised the world price of oil in 1973 during the Yom Kippur War, and then again in 1979 during the Iranian revolution. The world enjoyed a brief respite following that period as: (a) the conservation measures adopted during this period caused efficiencies, and (b) non-OPEC countries discovered new oil fields, such as in the North Sea and

**Figure 1.  Real Crude Prices: January 1970 to July 2005**

West Texas Intermediate in constant (July 2005) U.S. dollars

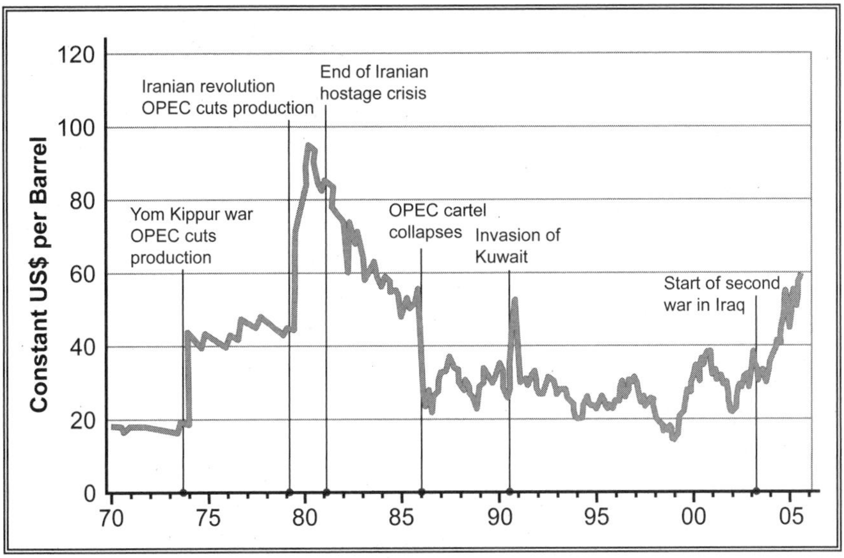

Sources: Federal Reserve Bank of St. Louis and Bureau of Labor Statistics

Prudhoe Bay, that added to the global supply. In 1990, Iraq's invasion of Kuwait broke a trend of falling prices and prompted another sudden price spike.

*What distinguishes the current spike from previous spikes is the fact that we stand, for the first time in modern history, at the pivotal point where global demand essentially equals oil production at full capacity.* Oil production is at 99% of full capacity and, as discussed below, several key oil reserve estimates are badly inflated. The ultimate world oil *supply* is completely inelastic.

Moreover, increased demand in traditional markets such as the U.S., the European Union, and Japan, plus recent rapid GDP growth in the giant emerging markets of China and India (10.5% and 8.5% annual growth, respectively), have irrevocably increased world oil *demand*. In other words, there is virtually no "give" in the system.

The fundamentals of this new conviction about rising oil prices are found in the sands of Saudi Arabia. In a recent book, *Twilight in the Desert,* Matthew R. Simmons, Founder and Chairman of an international energy investment banking firm, argues that the vast reserves of Saudi oil are much smaller than the sheikhs would have us believe. (In fact, it is a crime punishable by death to reveal state secrets of this type in Saudi Arabia.) Simmons concludes we will soon be facing a proverbial "high noon" in the desert: "The next generation of oil will be hard to extract and therefore more expensive. In two to three years, we will have conclusive evidence that Saudi oil is peaking."[7] As go the Saudis, so goes the world.

## SLIDING DOWN FROM HUBBERT'S PEAK

This situation has fueled a heated discussion about when we will reach the "tipping point" for the end of oil, known as "Hubbert's peak" or, more precisely, "Hubbert's Bell Curve," named for legendary geophysicist M. King Hubbert. While working for Shell Oil Company in 1956, Hubbert published a now-famous paper predicting the peak and decline of U.S. oil production in the lower 48 states.

Based on the amount and rate of past production, he argued that U.S. oil output would crest between 1965 and 1970. Hubbert was widely discredited at the time as a "fear monger." To the amazement of his many critics, Hubbert's predictions came true. Using the same model, Hubbert later projected that the peak in global oil production would occur as early as the year 2000.[8]

So, where are we on Hubbert's curve? The optimists, many of whom are employed in the oil industry, the U.S. Department of Energy, and the International Energy Agency, say we have at least 20 years or more to go before reaching global "peak oil."[9] The pessimists, including Hubbert himself, and astute observers like Simmons, Jeremy Rifkin, author of *The Hydrogen Economy*, and Kenneth S. Deffeyes, author of *Beyond Oil: The View from Hubbert's Peak*, believe we are already there.[10]

Inadvertently, the major oil companies have confirmed one significant piece of evidence buttressing our contention that oil will peak sooner rather than later: they have invested $112 billion in profits since 2005 to buy back their own stock instead of funding new exploration, development, or refineries. The oil companies understand very well—and who is in a better position to know?—that with little new oil to be easily discovered and with demand soaring, their remaining reserves will be even more valuable in the future world of $100 oil.

Even if oil does not peak for another 10 years, we must act now for several reasons.

First, whether the peak comes sooner or later, it will likely take at least a decade's lead time to wean the U.S. from Middle Eastern oil. As President Bush finally stated in his 2006 and 2007 State of the Union addresses, dependence on foreign oil is "a national security problem." In today's dangerous and unpredictable world, it is far, far better to act now.

Second, due to increased global demand, reduced U.S. demand for oil in response to higher prices will not significantly lower the global price of oil, as it did 1977-1985. Forced into action by the "second oil shock" of the Iranian revolution in those eight years, America implemented significant auto mileage and energy efficiency measures. "U.S. GDP rose by 27%, oil consumption fell by 17%, net oil imports fell by 50%, and net oil imports from the Persian Gulf fell by 87%. . . . The entire world oil market shrank by one-tenth, total U.S. energy consumption dropped by 17%, and OPEC's output fell by 48%, breaking its pricing power for a decade."[11] In other words, the U.S. was able to rapidly implement energy conservation measures and dramatically reduce oil consumption (and thus total global demand for oil), effectively undermining OPEC's control of oil prices, while at the same time achieving strong economic growth.

That was yesterday. Today, increased demand by China, India, and other developing nations will devour any surplus supply caused by U.S. efficiency measures or economic downturn, keeping oil prices relatively high. From now on, the global demand for oil will grow faster than production capacity, as one billion people—the "haves" of the modern societies—strive to maintain and increase their economic well-being, now dependent on oil. For most "have-not" nations, rising oil prices will derail development plans and increase human suffering. The only nations somewhat protected from economic hardships will be those that take definitive action to achieve energy independence from fossil fuels. For example, Brazil has replaced oil imports with ethanol produced from sugar cane and is now independent of all foreign energy sources—the first modern state to achieve this distinction.

Third, any of a series of possible geopolitical events could disrupt oil supplies, rapidly increasing post-peak oil prices. Foremost among these are continued disruption and destruction of oil pipelines in Iraq, the emerging civil war in Nigeria, an oil embargo by Venezuelan strongman Hugo Chávez, a terrorist attack on some segment of the global oil infrastructure, regional war in the Middle East sparked by the Iraq War or the ongoing conflict between Israel and Muslim nations, and, last, fall-out from international sanctions over Iran's nuclear program—not to mention the further destabilization of the region that would occur if Israel or the U.S. attacked Iran, as Vice President Cheney and other high-level members of the Bush Administration are urging.

Potentially the most serious blow would be a successful terrorist attack on Saudi Arabia's Ras Tanura installation, the largest oil terminal in the world. Every day, nearly 10% of the world's oil supply, more than eight million barrels per day (MBD), flows through this facility. Al Qa'eda calls oil the "umbilical cord and lifeline of the crusader community." Since 2004, it has incited attacks on key Persian Gulf installations, causing financial markets to assess an additional ~$5-$12/barrel risk premium.

In February 2006, suicide car bombers carried out a bold attack on the world's largest oil processing facility at Abqaiq, Saudi Arabia, about 25 miles inland from the Saudis' Persian Gulf coast— a target much easier to hit than the World Trade Center. While the attack was stopped by guards who fired on the bombers' cars, exploding the vehicles and killing the attackers, crude oil futures immediately shot up more than $2 a barrel on fears that the militants would again target the vital facility. This attack was viewed as new "in the sense that this is the boldest attempt to strike at the heart of a Saudi oil-production complex," said Eurasia Group oil analyst Antoine Halff.

One wonders what the outcome of the suicide attack would have been if instead of using a vehicle, the suicide bombers had rented a small private jet loaded with fuel—something Osama bin Laden has told us to expect.

In summary, one way or another, oil prices will increase faster than economic activity, causing widespread economic hardship. Obviously, oil prices do not rise in a straight line; they move up and down, sometimes because of market manipulation by the oil companies. But the general trend since 1999 has clearly been dramatically upward, resulting in nearly a four-fold increase in oil prices from less than $20/barrel in 1999 to nearly $80 per barrel in July 2007.

In many ways, the extraordinary success of Al Gore's *An Inconvenient Truth*, as both a book and a movie, is directly attributable to the growing public awareness that we are running out of time faster than anyone previously thought possible. It could be that we have a decade or less to avoid the "tipping point" for global disaster.

The global fuel system will change. The important questions are: *"In what way?" "How fast?"* and *"Through which new technologies?"* Or, as Paul Roberts notes, "The real question, for anyone truly concerned about our future, is not whether change is going to come, but whether the shift will be peaceful and orderly or chaotic and violent because we waited too long to begin planning for it."[12]

## THE CHINESE CATERPILLAR

Lester Brown, founder of the Worldwatch Institute and president of the Earth Policy Institute, has been described as "one of the world's most influential thinkers" by the *Washington Post*. Ted Turner refers to Brown's most recent work, *Plan B 2.0: Rescuing a Planet under Stress and a Civilization in Trouble*, as "a masterpiece." In fact, Turner purchased more than 3,000 copies and sent them to members of Congress and many CEOs.

Brown's central conclusion in *Plan B* is that "our global economy is outgrowing the capacity of the earth to support it, moving our early twenty-first century civilization ever closer to decline and possible collapse." His most compelling argument for this view is based on an analysis of China's stunning growth and its impact on the world economy.[13]

In this context, Brown further observes the changing role of the U.S. economy. Contrary to conventional wisdom, the U.S. is no longer the world's leading consumer nation. Recently, China replaced the U.S. as the globe's major consumer of basic commodities. China has surpassed the U.S. in consumption of four of the five basic commodities that Brown uses as indicators: grain, meat, coal and steel. Only in the consumption of oil does the U.S. still lead China by about a three-to-one margin (20.5 MBD versus China's 7 MBD). This gap also is closing, with negative consequences on a global scale.

The real shock to the global energy system, however, emerges in Brown's extrapolation of the future implications of what he calls the emergent "Chinese caterpillar," implacably devouring more and more oil to feed the energy needs of its vast population. If Chinese oil consumption were to equal that of the U.S., by 2031—less than 25 years from now—China would be using 99 MBD oil, which is nearly 18% more than the 84 MBD presently consumed by the entire world's population. Obviously, this can't possibly happen.

The number of cars in China has been growing by 19% a year, and by 2010, China is expected to have 90 times more cars than it had in 1990.[14] If China follows the U.S. pattern of three cars for every four people, China will eventually support 1.1 billion vehicles, well beyond the current global fleet of 800 million vehicles. Simply providing the roads, highways, and parking needed for those vehicles would necessitate paving an area roughly equal to China's current acreage for growing rice.

"The inevitable conclusion to be drawn from these projections is that there are not enough resources for China to reach U.S.-style consumption levels. The western economic model—*the fossil-fuel-based, automobile-centered, throwaway economy*—will not work for China's 1.45 billion people in 2031."[15] Nor will it work for India, nor for the other three billion people in the developing world who seek higher standards of living.

Of the 6.6 billion people in the world today, one billion use 85% of all generated energy, three billion use the rest, and 2.6 billion have virtually no energy at all. Based on the oil-addicted model of development, how can the "have-nots" ever hope to become "haves"?

How does China break its caterpillar consumption patterns copied from Western world views and oil consumption models that are no longer viable? How does China become a butterfly?

*Where do we go from here?*

## THE PROMETHEUS PLAN AND BEYOND PROMETHEUS

Given the unprecedented challenge the emerging energy crisis poses for the U.S. and the world, the only viable solution is a bold initiative that mobilizes the nation's vast resources around the bipartisan goal of energy independence. We therefore submit the Prometheus Plan, which uses conventional technologies to replace oil in the short and medium term, thereby achieving independence from Middle East oil by 2015. We also propose a Beyond Prometheus Strategy to further reduce oil consumption by rapidly commercializing advanced technologies to phase in and facilitate the transition to a hydrogen future.

Today, venture capital investment in efficiency and renewable energy technologies is soaring. Many technologies, like wind and ethanol, are already cost-competitive with conventional electric power and gas prices at the pump. What is lacking is the political will necessary to mobilize America on the same scale as President Franklin Delano Roosevelt's Manhattan Project, which built the atomic bomb during World War II, and President John F. Kennedy's

*"If we begin now, there is no reason why the next ten years cannot be the decade America declared and finally won our freedom from foreign oil dependency."*

— FORMER NEW YORK GOVERNOR GEORGE PATAKI, AUGUST 2006

Apollo Project, which put a man on the moon within 10 years during the Cold War.

**Prometheus Plan. The primary goal of the Prometheus Plan is to reduce U.S. oil consumption by 5 MBD by 2015 using conventional, practical, and climate-neutral technologies. This is equivalent to all the oil the U.S. is projected to import from the Middle East by 2015.**

The U.S. now consumes about 20 MBD of oil, and half of that is imported. Half of those imports come from OPEC, and in turn, half of the imports from OPEC come from the Middle Eastern members of OPEC. In other words, the Middle East now supplies 2.5 MBD (12.5%) of U.S. imports.

Unless the U.S. changes course, by 2015, it will be even more dependent on Middle Eastern oil than it is now. By 2015, predictions are that the U.S. will be consuming 25 MBD of oil, of which 60% (15 MBD) will be imported, with nearly 20% (5 MBD) coming from the Middle East. So by 2015, the 5 MBD of oil that the U.S. now imports from all OPEC nations are projected to come solely from the Middle Eastern, Persian Gulf members of OPEC.

Reducing our oil consumption would lessen our vulnerability to OPEC price increases, reduce OPEC's ability to control oil prices, and relieve geopolitical pressures in the volatile Middle East.

In order to reach the primary goal of achieving freedom from Middle Eastern oil, the Prometheus Plan contains the following specific objectives and recommendations:

- **Reduce oil use by 5 MBD by 2015.**

  Free the U.S. from dependence on Middle Eastern oil.

- **Cut transportation sector greenhouse gas emissions by 20% by 2015.**

  Cuts will come through transportation fuel efficiency and use of nonfossil fuels.

- **Increase fuel efficiency standards, saving 1.6 MBD by 2015.**

  Significantly improve average new passenger vehicle fuel economy standards to 40 mpg.

- **Make a rapid transition to biofuels, saving 1.6 MBD by 2015.**

  Use ethanol for flex-fuel vehicles, and biodiesel or pure vegetable oil for heavy-duty trucks.

- **Produce non-fossil fuels @ $1.50 per gallon (in constant dollars) by 2015.**

  Current price of Brazilian sugar-based ethanol delivered FOB New York is only $1.00.

- **Achieve massive implementation of 20% Renewable Energy Standard.**

  Standard will change residential, commercial, and industrial energy use.

- **Stimulate agriculture and biofuels business sectors.**

  Create billions of dollars in biofuels investments and new farm revenues.

- **Save or create nearly 2 million jobs by 2015.**

  Save or create one million rural jobs and one million auto and transport jobs.

- **Produce and sell at least 1 million hybrid electric vehicles a year by 2015.**

  Ramp up to annual sales of at least 1 million hybrid and plug-in hybrid electric vehicles.

- **Produce and sell at least 100,000 hydrogen fuel cell vehicles a year by 2015.**

  Create a platform for the long-term phase-in of a hydrogen economy.

To reduce oil consumption by 5 MBD by 2015 and build the platform for a hydrogen economy, we propose the strategy shown in Figure 2 below. We emphasize the transportation sector because that sector holds the greatest potential for rapid reductions in our oil consumption. The electric utility industry relies on petroleum to supply only about 2% of its energy needs.

## Figure 2.  U.S. Oil Savings Measures by 2015
### Achievable Oil Savings in Millions of Barrels of Oil per Day

| Oil Savings Measures | MBD |
|---|---|
| 1) **Auto Efficiency:** Rapidly increase the efficiency of using oil by:<br>• Raising fuel efficiency in new passenger vehicles to 40 mpg<br>• Accelerating oil savings in motor vehicles through:<br>  ◦ Fuel-efficient replacement tires and motor oil<br>  ◦ Efficiency improvements in heavy-duty trucks | 3.1 |
| 2) **Biofuels:** Accelerate growth of biofuels industry through major expansion of:<br>• Ethanol, mainly E85 from corn and sugar feed stocks<br>• Biodiesel, mainly B20 from vegetable oil feed stocks | 1.6 |
| 3) **Industrial, aviation, and residential sectors:** Maximize oil savings in all three sectors to supplement savings in transportation sector | .3 |
| 4) **Hydrogen Economy:** Phase-in through R&D and commercialization:<br>• Initially through annual sales of 100,000 hydrogen fuel cell vehicles | 0.0 |
| *Total Oil Saved within 10 Years of Implementation:* | **5.0** |

**Timetable.** Five MBD over 10 years requires an average annual reduction of 500,000 barrels of oil per day, equal to a 10% savings per year over current consumption levels.

**Beyond the Prometheus Plan.** As stated above, the longer-term objective of a strategy that goes beyond the 10 years of the Prometheus Plan (Beyond Prometheus Strategy) is to rapidly commercialize *advanced technologies* in order to phase in and facilitate the transition to a hydrogen future.

Since the end of World War II, the American people have not shown much appetite for conservation, so predicating a plan on reducing overall fuel use, instead of replacing fuels, might be unrealistic. However, we believe that as the U.S. heeds the imperative to stop climate change and move away from fossil fuels, the hydrogen economy presents an attractive alternative, especially if current trends in oil prices continue.

Obviously, before this transition can take place, we need to overcome significant challenges relating to technology and infrastructure. Primary among these challenges are the large-scale production and storage of hydrogen, the high cost of fuel cells, and the creation of a national infrastructure for the hydrogen economy.

To overcome these challenges will require a three-stage, *pedal-to-the metal* Beyond Prometheus Strategy. The principal components of this strategy are as follows:

- First, vast improvements in automobile efficiency through fuel-efficient and flexible-fuel vehicles in the short term, in hybrids and plug-in hybrids in the mid-term (2010-2015), and in advanced materials plug-in hybrids and fuel cell vehicles in the long term (2015-2025 and beyond).

- Second, acceleration of the domestic and international biofuels industry, primarily through corn-based ethanol in the short term; through corn- and sugar-based ethanol (sugar cane, sugar beets) in the mid-term; and ultimately through cellulosic biomass feedstocks, which will not compete with food or animal feed supplies, in the long term.

- Third, rapid phase-in and long-term transition to advanced-materials hydrogen fuel cell vehicles which use as feedstocks, cellulosic ethanol and/or hydrogen, the latter generated from distributed "trickle-charge" electrolysis plants.

All of the fundamental technologies required for this strategy are available today; no theoretical scientific breakthroughs are needed to achieve mass distribution and commercialization. By adopting this Beyond Prometheus Strategy, America could turn the dream of an oil-free future into a reality.

While describing the process of achieving total independence from *all forms of petroleum* (a principal contributor to global warming) is beyond the scope of this book, it is critical to understand that the steps taken in the next 10 years to eliminate U.S. dependence on OPEC oil will lay the foundation for a "beyond petroleum" economy in the future.

Why? It's simple. Few people remember that whale oil was the source of energy for most U.S. lighting needs until it was replaced by petroleum products in the 1850s. Once petroleum was refined for one purpose, it was quickly applied in a slightly different form (kerosene) to eliminate the need for more expensive whale oil, practically overnight. Similarly, once American industry has scaled up production, storage, distribution, and combustion of hydrogen in one application, hydrogen will readily begin displacing all other forms of energy still reliant upon dramatically more expensive and environmentally toxic fossil fuels (i.e., oil, coal, natural gas, and tar sands) from domestic and foreign sources.

At that stage, society will take its net savings and begin to work to reduce carbon dioxide concentrations in the upper atmosphere and to slow global warming with its attendant cataclysmic weather patterns. In fact, some thoughtful observers believe that the coming devastation from climate change may impel society to switch from fossil fuels *whatever the cost*, even before non-fossil fuel alternatives become significantly cheaper.

**Prometheus Plan Investment.** Based on data from a well-regarded independent, peer-reviewed study by the Rocky Mountain

24

Institute, we concur that it will cost approximately $180 billion to achieve the long-term objectives outlined in a Beyond Prometheus Strategy of eliminating dependence on all imported oil, not just Middle East oil. In *Winning the Oil Endgame*, Amory Lovins and his associates conclude that it will require an investment of "$180 billion over the next decade to eliminate oil dependence and revitalize strategic industries."[16] That's less than one-half the current cost of the Iraq War, started in large part to secure that country's oil. Currently, the U.S. pays more than that much for imported oil *with zero return*. The oil payments enrich OPEC rather than building infrastructure or creating jobs at home.

According to a report of the United Bank of Switzerland (UBS), *Global OilCo 2005*, the major oil companies will generate *more than $1 trillion in net cash flow from operations* between 2004 and 2008.[17] Because these are pure profits—calculated after deducting all other capital expenditures, buybacks, disposals, acquisition and dividend costs, private jet travel for executives, expense account lifestyles, and spending on lobbyists and politicians—this spectacular increase in returns can certainly be considered "excess profits." If governments—which already regulate, tax, and charter the very existence of these corporations—were to excise a trifling 18% of the corporations' next trillion in profits (leaving all of their historical profits untouched), it could use the revenue to fund the transition to new fuel sources.

**Prometheus Benefits.** Depending on how the Prometheus Plan strategies are implemented, the benefits will vary significantly. From any perspective, however, they are spectacular. These benefits include the following:

- Limiting the wealth flowing to Middle Eastern states that fund terrorism

- Reducing dependence on unstable, autocratic, and hostile governments

- Dramatically reducing carbon dioxide and harmful air emissions

- Rebalancing trade, reducing the deficit, and stabilizing the dollar

- Saving $133 billion in oil costs annually (assuming oil at $73/barrel), going forward after 10 years

- Saving one million high-wage automotive and transportation-related jobs

- Creating up to 2 million additional jobs in biofuels and new energy industries

- Increasing annual farm income by billions and revitalizing rural communities

- Providing the energy foundation for global security, prosperity, and equity

## JOHN F. KENNEDY'S EXAMPLE

The Prometheus Plan is far easier to achieve than President Kennedy's Apollo Project was because it relies *upon existing technology and resources*. The risks and stakes of today's energy crisis and war on terrorism are far greater than those that confronted President Kennedy at the height of the Cold War. In 1962, President Kennedy launched the Apollo Project. He challenged America to put a man on the moon in 10 years, to confront the mounting threat to U.S. and international security posed by Soviet dominance of space. At that time, the technology for a moon landing was in its infancy. No one knew for certain whether this ambitious goal could actually be achieved. No one had ever gone beyond the earth's orbit, let alone made a manned landing on the moon. The challenges were too great to even calculate. Nevertheless, the Apollo Project inspired the nation and resulted in extraordinary strategic and technological success, affecting almost every facet of modern life. It even, as it was hoped, totally revitalized the education system for engineering and the physical sciences.

Today, instead of Cold War threats and fears of nuclear annihilation or superpower confrontations, we face the more diffuse and

slow-moving dangers of terrorism, recession, economic chaos,
and the end of the American
dream as we know it. As in the
time of Roosevelt and Kennedy,
it is essential that America once
again provide bold domestic
and international leadership to

> *"One small step for a man; one
> giant leap for mankind."*
> — NEIL ARMSTRONG,
> ASTRONAUT AND
> COMMANDER,
> APOLLO II LUNAR LANDING

address a fundamental challenge to world peace, prosperity, and
progress. Through the Prometheus Plan, the U.S. can provide the
leadership required to reduce oil dependency, while averting a global
energy and economic catastrophe triggered by peak petroleum prices
and cataclysmic climate change.

## DOOM-AND-GLOOM PUNDITS

We are now surrounded by doom-and-gloom pundits, who
sincerely do not believe the American way of life will survive "the
converging catastrophes of the twenty-first century." For example, in *The
Long Emergency*, social commentator James Howard Kunstler predicts:

> The Long Emergency will change everything.
> Globalism will wither. Life will become profoundly
> and intensely local. The consumer economy will be a
> strange memory. Suburbia—considered a birthright
> and a reality by millions of Americans—will become
> untenable. We will struggle to feed ourselves. We may
> exhaust and bankrupt ourselves in the effort to prop up
> the unsustainable. And finally, the United States may not
> hold together as a nation. We are entering an uncharted
> territory of history.[18]

Certainly, those are potential dangers. Nevertheless, even
though the current energy system is entering its sunset years—in
fact because of it—our basic findings are overwhelmingly positive.
Civilization has already survived, indeed prospered, through several
profound energy transformations: from muscle power to wood; from
wood to coal and whale oil; and most recently from coal and whale

oil to petroleum and natural gas. We firmly believe it is within our collective power and wisdom to call forth the leadership needed to replace fossil fuels, minimize and eventually stabilize climate change, create a stronger and more secure global economy, and spread wealth to poor nations.

## LACK OF FEDERAL GOVERNMENT LEADERSHIP

Based on the experience of the past three decades, it is clear that the federal government has not been providing meaningful leadership to guide us through the coming energy crisis. In 1977, President Jimmy Carter made energy the central issue of his presidency, calling it "the moral equivalent of war." Conservatives and oil company "spin doctors" successfully portrayed him as a dour defeatist and pessimistic preacher, wearing a sweater in the unheated White House while lecturing Americans that they would have to learn to live with less. As a result, Carter squandered political traction and eventually lost the presidency. No one should underestimate the political risks in confronting Big Oil.

Part of the problem is the confusion Big Oil spreads throughout the voting public and among elected officials with its massive advertising budgets, paid for by excess profits. Conservation has often meant living with less and with lower expectations. This is *not* what we are suggesting. We believe the focus should be on energy efficiency, which means getting the same or more, but spending less. Major corporations such as 3M, DuPont, GE, and BP learned this lesson years ago. Wal-Mart is trumpeting its commitment to "go green" as very smart business sense. These corporations save hundreds of millions of dollars annually through energy efficiency programs. They will save many multiples more in the years ahead.

In President Ronald Reagan's view, "America did not conserve its way to greatness. America was a modern industrial state, not a hunting and gathering society. It needed more and more energy every year, and the mission of government was to provide that energy."[19] As energy prices fell in the 1980s, the Reagan administration froze the vehicle fuel efficiency standards, allowing auto manufacturers to build gas-guzzling, oversized sedans, light trucks, and SUVs that today represent half of all car sales. In the case of Ford, SUVs have constituted 90% of its profits. Much to its dismay, as its bond ratings fall to junk levels, it is learning that such a strategy is unsustainable.

Then came the first Gulf War. Conservation had been abandoned and the U.S. went to war over oil. In a new book by Senator Bryon Dorgan (D.-N. Dakota), in a section entitled "Oil Wars," he cogently discusses "the potential for military misadventures as countries seek to secure oil supplies." Senator Dorgan writes:

> If we do not wean ourselves from oil imports, we face not only skyrocketing prices and a devastated economy but the potential for military misadventures as countries seek to secure oil supplies.

> And let's face it: The unspoken agenda of America's military and political involvement in the Middle East is the oil supply. That is not to say that there are not other good reasons for our interest in the region, but oil is always a factor in our strategy.

> Always. The supply of oil is so important to us that we go to war for it. The first Gulf War was a war about whether we would allow Saddam Hussein to gain control of Kuwait's oil reserves—the fifth largest in the world. I know, they said it was about freedom. But we all know better. If Kuwait had been a country in central Africa and without oil, do you think we would have sent a half a million American troops to reclaim it?[20]

New Mexico Governor Bill Richardson, former U.S. Secretary of Energy, also has candidly discussed the role of oil in making foreign and national security policy, and has stated that oil provoked the first Gulf War.[21]

Since the 1970s, no Democratic or Republican administration has seriously attempted to curb America's growing addiction to foreign oil. Moreover, since the 2000 election, the Bush-Cheney administration has openly championed higher profits and greater tax breaks for the fossil-fuel industry by adopting the industry's fiction that we can "drill our way out of the problem."

## "FOLLOW THE MONEY"

George W. Bush is an oil man. He and Dick Cheney have close ties to the oil and other energy industries. Having served as co-chair of the host committee for the Republican National Convention in Houston in 1992, former Enron CEO Kenneth Lay exerted great influence in shaping energy policy in both Bush administrations. Enron and its employees gave $2 million to President Bush's campaign in 2000. Kenneth Lay was a member of the vice president's panel of energy advisors and had private access to the vice president. Lay also selected his own regulator from the Federal Energy Regulatory Commission. Former Enron employees or consultants who worked for or have strong influence in the second Bush administration include Lawrence Lindsey, Andrew White, Ed Gillespie, Theodore Kassinger, Marc Racicot, Ralph Reed, James Baker, Wendy Gramm, Robert Mosbacher, and Robert Zoellick.

Exerting enormous leverage over both the White House and the Congress, the fossil-fuel industry lobbied for and helped draft an energy bill in 2005 that was researched and written in a series of private industry meetings. In the years between the Bush-Cheney 2000 election and 2005, oil company profits exceeded the cumulative profits of the industry over the prior 14 years.

Most policies of the Bush Administration deepen our energy dependence. The Administration's predisposition to support the fossil-fuel industry may well be the cause of its failure to recognize the exigency of reducing carbon dioxide emissions and arresting global warming. The two positions go hand in hand: support Big Oil and resist meaningful attempts to halt global warming.

Early on, the Bush-Cheney team rejected U.S. participation in the multinational Kyoto Protocol to reduce greenhouse gases and slow global warming. It also rejected the theory of man-made climate change. In March 2007, a House committee released documents showing "hundreds of instances in which a White House

> *"We have to, in the next 10 years . . . decrease the rate of growth of $CO_2$ emissions. . . . If that doesn't happen . . . there's a great danger of passing some of these tipping points. If the ice sheets begin to disintegrate, what can you do about it? You can't tie a rope around the ice sheet."*
>
> – DR. JAMES HANSEN, NASA

official who was previously an oil industry lobbyist edited government climate change reports to play up uncertainty of a human role in global warming or play down evidence of such a role."[22] The official, head of the White House Council on Environmental Quality, even tried to stop Dr. James Hansen, NASA's top climate expert, from calling for prompt reductions in greenhouse gases linked to global warming.[23]

The Administration consistently has refused to raise CAFE standards. President Bush called for CAFE standards "reform" in his January 2007 State of the Union speech, but his proposal rejects legislatively mandated increases in favor of leaving the National Highway Traffic Safety Administration (NHTSA) with discretion over standards. His proposal requires no measurable mileage increases over time, and makes it harder for NHTSA to change the standard because the benefits of any change would have to be proven to outweigh costs. The present statutory language calls only for the consideration of "economic practicality." As the common legal expression says, *"res ipsa loquitur"—the situation speaks for itself.*

The Energy Policy Act of 2005 approved vast new subsidies for conventional energy sources: $6 billion for oil and gas, $9 billion for coal, and $12 billion for nuclear power. It awarded these subsidies at a time when oil companies were recording the highest quarterly profits of any corporations in history. Since the energy companies helped draft this legislation, it comes as no surprise that only $2.6 billion went to conservation and alternative fuels.

Even after the 2000 election, in which the fossil-fuel industries were among the top three financial contributors, energy corporations gave $115 million in campaign contributions to politicians running for federal office. By any measure, they have earned exceptional returns on their "investment."

For example, powerful oil and automobile industry lobbyists were able to use the 2005 Energy Policy Act to continue exemptions for SUVs from meaningful fuel efficiency standards, as well as tax *incentives that encouraged Americans to purchase them.* On top of this, and despite record gas prices and oil profits, the Bush-Cheney team blocked a one-year, $5 billion windfall profits tax for oil companies that the Senate passed in late 2005.[24]

## MORE MONEY TRAILS

As a result, we are trapped in a vicious circle: gargantuan oil company profits generate continuous self-serving advertising campaigns and enormous influence in the White House and Congress. This generates billions of dollars in subsidies and tax breaks, which in turn generate more excessive profits for the oil industry. These profits are used to pay for more lobbying and political donations in an ever-expanding circle.

It is difficult for most people to grasp the sheer size of the oil and gas industry. Today, about 425 companies in the developed world serve the demand for hydrocarbons. The major oil companies are the main players in this group, which includes explorers, producers, refiners, and distributors of oil, gas, and electricity. Their aggregate market capitalization approximates $3 trillion, and they constitute 10% to 12% of the entire world economy. By way of example of the size of these companies, Chevron supplies a mere 2% of global energy demand, yet its sales rank it as the eleventh largest company in the world.

The *UBS Global OilCo 2005* report predicted that these companies would generate an estimated $250 billion in net cash flow in 2006, and that between the time that the Bush-Cheney team took office in 2000 and the year 2006, the companies would generate more than $1.5 trillion in *net cash flow*, after all executive perks and dividends.

ExxonMobil, the biggest of the majors, announced $36 billion—*in profits*—for 2005. That's $3 billion every month, which if ExxonMobil were a country would make it the 90th richest nation in the world. Beginning in 1993 and continuing until he stepped down, ExxonMobil paid CEO Lee Raymond $144,000 every day, and recently rewarded him with a $398 million retirement package for tripling company profits.

Not surprisingly, ExxonMobil is regarded as the "Bad Boy of Oil" that ignores the coming energy crisis and current environmental problems and simply goes about its business. It has been among the top funders of climate skeptics and has the smallest investments in alternative energy.

With few new oil fields on the horizon and world demand rising, oil companies understand that their remaining reserves will continue to increase in value. Most major players, therefore, resist any significant energy initiatives that do not rely primarily on oil and other fossil fuels. However, some companies, such as BP, Chevron, and Shell, have already seen the handwriting on the wall. They are making a conscious decision to reposition themselves as "energy service companies" and are developing plans to incorporate sustainable energy resources into their product mix. If the other majors do not react quickly enough, rapidly growing alternative energy enterprises, such as GE and its FPL Group, are ready to fill the gap.

The outcome of decades of Big Oil's influence on Washington is that, in a very real sense, we in the West, especially the U.S., have become powerless *petroholics*. We are addicted to cheap oil, while OPEC, our dealer, is only too happy to supply our much-needed daily fix at ever-increasing prices. As a result, we are now mired in what *New York Times* columnist Thomas L. Friedman calls the era of *petrolism*, corrupt antidemocratic practices whereby oil rich nations—such as Iran, Nigeria, Russia, Saudi Arabia and Venezuela—can co-opt their citizens through public largesse and build up their internal security forces and military to keep themselves in power.

> *"Green is the new red, white, and blue."*
> - THOMAS L. FRIEDMAN, *INTERNATIONAL HERALD TRIBUNE*, 2006

We fully agree with Friedman that what America needs now is a president and a Congress with the guts not just to preemptively invade other nations, but to inspire energy efficiency, reward energy innovation, and lead an energy revolution here at home. This will take the adoption of the Prometheus Plan, which is based on a sound energy policy with real incentives for efficient cars and sustainable energy (biofuels, solar, and wind), rather than the business-as-usual, "welfare-for-oil-companies" policies in the Energy Policy Act of 2005.

In terms of true national security, becoming green is what we need. It is actually the most pragmatic, pro-growth, pro-active, preemptive, and patriotic policy we can pursue.

With adoption of the Prometheus Plan, the U.S. will take back its sovereignty from OPEC and regain control over its national destiny, while simultaneously reducing the threat of a catastrophic environmental breakdown from greenhouse-gas-driven climate change.

## COST OF OIL ADDICTION

In the absence of federal leadership, the business community and the states must lead the charge in addressing the negative impact of our dependence on foreign oil. The economic implications of this long-term addiction are staggering:

- For half of all households that received Bush income tax cuts of less than $500 per year, the increase in gas prices mean a $360.25 de facto gas tax, which wipes out 60% of that tax relief.

- A 2005 study by the International Center for Technology Assessment found that by quantifying the external costs of using gasoline-powered vehicles, including the cost of maintaining a permanent military presence in the Middle East, the real per-gallon cost of gas is actually between $5.60 and $15.14.

- The non-war cost of securing our access to Middle Eastern oil—deploying U.S. forces in the Persian Gulf, patrolling its waters, and supplying military assistance to Middle Eastern countries—is estimated at $50 billion per year.

- In 2006, oil imports cost $270 billion, up from $229 billion in 2005.

- On our present course, in 10 years America will import nearly two out of every three barrels of oil, up from one out of every two barrels now.

- Oil imports account for more than one-third of the total U.S. trade deficit and therefore are a major contributor to unemployment.

- The cost of the Iraq War is already more than $450 billion, with no end in sight. The Bush Administration originally promised that the cost of the war would be covered by Iraqi oil production, then revised its costs estimates to predict that the war would cost Americans $50 billion-$60 billion.

- One recent study by Nobel Prize-winning economist Joseph Stieglitz and Harvard's Linda Bilmes that incorporates the indirect and human costs of the war put the long-term cost to the U.S. at between $1 trillion (the most "conservative" estimate) and $2.2 trillion (their "moderate" estimate).

- According to U.S. Comptroller General David Walker and the members of conservative and liberal think tanks with whom he has been traveling the country to address audiences, the federal fiscal picture is so bleak that if the U.S. does not change course, by 2040 the federal government will have funds for little more than interest on its mounting debt and some entitlement benefits—nothing for defense, homeland security, education, or anything else.[25]

- In order to fund this growing deficit, we are going deeply into debt to China and other Asian nations, who show up weekly at the U.S. Treasury auction. China recently decoupled its currency from the dollar, reflecting a growing global lack of confidence in the dollar's long-term stability. Russia has already converted a staggering portion of its monetary reserves into euros and other non-U.S. currencies.

- A study commissioned by the U.S. Department of Energy found that dependence on oil from unfriendly countries has cost the U.S. more than $7 trillion in present value dollars over the past 30 years—more than the cumulative cost of all wars since the Revolutionary War.

*Heard enough? What are we waiting for?*

## BUSINESS AS THE TRIMTAB FACTOR

Business cannot afford to stick its head in the sand and hope for the federal government to save it. Despite modest tax incentives for biofuels in the 2005 Energy Policy Act, the federal government has been and continues to be a large part of the problem and certainly not the solution.

As a result, American business leaders and state governments have a fundamental self-interest in mobilizing on the energy issue and taking concerted action to increase energy independence and constrain the influence of Big Oil. The business bipartisan goal must be nothing less than the establishment of a new and sustainable U.S. transportation fuel system so that the economy can thrive during the transition to non-fossil fuels. It will take the active engagement of business leadership to influence the federal government at the highest levels to change the course of the ship of state and to provide the signals, policies, and incentives necessary to implement the Prometheus Plan.

As members of the World Business Academy, we are well aware of the successful precedent for bipartisan business leadership at the national level that was inspired by Harold Willens' book, *The Trimtab Factor: How Business Executives Can Help Solve the Nuclear Weapons Crisis.*[26] Writing in 1984, Willens described the "trimtab" as the tiny rudder that turns the main rudder in order to change the course of a large ocean liner (in this case, an oil tanker) traveling at high speeds through the ocean. He argued that business could provide the trimtab for steering the U.S. out of the cold war stalemate and avoiding the threat of nuclear war.

Willens' work inspired the formation of Business Executives for National Security (BENS), a bipartisan organization that successfully lobbied throughout the 1980s for the ambitious tri-part agenda of changing our relationship with the Soviet Union and ending the cold war, preventing nuclear war, and getting more bang for the buck out of the military budget. Prominent Fortune 500 executives who supported BENS' objectives included Ted Turner (CNN), Tom Watson (IBM), Dick Monroe (Time Warner), and Stanley Marcus (Neiman Marcus).

Our insights on how business and concerned citizens can be mobilized to address the present danger of foreign oil dependency are informed by Willens' writings and our personal experience with BENS. We believe that the time has come to apply these insights to the task of alerting the business community to the greatest challenge we have faced: the global climate change and energy crisis that accompanies the end of cheap oil. This is the defining issue of our time and the greatest challenge of the 21st century.

## ENERGY COMMON SENSE

Published in 1776, Thomas Paine's *Common Sense* challenged the authority of the British government and the monarchy. We offer this current work as a challenge to the 30-year failure of U.S. policymakers to defend Americans' vital interests by making energy independence a cornerstone of national security.

The primary rationale for the Prometheus Plan is that America is already at war and under siege from hostile interests who are threatening to destroy or interdict our long petroleum supply lines which snake through the pipelines, ports, and refineries of the desert sands of the Middle East to fuel our prosperity at home. Furthermore, higher oil prices weaken democracies and encourage autocracy around the world. Or, as Thomas Friedman succinctly puts it, according to the First Law of Petropolitics, "The price of oil and the pace of freedom always move in opposite directions in petrol-ist states."[27]

Our current leaders have spent hundreds of billions of dollars on a Middle Eastern war that totally misses the point of how the energy and climate change crisis has overtaken the war in Iraq and the War on Terrorism as the *most vital* domestic and foreign policy issue of our time.

This is not an alarmist or fatalistic approach, but a realistic and optimistic one that recognizes that business, acting as the trimtab factor, can provide *the* catalyst for appropriate government action. This mission involves convincing business, political, and military leaders and concerned citizens that continuing to defend "security of supply" is not in our best interests. Rather, making a rapid transition to a "new energy economy" is essential to win our freedom from continued instability and turmoil in the Middle East and hostile oil-producing nations.

Like it or not, we are on a journey through turbulent times. If we act expediently, we can make adjustments prudently. If not, we face the daunting prospect of having to come together during the equivalent of a hurricane to "rebuild the ship at sea," as Willis Harman used to say. This would indeed be a titanic miscalculation.

Depending on what course of action we choose, a future historian looking back from 2015 will, it is hoped, observe how certain "information-rich" companies adapted and prospered during the coming transition. Unfortunately, without proper leadership, many enterprises lacking knowledge will find themselves at a competitive disadvantage and will flounder or fail.

We believe that survival goes to the most vigilant. The vigilant are those armed with the critical intelligence necessary to negotiate through times of traumatic change. If we act wisely, individuals, companies, and nations can use the energy crisis as a unique opportunity for co-creating energy abundance and a sustainable future for all inhabitants of the earth—both the haves and the have-nots.

Civilization stands at a major crossroads at which nothing less than our modern way of life is at stake. If we fail to meet this challenge, we may accelerate the end of the golden age of energy-intensive prosperity and the onset of the next Dark Ages. If we succeed, we may, in our time, witness the birth of an oil-free economy and secure a brighter and safer future for countless generations.

The choice is ours!

## Notes and References
## Chapter 1: The Choice Is Ours

1 For the purpose of this analysis, the term Middle Eastern oil refers to the major Middle Eastern oil-exporting nations of the Persian Gulf, which are (ranked according to amount of oil exports): Saudi Arabia, Iran, United Arab Emirates, Kuwait, Iraq, and Qatar. All of these countries export more than 1 million barrels per day (MBD) of oil.

2 See U.S. Department of Energy, Energy Information Administration, *Annual Energy Outlook 2006 with Projections to 2030* (Washington, D.C., 2006), 33-39, (www.eia.doe.gov/oiaf/aeo/) for a discussion of the economic effects of high oil prices. While the discussion acknowledges that oil price spikes may have caused the recessions of the 1970s and 1980s, it suggests that "in today's U.S. economy, sustained higher oil prices can slow short-term growth but are not likely to cause recession." The fallacy in this analysis is that it is based on an oil price reference case of $50-$60/barrel between 2006 and 2030, when in fact the $60 cap has already been breached and economic experts believe prices will spike to $100 or more in the near future.

3 Samuel P. Harrington, *The Clash of Civilizations and the Remaking of World Order* (New York: Touchstone-Simon & Schuster, 1997).

4 Paul Roberts, *The End of Oil: On the Edge of a Perilous New World* (New York: Mariner Books, 2004), 307-10.

5 The member nations of OPEC are Saudi Arabia, Algeria, Indonesia, Iran, Iraq, Kuwait, Libya, Nigeria, Qatar, United Arab Emirates, and Venezuela.

6 "Abu Dhabi Explores Energy Alternatives," *New York Times*, March 18, 2007.

7 Matthew Simmons, *Twilight in the Desert: The Coming Saudi Oil Shock and the World Economy* (Hoboken, NJ: John Wiley & Sons, 2005).

8 For a detailed discussion of "The Hubbert Method," see Kenneth S. Deffeyes, *Beyond Oil: The View from Hubbert's Peak* (New York: Hill and Wang, 2005), 35-51.

9 U.S. Department of Energy, *op. cit.*, 33.

10 See Deffeyes, *Hubbert's Peak: The Impending World Oil Shortage* (Princeton, NJ: Princeton University Press, 2001), and Jeremy Rifkin, "Sliding Down Hubbert's Bell Curve," in *The Hydrogen Economy* (New York: Jeremy P. Tarcher/Penguin, 2002), 13-36.

11 Amory Lovins *et al.*, *Winning the Oil Endgame: Innovation for Profits, Jobs and Security* (Snowmass, CO: Rocky Mountain Institute, 2005). Similarly, in recent years Europe has demonstrated that economic growth is not dependent on increasing per capita consumption of energy.

12 Roberts, *op. cit.*, 15.

13 Lester R. Brown, *Plan B 2.0: Rescuing a Planet Under Stress and a Civilization in Trouble* (New York: W. W. Norton, 2006), 3.

14 "Fueling the dragon: China's race into the oil market," Institute for the Analysis of Global Security, http://www.iags.org/china.htm.

15 Brown, *op. cit.*, 11.

16 Lovins *et al.*, *op. cit.*, xii.

17 United Bank of Switzerland, *Global OilCo 2005: The Very Good, The Bad and The Ugly* (New York: UBS Investment Research, 2005).

18 James Howard Kunstler, *The Long Emergency: Surviving the Converging Catastrophes of the Twenty-First Century* (New York: Atlantic Monthly Press, 2005).

19 Dennis Hayes, an officer in the Energy Department in the Carter Administration, quoted in Roberts, *op. cit.*, 219.

20 Byron L. Dorgan, *Take This Job and Ship It: How Corporate Greed and Brain-Dead Politics are Selling Out America* (New York: St. Martin's Press 2006), 120.

21 Kevin Phillips, *American Theocracy: The Peril and Politics of Radical Religion, Oil, and Borrowed Money in the 21st Century* (New York: Penguin Group (USA) Inc.), 68.

22 "Material Shows Weakening of Climate Change Reports," *New York Times*, March 20, 2007.

23 "Rewriting the Science," CBS News, March 19, 2006, http://www.cbsnews.com/stories/2006/03/17/60minutes/printable1415985.shtml.

24 "At Exxon Mobil, a Record Profit but No Fanfare," *New York Times*, January 31, 2006.

25 "U.S. Heading for Financial Trouble?" *CBS News*, March 4, 2007, http://www.cbsnews.com/stories/2007/03/01/60minutes/printable2528226.shtml.

26 Harold Willens, *The Trimtab Factor: How Business Executives Can Help Solve the Nuclear Weapons Crisis* (New York: William Morrow and Company, Inc., 1985).

27 Thomas L. Friedman, "As Energy Prices Rise, It's All Downhill for Democracy," *New York Times*, Op-Ed Page, May 5, 2006.

# 2

## Running on Empty: The End of Cheap Oil

*"The Stone Age didn't end for lack of stone, and the Oil Age will end long before the world runs out of oil."*

– Sheikh Ahmed Zaki Yamani, former Saudi oil minister

**Are we at the beginning of a long-term, cataclysmic, global energy crisis?** *Yes.*

- To overcome the crisis and achieve energy independence, business executives and all levels of government, nationally and internationally, must provide global leadership.

- This crisis presents humankind with the greatest environmental, economic, and geopolitical security risk in its history.

- A precarious equilibrium between declining oil reserves and rapidly increasing demand is the key driving force, exacerbated by volatile geopolitical factors.

- Saudi Arabia is a critical player in this crisis.

- "Business as usual" guarantees triple-digit oil prices and global socio-economic chaos.

## BAD NEWS, GOOD NEWS, AND BEST NEWS

Driven by unbridled capitalism and a thirst for growth and expansion and fueled by boundless creativity and innovative spirit, the Western world over the past 150 years has created the most challenging "bad news/good news" conundrum in the history of civilization.

The *bad news:* by burning fossil fuels such as coal and oil since the beginning of the Industrial Revolution, we have unleashed a dangerously high level of greenhouse gases into our atmosphere. These gases, consisting mainly of carbon dioxide, have initiated a sequence of climate change events that if left unchecked will soon create a world unlike any humanity has ever known. The danger is serious, and it is present *now.* The ramifications of this challenge are discussed in Chapter 4.

The *good news:* we are faced simultaneously with an emerging global energy crisis unprecedented since the beginning of recorded time. As with climate change, this energy crisis also will bring dire consequences if left unchecked. "Good news?" you might ask. "How can this be?"

Climate change is complex and its effects are diffused throughout the ecosystem. In contrast, we quickly experience the rapidly evolving effects of the energy crisis—especially the rising price of petroleum—on a daily basis as the consequences ripple through our national economies and personal pocketbooks. There is no mistaking the impact. As Bill Clinton discovered vividly during his first presidential campaign, the economy ultimately grabs our attention. We will shift, whether we like it or not, away from fossil fuels. The economic impact of rising oil prices will compel major national economies, including the U.S. economy, to switch to other fuels. Triple-digit oil prices—and make no mistake, that *is* what's coming—will compel that conversion. In this regard, Brazil is the picture of the national economy of the future precisely because it already has achieved energy independence.

The *best news* is that *if* we get it right—and that's a very big *if*—by addressing the energy issue effectively, we have an opportunity to create a better world for *all* living things on this planet. The reason is simple. The same technologies and policies that have the power to ward off the unacceptable economic outcomes of our energy crisis can simultaneously bring climate change under control. The technologies exist today. Many already are proven commercial realities. The policies are a matter of business leadership, common sense, and effective political will.

*It is absolutely critical that in choosing from among several possible strategies to address the energy challenge, we select only that strategy that can also bring climate change under control. Alternative strategies, such as using coal and tar sands, can alleviate our energy problem, but they will simultaneously worsen climate change. That would be a grievous misjudgment, the effects of which would be felt for centuries if not millennia.*

Because some politicians, scientists, and corporations have been demanding ever-increasing levels of data before making decisions about how to deal expeditiously and most effectively with climate change, we already have waited several decades too long. Lessening the effects of climate change may be the best we can hope for in the near term. That, however, is an outcome far better than any available from the two other alternatives—doing nothing, or adopting oil substitutes such as coal or nuclear power that will increase our environmental problems.

## OIL PRODUCTION STRAINED AT CAPACITY

In the end, it's about oil, the single largest contributor to global energy and to greenhouse gases. In 2005, oil provided about 35% of the world's total energy needs (see Figure 1)[1] and 95% of the fuel to run some 700 million cars roaming the planet. It also is responsible for the creation of 40% of all global carbon dioxide, one of the primary bad actors among the greenhouse gases in our atmosphere. By 2020, oil is projected to supply 60% of our global energy requirements while powering more than 1.25 billion cars. Oil is the primary fuel energizing our planet in more ways than we would care to think.

## Figure 1. World Total Primary Energy Supply, 2005
### By Fuel Source

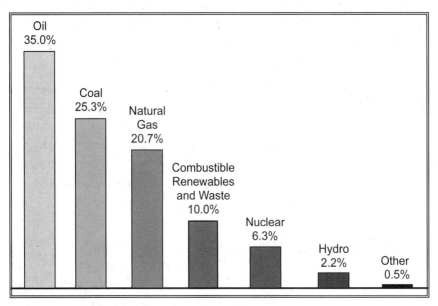

Source: International Energy Agency, 2006

With most oil going into consumers' fuel tanks, it is no surprise that the 2005-2006 spike in gasoline prices has caught our attention. And we are not very happy about it. In view of oil's critical role, one might wonder why industry or government did not foresee a price increase from $24/barrel in 2003 to over $78/barrel in July 2006, a 200% increase that occured within just three years. The false relief the public felt just prior to the November 2006 elections, when oil hovered down around $63/barrel, led to significant post-election disappointment as oil resumed its inexorable climb upward.

Barely a couple of weeks before oil reached $75/barrel in 2006, several Wall Street investment banking firms, including Citigroup, raised their 2006 oil futures forecast up to $60/barrel because of supply woes and the lack of spare production capacity. The $60 figure represented an 18% increase over the previous price and clearly the lowest price possible for the near future. In February 2006, investment bank Goldman Sachs warned that the cost of a barrel of oil could eventually top $100. We agree. In fact, we believe it will be above $100/barrel before December 2008. Moreover, any of several highly possible geopolitical events could cause this or a greater increase within days.

"Oil markets may have entered the early stages of what we have referred to as a 'super spike' period," Goldman Sachs analyst Arjun Murti noted. Some analysts such as William Browder, CEO of Hermitage Capital in Moscow, project potential near-term prices above $250/barrel under certain plausible scenarios.[2] Financer George Soros, who earned huge returns in the oil market, predicted that prices would increase significantly in 2007. So, what does all of this mean for the average American or, for that matter, for just about any global citizen?

In sharp contrast to the above plausible estimates, the *Annual Energy Outlook 2006* of the U.S. Department of Energy, Energy Information Administration (EIA) examined the long-term economic effects of high oil prices between 1980 and 2030. In its "reference" case, the EIA projected that world oil prices would stay fairly stable after 2006, staying within the $50-$60/barrel range for the next 25 years! Even the EIA's "high price" case did not predict oil prices of $78/barrel by mid-2006, nor $100 by 2030—let alone predict oil at $100 *or more* in 2008, where we think it will be.

It appears to us that something is influencing these overly optimistic EIA projections. No reasonable independent assessment of future oil prices could fail to see that in the future, solely because of the capacity limitations of global petroleum production, let alone "peak oil" issues, oil will be well in excess of last year's peak price of over $78/barrel.

## MIXED SIGNALS FROM OIL COMPANIES

Some oil-producing companies such as ExxonMobil argue there is plenty of oil in the ground, and the energy issue will resolve itself. Exxon has publicly stated that U.S. energy independence is not in the cards anytime soon. Senior Vice President Stuart McGill made this statement at an energy conference in Houston, a few days after President George W. Bush declared that America is addicted to

Middle Eastern oil.[3] "Realistically, [energy independence] is simply not feasible in any time period relevant to our discussion today," McGill declared, as he referred to what he called a "misconception" that the U.S. can achieve energy independence. "Americans depend upon imports to fill the gap," McGill said. "No combination of conservation measures, alternative energy sources, and technological advances could realistically and economically provide a way to completely replace those imports in the short or medium term." His logic is *totally wrong,* but we would expect that from a Big Oil executive.

For some years now, ExxonMobil has also maintained that global warming, which results in large part from burning fossil fuels such as oil, is not a critical issue.[4] We know that the company has paid scientists and consultants who intentionally misled the public for years on global climate change. So, one wonders what ExxonMobil really thinks about the future price of oil.

Other companies—namely, BP, Shell, Chevron, and Texaco—differ with Exxon. David O'Reilly, Chevron's CEO, has placed full-page ads in international publications stating that nearly half of the world's exploitable oil has already been extracted. More specifically, he has noted, "It took us 125 years to use the first trillion barrels of oil. We'll use the next trillion in 30." BP and Shell have similar public awareness programs on the energy issue and the climate change challenge and appear to be more responsible with their public relations budgets.

> "It took us 125 years to use the first trillion barrels of oil. We'll use the next trillion in 30."
> — DAVID O'REILLY, CEO, CHEVRON CORP.

Oil prices have escalated sharply in prior decades, but strictly on geopolitical grounds. For example, the Organization of Petroleum Exporting Countries (OPEC) dramatically raised the world price of oil in 1973 during the Yom Kippur War, and then again in 1979 during the Iranian Revolution.

We are now at the first point in history when the demand for oil is essentially equal to its production at approximately full capacity and about to pass this mark.[5] This has been caused by increased demand in major markets such as the European Union and the U.S., and most particularly by rapid growth in Asia, especially China and India, whose GDP increased in 2006 by 10.5% and 8.5%, respectively. China reported that during the first quarter of 2007, its GDP grew at an annual rate of 11.9%. All data indicate that India's 2007 GDP growth will equal or exceed its 2006 rate.

This precarious production-demand equilibrium has been exacerbated by our inability to find more cheap oil, even with access to numerous advanced technologies developed over the last two decades. Let's look at the data.

## DECLINING OIL RESERVES

In the decade between 1981 and 1991, global oil reserves increased by 43%, from 700 billion to 1 trillion barrels. But in the succeeding decade, despite advances in technology, reserves increased by a mere 3%, to 1.03 trillion barrels. During much of the latter period, the world was consuming two barrels of oil for every barrel found.

We can readily see the impact on major suppliers. In 2004, for the first time in history, several oil companies were unable to find new reserves that would replace the volume of oil they produced in the prior year. This is critical because reserves are a primary contributor to the asset value of these companies, and hence to their balance sheet.

Thus, Conoco-Phillips replaced only 60% of the reserves it exhausted in the prior year, Chevron 18%, BP 89%, ExxonMobil 89%, and Shell 49%. Exxon's reserve increase was primarily based on natural gas in Qatar, not oil. Shell lost its CEO in a corporate legal dispute, in which it was agreed that the company had overstated its reserves by 25-30% for several years. The company was twice forced under federal Securities Exchange Commission scrutiny to adjust its revenue numbers downward.

Not surprisingly, 2004 foreshadowed a dramatic decline in oil reserves. Global production for the year was 30.5 billion barrels.

That's 84 million barrels per day (MBD), but only 7.5 billion barrels of new oil were discovered that year—*that's more than four barrels consumed for every barrel found.*[6] To be sure, we are not running out of oil, just out of cheap oil. We are having a difficult time finding more, even with the most advanced technologies developed over the past decade.

The public felt false euphoria at the discovery of a large deep deposit in the Gulf of Mexico. The estimate of that well's capacity is somewhere between 3 and 15 billion barrels (a wide range!). At the high end of the range, this represents less than a 2% addition to world reserves and will not be brought on-stream until 2013 at the earliest, when global demand will already have outstripped supply. Last, but not least, the lowest estimate we have of the cost to recover that oil is $65/barrel. That's before refining, transportation, retail costs, and taxes.

## The View from Hubbert's Peak

As noted in the previous chapter, in the 1950s geophysicist M. King Hubbert developed a mathematical model that correctly predicted U.S. oil production in the lower 48 states would reach its peak production rate by 1970.[7] That is to say, barrels pumped per day would reach a maximum quantity and forever decline thereafter. *What is important is that the remaining half is both increasingly difficult and much more costly to recover.*

A number of well-known geologists have taken up Hubbert's work and applied his model to global oil production.[8] Projections of the year in which the world will reach global peak production vary from 2005 to 2020.[9] Once again, there is disagreement among geologists whether these projections are correct. Much of this disagreement has to do with how much oil is left in the ground.

For example, near-term "peak pessimists" like Colin Campbell would say that our initial God-given oil in the ground is two trillion barrels.[10] Most geologists agree that as of mid-2007, we will have used about 1 trillion billion barrels of oil since Colonel Edwin L. Drake drilled the first oil well in Titusville, Pennsylvania, in 1859.

That leaves one trillion barrels of reserves in the ground, or about half of oil consumed to date. Most geologists also agree that the world is currently burning about 30 billion barrels per year. It doesn't take much arithmetic to see that based on these assumptions (i.e., having used one trillion barrels), Hubbert's Peak is occurring about now.

There are dissenting views. For example, the U.S. Geological Survey would agree with most of this analysis. However, it would argue that the world started with three trillion barrels of oil. The extra trillion barrels, it says, are yet to be discovered, but it has no proof or data that would locate, much less prove, the existence of this oil. To put the U.S. Geological Survey assessment in perspective, this extra trillion barrels is more than all of the oil in the Middle East, Africa, and Asia combined. It is *four* Saudi Arabias. It is therefore not surprising that absent technological indicators for this extra trillion barrels of oil, a number of geologists do not accept this optimistic assessment.

## THE DEMAND DEMON

Demand is the new demon vexing the world of energy and oil. The oil shocks of the 1970s were geopolitically inspired, and high oil prices eventually fell to values dictated by market forces rather than by sheikhs, shahs, and demagogues. But over the past couple of decades, rapidly increasing demand from Europe, the U.S., and most especially Asia—particularly China and India—has created our current global oil crisis. If we assume just modest growth, the growing gap between supply and demand becomes clear.

Let's take an example offered by Matthew Simmons, a merger and acquisition banker and one of the leading independent energy analysts in the U.S.[11] In 2005, the world used 84 MBD of oil. Let's make the modest assumption—one might say, both conservative and unrealistic—that the need for global energy grows by 2% per year. By 2010, we will require 93 MBD to accommodate this growth. Most analysts agree that the combined output of the former Soviet Union countries and other non-OPEC producers could supply a maximum

49 MBD of this annual future demand, so that OPEC would have to supply the remaining 44 MBD to meet annual world demand in 2010. Today, OPEC supplies less than 30 MBD, and those countries are pumping at nearly full capacity. The

> *"The next generation of oil will be hard to extract and therefore more expensive. In 2-3 years, we will have conclusive evidence that Saudi oil is peaking."*
>
> — MATTHEW R. SIMMONS, AUTHOR, *TWILIGHT IN THE DESERT*, 2005

pertinent question is, "Can they deliver the additional 14 MBD?" Many who follow the industry say they cannot. Even comments from OPEC executives leaked to the press indicate they cannot meet this target.[12]

The International Energy Agency predicted that by 2020, to meet projected demand, the OPEC cartel would have to boost its output to 50 MBD from its current level of almost 30 MBD. After a meeting of OPEC executives in July 2005, senior Saudi energy officials privately warned their U.S. and EU counterparts that OPEC would have an "extremely difficult time" producing at that rate.[13] Saudi Arabia currently pumps about 10 MBD and has assured consuming countries that it could achieve up to 12.5 MBD by 2009 and maybe even 15 MBD in the long run. But a senior Western energy official warned, "They said it would be extremely difficult to move beyond that figure."

More recently, in July 2007, the International Energy Agency projected that global demand for oil in 2008 would increase from 80 MBD to 88.2 MBD. That is almost 50% more barrels a day than the U.S. Department of Energy projects. In July 2007, the National Petroleum Council issued a major report that stated, "It is a hard truth that the global supply of oil and natural gas from the conventional sources relied upon historically is unlikely to meet projected 50-60 percent growth in demand over the next 25 years."

We need only look back to February 2005 to see Russia turning off natural gas pipelines to the Ukraine and parts of the EU, or Iran's response to nations of the West challenging its entry into the "nuclear club." Energy has become a weapon of war and terror. Businesses and governments should be very concerned.

As a consequence, the world's feeding frenzy for oil presents a triple challenge to our future. It is a global threat to our *environmental*, our *economic*, and our *geopolitical* security. With no plan in place to effect an expeditious transition away from its petroleum-based economy, the U.S. will experience devastating consequences sooner than most think.

## Environmental Security

The world runs on oil, and the U.S. consumes about 25% of global production. Therefore, it's not surprising that the U.S. contribution to greenhouse gases is about 25% and rising annually. As a consequence, things are heating up—quickly—in more ways than one.

For example, could it be that our weather over the past decade is just an aberration? Why, for example, have hurricane and typhoon intensities worldwide increased 100% since the 1970s?[14] Why are ocean levels rising 50% faster than a decade ago?[15] Why did the Greenland Ice Sheet diminish faster in 2005 than in any previous year in recorded history?[16] Why are large numbers of polar bears drowning in the Arctic Sea?[17] Could all this be due to the most rapid change in climate since our species began to populate this planet?

A team of more than 2,000 scientists from more than 100 countries answered this question with an unqualified *yes*. And if we don't do something about it soon, they tell us, it will change the way we live and do business for generations to come.

Formed in 1988, this team of climate scientists, called the Intergovernmental Panel on Climate Change (IPCC, or Climate Change Panel),[18] has been cautioning industry, governments, and the public to take note of a few key findings:

- Global warming of the climate system is now unequivocal.

- Since 1970, the earth's average temperature has continued to rise.

- The increase during each decade was greater than the preceding one.

- 11 of the warmest years in recorded history have occurred in the last 12 years—all but one a record-breaker.

- The seven warmest years since recordkeeping began in 1880 have occurred in the past nine years.

- 2006 was the hottest year in history.[19]

The Climate Change Panel tells us that this heating is due to a marked increase in the concentration of greenhouse gases in the earth's atmosphere, carbon dioxide being a major culprit. Other gases, including methane and nitrogen oxides, primary fossil-fuel combustion by-products, are worse culprits (see Figures 2 and 3).

Methane is of extreme concern. As permafrost melts, it releases dramatically increased levels of methane into our already overly methane-saturated atmosphere. For example, the range of ambient

## Figure 2. Global Greenhouse Gas Concentrations

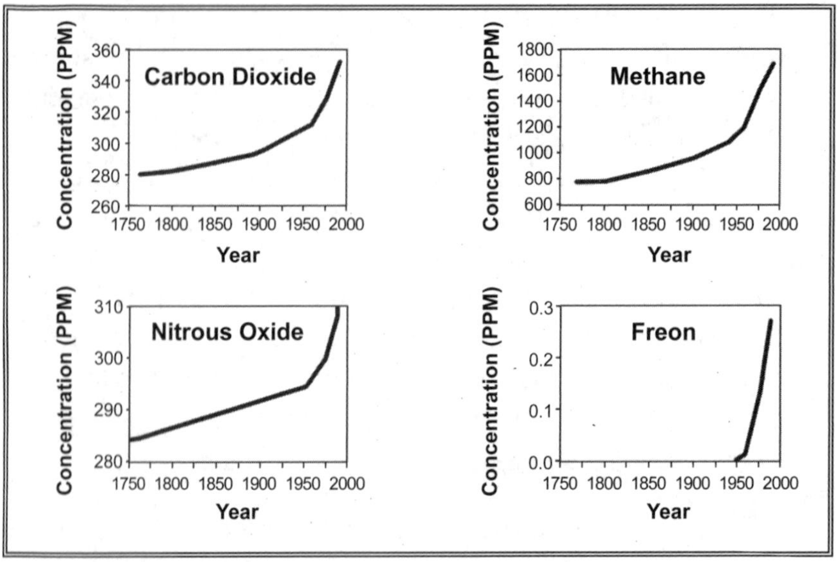

Source: Intergovernmental Panel on Climate Change, 2001

54

**Figure 3. Global Emissions of Nitrogen and Sulfur Oxides from Fossil Fuel Combustion**

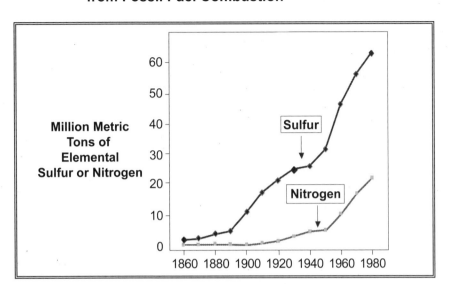

Source: J. Dignon and S. Hameed, *Journal of Air Pollution Control Association,* 1989

methane in the pre-industrial world atmosphere was 320-790 parts per billion. According to the Climate Change Panel, this number had more than doubled to 1774 parts per billion by 2005. And, the warmer it gets, the more the permafrost melts and releases methane, making it still hotter in an ever more vicious cycle.

Our challenge to reduce fossil fuel consumption is striking if you compare GDP per person data for India and China with that of the U.S. The per-person GDP of India, China, and the U.S. is, respectively, $3,700, $7,600, and $43,500.[20] The disturbing question is what will this world look like as these two waking giants continue catching up to the U.S.? Researchers at the Worldwatch Institute have calculated that we would need the resources of at least *two planet Earths* just to stay even and sustain the three economies at comparable standards with the same "fossil fuelish" approach to energy.[21] They conclude that it is essentially impossible for both of these continents to achieve the same per-person GDP as the U.S.

## Economic Security

Our global economic future does not look nearly as rosy as some political pundits and industry leaders would have us believe. Increases in oil prices have preceded nine of the 10 global recessions since World War II.[22] If the emerging energy-climate scenario is left unchecked, the world will face a recession and economic collapse unlike any we have ever experienced. And no country will be immune to the aftermath, although some nations like energy-independent Brazil will enjoy substantial competitive advantages as the price of oil continues to rise.

The developed world runs on oil, and its energy content finds its way into a significant fraction of the cost of all our products and services. Virtually every product we grow, make, import, distribute, or sell relies on oil for multiple phases of the production cycle, including the ubiquitous cargo planes and trucks that deliver our material "stuff."

In "Changing the Oil Economy," the Worldwatch Institute notes that numerous everyday items are made from petroleum-based raw materials, including: radios, shower curtains, shampoo, contact lenses, toothbrushes and toothpaste, drugs and pill capsules, fabrics, shoes, automobiles (the carpets and upholstery, insulation, fan belts, battery cases, safety glass and seatbelts, speakers, tires, dashboards, paint, antifreeze), umbrellas, CDs, tennis rackets and balls (and the cans they come in), credit cards, ballpoint pens, cameras, film, cell phones, and countless cosmetics.[23]

The prices for fuel, cars, food, clothing, housing, and health care—just about everything you need or can imagine, except your personal paycheck and company revenues—will escalate significantly. The result will be rapidly increasing inflation, unemployment, and lower capital investment. Tax revenues (on an adjusted basis) will decline, and budget deficits will continue their dramatic increase, driving up interest rates. Not a pretty picture.

The economic incentives to get away from our oil-driven economy are huge. Every day, the U.S. imports more than 10 million barrels of oil, about 50% of its daily requirement. At $75/barrel that's an annual contribution to our current account deficit—$850 billion in early 2007—of about $275 billion, or more than 30%. And the U.S. Department of Energy projects that if we do nothing to change the situation, our dependence on foreign oil will increase to 70% by 2020, even as the price continues to escalate for every single barrel.

Consumers already pay much more for gasoline than they realize. For example, in the U.S. the price of gasoline rose to well over $3/gallon in April 2006, and remained near $3/gallon in much of the U.S. in mid-2007.

Of course, this is not high by EU standards. But this price does not include tax subsidies to the oil industry such as: oil depletion allowances; subsidies for extraction, production, and the use of petroleum; the increasing cost of protecting oil supplies in the Middle East ($50 billion per year *excluding* the Iraq war);[24] health care costs for treating respiratory illnesses caused by oil-induced air pollution; and the heightened hurricane and disaster costs associated with climate change.

The U.S. International Center for Technology Assessment estimates that these externalities add more than $11 per gallon.[25] That's a total price to the consumer of more than $14 per gallon of gasoline, and this does not include the financial cost to the American public of the Iraq war, which as of March 2007 was more than $450 billion (not including future health care costs and the so-called "Dark Budget" which bring this figure to more than $1 trillion), with no end in sight.[26] This pump price for gasoline is nothing compared to what could occur if we do nothing to avoid, or at least minimize, the impact of rising oil prices.

## GEOPOLITICAL SECURITY

Although the U.S. now consumes 25% of all global oil, it has only 3% of global reserves. Currently, 65% of global oil reserves lie in the Middle East, primarily in Saudi Arabia, Iran, Iraq, United Arab Emirates, Kuwait, and Libya. It has been estimated that 20% of this oil is owned by nations known or suspected to be sponsors of terrorism.[27] By 2020, 80% of all global reserves are projected to be in the Middle East, with a significantly higher percentage expected to be owned by terror-sponsoring nations. Today, the U.S. imports 50% of its oil, with 2.5 MBD, or 20% of this oil coming from the Persian Gulf. Saudi Arabia exports the largest fraction of Persian Gulf oil to the U.S. It is one of America's top five suppliers (see Figure 4).

**Figure 4. Top Five U.S. Oil Suppliers**

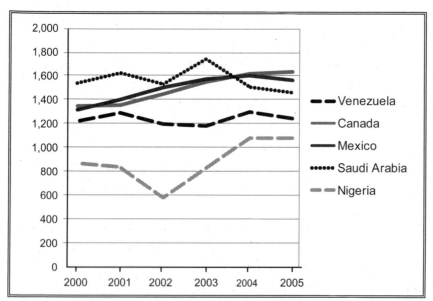

Source: U.S. Energy Information Administration, *Annual Energy Review*, 2006

Because global oil demand now is essentially equal to global supply at full production rates, any of several highly possible geopolitical scenarios involving oil-rich nations could elevate the price of oil overnight to well over $100/barrel. For example, as a consequence of the international dispute over its nuclear program, Iran, with the second-largest oil reserves in the world after Saudi Arabia, could declare an oil embargo, as OPEC did in 1973. Venezuela's strongman Hugo Chávez already has threatened such an embargo. Civil war could escalate in Nigeria. Unrest and violence in Algeria could seriously disrupt its production. Intensified attacks on the oil infrastructure in Iraq are another high possibility. And most serious would be a strike on the Saudi Arabian oil infrastructure. To understand this point, it is important to look at Saudi Arabia and its critical role in the global oil picture.

## POLITICAL SPIN ON SAUDI OIL RESERVES

The Saudis, who control 25% of the world's reported oil deposits—263 billion barrels—are the king of reserves. Iran with its 133 billion barrels is a distant second (excluding Iraq). The Saudis' current production is 10 MBD with a spare capacity of about 2 MBD, essentially the only extra capacity left in the world. Indeed, Saudi Arabia is the only source that can make up for shortfalls or disruptions, just as it did in 2003 when production problems occurred in Nigeria, Venezuela, and Iraq.

More than 90% of the entire Saudi production comes from just six oilfields with projected productive lifespans of 30 to 50 years. Among these fields, Ghawar, the world's largest onshore field, accounts for about 50% of Saudi production. Safaniya, the world's largest offshore field, is also a major contributor. Furthermore, by 1981 all of these fields' production had peaked, and the output rate is now decreasing (see Figure 5).

A key characteristic of the Saudi oilfields, beyond their sheer size, is the very high pressure in their reservoirs. Drill a hole in the right spot in the desert, and oil comes gushing forth. But it is a well-known geological fact that this high pressure makes these fields highly susceptible to damage if they are pumped too quickly.[28] In a nine-year period between 1965 and 1974, the Saudis increased their production by nearly 400%. An increase of that magnitude had never been attempted before. It has been speculated that this decision was made by the foreign oil partners and operators (Chevron, Texaco, Mobil, and Exxon) who believed that the Saudis were about to ask them to leave the country (which they did in 1979). It has been posited that the oil companies may have wanted to capture sizeable quantities of low-cost oil while they were operating partners. It is highly possible that this extreme production rate damaged the Saudi fields.[29]

**Figure 5. Six Fields Produce 90% of Saudi Arabia's Oil**

| Oil Field | Year Production Began | Year Production Peaked | Peak Oil Production (MBD) |
|---|---|---|---|
| Ghawar | 1951 | 1981 | 5.694 |
| Safaniya | 1957 | 1981 | 1.544 |
| Abqaiq | 1956 | 1973 | 1.094 |
| Berri | — | 1976 | 0.808 |
| Zuluf | 1973 | 1981 | 0.658 |
| Marjan | 1974 | 1979 | 0.108 |

Source: Robert Czeschin, *Czeschin Oil & Energy Investment Report*, August 30, 2005

To make matters worse, as early as 1956, the Saudis began to inject high volumes of seawater into their wells at Abqaiq. This form of secondary oil recovery is normally practiced only when a well is aging and decreasing in output. The water is used to push trapped oil out of the well. In a sense, the Saudis were practicing primary and secondary recovery simultaneously, which again is not good for the life of the wells and the oil fields.

The actual value of Saudi reserves has often been called into question. For that matter, this can be said for the oil reserves of all OPEC members. Each member is allowed to produce an annual quantity of oil that is directly related to that member's reserves. The last time Saudi reserves were subjected to an independent audit was in 1978, the year before the Saudis took over complete control of production from their Western partners (see Figure 6). At the time, their reserves were 110 billion barrels. The very next year, the Saudis "announced" that their reserves had increased to 160 billion barrels. In 1988, after their reserves had stayed flat for nine years, they abruptly "announced" another major increase in reserves again, this time by over 100 billion to 263 billion barrels. They report this same number today. *None of these "announced" increases included the discovery of a major new find or giant field.* Curious, isn't it?

## Figure 6. Saudi Arabian Oil Reserves

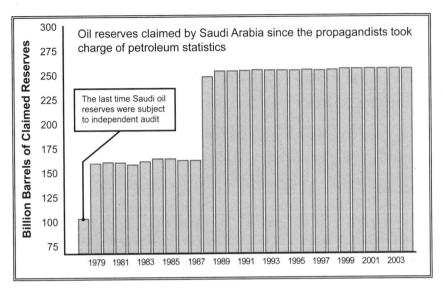

Source: Robert Czeschin, *Czeschin Oil & Energy Investment Report*, August 30, 2005

To a neutral observer, it seems *very* peculiar that Saudi reserves have remained flat for the past 18 years, yet during this period the Saudis have supplied the world with nearly 50 billion barrels of oil. How can their reserve base have remained unchanged? Where did these 50 billion barrels come from? It is further disconcerting that in 1979, Saudi Oil Minister Sheikh Yamani, apparently concerned that the West would have a clear picture of the declining condition and pumping rates of the Saudi fields, slammed the door shut on all further releases of oilfield data and any independent audits. It is no wonder that Western oil analysts are nervous about what might be the actual oil reserve figures for Saudi Arabia and for other OPEC countries. This issue is particularly critical today when production and demand are essentially at parity. It has cast the world into a shadow of uncertainty with respect to its future energy supply.

In 2005, *New York Times* columnist Peter Maass interviewed Sadad al-Husseini, the recently retired head of the Saudis' exploration and production operations.[29] Husseini explained that the Saudis cannot replace reserves fast enough to keep up with global demand.

He pointed out that as with all other producers, Saudi Arabia depletes its oil reserves every time it pumps a barrel of oil. Therefore, just to stay even and maintain its reserve base, it must replace the oil it pumps from declining fields. Husseini reminded us that the world is increasing its appetite for oil by 2-3 MBD every year, so if you are to cover declining reserves *plus* pump for new demand, that's a total of 4-6 MBD. Husseini said that if the demand-depletion pattern continues, the world will have to open enough new fields or wells to pump annually at this 4-6 MBD rate. "That's a whole new Saudi Arabia (which pumps 10 MBD) every couple of years," he said. "It's not sustainable."

When Maass asked Husseini if Saudi Arabia could ever get to 20 MBD, as some politicians and energy analysts in the West project or "hope" it will, he thought for awhile and finally answered with an unqualified "No!"

## MIDDLE EASTERN OIL AND TERRORISM

Saudi Arabia is a prime target of terrorist groups. Their strategy is to deal a crippling economic blow to the Western world. More than 65% of Saudi oil is processed in a single large facility at Abqaiq, 25 miles inland from the Gulf of Bahrain.[30] Most of this oil is then shipped from two major export terminals on the Persian Gulf—Ras al-Ju'aymah and Ras Tanura (the world's largest offshore terminal, through which 10% of global oil supply—nearly 8.5 MBD—flows daily). The Saudis also have a terminal on the Red Sea called Yanbu which is connected to Abqaiq by a 750-mile pipeline across the desert. It is essentially unprotected and an easy target for terrorists.

Terrorist attacks on these facilities could readily take 50% of the Saudi oil off the market for much more than six months. Robert Baer, a former Middle East CIA field officer, said, "Such an attack would be more economically damaging than a dirty nuclear bomb set off in midtown Manhattan or across from the White House in Lafayette Square." He further noted that this "would be enough to bring the world's oil-addicted economies to their knees, America's along with them."

Other aspects of the oil infrastructure are of concern with respect to terrorist opportunities. Today, more than 60% of global oil is shipped on about 3,500 tankers through a small number of what have come to be known as "chokepoints." "There is the Strait of Hormuz, through which 13 MBD of oil is moved; Bab el-Mandab, which connects the Red Sea to the Arabian Sea; and the Strait of Malacca, located between Indonesia and Malaysia."[31] About 80% of Japan's oil passes through Malacca, as well as 50% of the oil bound for East Asia and 65% of all global liquefied natural gas (LNG). Most of these chokepoints are located in Islamic fundamentalist environments. The Strait of Hormuz is controlled by Iran, and Bab el-Mandab by Yemen, Osama bin Laden's ancestral home.

Islamic terrorists now understand that they need not risk travel to Western nations to inflict a devastating blow such as 9/11. Taking several million barrels of oil production instantly off the world market by an effective attack on installations within their own country or neighboring countries in the Middle East can have an even greater economic impact, crippling businesses and driving Western economies into a devastating tailspin.

Lord John Browne, former CEO of BP, was recently interviewed by *Fortune* magazine and asked if oil could spike to $100 a barrel.[32] He replied, "It is a sensitive balance at the moment. If something were to go out of the supply chain—Venezuela, Nigeria, Iraq, Iran, or Saudi Arabia—obviously it would tighten supplies, and there would be a reaction. Let's hope that doesn't happen."

We have already seen what can happen in the U.S. During the 1973 Arab Oil embargo, oil prices quadrupled in a matter of weeks. Unemployment doubled, as more than 500,000 people lost their jobs, and the GDP declined by 6%. At the time, only 28% of U.S. oil was imported, so with the current level of more than 50% of our oil imported, the economic impact would likely be catastrophic.

Terrorism will not go away anytime soon. Former CIA Director James R. Woolsey tell us that even our "friends," the Saudis, have invested between $70 and $100 billion over the past 30 years in spreading fundamentalist Wahhabi beliefs throughout the world.[33]

This doctrine is fanatically hostile to Shi'ites and Sufi Muslims, Jews, Christians, women, modernity, and many Western institutions. It plays a core role in Islamic fundamentalist terrorism and was a key support system for launching the Taliban.

## WHERE DO WE GO FROM HERE?

The implications of the facts cited in this chapter are as clear as the need for action. Oil increasingly will become more expensive, with per-barrel prices easily rising to triple digits. It has also become a powerful weapon of war. To continually expand our dependence on oil on the assumption that Mother Earth will provide whatever we need is both reckless and irresponsible.

In his award-winning book, *The Prize: The Epic Quest for Oil, Money & Power*, Daniel Yergin refers to the twentieth century as "the century of oil."[34] He documents how we have become a "Hydrocarbon Society" and refers to us "Hydrocarbon Man" living in "The Hydrocarbon Age." If this anthropological characterization is true—and we certainly believe it is—then the great *transition* of the 21st century will be to switch the planetary fuel system from fossil fuels to inexhaustible, inexpensive, and abundant renewable fuels. The great *challenge* of the 21st century is to execute the *transition* with a minimum amount of societal pain.

In meeting this challenge expeditiously, it would be most beneficial if the two major global players would immediately change the way they view the world. The U.S. should get serious and develop an effective energy policy. The EU should forge a regional energy security plan, something that to date it has failed to do.

In taking these steps, the U.S. and the EU would provide the vital leadership and political will that the rest of the world so desperately needs to address the global energy crisis and to limit the impact of an even more menacing challenge—human-induced climate change.

# Notes and References
# Chapter 2: Running On Empty

1 Estimates vary. *See also* Thomas Prugh, Christopher Flavin, and Janet L. Sawin, *State of the World 2005* (New York: W. W. Norton), 102.

2 Nelson Schwartz, "Ready for $262 oil?" *Fortune,* April 11, 2006.

3 *Ibid.*

4 Jeffrey Ball, "Exxon Denies Fossil Fuels Cause Global Warming," *Wall Street Journal,* June 15, 2005, and Paul Krugman, "Enemy of the Planet," *The New York Times,* April 17, 2006.

5 One might argue that a similar situation occurred during the early history of the automobile. Henry Ford ran his first cars on ethanol and only later on gasoline. For a while, there were concerns that there would not be sufficient gasoline for the rapidly increasing number of cars. This concern was addressed technically in 1936 by entrepreneur Eugene Houdry, a French race car enthusiast. He invented catalytic cracking, which significantly increased the yield of gasoline and diesel fuel from petroleum. This invention and the discovery of oil in Texas and the Middle East relieved any demand issue until the present day.

6 Lester Brown, *Plan B 2.0: Rescuing a Planet Under Stress and a Civilization in Trouble* (Earth Policy Institute, 2006), 24.

7 Kenneth S. Deffeyes, *Hubbert's Peak: The Impending World Oil Shortage* (Princeton, NJ: Princeton University Press, 2001).

8 Kenneth S. Deffeyes, *Beyond Oil: The View From Hubbert's Peak (Ferrar, Straus & Giroux, 2005).*

9 Stephen Leeb and Donna Leeb, *The Oil Factor* (New York: Warner Business Books, 2004); Gal Luft and Anne Korin, "Terror's Next Target," *Journal of International Security Affairs* (December 2003), http://www.iags.org/n053004a.htm.

10 Colin Campbell, see http://www.hubbertpeak.com/de/lecture.html.

11 Matthew Simmons, *Twilight in the Desert: The Coming Saudi Oil Shock and the World Economy* (Hoboken, NJ: John Wiley & Sons, 2005).

12 Peter Maass, "The Breaking Point," *New York Times,* August 21, 2005.

13 Carola Hoyos and Neil Dennis, "Saudis Warn of Shortfalls as Oil Hits $61," *Financial Times*, July 6, 2005.

14 NOAA Geophysical Fluid Dynamics Laboratory, "Global Warming and Hurricanes" http://www.gfdl.noaa.gov/~tk/glob_warm_hurr.html.

15 Susan Heavey, Reuters, "Oceans, Greenhouse Gases Rising Faster," *The Epoch Times*, http://www.theepochtimes.com/news/5-11-23/34925.html.

16 Stefan Lovgren, "Greenland Melt May Swamp LA, Other Cities, Study Says," *National Geographic News*, April 8, 2004.

17 Will Iredale, "Polar bears drown as ice shelf melts," *The Sunday Times (UK)*, December 18, 2005.

18 IPCC, "Mandate and Membership of the IPCC," http://www.ipcc.ch/about/about.htm.

19 National Climatic Data Center, as reported by CBS News, January 7, 2007, "2006 Breaks U.S. Temperature Record."

20 Central Intelligence Agency of the United States, *The World Factbook*, Rank order GDP per capita, 2006 est.

21 Prugh, Flavin, and Sawin, *op. cit.*

22 Jon E. Hilsenrath and Marcus Walker, "Oil Prices Start to Pinch, Stirring Concern Over Economic Impact," *Wall Street Journal*, June 4, 2004.

23 Prugh, Flavin, and Sawin, *op. cit.*, 101.

24 Scott Peterson, "For Oil and Allies, US Offers a $50 Billion Solution," *Christian Science Monitor*, August 6, 1997, and Tim Weiner, "Russia and France Gain on US Lead in Arms Sales, Study Says," *New York Times*, August 4, 1998; F. Gregory Gause III, "Arms Supplies and Military Spending in the Gulf," *Middle East Report* 204 (July-September 1997), 12-14.

25 Andrew Kimbrell, *et al.*, *The Real Price of Gasoline* (Washington, DC: International Center for Technology Assessment on 1998), 39.

26 National Priorities Project, Cost of War, http://nationalpriorities.org/index.php?option=com_wrapper&Itemid=182.

27 James A. Cusumano, *The Energy-Climate Crisis Is Your Business, Part 3: Creating a Brighter Future,* Project Earthrise Energy Taskforce, World Business Academy, March 2, 2006.

28 Peter Maass, "The Breaking Point," *The New York Times,* August 21, 2005. "This process is unpredictable; reservoirs are extremely temperamental. If too much oil is extracted too quickly or if the wrong types or amounts of secondary efforts are employed, the amount of oil that can be recovered from a field can be greatly reduced; this is known in the oil world as 'damaging a reservoir.' A widely cited example is Oman: in 2001, its daily production reached more than 960,000 barrels, but then suddenly declined, despite the use of advanced technologies."

29 *Ibid.*

30 Gal Luft and Anne Korin, *op. cit.*

31 *Ibid.*

32 Nelson Schwartz, "Normal Capitalism or Obscene Profits?" *Fortune,* March 6, 2006, 13.

33 George P. Schultz and R. James Woolsey, "Oil Security," The Committee on the Present Danger, 2005.

34 Daniel Yergin, *The Prize: The Epic Quest for Oil, Money, and Power* (New York: Simon & Schuster, 1991), 14.

# 3

## GEOPOLITICS OF SCARCITY:
## OIL UNDER SIEGE

*"If you don't worry about oil interruptions, you are living in a fool's paradise."*

- JAMES R. WOOLSEY, FORMER DIRECTOR, CENTRAL INTELLIGENCE AGENCY

**Will the geopolitics of oil create the next energy crisis?**

- Iraq, Iran, Israel, Nigeria, Saudi Arabia, and Venezuela all pose grave risks.

- It's happened before: OPEC boycott, Iranian Revolution, Gulf War I.

- By 2031, China could consume more oil than the world produces today.

- A fundamentalist takeover of Saudi Arabia would imperil the "swing supply.

## ENERGY WAR GAMES AT DAVOS

In March 2006, a *CNN/USA Today/Gallup* poll found that most Americans feared for the vulnerability of our oil supply. In fact, nearly three-quarters believed terrorists will attempt a major attack on oil installations somewhere in the world within the next year. Such concerns are well-founded.

Weekly news headlines highlight the international hot spots that supply oil to the U.S. Samples from early 2006 read: "Attack on huge Saudi refinery foiled." "Crude oil prices jump \$2 amid terrorist fears." "Iran threatens to use oil in case of nuke standoff." "Nigeria: the next quagmire." "Iraq war's result so far seen as chaos, insecurity." "Chávez: Bush to blame if I'm assassinated." Add to that, "Middle East at War" headlines in July as Israel attacked Lebanon in response to Hezbollah kidnappings.

A new and precarious equilibrium exists in the world today, between declining oil reserves and rapidly increasing demand, exacerbated by the fast-growing economies of China and India. It is highly likely that geopolitical tensions will be the catalyst that destroys this delicate balance and triggers the next global energy crisis, pushing oil prices over \$100/barrel and creating a severe chaotic economic tailspin the full extent of which no one can predict. The result will be a permanent energy crisis far, far worse than anything America or the West experienced in the 1970s. The financial effects will be devastating.[1]

What are the probabilities of such an event? What are the chances political turmoil in petroleum-rich trouble spots such as Iran, Iraq, Nigeria, Venezuela, or Saudi Arabia—five of the world's top 10 oil exporters—could set off an energy-driven financial crisis? Technically speaking, it is impossible to assign statistical probabilities to these events. However, that doesn't stop the gamblers on tradesports.com from setting at almost even money the odds of an overt air strike on Iran's nuclear facilities by the U.S. or Israel between now and the end of 2007.

For discussion purposes, let's conservatively estimate the odds at only one chance in 10 (1/10) of a political crisis occurring in just one of the oil exporting nations that would cause a significant reduction in world oil flow over the long term. Then, the probability of *any one of these five events occurring* is: 1/10 + 1/10 + 1/10 + 1/10 + 1/10 = 5/10 = ½ = 50%. Thus, the odds of a significant disruption of oil that would drive the price above $100/barrel are 50/50, in effect 1:1.

These very forces, together wth an increasingly apparent exhaustion of some of the world's largest oil fields, have already placed a risk-premium on petroleum and pushed oil above $78/barrel.

Unfortunately, as this chapter shows, a major oil conflict between industrialized and developing nations has occurred once a decade in every decade since the 1940s. Based on this historical evidence, we should assume going forward that similar confrontations will flare up again and again until we achieve global independence from Middle Eastern oil.

In any prediction, we must deal with the knowns (such as high-tension geographical zones), and the wildcards (such as the exact year in which oil peaks, and possible hurricane destruction of U.S. Gulf Coast infrastructure and refineries). Even more challenging is the realization that the trickiest elements are the factors of which we are not yet even aware. This greatly complicates the problem of calculating the odds of a significant disruption in oil flow.

Some believe that heavy oils in Canada (Athabasca tar sands) or Venezuela (Orinoco belt) or new finds in Saudi Arabia could resolve global oil shortages. This is highly unlikely. Unfortunately, the aggregate predictable yield for U.S. oil from all those sources will not provide meaningful relief from the international shortfalls that will occur in the future (see Chapter 6, Coal, Natural Gas, Tar Sands). A giant new oil field is not likely to be discovered in an area previously overlooked by geologists. According to the U.S. Geological Service, global discoveries of giant oil fields peaked in 1962 and have been declining ever since. And even so-called "large finds" (such as, potentially, the Jack Well, which could add 0.5 to 1.8% to global reserves) are likely to be found only in extremely remote areas, or so far below the sea that they will be so costly to extract that they will further drive up the price of oil.

Another unknown is the geopolitical future in the Middle East. A sweeping diplomatic breakthrough ending once and for all the war on terror and concluding the conflict between the West and Islam seems impossible to envision at this time. The war in Iraq has increased terrorism, instability, and turmoil in the Middle East. All neutral observers and major segments of the U.S. military believe that certain current policies are making the Middle East less stable every day and actually are increasing the number of terrorists.

While we may fervently hope that dire predictions of future constraints on the availability and price of oil do not come true, the evidence strongly suggests one or more will. Some of the most compelling evidence is found by examining the nearly half-century-long conflict over oil between the consuming nations of the developed world and the producing nations of the developing world. This history is essential to understanding how the current geopolitics of scarcity will accelerate the next energy crisis. If we are in the midst of a global clash of cultures, which it certainly appears we are, the "oil lifeline" to the West will continue to be threatened by accelerating geopolitical instability in both the Middle East and Malaysia.

Two milestone events took place 30 years apart: the first summit meeting of OPEC in 1975 and the Energy Crisis Simulation games at the World Economic Forum in 2006.

Anthony Sampson opens his prophetic book, *The Seven Sisters: The Great Oil Companies and the World They Shaped,* describing the arrival of the delegates at the first public OPEC conference at the Palace of Nations outside Algiers in March 1975.[2] Dressed in their national regalia, the delegates marched under a triumphal arch with a "pomp and fervor which suggested either a victory march or a revivalist meeting." Actually, the assembly was a pronouncement of both victory and revival.

Striding past the Algerian guard of honor, the world's new dignitaries arrived: The Sheikh of Abu Dhabi in his dazzling white robes. General Lara, the tiny president of Ecuador, with his medal ribbons and gold lace. Carlos Andrés Pérez, President of Venezuela and father of OPEC, with his signature Bolivar-like sideburns. Saddam Hussein, the strongman of Iraq, his face set in a stony glare. The Shah of Iran, well-groomed like a banker, joining this cult of rulers and revolutionaries. Sheikh Zaki Yamani, the Saudi Arabian oil minister, in his signature flowing white robes and Bedouin headdress.

On the rostrum, Houari Boumédienne, president of the host country, was making one of his famous marathon speeches, lacing his arguments with florid appeals to "Your Majesties, Brothers." Above him, hung a mystical symbol of four incomplete circles, which only with difficulty could be deciphered as the magic word: OPEC.

As if in prayer, Boumédienne reiterated his favorite themes: "Oil was not merely a fuel, but the source of life itself. The oil-producing countries must be the spearhead of the revival of the Third World, and the means to an equitable new system of world justice."

What struck Sampson most was not the magnificence of the assembled potentates, but the nature of this unpredictable black fluid that had turned the world on its head and left Western officials on the outside looking in, staring like hungry children with their noses pressed against a toy store window at Christmas. Sampson described the scene:

> Certainly the arrangements of the conference suggested some kind of revolution. While the delegations from the Middle East or Latin America marched in and out, driven off in their shining black Citroëns to banquets and private meetings, the Western diplomats and journalists came in by the side doors, milling around the crowded convex space outside the circumference, trying to pick up news of what Venezuela had said to Algeria, or what Saudi Arabia thought about Libya.[3]

Now, fast forward 30 years to the World Economic Forum meeting at Davos, Switzerland, in January 2006. Here, nestled in an idyllic Swiss Alpine village, the Forum hosts an annual, by-invitation-only summit of chief executives of the world's biggest corporations ($1 billion sales, minimum), presidents, and prime ministers, plus select intellectuals, journalists, and celebrities. There are few places in the world where, within a few steps between conference halls, one can go from hearing Bill Clinton expounding on climate change, to Bill Gates calling on world leaders to fund a new TB plan, to Zhou Xiaochuan, governor of the People's Bank of China, speaking on improving corporate governance.

But the 2006 meeting found the chieftains of industry and heads of state peering out through frosty windows, from their melting perches in the snow-covered Swiss mountains. Although energy issues were not even on the agenda in 2005, this year they emerged front and center with a vengeance. Sessions included: The End of the Era of Easy Oil; The Future of Alternative Energy; The New Nuclear Calculus; and New Energy Security Institutions.

As far as energy and its impact on economic growth were concerned, the world leaders at Davos recognized they were waging a losing, rear-guard action in an energy war that had started three decades earlier in the desert of Algeria. This was the focus of a Forum session with the ominous title "Energy Simulation: Concerted Terrorist Attacks Create Price Shock." The session simulated energy war games in response to a possible oil supply disruption from terrorist attacks, in which a CEO advisory board, set up by G-8 leaders, reviews and makes recommendations on two potential crisis situations.

Simulation 1 contemplates simultaneous attacks on key choke points in the global energy supply chain in the dead of winter. Oil prices exceed $120/barrel and are expected to stay at this level for the medium term. About 5% of the world crude oil supply is taken off the market for at least four months, while repairs are made. Thirty-five tankers are stranded.

In Simulation 2, two months later, terrorists attack soft targets, like housing complexes and hotels, throughout the Persian Gulf region. Oil soars to $135/barrel on fears of further attacks. With at least 5% of the world's crude supply disrupted—equal to 4.2 million barrels per day (MBD) in terms of 2005 output—continued uncertainty about the future security of supply leads to long-term high oil prices.

Faced with the prospect of sporadic, yet sustained terrorist attacks on soft targets in key oil-producing nations, the CEO Advisory Board was forced to consider a series of dire effects: potential disruptions of existing oil producing facilities; exodus of the expatriate workforce; difficulty in attracting investment to enhance oil production; continued high prices; and macroeconomic fallout.

Do the energy war games at Davos go far enough? We think not.

Terrorist attacks represent only one way in which oil supplies can be interrupted. Direct confrontations with governments of oil-producing nations—in the form of negotiation stalemates, nationalization, boycotts, embargoes, and outright acts of war—all pose more fundamental challenges to stable oil prices and a steady supply of oil.

Not only have such political conflicts over oil occurred during the past 30 years, but they also have happened over and over again, with surprising regularity, since the 1930s. Together, these ongoing conflicts have created a geopolitics of scarcity, placing U.S. oil supply lines under siege in Latin America, Africa, and the Middle East.

## GEOPOLITICS OF OIL

In *The Prize*, Daniel Yergin observes, "It is the twentieth century that has been completely transformed by the advent of petroleum."[4] He describes three great themes that underlie the story of oil: the rise of capitalism and modern business; the national strategies and global politics of power; and the evolution of our current hydrocarbon society. Yergin rightfully focuses on the emergence of petroleum during the *first half of the 20th century* as a key element of national power in World War I, and the strategic role that petroleum played in the outcome of World War II. However, we would like to call attention to the lesser known, but equally important "greasy conflicts" brewing between the industrialized nations and the oil-producing nations during the *latter half of the 20th century*. Understanding these conflicts is essential to anticipating and understanding the new geopolitics of scarcity that is rapidly reshaping the world order.

These conflicts initially flared between the oil-producing nations and the original Seven Sisters, the great companies that built the global oil industry in the twentieth century: Exxon (Esso), Shell, BP (British Petroleum), Gulf, Texaco, Mobil, and Socal (Chevron). But, inevitably their home governments—the U.S., Great Britain, and the Netherlands—were drawn into the fray.

As Figure 1 shows, beginning in the late 1930s, *every decade of the 20th century has been jarred by petroleum confrontations*, initiated by emerging nations and other players struggling to enhance control over their black gold. These include Mexico in the 1930s and 1940s, Venezuela and Iran in the 1950s, OPEC in the 1960s, Libya and OPEC in the 1970s, Iran in the 1980s, and Iraq in the 1990s.

**Figure 1.  Developed versus Developing World Oil Conflicts in the 20th Century**

| Year | Entity | Leader | Confrontation | Outcome |
|------|--------|--------|---------------|---------|
| 1938 | Mexico | Cárdenas | Expropriation | Capitulation |
| 1950s | Venezuela | Perez Alfonso | 50/50 Deal | Capitulation |
| 1953 | Iran | Mossadeq | Nationalization | Overthrow |
| 1960s | OPEC | Alfonso/Tariki | Participation | Capitulation |
| 1973 | Libya | Qadaffi | Expropriation | Capitulation |
| 1973 | OPEC | Yamani | Embargo | Recession |
| 1979 | Iran | Khomeini | Revolution | Recession |
| 1990 | Iraq | Hussein | Kuwait Invasion | Gulf War I |

# MEXICAN EXPROPRIATION, 1938

In 1938, Mexican President Lázaro Cárdenas expropriated all holdings belonging to U.S., British, and Dutch oil companies.[5] This unprecedented act came after the oil companies defiantly refused an order from the Supreme Court of Mexico to negotiate with oil field workers, who had gone on strike over abysmal living and working conditions. The oil companies protested vehemently and asked President Franklin D. Roosevelt to intervene, even pressuring him to invade Mexico. President Roosevelt refused. He had proclaimed the Good Neighbor Policy and knew that the U.S. would need Latin American allies and raw materials for the coming war in Europe.

In retaliation, the American, British, and Dutch oil companies, with essential refineries and distribution systems, boycotted the nationalized oil. American Ambassador Josephus Daniels predicted Mexicans would "drown in their own oil." Mexico, however, persevered throughout the 1940s and founded a new national oil company, Petroleos Mexicanos, PEMEX. Today, PEMEX is the crown jewel of national pride, the largest company in Latin America, and the primary source of hard currency for Mexico.

The Mexican expropriation was the first successful confrontation between a developing nation and the oil cartel. It was the shot heard round the oil-producing world, inspiring additional challenges. Yet, at the time, few observers perceived that Mexico would be the first in a chain reaction that spread next to Venezuela and ultimately to the Middle East. In time, this chain reaction would unify most of the oil producers against the oil companies.

## VENEZUELA'S FIFTY-FIFTY DEAL, 1950s

In 1945, a sophisticated new breed of oil minister emerged in Venezuela. Perez Alfonso was an academic economist who understood the international economics of oil. In time, he would become president of Venezuela and the chief architect of OPEC. With an eye on Mexico's success and an understanding of how the wartime pressures for uncontested oil made the governments of the U.S. and Europe reluctant to back up the oil companies, Alfonso realized the time was ripe for peacefully negotiating a new partnership.

Venezuela demanded and received a fifty-fifty share in all oil profits. The companies soon realized this arrangement provided them with a new kind of security. It made them partners with the government and thus far less vulnerable to radical and nationalistic attacks. It also marked the beginning of the shift from confrontation to collusion between the oil companies and their host regimes. As this fifty-fifty arrangement provided a viable basis for oil stability during the 1950s, it soon crossed the Atlantic and became the rallying cry for the Arab oil exporters.

## OPEC ESTABLISHED, 1960s

The early 1960s saw the birth of OPEC, which originated in meetings among Saudi Arabia, Iran, Iraq, Kuwait, and Venezuela. Together, they accounted for 80% of the world's oil exports. The alliance was spearheaded by Perez Alfonso and Abdullah Tariki, the new oil advisor in Saudi Arabia. Like Alfonso, Tariki represented the new generation of oil ministers. He had been educated at the University of Texas, had worked for Texaco, and had a first-hand knowledge of U.S. oil and anti-trust regulations. The catalyst for OPEC was a series of price concessions that the oil companies, led by Exxon, demanded from the Arab nations. This poisoned the atmosphere in the Middle East. The major oil producers believed they had to form "a cartel to confront the cartel" of "Big Oil" greed to avoid being forced to make additional future concessions. Little by little, throughout the 1960s, the oil companies capitulated.

First, OPEC prevented further price reductions. Eventually, under the emerging leadership of the Saudi Arabian oil minister Sheikh Zaki Yamani, OPEC articulated the goal of shared ownership of the oil concessions. So, in the late sixties, OPEC moved from negotiating favorable crude oil prices toward the idea of gradual nationalization, under the tactful concept of "participation."

The Harvard-educated Yamani believed the oil-exporting nations should forego militant confrontation and leverage their way into the global oil system—without disrupting it. They would build up their national oil companies and take over a major share of oil revenues. OPEC nations chose not to try to fight the cartel companies but to become a cartel themselves. Oil executives soon realized that without access to oil, they would have no oil companies, and without playing ball, they would eventually be nationalized. In a

> *"With the possible exception of Croesus, the world will never have seen anything like the wealth which is flowing and will continue to flow into the Persian Gulf."*
>
> —JAMES AKINS, APRIL 1973

major shift in the global balance of power, the oil companies capitulated to participation. This solidified OPEC, vastly enriched the oil producers, and forged a new collaboration between the oil companies and the oil regimes. It also set the stage for the major confrontations between OPEC and the West that would precipitate the oil crises of the 1970s.

## LIBYAN NATIONALIZATION, 1973

In 1973, on the eve of the Arab-Israeli War, Muammar al-Gadaffi unilaterally announced he would nationalize 51% of the holdings of all oil companies operating in Libya, including subsidiaries of Exxon, Mobil, Texaco, Socal, and Shell. Two days later he doubled the price of Libyan oil and threatened to cut off all exports to America if Washington continued to support Israel. Soon afterward, the ministers of the Arab oil nations met at OPEC headquarters in Vienna to discuss using oil as a weapon to change U.S. policy. President Nixon publicly warned Gadaffi about the dangers of an oil boycott, defiantly reminding him of the fate of Iranian Prime Minster Mossadeq, who had been deposed by the CIA and Churchill's government 20 years earlier for nationalizing British oil holdings. But the U.S. president failed to grasp a fundamental sea change in the world oil markets over the previous decade: power had shifted from consumers to producers. Oil company middlemen were now beholden to the producers of oil.

## OPEC EMBARGO, 1973

In the crisis atmosphere of October 1973, Egypt and Syria invaded Israeli-occupied territory. The Arab members of OPEC announced they would meet to discuss the use of oil as a weapon.

As the U.S. rushed to re-arm Israeli to prevent almost certain defeat, Arab OPEC leaders flew to Washington to announce both unilateral price hikes and the possibility of an oil embargo unless the U.S. agreed to stop supporting Israel. Not only did the more conservative Saudis join the embargo, they also implied that the next steps would bring nationalization and possibly a break in diplomatic relations with Washington. As the price of oil quadrupled in just over two months, America plunged into its first major oil-driven recession. This particular recession was so severe that it crippled the economies of the Western democracies and thereby reduced the quantity of oil those countries consumed. The drop in demand became so great that it broke OPEC's ability to maintain its pricing structure. Unfortunately, a similar scenario will not bring the end to the next oil-driven recession because China, India, and the rest of Asia will continue to accelerate their consumption even if the rate of consumption in the U.S. were to drop.

## IRANIAN REVOLUTION

Six years later, in June 1979, the second OPEC oil crisis of the decade erupted in the U.S., undermining Jimmy Carter's presidency and ruining his chances for re-election. The Iranian Revolution deposed the Shah of Iran, the key to the West's hopes for political moderation and stability in the Middle East, and replaced him with the militant Islamic cleric Ayatollah Khomeini. Iran's oil supply was disrupted for months, OPEC increased oil prices, gas prices skyrocketed, and hundreds of billions of petrodollars were transferred to Middle Eastern nations. In the U.S., this resulted in severe gas shortages, long lines at filling stations, double-digit interest rates, high inflation, high unemployment, and economic stagnation.

As a result, President Carter's approval rating dropped to 25%, even lower than President Nixon's during the Watergate hearings. This novel ongoing energy crisis catapulted foreign nations previously peripheral to international politics into positions of great wealth and influence and created a sobering crisis of confidence in industrial nations whose growth was linked to cheap oil.

# GULF WAR I, 1990

All three major U.S. recessions of the late twentieth century have been caused by geopolitical events rather than supply shortages. These events included the 1973 Arab-led OPEC oil boycott to protest U.S. support for Israel; the 1979 Iranian Revolution; and most recently, the 1990 first Gulf War, which President George H.W. Bush launched in response to Saddam Hussein's invasion of Kuwait.

In 1989, Hussein had just finished a long and costly war with Iran. He needed to sell as much oil as possible to replenish his depleted treasury. Neighboring Kuwait, fearing its bellicose neighbor, flooded the market with oil to keep prices down. Hussein considered this an act of "economic war" and in 1990 sent troops pouring over the Kuwaiti border. He launched this invasion on the grave miscalculation that the U.S. would not risk war over oil. By the 1990s, oil addiction and dependency on oil imports dominated the U.S. economy. Perceiving its oil lifeline in jeopardy, the U.S. rapidly mobilized for Gulf War I, drove Hussein's forces from Kuwait, and invaded Iraq.

Significantly, this was the first war in world history that was exclusively about oil. Hussein had invaded over oil. Economists worried over the loss of Kuwaiti oil. The U.S. reacted so quickly because the world could not tolerate Hussein's imperial ambitions to control the combined oil resources of Kuwait and Saudi Arabia (widely assumed to be next on Hussein's "hit list"), which together accounted for nearly 30% of world exports. It was the spike in oil prices that resulted from Gulf War I that plunged the U.S. into another recession and gave Democratic candidate Bill Clinton the issue he needed ("It's the economy, stupid!") to defeat President Bush's bid for reelection. Ironically, President Bush protected his oil industry associates and Saudi Arabian partners at the cost of his own presidency.

The oil conflicts of the past-half century have set the stage for a potential oil-triggered global economic collapse in the next 10 years that could rival the Depression of the 1930s. Figure 2 shows the high concentration of world oil exports: the top five countries control 61%. More ominous is that 45% of all oil exports come from five geopolitical "hot" spots: Iran, Iraq, Nigeria, Venezuela, and Saudi Arabia. Because of the continuing second Iraq war, Iraq's daily output remains far below and less reliable than its pre-war production of 2.5 MBD and even below what Iraq requires for domestic use. In addition, Russia has already demonstrated its willingness to use oil and gas as a political weapon, as witnessed by the temporary cutoff of natural gas supplies to the Ukraine and Europe in the summer of 2005. It has also nationalized and consolidated the major petroleum companies, Yukos and Gazprom, and raised prices to Belarus and Ukraine by well over 100% since 2005.

## Figure 2.  Top World Oil Net Exporters, 2004*
### (OPEC members in italics, hot spots in bold)

|     | Country | Net Oil Exports (MBD) |
| --- | --- | --- |
| 1) | *Saudi Arabia* | 8.73 (22.8%) |
| 2) | Russia | 6.67 (17.4%) |
| 3) | Norway | 2.91 (7.6%) |
| 4) | *Iran* | 2.55 (6.7%) |
| 5) | *Venezuela* | 2.36 (6.2%) |
| 6) | *United Arab Emirates* | 2.33 (6.1%) |
| 7) | *Kuwait* | 2.20 (5.7%) |
| 8) | *Nigeria* | 2.19 (5.7%) |
| 9) | Mexico | 1.80 (4.7%) |
| 10) | *Algeria* | 1.68 (4.4%) |
| 11) | *Iraq* | 1.48 (3.9%) |
| 12) | *Libya* | 1.34 (3.5%) |
| 13) | Kazakhstan | 1.06 (2.8%) |
| 14) | Qatar | 1.02 (2.7%) |
|     | **Total** | **38.32 (100%)**\*\* |

\* Table includes all countries with net exports exceeding 1 MBD in 2004
\*\* Rounded from 100.2%
Source: U.S. Energy Information Administration, 2006

## THE VENEZUELAN STRONGMAN

The relationship between the U.S. and Venezuela has been strained since populist President Hugo Chávez was elected in 1998. He was re-elected in 2000 and 2006, each time with 60% or more of the vote. On several occasions, Chávez has directly threatened an oil embargo of the U.S.

A sudden cut-off of Venezuelan oil, which accounts for about 15% of U.S. imports, would precipitate steep price spikes and shortages. Amidst recent oil price increases and market jitters, it would probably take a cut-off of less than one-third of Venezuelan exports to the U.S. (shipped to China and India instead) to push U.S. gas prices up to the $4-$5 per gallon range.

Venezuela has played a key role in world oil production and exports since the 1940s. At that time, Venezuela filled the gap left by the Mexican oil nationalization and provided critical petroleum supplies to the Allies during World War II. Venezuela today has 7.4% of the world's total proven reserves (77 billion barrels) compared to Saudi Arabia's 25% of world reserves (262 billion barrels). Venezuela produces 4% of world oil output (3.5 MBD) compared to 12% (10 MBD) for Saudi Arabia. Venezuela is one of the top five oil exporters in the world, with 6.2% of total world exports (about 2.4 MBD). Of great significance for potential supply disruptions and short-term production swings is that Petroleos de Venezuela SA (PDVSA), the national oil company, has a refining capacity that is *higher than that of any other oil company in the world* except for ExxonMobil. In addition, PDVSA is the sole owner of Citgo, a U.S refining and marketing firm that operates 14,000 gas stations in the U.S.

Short of military intervention by the U.S. or an oil boycott by Venezuela, diplomatic relations between the two nations could not get much worse. Chávez has repeatedly complained about the Bush administration's overt support for groups who have attempted to overthrow him, and its backing of a short-lived coup against him in 2002, during which he was imprisoned in his own country by pro-U.S. forces. Bush denounces Chávez as a radical and revolutionary who supports left-wing movements throughout Latin

America—"Castro with oil." In return, Chávez labels Bush "the greatest terrorist in the world" and in a U.N. speech in October 2006, evidenced his disdain for President Bush by calling him "the devil." Clearly, Chávez feels extreme hostility toward the Bush

> "The United States should know that if they go over the line, they are not going to have Venezuelan oil."
>
> — HUGO CHÁVEZ,
> PRESIDENT OF VENEZUELA

administration and would relish the opportunity to drive home his enmity with oil as his weapon of choice.

To add to the tensions caused by Chávez's belief that the Bush administration overtly supported an attempt to overthrow him and put him in prison, he has heard even more threatening comments from some of the Administration's most prominent supporters. In early 2006, Pat Robertson, a right-wing religious leader, called for the assassination of Chávez so that the U.S. would not have to spend $200 billion on another oil war. It is telling that, while Sean McCormack, a U.S. State Department spokesman, called Robertson's remarks inappropriate, he stopped short of condemning them or demanding a retraction.

In this tense atmosphere, Chávez has decreed that all foreign oil companies with contracts to pump oil in Venezuela must pay increased royalty rates of 50% and must also comply with a new law requiring them to form joint ventures with Petroleos de Venezuela. Under the law, the government will own a majority share of all joint ventures with foreign firms. Chávez has also claimed that the foreign oil companies owe more than $3 billion in unpaid taxes and has initiated tax evasion probes to collect these funds. Tax evasion was precisely the weapon used by Vladimir Putin to effectively nationalize Yukos, Russia's largest oil company.

As the fifth-largest oil exporter in the world, Venezuela currently sells half of its 3.5 MBD of production to the U.S. (Venezuela's massive and often specialized refinery structure processes crude oil pumped from other countries as well as its own.) It is clear Chávez is aggressively seeking new markets for oil exports, so that he will have the option to cut off oil sales to the U.S. in the future. To this end, Venezuelan oil shipments to China have increased five times in a framework of long-term oil contracts. India has been given rights to purchase oil *and* build a refinery there. Chávez is also seeking new customers in other Asian markets, all of which (with the exception of Indonesia and Malaysia) are consuming much more oil than they are producing.

There is an old adage that "the enemy of my enemy is my friend." So, it is not surprising that Chávez recently visited and sided with Iran, claiming that the Bush administration is falsely accusing Iran of trying to build a nuclear bomb and is using that as a pretext to an attempt to control Iran's oil reserves.

Unfortunately, President Chávez with his huge oil wealth and 70% domestic approval rating will constantly be looking for ways to assist other nations in their efforts to obtain the "upper hand" over the U.S., whom he views as a "terrorist state." And, remember, this skillful and charismatic leader, who sees himself as the new Bolivar of South America, controls 15% of all U.S. oil imports. We believe this spells certain trouble for the U.S. in the years ahead, as producer power grows and consumer nations become even weaker and more dependent.

## The Iranian Mystic

In March 2006, OPEC's No. 2 oil producer, Iran, threatened the West that it "will use any means" necessary, including employing oil as a weapon, if the U.N. Security Council imposes sanctions because of the Iranian nuclear program which the U.S. suspects Iran is using to produce nuclear bombs for ultimate proliferation throughout the Muslim world. While the U.S. is not a direct importer of Iranian oil, these explicit threats by Iran to escalate the crisis over its nuclear program "beyond Europe's control" could have economic repercussions that reach far beyond France and Germany, Iran's largest trading partners.

The appointment/election of Mahmoud Ahmadinejad as president of Iraq in 2005 has dramatically ramped up the rhetoric of confrontation within the highly volatile Middle East. Educated as a revolutionary, trained as a killer, and decried as a fanatic, Ahmadinejad has gone out of his way to provoke international outrage. He has denied the existence of the Holocaust, called for the destruction of Israel, and berated the "false superpowers" who are trying to prevent Iran's legitimate ambitions to develop

> *"If (they) politicize our nuclear case, we will use any means . . . . We have control over the biggest and most sensitive energy route in the world."*
>
> — IRANIAN INTERIOR MINISTER MOSTAFA POURMOHAMMADI

nuclear power. Ahmadinejad has linked his movement to the preparation of the way for the mystical return of the Imam Mahdi, a highly charismatic Islamic religious figure who vanished some 1,000 years ago. While Ahmadinejad's appeal is strongest among the "war generation" that successfully fought off Saddam's forces in the Iraq-Iran war of 1980-88, his defiance of the West over Iran's nuclear ambitions has generated broad popular support.

In raising the possibility that Iran would use its oil and natural gas resources as weapons in the international standoff, Iranian Interior Minister Mostafa Pourmohammadi noted Iran's strategic location near the Strait of Hormuz, a key chokepoint for the vital Persian Gulf oil route through which a quarter of the world's oil supply moves each day (see Figure 3.) "If (they) politicize our nuclear case, we will use any means. We are rich in energy resources. We have control over the biggest and most sensitive energy route in the world," Pourmohammadi told the official Islamic Republic News Agency. Should Iran blockade the Strait, it could stop international oil shipments from *the key* exporting nations, including Iraq, Kuwait, Bahrain, Saudi Arabia, Qatar, and the United Arab Emirates. *Any sustained stoppage* of oil flowing through the Strait would rapidly bring the economies of the Western democracies to their knees.

Oil flow optimists say that such a move would be an economic disaster for Iran itself, and thus such threats are hollow. In a world of suicide bombers and leaders who draw inspiration from divine communications or submit their nations to severe economic deprivation, such logical cause-effect analyses based on material considerations have a distinctly Western tone. We are concerned that the "clash of cultures" may produce illogical results based upon fear and perceived religious mandates. Make no mistake, an Iran that perceived itself threatened would be capable of numerous attempts to block the flow of Middle Eastern oil to the Western democracies.

**Figure 3. Strait of Hormuz and Saudi Arabian Oil Industry**

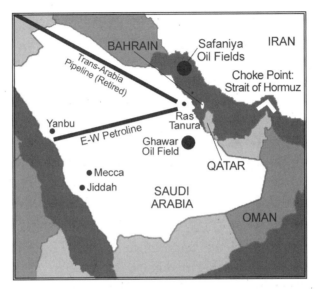

Sources: Compiled by PBS based on data provided by U.S. Energy Information
    Administration; British Petroleum; BBC News Online; CIA World Factbook;
    and U.S. Department of State

Iran insists it has the right to engage in peaceful uranium enrichment under the Non-Proliferation Treaty (NPT), the key safeguard of the global system designed to stop the spread of nuclear weapons. U.S. and European opposition to Iran's enrichment program for nuclear power is creating another potential flashpoint in the region.

Certainly President Bush's surprise announcement in March 2006 that the U.S. will provide commercial nuclear power technology to India (which for three decades has steadfastly refused to sign the NPT) both unilaterally reverses 50 years of established arms control policy and undermines the international case against Iran.

Furthermore, speculation is rampant of a possible U.S. or Israeli preemptive military strike against Iranian uranium enrichment facilities at Natanz, similar to the successful Israeli air strike against Iraq's Osirak reactor in 1981. Such a strike would further destabilize the region, possibly leading to a new round of OPEC sanctions. Likewise, the outbreak of a shooting war between Israel and Hezbollah in southern Lebanon in July 2006 must be viewed in the broader context of regional hostilities that could easily spill over to the other "tinderbox" regions of the Middle East.

Any action by Iran, the world's No. 4 oil exporter, to suspend its oil shipments could send crude oil prices rocketing to over $100/ barrel.

## CHAOS IN NIGERIA

Some analysts describe Nigeria as "the next Iraq."[6] With nearly 10% of U.S. oil imports coming from Nigeria, this sub-Saharan OPEC nation has become America's fifth-largest supplier of imported oil. As such, it ranks closely behind Saudi Arabia, Venezuela, Canada, and Mexico in importance. Overall, Nigeria exports 2.2 MBD of oil into the global market.

Since January 2006, attacks by rebels from the oil-rich Niger Delta have cut Nigeria's oil exports by over 25%—by over 800,000 barrels per day.[7] Continuing rebel attacks and the kidnapping of over 100 oil and other foreign workers have cost the Nigerian government billions of dollars in lost oil revenues and have sharply cut new investment. The militants, members of the Movement for the Emancipation of the Niger Delta, have already blasted oil and gas pipelines, damaged a key oil loading terminal, and threatened to fire rockets at international oil tankers. One of the group's leaders has boasted that he has "the oil industry by the balls." An oil-industry security official said, "Either bodies are going to pile up or we are going to see an oil shock, or both."[8]

This is not a sporadic outburst but the continuation of a *decade* of protests against oil exploitation and pollution by bitter Delta Nigerians. These Nigerians live in extreme poverty, often lacking electricity, running water, and decent schools or jobs, *despite* the oil wealth generated by their region of the country. Unlike the situation in Iran and Venezuela, the potential chaos in Nigeria stems from the deep and simmering outrage that residents feel against the oil companies and their own government, which has corruptly pocketed the proceeds of oil leases, despoiled the environment, and imposed a brutal crackdown on protest leaders.

The nation's oil-producing region is beset with insurgencies and criminality, some originating in the national government itself. In 2005, two Nigerian rear admirals were court-martialed for their role in the attempted theft of thousands of tons of Nigerian oil by an international crime syndicate operating in Russia and Eastern Europe.

Ever since American troops were ambushed and killed in Somalia during the first term of the Clinton presidency, American policy has operated under the firm rule of never putting U.S. soldiers on the ground in Africa. While this has prevented humanitarian missions in Rwanda and Liberia, the policy is under review by the influential Council on Foreign Relations because of the tacit principle of protecting American oil supply at any price. A recent Council report notes, "The suppression of dissent in the Delta, together with armed violence and the existence of armed militias make for a potentially explosive combination." [9] If Iraq has become a sandstorm for the U.S., Nigeria may soon become a tar pit.

## The House of Saud

Without question, the secret "oil-for-security pact" forged between Saudi Arabia's royal family and President Franklin D. Roosevelt during World War II remains the linchpin for U.S. interests in maintaining a stable and secure supply of oil from the Middle East. More recently, the Saudi-U.S. relationship has been further enhanced by the Carlyle Group's role in investing Saudi wealth, initially in American arms production and recently through a series of private sector investments. The Carlyle Group is under the blue-ribbon leadership of former President George

H.W. Bush, former Secretary of State Henry Kissinger, and other notables.

The Saudis are by far the number 1 exporter of oil in the world (exporting 8.73 MBD), the number 1 supplier of U.S. oil imports (providing 63% of U.S. net imports from the Persian Gulf), and holders of 25% of the world's proven oil reserves. At present, the "war on terror," the strife in Somalia, the War in Iraq, the recent Israeli military excursions into Lebanon and Gaza, and the rise of Islamist violence against Westerners have created the most severe challenge faced by the Saudi royal family in its 100-year history. Moreover, these factors have strained the U.S.-Saudi alliance within the general U.S. *and* Saudi populations.

With overall U.S. oil imports expected to rise from 53% of U.S. consumption in 2000 to 70% by 2025, America is becoming ever more dependent on Saudi Arabia and a Gulf region that is volatile, militarized, distant, unstable, and hostile to the West and American values. After the death of King Fahd in August 2005 and the official installation of his half-brother, Abdullah, as the new ruler, Saudi Arabia's fragile monarchy faces a "slow-motion insurrection" from rising Islamic fundamentalism.[10]

Tensions have been significantly exacerbated by President George W. Bush's soon-to-be half a trillion-dollar war in Iraq. Four years after the U.S. invaded Iraq, the region has witnessed an acceleration of chaos and insecurity. An ever-larger portion of the Muslim world has become radicalized. Iraq, Afghanistan, and significant portions of northwestern Pakistan have become havens for terrorists. The deepening Sunni-Shiite civil war has spread a sense of apprehension throughout the region.

Because Iraq had the world's second-largest proven oil reserves, it was naively hoped that its untapped oil fields—which could reach 200 billion barrels—would pay for reconstruction and nation-building. Unfortunately, hundreds of billions of American tax dollars later, *Iraq's oil is still flowing well below prewar levels*—when it flows at all. As noted earlier, Iraq now produces less oil than it requires even for its own domestic energy needs. There is not enough electricity in

Baghdad. How much longer do we have before Iraq further reduces its oil shipments to the rest of the world when its domestic economy is in shambles?

Terrorist attacks have routinely disrupted both Iraqi production and exports. For example, in March 2006, suicide boat attacks on the al-Basar terminal resulted in the loss of nearly 1 MBD, equal to two-thirds of Iraq's total oil exports.

At this rate it will take a decade or more before the Iraq oil industry can recover from the 2003 U.S. invasion, and export to world markets in substantial quantities. As the U.S. eventually withdraws its forces, the civil war will predictably end with Iran's allies controlling the south of the country while the Kurds consolidate their control of the north. Clearly, despite its vast reserves, Iraq will not be a major oil player for exports or new reserves in the near future.

Heightened militancy, terrorism, and extremism in Saudi Arabia and the Middle East rank high among the vortex of unintended consequences that the invasion of Iraq has accelerated. In November 2004, 26 prominent Saudi clerics signed a *fatwa* urging the Iraqis to rise up against the Americans and encouraged all Muslims to go and fight the Americans occupying Iraq. A fundamentalist takeover of Saudi Arabia could result in that nation's turning its back on capitalism and international trade and a long-term reduction or suspension of oil shipments to the U.S.

As Figure 3 shows, most of Saudi Arabia's oil resources and infrastructure are concentrated in the east, close to the conflict-prone Persian Gulf. Oil exports are typically shipped through the Strait of Hormuz, the strategically vulnerable bottleneck near the Gulf's outlet to international waters. Of the eight largest oil and gas fields that contain more than half of Saudi oil reserves, the two biggest, Ghawar (the world's largest oil field) and Safaniya (the world's largest offshore oilfield), are near or in the Persian Gulf itself. Two-thirds of Saudi Arabia's crude oil is exported from the Gulf via the Abqaiq processing facility. Saudi Arabia's two primary oil export terminals are located at Ras Tanura (the world's largest offshore oil transfer facility) and Ras al-Ju'aymah, both in the Gulf as well. Another terminal lies in Yanbu, a port city on the Red Sea.

Saudi Arabia's oil facilities provide inviting and high-profile targets to terrorists. In February 2006, suicide bombers carried out a foiled attack on the world's largest oil processing facility at Abqaiq. Had the suicide squad used a small private plane instead of an automobile, they could well have succeeded in severely damaging that enormous refinery. Similarly, a successful attack on the pipelines feeding the Saudis' Ras Tanura oil installation could immediately disrupt 10% of the world's oil supply. As noted previously, an Iranian blockage of the Strait of Hormuz would disrupt the oil exports not only of Saudi Arabia, but of Iraq, Kuwait, Qatar, and the United Arab Emirates, as well. The U.S. Energy Information Administration projects that oil exports through the Strait will dramatically rise if pumping is increased in the Middle East. The Strait will remain the most vital link (some would say the "linchpin") in U.S. and global oil supply.

In these volatile times, the U.S. relies heavily on the "sole Saudi pillar" for world oil stability. According to a former U.S. Energy Information Administration chief economist, even a few months' disruption of Saudi exports "would spell disaster" and "throw the global economy into chaos." No reasonable observer believes the Middle East is a stable region. Yet, it is upon this wildly chaotic hotbed of Islamic fundamentalism that the U.S. has placed its *total* dependence. This is inherently unwise and dangerous beyond any reasonable doubt. We believe it is a time bomb ticking. We believe the U.S. must act *now* to dramatically reduce its dependence on Middle East oil.

## CHINA AND INDIA: THE PERFECT STORM

Worldwatch Institute observers describe "the great leap forward" taking place concurrently in China and India as an event without precedent in world history—on par with the rise of Rome and the discovery of the New World.[11]

With 2.4 billion people (equal to 40% of the world's population), these two no-longer-sleeping giants threaten to overwhelm the already strained balance between human consumption and the earth's natural resources. For example, it is projected that by 2015, China could be the world's largest automobile manufacturer, over-taking both the U.S. and Japan, which currently each turn out about 8 million cars per year. This holds obvious implications for rapidly increasing global demand for oil. Already, China and India have turned not only to the Middle East, but to Africa, Latin America, the former Soviet Union, and beyond, in search of oil to fuel their domestic automobile-trucking fleets and their growing economies.

Both China and India have launched this great transition to modernization because of intensive investments in human resources and intellectual capital. Whereas India's growth is based mainly on technology, China's economic miracle has been built on a burgeoning manufacturing sector. China now makes everything from clothing to consumer goods and is rapidly moving into computers and high-tech manufacturing.

China and the U.S. are locked in a symbiotic relationship. Low-cost Chinese consumer goods are essential to the American middle-class lifestyle. In turn, U.S. trade dollars fund China's insatiable need for raw materials. To put this into perspective, consider that 80% of Wal-Mart suppliers are located in China. In 2004, Wal-Mart alone accounted for almost 10% of the $197 billion in goods the U.S. imported from China.

China is on the verge of reshaping the world economy and the biosphere. Just as the 20th century was "the American century," so the 21st century will be "the Chinese century."

As Figure 4 shows, China's and India's economic expansions have been primarily fed with home-grown, conventional energy resources: coal and biomass (firewood and agricultural wastes) and hydroelectric. Coal currently accounts for two-thirds of China's energy supplies and one half of India's.

Compared to the energy-intensive economies of the U.S., Germany, and Japan, oil use in China is a modest 1.9 barrels per person per year. India consumes only 0.9 barrels per person per year. In both countries this ratio *and* the absolutely total number

**Figure 4. Oil and Coal Trends in China, India, Germany, Japan, and the United States, 2004**

| Country | Coal Use | Oil Use | Oil Use Per Person | Net Oil Imports | Share of Oil Imported |
|---|---|---|---|---|---|
| | Million tons of oil-equivalent | Million barrels per day | Barrels per year | Million barrels per day | Percent |
| China | 957 | 6.7 | 1.9 | 3.2 | 48 |
| India | 205 | 2.6 | 0.9 | 1.7 | 65 |
| Germany | 86 | 2.6 | 11.9 | 2.6 | 100 |
| Japan | 121 | 5.3 | 15.2 | 5.3 | 100 |
| USA | 564 | 20.5 | 25.3 | 13.3 | 65 |

Source: Worldwatch Institute, *State of the World 2006*

of barrels consumed shows dramatic growth. China's oil use is growing by 7.5% a year, seven times the U.S. growth rate. China's energy system is stressed beyond capacity in trying to cope with increases in GDP of 10.5% per year. When peak demand exceeded supplies in 2004, the mainland experienced rolling blackouts and manufacturing stoppages—in a country where political survival is dependent on keeping the manufacturing base growing.

As a result, both China and India have followed the example of the West and Japan, turning to imported oil to fuel growth. In 2007, China displaced Japan as the world's second largest oil importer, and Chinese oil imports are growing by 30% a year.

As Chris Flavin and Gary Gardner of the Worldwatch Institute note, "If over the next several decades both countries [China and India] were to reach even half of U.S. levels of consumption—about the current level of Japan—they alone would be using 100 MBD . . . . That would imply total worldwide oil consumption in 2050 of well over 200 MBD. Few geologists believe that output will reach even half those levels before beginning to decline."[12]

> *"In 2005, China used 26% of the world's crude steel, 32% of the rice, 37% of the cotton, and 47% of the cement."*
>
> — CHRIS FLAVIN AND GARY GARDNER, WORLDWATCH INSTITUTE

Whatever the long-term consequences for oil demand may be, the simultaneous arrival of China and India on the world economic stage exacerbates the volatile, short-term geopolitics of oil and establishes the ideal conditions for a "perfect storm" of scarcity, instability and skyrocketing prices in world oil markets. These conditions include:

- World oil demand growing faster than production is increasing;

- A recent doubling of China's and India's rates of oil consumption;

- Limits reached on Saudi Arabia's role as the swing producer;

- Political volatility between U.S. and key oil exporters;

- U.S. losing control of oil supplies vulnerable to external political forces;

- Skyrocketing oil prices: more than $78/barrel in 2006 and estimated to surpass $100 by 2008; and

- Middle East instability, terrorism, and the West's tenuous oil umbilical cord.

In early 2004, in a book entitled *The Oil Factor*, Stephen Leeb predicted that oil prices would reach $100/barrel within a few years.[13] At the time, most experts found this to be outlandish. In fact, annual peak oil prices have soared in the past decade: the price of a barrel went from $10 in 1998, to $30 in 2003, to above $78 in 2006 and 2007, and is now estimated to exceed $100 in 2008—which could eventually mean gas pump prices in the U.S. at or above $10/ gallon.

*If we continue to do business as usual,* the stage is set for long-term oil prices at $100 to $200/barrel, an unprecedented energy crisis, and potential economic collapse. This is not a Chicken Little alarm. Leeb warns, "An economic crisis is near at hand in America today, the kind of dramatic, earth-shattering crisis that periodically threatens the very survival of civilization." He joins a small but rising chorus of expert opinion that the coming energy crisis will pose the greatest problem ever faced by our civilization.[14]

The geopolitics of scarcity will accelerate the end of easy oil and the coming energy-driven economic crisis. In numerous parts of the world, America's vital oil supplies are under siege by insurgents, terrorists, and hostile governments. The "good guys" cannot always win the battle of oil security versus terrorism. Current U.S. policy is fostering terrorism, "petrolism," and oil insecurity. Time is short. We must act now to avert potential economic collapse and a grim future. We have been warned, and we have ever less time to respond. Action to *dramatically* decrease U.S. dependence on imported oil is the number 1 national security mandate. And as discussed in the next chapter, we have no alternative but to address this energy challenge in a manner that is completely compatible with mitigating the interdependent crisis of climate change.

# Notes and References
## Chapter 3: Geopolitics of Scarcity

1 For an elaboration of this argument, see Stephen Leeb, *The Coming Economic Collapse: How You Can Thrive When Oil Costs $200 a Barrel* (New York: Warner Business Books, 2006).

2 Anthony Sampson, *The Seven Sisters: The Great Oil Companies and the World They Made* (New York: Viking Press, 1975). This description of the OPEC conference is based directly on Sampson's first chapter, "Who Controls?"

3 *Ibid.*, 2-3.

4 Daniel Yergin, *The Prize: The Epic Quest for Oil, Money, and Power* (New York: Simon & Schuster, 1991), 13.

5 Jerry B. Brown, "The Mexican Oil Expropriation," *Caribbean Review*, 10:3, 1981.

6 G. Pacal Zachary, "Nigeria: The Next Quagmire"? *AlterNet*, 2006, www.alternet.org/story/33282.

7 S. Hanson, "MEND: The Niger Delta's Umbrella Militant Group," Backgrounder, March 22, 2007, Council on Foreign Relations, http://www.cfr.org/publication/12920/.

8 *The Economist*, March 17, 2007, 52.

9 *Ibid.*, 1.

10 G. Dyer, "If Saudi Arabia Falls," GBN Global Perspectives, Emeryville, CA, Global Business Network, June 2, 2004.

11 Chris Flavin and Gary Gardner, "China, India and the New World Order," *State of the World 2006*, 3.

12 *Ibid.*, 10.

13 Stephen Leeb and Donna Leeb, *The Oil Factor* (New York: Warner Business Books, 2004), 1.

14 For example, Lester Brown, *Plan B 2.0: Rescuing a Planet Under Stress and a Civilization in Trouble (New York: W.W. Norton, 2006)*; Paul Roberts, *The End of Oil: On the Edge of a Perilous New World (New York: Mariner Books, 2004)*; Richard Heinberg, *The Party's Over: Oil, War, and the Fate of Industrial Societies* (Gabriola Island, BC, Canada: New Society Publishers, 2005); and James Howard Kunstler, *The Long Emergency: Surviving the Converging Catastrophes of the Twenty-First Century* (New York: Atlantic Monthly Press, 2005).

# 4

## CLIMATE CHANGE:
## CLOUDY WITH A CHANCE OF CHAOS

*"There is a kind of optimism built into our species that prefers to live in the comfortable present rather than confront the possibility of destruction. It may happen, but not now, and not to us."*

—RICHARD FORTEY, PALEONTOLOGIST AND AUTHOR

**Is climate change really a critical global issue?** *Absolutely!*

- Carbon dioxide levels in our atmosphere are higher than at any time in the past 740,000 years. Short of nuclear war, climate change is likely to be the most critical challenge of the 21st century. It will cause trillions of dollars in damage and incalculable human suffering, expanding desertification, the spread of disease, famine, and more.

- If we do nothing, the earth's average temperature probably will rise by 2 to 4.5°C (3.6 to 8.1°F) by 2100. In a worst-case scenario—melting of the East Antarctic Ice Sheet or the Greenland Ice Sheet—sea levels could rise by as much as 65 meters (213 feet).

- Other consequences of a "business-as-usual" scenario include increased storm devastation, droughts, intense heat waves, species extinction, ocean acidification, and extinction of marine life.

- The results—massive migration of humans and other species, global economic collapse, and intense civil unrest.

- The Prometheus Plan could significantly mitigate the consequences of climate change if we begin immediately with dedicated political will.

## WHAT WILL WE TELL THE CHILDREN?

What *will* we tell the children when they ask why we didn't do something? Why didn't we take some kind of action? Will we cower and respond defensively, perhaps defiantly? "It was just too complex. We didn't understand it. There really wasn't enough evidence to make a good decision."

Or, will we pass the blame to someone else? Would we tell our children the following story?

It was those scientists! It was too complicated; they never made themselves clear. And besides, it was really a political thing. Why, even President George W. Bush firmly advised us, "No one can say with any certainty what constitutes a dangerous level of warming and therefore what levels must be avoided."[1] There was simply no leadership, none at all. How could we possibly have known what to do?

But then everything changed; it seemed like it happened overnight. It started back in 2005. Mississippi and Texas were smashed and New Orleans inundated by Hurricane Katrina, and as they were picking up the pieces, they were slapped again with a reminder by Rita. But those hurricanes were a midsummer breeze compared to what happened in the years that followed.

Before we knew it, our global climate had changed dramatically, and we were overtaken by the forces of unimaginably unstable weather patterns from every direction—cataclysmic hurricanes and typhoons, coastal storm surges, desertification where there once had been adequate precipitation, and rapidly melting glaciers in Alaska, Greenland, the Arctic, and the Antarctic. The coastline of the U.S. was changed beyond recognition. Miami, New Orleans, Boston, New York, San Francisco, and Los Angeles—well, you know, they're just not the same places anymore—not the way they used to be. Millions of people were displaced from cities now partially under water. How could anyone know that sea levels would rise so quickly? We thought even if those scientists were right, it surely would be hundreds of years in the future. Why should we be concerned?

And those poor folks in Northern Europe: they've had to leave their homes and migrate south to warmer climates to escape a permanent Siberian deep freeze. The Gulf Stream, part of our global heat conveyor system—it just shut down. Yes, I know there was a Pentagon study back in 2005 warning it could happen. Well, who knew it would be so soon? London, Paris, Brussels, Berlin, and more—all have suffered severe population decreases. And I shudder to recall what happened in Asia. Bangladesh—almost the whole country—it's gone, under the sea.

Our food supply was also hit hard. Wheat, corn, and many other crops were devastated on several continents. More people are starving today than ever in the history of civilization. And we were supposed to be the most technically advanced species since life began on this deeply troubled planet. I tell you, kids, there is a bit of a silver lining. I hear that folks up in the Canadian Far North are experiencing much warmer weather. They're actually beginning to have some success with a wide variety of crops they never could grow at those latitudes.

Here we are in 2030, just 25 years after it all seemed to start, and sea levels are still rising fast, as the glaciers at the poles continue to melt more rapidly. We're trying to stop them, but now they tell us that we've passed something called a "tipping point," and it's probably too late to do much good.

Look, kids, you ought to be grateful. At least we have a roof over our heads and some food to eat. I know that's

101

not much consolation. Since all of the financial markets crashed in 2010, millions of people have been out of work around the world. What can I tell you, kids? What can I tell you?

Sound like fiction? We hope so. Could it happen in our lifetime? Yes. Will it? It need not. Nonetheless, numerous well-informed scientists are convinced that if we continue to do nothing about climate change, we soon will have no chance to reverse what could be the most devastating change in the earth's environment since the genesis of homo sapiens.

And it will touch all of us. As Tim Flannery reminds us in *The Weather Makers*, his tutorial on climate change, 70% of all people alive today will still be alive in 2050.[2] What will you tell your children? Or as Nikita Lopoukhine, former director general of the National Parks in Canada, said in a recent editorial, "Have a hot, dry, stormy life, kids!"[3]

> *"It ain't what you don't know that gets you in trouble. It's what you know for sure that just ain't so."*
> — MARK TWAIN

## OUR BRAVE NEW WORLD

A critical question all of us should ponder is whether sustainable growth is possible in the 21st century. By *sustainable growth*, we mean *meeting today's global economic and environmental needs while preserving the ability of future generations to meet theirs.* On one hand, governments, industry, and large segments of society champion continuous growth even if that growth is destroying the planet. On the other hand, constituencies such as scientists, environmentalists, and government regulators are pushing back with equal passion for cautionary controls that would make that growth sustainable.

To understand how we got here, it is helpful to look back at the inception of this "brave new world" of ours. It started and took off incredibly quickly in the early 19th century with the Industrial Revolution. Fed by unquenchable technological curiosity and creativity, enabled by a capitalist growth-oriented society, and fueled by a drive for exploration, innovators and entrepreneurs launched an era that saw the greatest explosion in social progress and material wealth in human history.

There is, however, a very different way to view this development. Author Robert Newman cautions, "It's either capitalism or a habitable planet—you can't have both." Newman and others like him hold that our economic system is unsustainable by its very nature, and that the only meaningful response to climate chaos and peak oil is major social change. Newman passionately proclaims, "Capitalism . . . is predicated on infinitely expanding markets, faster consumption, and bigger production on a finite planet. And yet this ideological model remains the central organizing principle of our lives, and as long as it continues to be so, it will automatically undo (with its invisible hand) every single green initiative anybody cares to come up with."[4]

We disagree. Without question, the capitalist model and its attendant GDP growth have produced numerous positive outcomes for society. For example, during the 20th century, global population increased fourfold, from 1.5 to 6.3 billion people. At the same time, global GDP, or production of goods and services, increased by a factor of almost 75, from $0.6 trillion to $44 trillion, bringing prosperity and well-being to a multitude of people throughout the developed world. That's capitalism in action. However, we need a capitalist free market system that is disciplined with the wisdom to address future needs as well as present ones. We are capable of sustained growth which reconstructs our planetary environmental systems. In fact, that's the *only* way growth will continue to occur.

The enormous growth of the 20th century was accompanied by explosive technological progress in transportation, communication, education, and health care. For example, if you were born in 1900 in the developed world, your life expectancy was 40 years. In 2000, life expectancy increased to almost 80 years. Some of this longevity enhancement is due to the discovery of the power of simple sanitary methods. And much is based on significant technological advances. Thus, certain diseases are no longer a threat to people in the developed world—malaria, polio, typhoid, tuberculosis, and most bacterial infections, for example.

As we saw in Chapter 2 (see Figures 2 and 3), with the advent of the Industrial Revolution, the burning of fossil fuels has stuffed the earth's atmosphere with large volumes of toxic pollutants—particulates, nitrogen oxides and sulfur oxides, and a host of greenhouse gases, including methane, nitrous oxide, chlorofluorocarbons, and the major culprit, carbon dioxide ($CO_2$). The volumes of these harmful gases are large and growing so rapidly that to address this problem for the long term, we can no longer depend only on environmental service technologies such as disposal, recycling, and treatment. *Pollution prevention* must be a key strategic component of any effective growth plan for all nations. Ironically, it is often also the most economical solution, because prevention almost always results in a significant increase in energy and production efficiencies.

The most challenging of all pollution prevention problems in our current growth- and consumption-oriented society is the design and implementation of a strategy to control and, it is hoped, reverse, the negative impact of climate change by minimizing and eventually eliminating greenhouse gas emissions. Climate change is complex and difficult to evaluate objectively because it is deeply entangled in political and economic issues. Ironically, it is intimately connected to, and is an unfortunate by-product of, the very success and progress of our civilization. We are now wiser and can understand the nature and consequences of climate change. Fortunately, we now have the technological capabilities to meet our need for clean energy in a manner that does not negatively affect the environment.

Without the incredible technologies birthed during the Industrial Revolution, it would have been impossible to achieve all that society has achieved. Most of the technological engines of growth, however, were fired by fossil fuels. Furthermore, although global warming was predicted with limited data in 1905 by Swedish physical chemist Svante August Arrhenius,[5] there was really no way we could have known of the downside of fossil-fuel consumption until the early 1980s. Even Arrhenius thought that our atmosphere was so large that the effects of global warming would be inconsequential.

Because of this history and associated political-economic ramifications, we believe it will take immense courage, political will, and a boldly creative plan—the Prometheus Plan—to address these challenges. We must move the U.S. and through its leadership, the rest of the world, away from fossil fuels and in a safer and more sustainable direction.

## NATURE'S CHALLENGE

Our challenge is enormous, and the time is short if we are to make a difference. In brief, we now know that the $CO_2$ concentration in our atmosphere was nearly constant for 10,000 years. Then, suddenly, in direct parallel to the birth and growth of the Industrial Revolution, the $CO_2$ concentration increased over the past 150 years by 36%, from 280 parts per million (ppm) to 380 ppm (see Figure 1).

From analyses of the gas composition in ancient ice cores drilled in Greenland, the Arctic, and the Antarctic, we know that the $CO_2$ level is the highest it has been in more than 740,000 years. Since 1970 the average temperature of the earth has increased by 0.8°C, or about 1.4°F (see Figure 2).

## Figure 1. Atmospheric Concentrations of Carbon Dioxide, 1000-2004

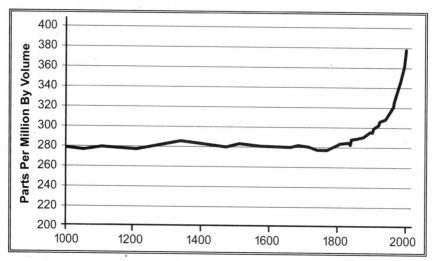

Source: Scripps Institution of Oceanography

## Figure 2. Average Global Temperature, 1880-2005

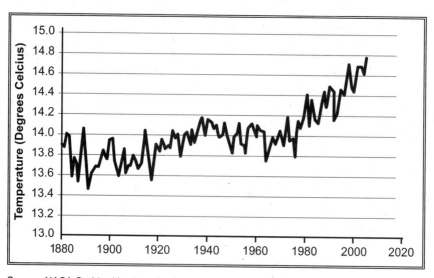

Source: NASA Goddard Institute for Space Studies, 2005

In addition to $CO_2$ concentration, we now can also measure the average temperature of the earth going back hundreds of thousands of years. Scientists have accomplished this by determining the ratio of two isotopic forms of oxygen (oxygen-16 and oxygen-18) found in bubbles trapped within ancient ice cores. This ratio is related to the precise temperature at the time the ice was formed. Even over the past 1,000 years, the results are provocative, as they quantitatively demonstrate that the earth's current temperature is the highest it has been—and it is rapidly rising[6] (see Figure 3).

**Figure 3. Average Global Temperature, Last 1,000 Years**

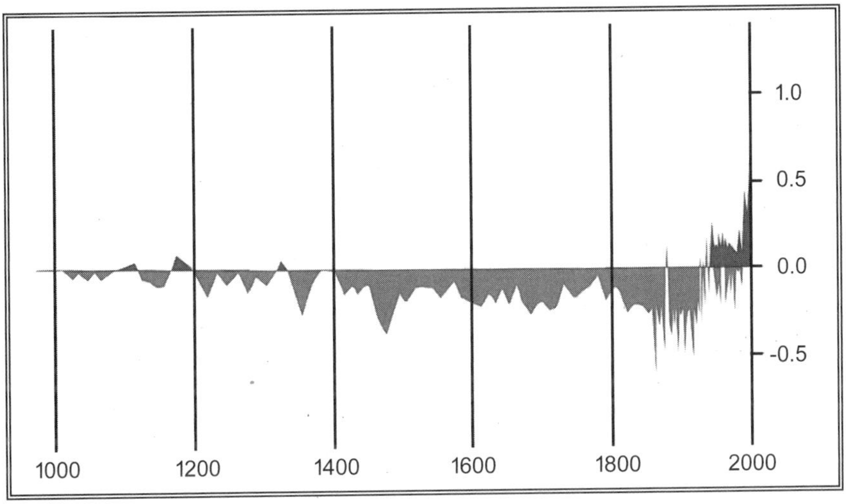

Source: Intergovernmental Panel on Climate Change, *Summary for Policymakers*, 2001

Furthermore, when scientists measured both the $CO_2$ concentration and temperature over a 600,000-year span in the Antarctic ice, they find that *at no point did the concentration of $CO_2$ exceed 300 parts per million*, as compared to today's level of 380 ppm, which is rapidly rising. Also, there is nearly a direct correlation between temperature and $CO_2$ concentration, even going back hundreds of thousands of years (see Figure 4). The higher the $CO_2$ concentration, the higher the temperature. And at our current rate of use of fossil fuels, our atmospheric $CO_2$ concentration will be greater than 600 ppm within 45 years, with correspondingly higher temperatures—unless we take immediate action to ameliorate this problem.[7]

**Figure 4. Comparison of $CO_2$ Concentration with Global Temperature**

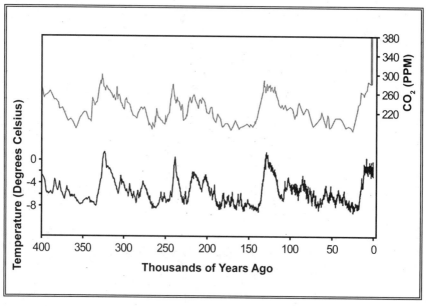

Source: U.S. Environmental Protection Agency, *Climate Change Science Images*

In 1988, climate scientists became sufficiently alarmed that the U.N. formed the Intergovernmental Panel on Climate Change (IPCC, or Climate Change Panel), a group comprising the foremost leading climatologists and scientists around the world, who now report twice each decade on climate change. The Climate Change Panel's fourth report, issued in February 2007, was clear and even more unequivocal than its third report issued in 2001—human beings are having an impact on climate change. In recent reports, Climate Change Panel scientists have told us with ever-increasing confidence levels that during this century, we can expect the earth's surface temperature to continue to rise. It is clear from the February 2007 report that their earlier predictions of startling increases in global temperatures were too optimistic. By 2100, the earth's surface temperature will have risen between 1.1°C and 6.4°C (2°F and 11.5°F) (see Figure 5).[8] The 2007 IPCC report states that there is very high probability that the temperature increase by 2100 will be between 2°C (3.6°F) and 4.5°C (8.1°F).[9] This level of warming will likely deliver an ice-free Arctic and a 30% drop in rainfall in subtropical regions.

**Figure 5. Average Global Temperature, 1880-2005 with Projection to 2100**

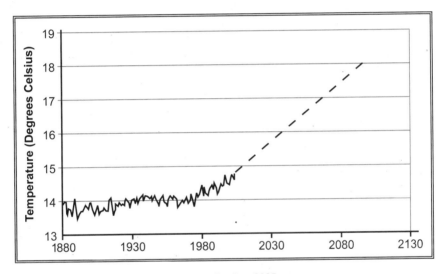

Source: NASA Goddard Institute for Space Studies, 2005

This does not seem like much of an increase, but we know from historical records that it will have a profound impact on climate. For example, *the last ice age was triggered by a mere 1-1.7°C (2-3°F) decrease in temperature.* We also know that *climate change is now occurring at least 50% faster than we had thought.*[10] Some of the effects we are currently observing are as follows:

- In 2003, the 3,000-year-old, 80-foot-thick, 150-square-mile Arctic Ice Sheet collapsed.

- Deadly heat waves, such as the one that hit Europe in August 2003 and claimed more than 30,000 lives, have occurred with greater frequency.

- In 2004, the Greenland Ice Sheet was found to be melting at dangerously increasing rates.

- Increasing ocean temperatures are creating more frequent and more severe storms than in all of recorded history. Until recently, meteorology textbooks stated that it was impossible for a hurricane to appear in the South Atlantic. In 2004, however, Brazil endured its first hurricane, ever. The year 2004 also set the all-time record for tornadoes in the U.S.

- Since 1900, oceans have risen by 20 centimeters (8 inches) because of thermal expansion and glacier melting, and that will increase to 43 centimeters (17 inches), even if the average global temperature were not to change.

The projected temperature changes, which now have an even higher probability of occurring than that stated in the prior IPCC report, are very disconcerting. An increase in temperature of 4-8°C (7.2-14.4° F) could collapse the West Antarctic Ice Sheet and raise our sea levels by 5 meters (16.4 feet). These drastic changes would lead to inundating flooding of coastal areas; severe storms; increased ocean acidification; intense heat waves, droughts, and famines; and global disease. As global populations surge across political borders in search of dry land, food, and clean water, global chaos would ensue, and we would be faced with the most significant environmental, economic, and civil security challenge in recorded history. It would be an extremely unpleasant world in which to live.

Let's take a closer look at the history of climate change and the mounting evidence for an unacceptable future. We start by clarifying the nature of global warming, a critical piece of climate change.

## GLOBAL WARMING IN A NUTSHELL

"Global warming" is the term commonly known and used by most people and the media with respect to alteration of climate conditions, although "climate change crisis" is probably a more accurate term. In fact, warming is a major part of climate change, but the final global conditions can be a mix of extremes—warming in colder areas, cooling in warmer areas, desertification in wet areas, flooding in deserts, and so forth. In all cases, wild climate swings will continue to puncture the myth that we can still predict the weather. The end result is a major negative impact on all living species, including humankind. So what is this thing called "global warming"?

Like a window pane, our atmosphere is essentially transparent to solar radiation in the visible and ultraviolet regions of the electromagnetic spectrum, which stretches from short wavelengths to long wavelengths, namely: cosmic rays→gamma rays→X-rays→ ultraviolet rays→visible rays→infrared rays→microwave rays→radio waves. Solar radiation in the ultraviolet and infrared regions heats the earth's surface, which in turn reflects infrared radiation back into the atmosphere. A portion of these infrared rays is absorbed in the atmosphere by greenhouse gases such as carbon dioxide, water vapor, and methane, among others. Another portion is reflected back to earth by the atmosphere, heating the earth's surface. The rest of the infrared radiation escapes into space.

For a gas in the atmosphere to absorb this infrared radiation, its molecules must have specific physical properties. They must be asymmetrical so that a positive charge can accumulate at one end of the molecule and a negative charge at the other. This creates what is known as a "dipole moment," and it is this property of the molecule that enables absorption of the infrared heat waves. Some molecules have a larger dipole moment than do other molecules and, therefore, absorb more heat. This aspect, among other properties, makes some molecules much more effective greenhouse gases than others, which is why methane carries as much as 60 times more destructive capacity than carbon dioxide as a greenhouse gas (its destructive capacity fades over time).

The earth needs a certain level of global warming, or there could be no life on this planet. For example, Mars has essentially no atmosphere, so a greenhouse effect is not possible. Therefore, the planet is very cold because virtually all of the sun's radiation is completely radiated back into space. However, Venus, which has a dense atmosphere of carbon dioxide (a greenhouse gas), is very hot, with surface temperatures greater than 500°C, hot enough to melt lead. As a consequence, neither Venus nor Mars support life as we know it. Neither extreme is survivable by human beings.

> *"My colleagues and I now take the threat of global warming seriously. The time to consider the policy dimensions of climate change is not when the link between greenhouse gases and climate change is conclusively proven, but when the possibility cannot be discounted and [must be] taken seriously by the society of which we are a part. We in BP have reached that point."*
>
> — LORD JOHN BROWNE, FORMER CEO, BP
> STANFORD UNIVERSITY, MAY 1997

The important greenhouse gases in the earth's atmosphere are water vapor, carbon dioxide, methane, freons (chlorofluorocarbons—CFCs), and nitrous oxide (the "laughing gas" used by dentists). Water vapor is an important greenhouse gas, and because it is responsible for intermittent formation of clouds in our atmosphere, it makes modeling of global warming a significant challenge. The hotter planet earth becomes, the greater the amount of water vapor in its atmosphere and the greater the atmospheric warming effect. Carbon dioxide is next in importance. We determine the historical levels of $CO_2$ in the atmosphere by drilling and analyzing ice cores in Greenland. Each year, the snowfall is compacted into ice, trapping air bubbles that provide a historical fingerprint and record of the concentration of various gases in the atmosphere through the ages.

Carbon dioxide is emitted from a number of sources on earth, and it is re-absorbed by others. Most of these emissions and re-absorptions are natural processes. For example, Yellowstone National Park, with its geysers and other volcanic activity, emits 44 million metric tons of $CO_2$ each year, about 10 times the annual quantity released by one medium-sized power plant burning fossil fuels.[11] Although human beings are responsible for a much lower level of $CO_2$ emissions, that level is sufficient, and increasingly so, to push the atmospheric conditions out of balance and past a tipping point that can initiate a cascade of devastating effects from climate change. Leaking Russian natural gas pipelines are responsible for about 59 million tons of $CO_2$-equivalent per year.[12] The average human being on the planet generates about one metric ton of $CO_2$ per year, most of it through the burning of fossil fuels such as coal, oil, and gas. In developed nations, $CO_2$ emissions are much higher (e.g., in the U.S., the amount is five metric tons per person per year). As countries become increasingly developed, they require the input of much larger per capita amounts of energy, most of which has been generated by burning fossil fuels.

Political factors often play a key role in $CO_2$ emissions. For example, cement kilns produce about 7% of annual global $CO_2$ emissions.[13] After signing the Kyoto Protocol, Japan outlawed the manufacture of cement, so it imports cement (mainly from Taiwan). Taiwan burns old tires as a primary fuel in its cement plants, and this creates huge levels of air pollution. There are far more efficient ways to use old tires, and there are methods to create cement that emit only a fraction of the $CO_2$. And the $CO_2$ emitted from cement plants can be captured rather than vented to the air. The tires, in turn are exported to Taiwan from the U.S., where tire burning is illegal.

The other greenhouse gas of great concern is methane, which is the primary constituent of natural gas. We would surely muster the political will to cut carbon emissions if there were wider public awareness of just a few facts about methane:

- Its destructive potential is far greater than $CO_2$.

- The 2005 atmospheric concentration of methane far exceeds the natural range of the last 650,000 years.

- Vast quantities of methane could be released by melting permafrost and warming oceans.

- More permafrost has already melted than at any time in the past 100,000 years.

- Siberia, the land of permafrost, is warming faster than any place on earth.

- Some scientists think that global warming caused by a sudden surge of methane and $CO_2$ into the atmosphere was a primary contributing cause of the last major climate change 55 million years ago and the ensuing species extinction.

Methane still remains a sleeper story in the press. Carbon dioxide has received far more media attention, but that must change.

Whereas $CO_2$ persists in our atmosphere for about a century before it is finally re-absorbed by the earth, methane lasts for only about 10 years before it is oxidized to $CO_2$ and water vapor. When methane's lifetime in the atmosphere, its heat-trapping potential, and the fact that it is ultimately oxidized to $CO_2$ and water vapor (both strong greenhouse gases) are taken into full account, methane is actually 60 times more potent than $CO_2$ as a greenhouse gas.

The biggest stores of methane exist in two places: permafrost regions of our planet, and deep within our oceans as a high-pressure form of a water-methane compound called methane hydrate or methane clathrate. (The term "clathrate" comes from the Greek, meaning "claw," as the methane is held in place by a solid claw-like structure formed by water at low temperatures and high pressures). The carbon content in methane clathrate buried deep in our oceans is greater than that contained in all of the coal in the world.[14]

If the oceans or permafrost regions of the earth were to warm sufficiently, this stored methane could be released almost instantly in a huge explosive event. This would cause rapid major global warming. It is thought that several of the previous species' mass extinctions on earth occurred because of this process.[15] One such example is the Permian extinction some 251 million years ago, when 95% of all marine life and 70% of all land animals perished. And it happened very quickly.

As Nicholas D. Kristof recently observed, "The history of

climate change shows that it does not evolve slowly and gracefully, it lurches. There are tipping points, and if we trigger certain chain reactions, then our leaders cannot claim a 'mulligan.'[16] They could set back our planet for, say, 10 million years."[17]

In northern Siberia the ground has been permanently frozen thousands of feet deep. The surface layer, which is as much as 260 feet deep and contains 50% ice, once consisted of grasslands where wooly mammoths roamed. Siberian permafrost has been melting slowly since the end of the last ice age, about 10,000 years ago. Recent work, however, has shown that the rate of melting is accelerating.[18] As permafrost melts further, there is concern that it could release gigatons of additional methane. The top 200 to 300 feet of the permafrost contains more than 500 gigatons of carbon (as methane), two and half times all of the carbon that is contained in the world's tropical forests. Larry Smith, a hydrologist at the UCLA, has reported that the west Siberian peat bog could contain one-quarter of the world's total below-ground methane deposits—70 billion tons of methane.

Western Siberia is heating up faster than any other place on earth, some 3°C in the past 40 years. This is the highest jump recorded on the planet. Already, one square kilometer of permafrost in western Siberia has melted—*something that hasn't happened since the wooly mammoths roamed the earth.* The slow thaw of this trapped methane is a terrifying prospect.

We already have unnaturally high levels of methane. The Climate Change Panel's February 2007 report states that the concentration of methane in the global atmosphere has increased from a pre-industrial level of about 715 parts per billion (ppb) to 1774 ppb in 2005. It also states that, as determined from ice cores, the 2005 atmospheric concentration of methane far exceeds the natural range of the last 650,000 years.

Melting permafrost and warming oceans are not the only sources of methane.

Other significant sources include mammal digestion (primarily by cattle), leaking gas wells, and various insects. It has been estimated that termites, which emit large volumes of methane as a consequence of their metabolic system, produce about 20% of the methane in our atmosphere.

The following brief history of climate change describes the role of methane and $CO_2$ in the last major climate change about 55 million years ago. As the philosopher George Santayana famously remarked, "those who cannot remember the past are condemned to repeat it."

## A BRIEF HISTORY OF CLIMATE CHANGE

Climate change is not new. Ever since the earth formed some 4.5 billion years ago, living organisms, ranging from bacteria to mammals, have played a role in initiating and moderating climate change by controlling the level of heat-trapping gases in our atmosphere—absorbing them during life and releasing them upon death. Over numerous millennia, epochs, and eras, temperatures have several times gone from simmering to freezing, dramatically changing the landscape and the nature of life on earth.

Ever since we moved beyond our bacterial ancestors some hundreds of millions of years ago and complex life forms evolved, the $CO_2$ associated with their life and death has kept temperatures above freezing. In fact, without $CO_2$ and other greenhouse gases, the earth's average surface temperature would be a deathly -18°C (-0.4°F). Over the past 10,000 years, our global thermostat has been set at a comfortable 15°C (59°F).[19]

It hasn't always been that comfortable. When $CO_2$ significantly decreased in the atmosphere about 710 million years ago (for reasons we don't yet understand) and then again 600 million years ago, the earth went into a rapid deep freeze, with solid mountains of ice forming smack up to the equator. As a consequence of this freeze, a large number of the species on the planet were exterminated.[20]

Then, some 540 million years ago, many living species, as part of their natural evolutionary process, began to acquire skeletons with a large component of carbonate in their structures. To form the carbonate molecular structure, huge volumes of $CO_2$ were extracted from the earth's atmosphere and environment, and since then there have been only two major ice age periods—the first between 355 and 280 million years ago, and the second during the past 33 million years. Scientists are not sure why this was the case, but they believe it may have to do with the evolution of shell-forming surface plankton in our oceans (a shell is a carbonate structure). The plankton appears to have acted as a huge absorption sink and buffer that stabilized the $CO_2$ concentration in our atmosphere and, therefore, the earth's surface temperature.[21]

The last major climate change that may be a good model for what we can expect from the current changes on earth occurred about 55 million years ago. There was a sudden surge of $CO_2$ and methane gases from the depths of our oceans, most likely produced by bacteria. This large volume of $CO_2$ rose into the earth's atmosphere, rapidly increasing the average global surface temperature by 5°C (9°F) over a period of just years or decades. From deep-sea core drillings, scientists have determined that the oceans belched an enormous 1,650-3,300 gigatons of carbon-containing gases into the atmosphere, elevating the concentration of $CO_2$ from 500 ppm to 2,000 ppm. By comparison, our current annual global emission of $CO_2$ is about 26 gigatons. This seemingly modest shift in temperature caused massive extinction of numerous species on the planet.[22]

Piecing together all of the evidence, Norwegian scientists now believe that one of the largest deposits of fossil fuels, probably mostly natural gas (methane), was ejected with molten magma from a huge fissure in the ocean depths. As the gases and molten magma made their way to the surface, the hot methane combined with dissolved oxygen in the sea to form $CO_2$ and then exploded through the sea's surface with nuclear force, creating a huge increase in $CO_2$ in the atmosphere.[23] The ocean, robbed of life-supporting dissolved oxygen, was subsequently not a very hospitable place for many species. To make matters worse, some of the $CO_2$ combined with sea water to form carbonic acid, thereby lowering the pH (increasing acidity), and extinguishing many of the creatures in the deep sea. It took 20,000 years for the earth to re-absorb the additional carbon from our atmosphere; it was apparently soaked up by surface plankton in the sea.

Following this cataclysm, the earth over the past 55 million years has slowly cooled, occasionally experiencing a modest ice age here and there, triggered by changes in greenhouse gases and shifts in the earth's processional or wobbling orbit, the latter causing changes in the amount of solar energy penetrating the poles. Indeed, we can tell from analyses of ice-core and deep-sea drilling that the concentration of greenhouse gases was low at the beginning of each ice age and surged to high levels at the end.

> *"We don't have a lot more time to deal with climate change."*
> — HENRY M. PAULSON, JR, SECRETARY OF THE U.S. TREASURY AND FORMER CHAIRMAN AND CEO, GOLDMAN SACHS GROUP

Our last ice age ended about 10,000 years ago. And by 8,000 years ago, the earth's global climate settled into what paleontologist Tim Flannery calls the "long summer." It is highly likely that this constancy in moderate global temperature facilitated the genesis of civilization as we know it. It was then that agriculture and urban settlements were "invented," flourished, and spread throughout the world. It is ironic that those same "inventors" are now responsible for the next surge in greenhouse gas escalation and the consequent rise in global temperatures.

## THE KEELING CURVE

If there is any doubt that $CO_2$ is rapidly rising and affecting the entire metabolism of Planet Earth, we need look only at what has become known as the Keeling Curve. During the 1950s, climatologist Charles Keeling, under the direction of Professor Roger Revelle of Harvard University, began recording the $CO_2$ concentration on the summit of Mt. Mauna Loa in Hawaii. (Results are shown in Figure 6.)

## Figure 6. The Keeling Curve

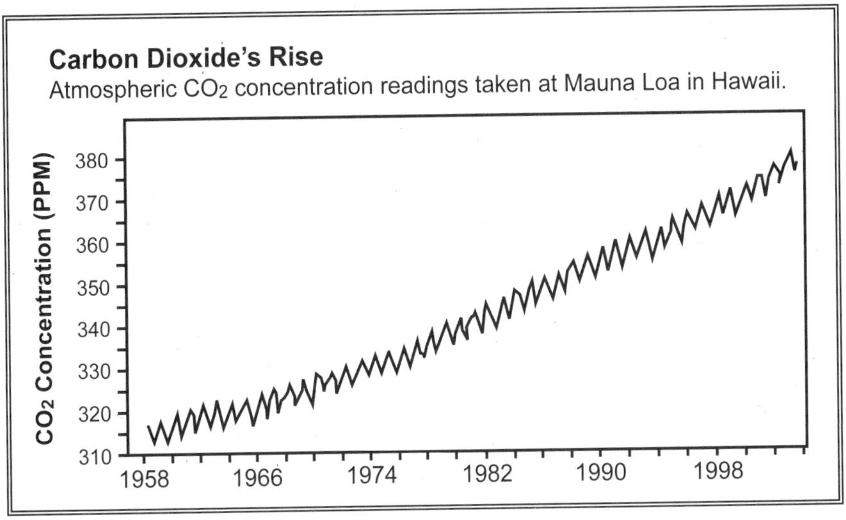

**Carbon Dioxide's Rise**
Atmospheric $CO_2$ concentration readings taken at Mauna Loa in Hawaii.

Source: C.D. Keeling, *et al.*, Scripps Institution of Oceanography

There are two points to be made about this landmark study. First, the global concentration of $CO_2$ is increasing significantly each year. Second, and equally profound, one can actually see the respiration of our beautiful planet in the fine structure oscillations of this graph. In the Northern Hemisphere, which contains most of the earth's vegetation, new greenery inhales $CO_2$ from our atmosphere each spring to facilitate its growth. This is shown as a small annual decrease in $CO_2$ concentration. Then in autumn, subsequent to the death and decomposition of this greenery, $CO_2$ is released back into the atmosphere, as indicated by an increase in $CO_2$ concentration. This inhalation-exhalation respiratory process is responsible for the oscillations in the curve in Figure 6, and it endows a true sense of life to the earth and is in accord with James Lovelock's Gaia concept of the earth as a living organism.[24] The relevant and unfortunate finding from the work of Keeling and Revelle is that each annual exhalation ends with an increase in the concentration of $CO_2$ that remains in the atmosphere. Hence, the curve's upward trend each year.

So, climate change and global warming are not new, and a certain level of warming was absolutely critical for the genesis, evolution, and the well-being of all living species on the planet. What *is* new, however, is its rapidity. Most warming-freezing cycles occurred over tens of thousands of years. What we are seeing today is transpiring much faster. The best model we have is the change that happened some 55 million years ago. Tim Flannery provides an incisive summary of the challenge we face:

> Earth has now been in an icehouse phase for millions of years, whereas 55 million years ago it was already very warm, with $CO_2$ levels around twice the level they are today. There were no ice caps then, and presumably fewer cold-adapted species—certainly nothing like narwhals and polar bears. Nor was this warmer world likely to possess the wondrous, stratified slices of life we find today on mountains and in the depths of the sea. Thus, our modern earth stands to lose far more from rapid warming than the world of 55 million years ago. Back then the warming closed a geological period, while we might through our activities bring an end to an entire era.[25]

In his book *Collapse*, Jared Diamond demonstrates how great ancient societies collapsed in ruin when they ignored environmental signals and the critical role of their resource base. In a prescient comment concerning the destruction of these civilizations, paleoclimatologist Peter deMenocal of Columbia University notes, "The thing they couldn't prepare for was the same thing that we won't prepare for, because in their case they didn't know about it and because in our case the political system can't listen to it."[26]

## The Culprits: Greenhouse Gases

The primary greenhouse gases heating our planet are shown in Figure 7. Of all of the gases beyond water vapor, $CO_2$ is most significant because it is present in the largest concentration and contributes directly or indirectly to about 80% of the earth's global warming. About 56% of all of the $CO_2$ that has been liberated by human beings burning fossil fuels is still present in our atmosphere.[27] For the past couple of decades, humanity has generated about 14.6 gigatons of carbon dioxide annually by burning fossil fuels, a figure that has now surpassed 20 gigatons per year.[28] Oceans have absorbed nearly 50% of all of the carbon emitted by humans since 1800, while during that same period, life on land has contributed to the net carbon in our atmosphere. Oceans are the major carbon sinks on this planet.[29]

## Figure 7. Greenhouse Gases in the Earth's Atmosphere

| GHG | Formula | Concentration (ppm) | $CO_2$ Equivalence | GW Contribution (%) |
| --- | --- | --- | --- | --- |
| Carbon Dioxide | $CO_2$ | 380 | 1x | 80 |
| Methane | $CH_4$ | 1.5 | 60x | 15 |
| Nitrous Oxide | $N_2O$ | < 1 | 270x | |
| Dichloro-trifluor-ethane | "CFC" | << 1 | 10,000x | |

Source: Tim Flannery, *The Weather Makers*, 2005

$CO_2$ is responsible for an effective and important atmospheric-heating mechanism involving water vapor. It does this by absorbing the sun's rays and to some extent heating the surface of the earth. This heating stimulates evaporation of water into the atmosphere. Most people are unaware that water is a more effective greenhouse gas than $CO_2$. The atmosphere is warmed further, and then more water is absorbed into the atmosphere. This is referred to as a "positive feedback loop" and is a potent part of the overall mechanism for global warming and climate change.[30] Anyone who has walked the streets of New York City on one of those hot muggy August days has experienced this mechanism in full force.

> *"We've known for some time that we have to worry about the impact of climate change on our children's generation. But now we have to worry about ourselves as well."*
>
> — MARGARET BECKETT, BRITISH FOREIGN SECRETARY

As discussed above, at this moment in geological history, methane is a secondary contributor to climate change compared to $CO_2$. However, methane caused significant climate change millions of years ago, and it could do so again.

Nitrous oxide and dichlorotrifluoroethane are present in our atmosphere at much lower levels than $CO_2$ but they are important to monitor because they are so much more effective than $CO_2$ in warming the planet. Dichlorotrifluoroethane is particularly an issue because developing countries such as China continue to use it in the manufacture of refrigeration units, and the gas was outlawed globally by the Montreal Protocol as a means to avoid continued diminishment of our stratospheric ozone layer.

If we study the overall picture of greenhouse gases, the best data climatologists have tell us that to avoid catastrophic climate change we must reduce our $CO_2$ emissions, or its equivalent in other greenhouse gases, into the atmosphere by at least 70% by 2050.[31] This, of course, is well beyond the Kyoto Protocol, which at this point is almost symbolic with respect to what really must be done to have a meaningful impact. Estimates indicate that even if the Kyoto Protocol were successfully implemented, an increase in global temperature of 1.8 to 4°C (3.2 to 7.2° F) by 2100 would be reduced by only 0.02-0.28°C (0.04-0.50°F) by 2050. Another way to look at the challenge before us is shown in Figure 8.

**Figure 8.** History and Projection for $CO_2$ Concentration

| Year | $CO_2$ Concentration (ppm) | Gigatons (Carbon) |
|---|---|---|
| 1800 | 280 | 645 |
| 2005 | 380 | 875 |
| 2100 Target | 560 | 1,290 |

Source: Tim Flannery, *The Weather Makers*, 2005

Suppose that by 2100 we wanted to limit the amount of $CO_2$ in our atmosphere to twice that present before the Industrial Revolution (i.e., twice 280 ppm, or 560 ppm). That is considered by most climatologists as the maximum level of $CO_2$ concentration permissible to avoid catastrophic climate change. This concentration corresponds to limiting all future human-generated greenhouse gases to 1,290 - 875 = 415 gigatons of carbon (see Figure 8). Therefore, for the rest of the century, our emissions of greenhouse gases must be low enough to limit the annual atmospheric increase of the gases to no more than 4.37 gigatons (some of the greenhouse gases already in the atmosphere will be transformed into safe gases). But, as noted, we have been producing on average more than 20 gigatons per year globally since the 1990s. Consequently, the target will be an *extremely difficult* one to meet without immediate, accelerated replacement of fossil-fuel energy. To motivate us to do this, let's look at the specific evidence for climate change.

## RISING SEA LEVELS

The 2007 fourth report of the Intergovernmental Panel on Climate Change was clear in linking human activity to climate change. High on the list of growing concerns are new ice-core drilling data that show that $CO_2$ levels in our atmosphere are higher today than any time in the past 740,000 years and probably for a considerably longer period than that. We also know that most of the increase has occurred since the beginning of the Industrial Revolution in the early nineteenth century (Figure 1).

It is now well established that with increased $CO_2$ levels come rising global temperatures (Figure 4). This trend has been confirmed by British researchers who found climate $CO_2$ level correlations over the past 740,000 years from Antarctic ice cores drilled from a depth of 3 kilometers (1.8 miles).[32] They found that the concentration of $CO_2$ has varied between 200 ppm during the cold ice ages and 270 ppm for warm tropical periods.

The current level of 380 ppm of $CO_2$ in the atmosphere is not only higher than any time over the past 740,000 years, but may be approaching the level present 55 million years ago when the entire earth was a tropical planet. There were no polar ice caps then, and sea levels were 80 meters (260 feet) higher than they are today.[33]

The Climate Change Panel's best estimates are that the earth's average global temperature could rise between 2.0 and 4.5°C (3.6 and 8.1°F) during this century. More and more data from northern regions such as Canada, Alaska, Siberia, Greenland, the Arctic, and Antarctica suggest that the earth's temperature will likely approach the higher level of this range, in part because massive glaciers are melting much faster than expected.

For example, a study by scientists at the University of Colorado has shown that the melting of large glaciers on the west coast of Alaska and in northern Canada is accelerating.[34] Recent studies show that glacial melting rates have more than doubled and are climbing rapidly. In related studies, the U.S. Geological Survey has shown that glaciers are melting in all 11 of Alaska's glaciated mountains (Figure 9).

**Figure 9. Baked Alaska—Toboggan Glacier
Prince William Sound**

Source: *U.S. Geological Survey*

Another USGS study of the glaciers in Glacier National Park in the U.S. has found that of the 150 glaciers that existed in the park in 1850, only 50 are left, and they will be gone within the next three decades.[35] In fact, it is now established that nearly all of the mountain glaciers in the world are melting, many of them at an increasingly rapid rate.[36] This has never before occurred during humanity's presence on this planet.

One of the authors of this book has spent time on the summit of Africa's magnificent Mt. Kilimanjaro, at a height of 5,895 meters (19,340 feet), exploring its glaciers and its latent volcanic activity. It is most disconcerting that between 1989 and 2000, this incredible African monolith lost 33% of its ice fields and glaciers.[37] New studies project that the "snows of Kilimanjaro" will be completely gone by 2015. The consequences for the people living at the base of this mountain will be dire, given that glacial melt forms the basis of their year-round fresh water. Clearly, a local catastrophe is in the making.

Of more serious global concern is what is happening in the Arctic. Recent research by the Arctic Climate Impact Assessment, an international team of 300 scientists, has demonstrated that in regions surrounding the Arctic, winter temperatures have already climbed by 3-4°C (5.4-7.2°F) over the past 50 years.[38] The rate of disappearance of the Arctic Ice Sheet can be seen in Figure 10, which shows satellite photos taken by the Arctic Climate Team over the past two and a half decades. Just as ice melts in a cocktail and does not raise the liquid level, if all of the ice on the Arctic continent melts, it will not raise sea levels, because most of it is already in the sea.

**Figure 10. The Arctic Ice Sheet is Melting**

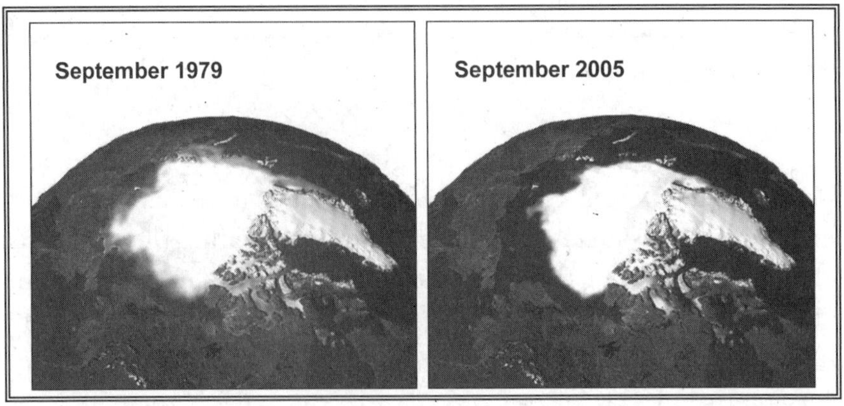

Source: NASA, 2005

However, there are two serious concerns here. First, warm temperatures are likely to thaw the permafrost. As discussed above, melting permafrost could release disastrous levels of methane. Boreal and alpine permafrost is estimated to contain 350-450 gigatons of locked-up carbon as $CO_2$ and methane.[39]

Second, and equally problematic, is the melting of Arctic Sea ice. This could accelerate the melting of the Greenland Ice Sheet, which is an ice mass nearly the size of Mexico and more than a mile thick in places. It all rests on a land mass, and, therefore, its melting would raise our seas by 7 meters (23 feet).

Melting Arctic ice would also decrease the salinity of the North

Atlantic Ocean, and this could have a devastating impact on ocean currents, all of which moderate global weather patterns (see "Europe In A Siberian Freeze" below).

In fact, recent satellite data show that Greenland's glaciers are slip-sliding away.[40] In western Greenland, the heights of some glaciers are dropping 15 meters (49 feet) per year. Losses are even greater along the southeastern coast. The surface of Helheim Glacier has decreased by 50 meters (164 feet) over the past two years, and during that same period, Kangerdlugssuaq Glacier fell by 80 meters (262 feet). The latter two glaciers drain almost 10% of Greenland's ice sheet. In addition to melting, they are flowing increasingly faster, three times faster than in 2001, when they were measured at flow rates that were the same as in 1996 and 1988. The glacier melting rate has begun to accelerate.

**Figure 11.  Falling Ice Sheet**

Source: AP photo/Natacha Pisarenko

Similar challenges are apparent on the Antarctic continent, which holds more than 90% of all the ice on Planet Earth.[41] On the West Antarctic Ice Sheet, three of the continent's biggest glaciers (around Pine Island and West Antarctica) are rapidly disappearing. They are losing about 54 cubic miles (250 cubic kilometers) of ice per year—picture a cube of ice 3.8 miles (6.3 kilometers) on each of its six edges. That's approximately the amount of water used in the entire U.S. in a five-month period. These glaciers drain more than 30% of the West Antarctic Ice Sheet. The last time this ice sheet melted was about 100,000 years ago. If it were to melt completely, it would raise global sea levels by 8 meters (26 feet). Worse yet, if the West Antarctic Ice Sheet melted, it would likely destabilize and melt the East Antarctic Ice Sheet, which contains enough water to raise our sea levels by 65 meters (213 feet).[42]

There are also indications that parts of the Antarctic ice pack are actually increasing because of increasing snowfall. This effect is predicted by the climate models and supports the conclusion that we are in the mode of global climate change. In a 2.7-million-square-mile region of the ice sheet, which is the coldest area on earth, it is normally too cold for snow to form. Additional snowfall confirms warmer temperatures.[43] As the atmosphere warms, it holds more moisture, leading to greater snowfall. Since this moisture must ultimately come from oceans, this increasing ice sheet in Antarctica would diminish the total rise of 65 meters (213 feet) in sea levels if the entire ice were to melt. However, this effect is modest and would reduce the rise in sea level only by about 7%.[44]

Even if we look at a sampling of several delta regions around the world, a recent study shows that a business-as-usual scenario will lead to displacement of more than 8 million people: Bengal delta, Bangladesh, 3.4 million; Mekong delta, Vietnam, 1.9 million; Nile delta, Egypt, 1.3 million; Yangtze delta, China, 0.5 million; Mississippi delta, U.S., 0.5 million; Godvari delta, India, 0.5 million.[45] Many millions more will become "climate change refugees" as they abandon less habitable areas for lands where human beings can hope to survive.

Glacier melting presents other challenges, as well. For example, the Himalayan glaciers that rest on the Tibetan Plateau have been dangerously affected by global warming. This area contains 100 times as much ice as the Alps and provides more than 50% of the drinking water for 40% of the world's population.[46] This water runs rapidly through seven of the largest Asian rivers, all originating on the Tibetan Plateau. The melting of large quantities of this fresh water source, causing it to gush aimlessly down to the sea at speeds too rapid to harness, would put more than 2.5 billion people at severe risk.

## EUROPE IN A SIBERIAN FREEZE

A potential "by-product" of glacial melting would be to shut down our ocean thermohaline circulation (see Figure 12).

**Figure 12.** **The Atlantic Heat Conveyor**

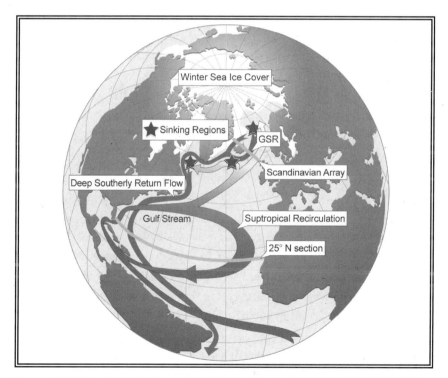

Source: Detlef Quadfasel, "Anthropogenic Effects of Tropical Cyclone Activity," MIT, 2006

For example, the Gulf Stream is actually a water current "conveyor belt" that moves huge volumes of water and heat globally from the tropics toward the poles in a delicate equilibrium between the melting and freezing of water. This same Gulf Stream keeps Western Europe from freezing over. The conveyor belt is driven by the formation of ice in the North Atlantic Ocean, which leaves behind dense seawater that has a higher than normal salt content. It rapidly sinks to the ocean depths. The cold stream rises again as it is heated in the oceans of the tropics. This conveyor could shut down if the ocean becomes too warm for ice to form or if the dense salty water is diluted by large volumes of fresh water from melting glacier ice.

The ocean circulator appears to have only two modes of operation—on and off. Terry Hughes, a glaciologist, has said that under certain conditions the heat conveyor could shut down in a matter of days.[47] This happened most recently 12,000 years ago. Europe would rapidly chill to a Siberian-style freeze that would more than overcome the projected impact of global warming temperatures in that part of the globe. Alaska would warm faster, and it is likely that without the heat movement of this conveyor, the monsoon rains would fail, adversely affecting agriculture throughout Asia. There is a planetwide network of these ocean currents, or thermohaline conveyors, which perform similar functions throughout the oceans.

The potential impact of a failing thermohaline conveyor was highlighted by a recent Pentagon study that caused a significant international stir.[48] Also quite disconcerting are the results of research into the thermohaline conveyor by Harry Bryden of the Southampton Oceanography Centre in the UK.[49] Bryden has found that ocean circulation in the North Atlantic is "stuttering," and there is a 30% reduction in the warm currents that carry water north from the Gulf Stream and give Western Europe its relatively balmy climate. He and his team have found that while one area of sinking water on the Canadian side of Greenland still seems to be functioning as normal, a second stream on the European side has partially shut down and is sending only 50% as much deep water to the south. At this time, it is not clear whether this is a temporary decrease or portends a more dramatic change.

## U.S. COASTLINE SUBMERGED

With modern technology we can "look" back over 55 million years, and the picture we see is not reassuring. At that time, $CO_2$ levels appear to have been above 1,000 ppm and sea levels more than 50 meters (164 feet) higher than today. As noted earlier, $CO_2$ levels decreased over time as marine life absorbed carbon through photo-synthesis and carbonate-based skeleton formation. The carbon was ultimately buried as the organisms died and sank to the ocean floor. This reduction in $CO_2$ levels lowered the temperature of the earth's atmosphere and allowed ice sheets to form in Antarctica about 40 million years ago. By four million years ago, $CO_2$ levels had dropped to less than our pre-industrial level of 280 ppm, and permanent ice sheets covered the Northern Hemisphere. As subsequent glacial periods waxed and waned, $CO_2$ levels and the earth's temperature were tightly and directly linked. When both increased, there were stable warm periods with high sea levels, and conversely, when both decreased, there were glacial ice ages and low sea levels.

*At no time in the past 10 million years did our $CO_2$ levels exceed the current value of 380 ppm.* In fact, 10 million years ago, the earth's average temperature was several degrees higher than today—there were no ice sheets in Greenland—and sea levels were several meters higher. Florida was nearly non-existent.

As we move closer to the present, the geological records of some 120,000 years ago provide a telling story. The climate was warm, similar to today, and sea levels were several meters higher than they are now, even though $CO_2$ levels remained lower than today's post-industrial level of 380 ppm. Closer yet to the present, the past 10,000 years have provided a relatively stable climate that has fostered the birth of human civilization.

What all of this tells us is that given the recent rapid rise in the $CO_2$ level in our atmosphere, we should expect climate changes. Also, we should note that in the past, dramatic changes in climate have sometimes occurred within just a few decades. With the onset of the Industrial Revolution we have become preoccupied with and driven by the allure of growth. And as a civilization, we have become comfortable and secure with a stable climate over the past 10 millennia *that we have come to take for granted*. Given the large increases in the $CO_2$ levels we currently observe, this long stable period appears to be coming to an end. The expectation of *no* change in climate is an unreasonable and dangerous conclusion.

Currently, numerous island nations face complete devastation by rising seas. The Maldives, Tuvalu, Fiji, and more than 26 other island nations are at risk. More than 11,000 citizens of Tuvalu have asked New Zealand to accept them after they were refused entry to Australia. Their island home is being inundated by rising seas.[50] The 400-year-old village of Shishmaref in northern Alaska is gradually being abandoned due to storm surges, melting permafrost, erosion, and loss of wild food sources. Accelerated melting of glaciers and large increases in sea levels should be viewed as probable events, not hypothetical possibilities.[51] Many such events already have begun to make once idyllic portions of our biosphere, like Tuvalu, completely uninhabitable.

## SEVERE STORMS

Her name was Katrina. She started as a simple storm, just a Category 1 on a scale of 1 to 5. On August 25, 2005, residents of Miami breathed a sigh of relief as Katrina blew by, but that was short-lived as she sucked up energy from the warm waters of the Gulf of Mexico and grew rapidly over a couple of days to a full-fledged, devastating Category 5 hurricane. Katrina weakened only a bit to 4 as she slammed into the Mississippi and Louisiana coastline. She destroyed the levees at Lake Pontchartrain, inundating New Orleans with up to 20 feet of flood waters and plunging the city into mayhem. By December 31, the National Climatic Data Center estimated hurricane damage in the U.S. for the year was more than $100 billion. Swiss Reinsurance Co. said its net profit for 2005 fell 41%, as claims hit $760 million.[52] Katrina damaged oil rigs and refineries responsible for supplying 25% of U.S. oil production. When it was over, nearly 2 MBD of oil and 5.2 billion cubic feet of gas per day went offline. Was this just a freak occurrence or a harbinger of things to come—increasingly ferocious storms, a consequence of global-warming-induced climate change?

Until 1996, there seemed to be a consensus that increased $CO_2$ levels and global warming would have only minimal effects on hurricane intensity. But that is no longer the case, and numerous scientists, after detailed studies, have broken ranks with this view. The prevailing view now is that the surge in global temperature over the past three decades has made hurricanes more severe. Damage from climate-change-induced weather catastrophes has increased geometrically—$75 billion during the period 1980-89; $290 billion during 1988-97; and nearly $750 billion during 1998-2005.[53]

Worldwide, there are about 85 tropical cyclones each year, of which two-thirds reach hurricane force.[54] So far, the number has not varied much each year, but the distribution and intensity of the storms has. A hurricane starts as a small cyclic column of warm humid air rising from the surface of a tropical ocean. As the saturated air rises, water vapor condenses in the cooler upper atmosphere. As this vapor condenses, heat is released. This is the heat that was absorbed from the ocean surface to generate the rising water vapor. It is also the fuel that energizes and drives hurricane formation and growth.

Hurricanes contain "nuclear" amounts of energy. Typically, they release more than 10 million trillion joules per day.[55] That is equivalent to approximately a million Hiroshima atomic bombs. Fortunately, most of this energy is released in driving air upward, rather than sideways, or we would really be in trouble. Climate theory and computer models tell us that as the world gets warmer, higher-temperature surface waters will fuel hurricanes, increasing their wind speed and water fall. The initial mini-cyclone of warm air forms when the surface sea temperature exceeds 26°C (79°F). Every fraction of a degree above this threshold energizes hurricane formation exponentially. When Katrina reached Category 5, the surface temperature of the Gulf of Mexico was 30°C (86°F), only 4°C (7°F) above the temperature necessary for hurricane formation.

Using the maximum wind speed and lifespan of a storm, Kerry Emanuel, a tropical meteorologist at Massachusetts Institute of Technology, developed a formula for what is now called the power-dissipation index (PDI).[56] The PDI is directly related to the total devastation a hurricane can wreak on buildings and general construction. The results of his study show that damage increases exponentially with wind speed. Thus, a hurricane with winds of 148 miles per hour (247 kilometers/hour) can produce up to 250 times more damage than one with wind speeds of 74 miles per hour (123 kilometers/hour). In a study of storms over the past 30 years, Emanuel found that the PDI has doubled. This increase is directly related to increases in sea temperatures and likely reflects the effect of global warming (Figure 13).

**Figure 13. Hurricane Intensity vs. Sea Temperature**

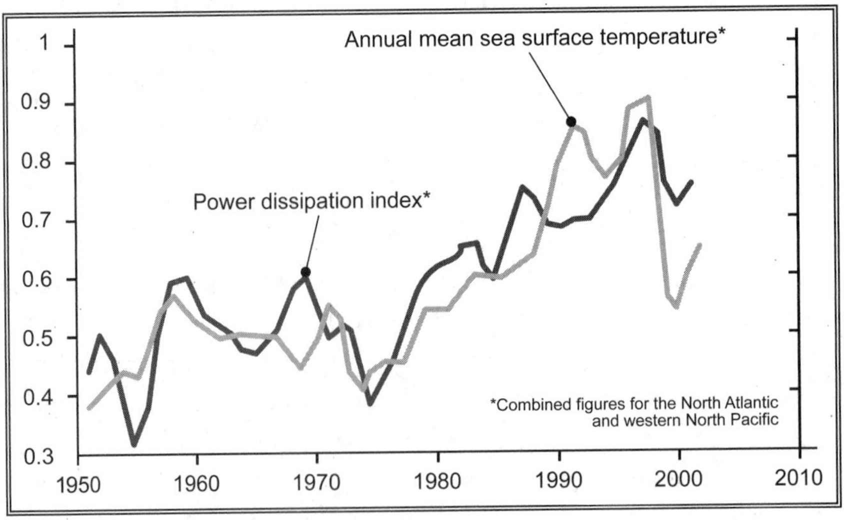

Source: Kerry Emanuel, *Nature 436*, August 4, 2005

Emanuel also concluded from his studies that, on average, storms are lasting 60% longer, with wind speeds increasing by as much as 15%. These studies show that the destructive power of hurricanes has increased by more than 70% over the past three decades.[57] Emanuel reluctantly sums up his disturbing findings: "We will have some quiet years, but unless we have a really big volcanic eruption [to temporarily cool the earth's atmosphere], we'll never see another quiet decade in the Atlantic in our lifetime or that of our children."[58]

Greg Holland, a climatologist at the National Center for Atmospheric Research, found from satellite data since 1970 that the number of hurricanes in categories 4 and 5 has doubled, while the number of storms in categories 1 and 3 has decreased.[59] The larger hurricanes now occur 20-35% more often than smaller storms do.

To be sure, the data concerning hurricanes are complex, and the debate on their interpretation rages on. William Gray, a senior hurricane scientist, does not believe global warming is responsible for the increased ferocity of hurricanes. He believes the current era of intense storm activity will eventually end as a result of changes in salinity and currents in the Atlantic. He also feels that sometime in the next decade or two, the earth will enter a cooling period. His views are those of only a very small minority of experts.

Although the hurricane picture is complicated and difficult to model, the data over the past few decades appear to confirm the reality of increasing hurricane intensities and the direct connection of these intensities to global warming.

## Ocean Acidification

Of the $CO_2$ formed by burning fossil fuels, 40% stays in the atmosphere, 30% is absorbed by vegetation on land, and 30% dissolves in our oceans, which is not good for marine life and, therefore, not good for us, as well.

When $CO_2$ dissolves in sea water, it forms carbonic acid, $H_2CO_3$, the same weak acid found in carbonated beverages. Just as all acids do, carbonic acid dissociates in water to hydrogen ions $H^+$, which are responsible for acidity. The pH scale is actually a measure of hydrogen ion concentration or acidity. A value of 7 is neutral, where the concentration of hydrogen ions (causing acidity) is just equal to the concentration of hydroxyl ions, OH⁻ (causing alkalinity). The pH scale is inversely and exponentially proportional to acidity. Thus, a drop of one pH unit, say from 6 to 5, corresponds to a tenfold increase in the concentration of hydrogen ions, i.e., in acidity.

The pH of pristine seawater is between 8.0 and 8.3. It is slightly alkaline.[60] Absorption of $CO_2$ in our oceans has already dropped the pH by 0.1 units since the beginning of the Industrial Revolution. At the current rate of change, it will fall an additional 0.3 pH units by 2100. Several centuries from now, the pH will easily be lower than at any time in the past 300 million years.[61] These shifts seem small, but there is ample cause for concern. Recent experiments demonstrate that we are already beginning to interfere with skeleton formation in critical species such as phytoplankton, commonly found floating near the surface of oceans. These tiny species are a major food source for fish and marine mammals, including whales. Similar negative impact has been found for ocean coral reefs, a large fraction of which have been acid-bleached and are in ultimate danger of complete destruction.

Coral reefs are the nurseries for all marine life and for ocean health. Should coral reefs continue to suffer more damage (as they are now), we could lose the entire aquatic system of planet earth which acts as the ultimate incubator of cellular life as we know it. Humans and all other life forms on earth were incubated in this nursery we call the oceans. Without coral reefs, our oceans could "die" and with them, every form of life on the planet. More vital than rain forests for the survival of our planetary ecology, ocean coral reefs are now moving toward extinction, with all that that implies.

As noted earlier, low pH (acidic) conditions prevailed some 55 million years ago when the earth was much warmer than today. The consequence of this increased acidity was massive extinction of most marine species. It took several hundred thousand years for the oceans to recover.

All of this points to the negative impact of continuing to burn large volumes of fossil fuels and bloating our atmosphere with $CO_2$. It also speaks volumes against wasting time and resources on deep-sea sequestering of $CO_2$ from "clean" coal plants.

"Clean coal," which some might say is an oxymoron, is a term used frequently by the current administration in Washington and the coal industry. It is a technology that has yet to be commercially developed, and is heavily supported financially by the U.S. government. In this technology, coal is gasified by pulverizing it and heating the resultant powder to very high temperatures with oxygen and steam. The particulate matter, or ash, is then removed from the gases, as is the resultant $CO_2$. The other gases formed, carbon monoxide and hydrogen,[62] can either be burned in a power plant directly or converted further with a catalyst to nearly pure hydrogen, which can then be burned or used in a fuel cell for power generation. By-product $CO_2$ is buried ("sequestered") deep in the ground or the ocean.

Two major issues are associated with this technology. First, the process is very expensive. A typical coal plant costs $780 million to build, whereas a "clean coal" plant will cost at least $1 billion, and most probably, significantly more.[63] Furthermore, one must factor in the cost to sequester huge volumes of $CO_2$. And finally, there is no guarantee that this $CO_2$ will not "burp" to the surface of the earth someday, causing catastrophic effects, let alone increased global warming. Early tests show that the shale rock used to "hold" the $CO_2$ actually changes composition over time, leading to greater porosity of the rock and an increased likelihood of its "burping" $CO_2$ back to the surface. If the administration's billions of dollars for support of "clean coal" technology were to be directed to commercialization of alternate non-fossil-fuel technologies, there would a much greater benefit to all constituencies. Simply stated, "clean coal" doesn't exist in any form and won't for many decades into the future, if ever. It is a marketing slogan for very narrow special interests willing to risk irreparable damage to the biosphere in pursuit of short-term financial gain.

## Heat Waves, Droughts, and Famines

Between 35,000 and 50,000 people died in the August 2003 European heat wave, which hit Paris particularly hard. In the summer of 1995, nearly 800 Chicagoans died from an intense heat wave in that city. In addition to the unfortunate loss of human life, both of these heat waves cost their respective governments billions of dollars.

Are these heat waves harbingers of global climate change? A recent study asserts that this is the case.[64] It predicts that future heat waves will be more intense, more frequent, and will last longer as we progress into the 21st century. Furthermore, researchers show that the heat waves coincided with a specific atmospheric circulation pattern that was intensified by ongoing increases in greenhouse gases, indicating that future heat waves over Europe and North America will be more severe.

Billions of people will also be at greater risk because of droughts and famines as a consequence of climate change. "By 2025, half the world's population will be living in areas that are at risk from storms and other weather extremes," the World Water Council predicts, citing evidence gathered by U.N. experts and others. The economic cost will be huge, especially for developing nations. The Council predicts:

> The expected climatic change during the twenty-first century will further intensify the hydrological cycle, with rainy seasons becoming shorter and more intense in some regions, while droughts in other areas will grow longer in duration, which could endanger species and crops and lead to a drop in food production globally. . . . Droughts are becoming more severe and widespread. . . . Up to 45% of reported deaths from natural disasters between 1992 and 2001 resulted from droughts and famines. The most vulnerable communities are impoverished peoples occupying marginal rural and urban environments.[65]

Africa's most precious crop, maize, is currently struggling in the face of climate change. In recent years, climate change has cut maize yields by 50% in southern Africa.[66] African agriculturists are considering a switch to more traditional crops such as sorghum and cassava.

## GLOBAL DISEASE

Climate change is also responsible for increases in the frequency and virulence of infectious disease.[67] Our earth's warming climate over the past 30 years is estimated to have contributed to 150,000 deaths and five million illnesses each year, according to the World Health Organization.[68] Many human diseases are directly linked to climate change, from cardiovascular mortality and respiratory illnesses caused by heat waves, to increased transmission of infectious diseases and malnutrition because of crop failures and expanded habitats for pathogen-carrying insects, such as malarial mosquitoes. Ironically, the people of underdeveloped nations are those most vulnerable to climate change, and yet have had the least to do with causing it. The following is but a small sampling of global disease incidences attributable in large part to climate change:

- In the North West Frontier Province of Pakistan, a regional increase in annual mean temperature of 0.5°C since 1978 has contributed to the increase in malaria cases from a few hundred in the early 1980s to 25,000 in 1990.

- An extended season of malaria and dengue activity has been observed in Argentina.

- Epidemic malaria has occurred at high altitudes over the past decade in Rwanda, Zambia, Swaziland, Ethiopia, and Madagascar. Increased temperatures or rainfall or both have significantly contributed to these epidemics. One epidemic in highland Madagascar in 1988 killed more than 100,000 people.

- Dengue has appeared at higher altitudes than previously reported in Costa Rica (at 1,250 meters, or 4,100 feet), and in Colombia and India (at 2,200 meters, or 7,216 feet). The previous range was temperature-limited to approximately 1,000 meters (3,280 feet) above sea level. In Mexico, the dengue virus has been detected at 1,600 meters (5,248 feet); transmission of dengue was unknown above 1,200 meters (3,936 feet) before 1986. The above cases lie near or above the altitude or latitude limit of transmission and would be vulnerable to the small increases in temperature that have occurred across these regions.

- Other examples of climate-related changes in the prevalence or distribution of pathogens and their vectors include the resurgence of Mediterranean spotted fever in Spain and Italy, the recent episode of African horse sickness in Iberia, the resurgence of plague in parts of southern Africa, increased incidence and geographic spread of algal blooms, outbreaks of opportunistic infections among seals, and the spread and establishment of pathogens and vectors in Switzerland.

- West Nile disease, previously unknown in the U.S. and Canada, has been seen in several recent breakouts.

As indicated, malaria is a particularly frightening prospect. Today, more than 4.4 billion people are at risk from malaria infection. This is projected to increase to 8.8 billion people by 2085 in the absence of global warming.[69] With global warming, this level will conservatively increase by at least 3%, i.e., by more than 260 million additional people in 2085. This is due to the increased range of mosquitoes, as higher altitudes become warmer and more hospitable to them. The countries most at risk are those where malaria is currently not a major factor, because immunity in human beings and animals in these countries is quite low.

## WHERE ARE WE AS A NATION—REALLY?

We are arguably at the most significant crossroads in the history of our civilization. The current U.S. administration and Congress finally recognize that a transition from our dependence on oil is important, although many of their members have yet to recognize that the solution is in non-fossil fuels. They still argue for burning more coal and building more nuclear plants. Furthermore, their actions—or inactions—support a position that would be fine if this transition occurs in an orderly manner over the next 50 years or so. The European Union, while more committed to action, has not progressed significantly beyond this position. And yet, it is the U.S. and the European Union that must provide global leadership to address a challenge as great as climate change.

Industry leaders such as Shell, BP, GE, and DuPont have made commitments to clean alternative sources of energy. They recognize that it can mean greater profitability, generally enhanced financial results, and preferable social benefits. As Jeffrey R. Immelt, chairman and CEO of GE, recently stated, "We think Green means Green. This is a time period where environmental improvement is going to lead toward profitability." But too many industry leaders still believe that there is plenty of oil in the ground, and that technology will save the day. So, their attitude is, "Let's continue to plan on burning more and more fossil fuels."

As for climate change, the current administration and a number of large corporations claim the need for much more research and data before they accept it is an issue that requires action. They argue, as President Bush has often done in the past, that any reasonable action would strain the American economy and, therefore, is unjustified at this time. They fail to recognize that the financial impact will be much more devastating if we continue to do nothing. As for climate-change skeptics, Donald Kennedy, internationally respected scientist and editor-in-chief of *Science* Magazine, summed it up well: "Consensus as strong as the one that has developed around this topic is rare in science." On June 21, 2004, 48 Nobel laureate scientists went a step further by stating, "By ignoring scientific consensus on critical issues such as global climate change, [President Bush and his administration] are threatening the earth's future." In February 2007, the American Association for the Advancement of Science, the world's largest scientific association, stated, ""The evidence is clear: Global climate change caused by human activities is occurring now and is a growing threat to society."[70]

Where are we really? In our view, climate change is real and humanity is a big factor in its formation. It is taking place at an ever-increasing and more danger-ous pace, not just for the U.S., but for all of humanity. We Americans

> *"Climate change is the most severe problem that we are facing today, more serious even than the threat of terrorism."*
>
> — SIR DAVID KING,
> BRITISH SCIENCE ADVISOR

are major contributors to this problem, and it is we who hold the solution. In its most fundamental essence, climate change is not a pollution problem, it is an energy problem.

The world must get off oil, coal, and, eventually, natural gas, and move to non-fossil fuels, if it is to survive in some form that approximates modern civilization. In many respects, we should be grateful that oil is rapidly approaching its peak and consequently increasing in price. It seems that historically only economic factors grab our attention and the attention of our political representatives. Climate change is complex and not yet appreciated by those who can and should provide leadership and the political will. Our lead-ers should do something constructive to immediately begin pulling us back from the brink of disaster. Climate change, arguably, is the most critical issue we will face in the 21st century. Nonetheless, it is the economic cost of our current foolish energy consumption patterns that will ultimately drive us to act. That's fine, as we have the opportunity to solve both problems with one stroke.

If oil production rates have not peaked, they surely will very shortly, and the global economic impact will be catastrophic to all nations, ultimately even to oil-producing countries. Over the past decade, globalization has tightly coupled international economic, energy, and environmental systems. These systems are stressed. A tipping point is close at hand, and it will not take much duress or chaotic behavior in any of these three systems to send the world into an economic and security tailspin. It may well be that a geopolitical event will force us to act before we feel the economic impact of peak oil. Whatever the catalytic event, the eco-political environment is right for it to occur in the very near future. With hope, we will have got our act together as a country and will provide the leadership and political will for which the world waits.

## CAPPING CARBON EMISSIONS

To reduce the rate of climate change, the National Commission on Energy Policy has proposed a flexible, market-based strategy of tradable emissions permits. The Commission recommended that "the U.S. government in 2010 would begin issuing permits for greenhouse gas emissions based on an annual emissions target that reflects a 2.4% per year reduction in [the] average greenhouse gas emissions intensity of the economy (where "intensity" is measured in tons of emissions per dollar of GDP)."[71]

Under this proposal, most permits would be issued at no cost to existing emitters, but at the beginning a small pool equal to 5% of all emissions would be auctioned to accommodate new emitters, stimulate the market in emission permits, and fund R&D of new technologies. The Commission proposal also includes a "safety valve mechanism" that allows additional permits to be purchased at an initial price of $7 per metric ton of carbon dioxide ($CO_2$-equivalent). The safety valve price would increase gradually by 5% per year to provide an increasing market incentive to reduce emissions.

The U.S. already has substantial experience with emissions trading. The Clean Air Act Amendments of 1990 established an acid rain trading program generally considered to be "the most effective comprehensive emission trading program to date."[72] As discussed in Chapter 13, a number of states are forming regional trading programs.[73]

Market-based mechanisms such as an emissions tax or tradable emissions permits rely on financial incentives that price the atmospheric release of specific amounts of carbon dioxide. This stands in contrast to traditional methods of capping standard emissions levels across the board for all companies or industry sectors. This traditional method lacks a financial incentive or market mechanism.

With an emission tax, on the other hand, a company is charged per ton of carbon dioxide it emits. Thus, the businesses continue reducing emissions until the cost of carbon dioxide emissions reduction is greater than the tax.

> "It is time to move from denial to action."
>
> — PAUL ANDERSON, CHAIRMAN AND CEO, DUKE ENERGY CORP.

Under an emissions trading system, the government places a total emission cap or quota on the emitters, in this case the electric power sector. It then distributes emission permits equal only to the level of the cap. Of course, the key here is the level at which the cap is set. And it is on this point that millions of lobbying dollars are spent to be sure the cap is set as high as possible for a given industry. Each company must have sufficient permits to cover its level of emissions and may trade (buy or sell) permits with other companies. Companies with low emission reduction costs have financial incentives to reduce emissions and sell excess permits to companies that have higher emission reduction costs. In this context, both pollution control innovators and traditional pollution emitting companies have incentives to find new and cheaper ways to reduce carbon dioxide emissions.[74]

A further benefit of the proposed carbon emission trading system is that it would create a new tradable asset. If carbon were priced at $25 per ton, the total value of all carbon emissions in 2000 would have been nearly $40 billion, compared to the total maximum value of about $3 billion for existing acid rain permits.

While reducing greenhouse gases poses several unique problems (taxes vs. permits, implementation, distribution, monitoring, and enforcement), today most economists and many environmentalists agree that some type of market-based mechanism should be incorporated into an effective strategy for controlling greenhouse gases, and especially carbon dioxide emissions. This is primarily driven by the fact that almost all industries favor this market-driven approach, and therefore it is the easiest to adopt, provided the carbon cap is not set too low.

However, there are a number of analysts who believe that requiring a polluter to be taxed for its emissions is the best way to cause the polluter to internalize the cost of global warming on its books, rather than externalizing that significant cost to society at large. Arguments for this strictly regulatory approach, i.e., "cap but no trade," are cogently summarized in a recent article by David Morris.[75] He suggests that, "So far, the real winners in emissions trading have been polluting factory owners who can sell menial cuts for massive profits and the brokers who pocket fees each time a company buys or sells the right to pollute." His arguments against cap and trade are four-fold:

### 1. Buying offsets encourages complacency.

Morris borrows a metaphor from author George Mobiot and compares the purchase of offsets, i.e., cap and trade, to the purchase of medieval indulgences. He suggests that "if we sin, we can buy absolution." He then argues:

> Using $10 per ton of $CO_2$ as the average offset price (current prices are as low as $3 per ton), the United States, which generates about 20 percent of the world's greenhouse gases, could buy complete absolution for about $50 billion a year. For that price it would announce to the world . . . that we are not responsible for *any* net new greenhouse gases. The cost is less than half the annual spending on the war in Iraq, a little over 5 percent of the Pentagon's annual budget.

### 2. Carbon trading is inherently susceptible to fraud and manipulation.

Morris correctly notes that global computerized trading is often non-transparent. For example, in a recent cap and trade deal concerning a $5 million incinerator in China, carbon offsets were sold to European investors for $500 million. Morris maintains that the profits from this transaction were likely divided among the factory's owners, a Chinese government energy fund, and the consultants and bankers who put the deal together.

## 3. Carbon trading encourages cheating and rewards low-cost cosmetic changes while undermining higher cost innovation.

Morris argues:

The greater the "baseline" emissions, the greater the payoff that can be derived from selling emission-reducing projects. Thus, there is a perverse incentive to emit as much greenhouse gas as possible today in order to make projects appear to be saving as much carbon as possible tomorrow.

## 4. Carbon trading separates authority and responsibility, undermining coherent, holistic community-based efforts.

Morris suggests:

Globalized carbon trading lends itself to similar criticisms of globalized trade agreements: the preemption of local and national authority, the separation of those who make the decisions from those who feel the impact of those decisions, the separation of those communities that receive the benefit from those who bear the cost.

Those who criticize the cap and trade approach of selling offsets strongly favor government regulation and setting a cap without any trade. Morris points to the following examples:

One alternative is good old regulation, which contrary to the popular wisdom, has worked very well, especially when the regulations are performance-based. The United States required 23 years to eliminate leaded gasoline, in part because it created a lead trading program. Without allowing trading, Japan eliminated lead in 10 years and China in three. The Corporate Average Fuel Economy regulation, enacted in 1975, did not allow trading but effectively doubled auto efficiency within 10 years. The 1970 Clean Air Act, without allowing trading, reduced emissions significantly through a regulatory approach.

Another program adopted about the same time as the $SO_x$ trading program might serve as a better model for implementing the Kyoto Protocol. The discovery of the depletion of atmospheric ozone led to the international Montreal Accord. Signatories agreed to phase out specific ozone depleting chemicals. The U.S. Congress coupled the phase-out requirement with a very high tax on chlorofluorocarbons, sending an important price signal it correctly predicted would accelerate phase-out.

In summary, Morris argues that, "Unlike carbon trading, investing to reduce local carbon emissions strengthens the local economy, encourages real innovation, and is a long-term, durable strategy."

While we are not negative on the cap and trade approach, we recommend a hard look at the cap without the trade. Time has proven the value of legal duties that cannot be traded away—indeed such laws are the foundation of the social and economic spheres of life in this country.

The EU's emission-trading scheme (ETS) should serve as a lesson to the U.S. of the potential weaknesses of cap-and-trade systems. In March 2007, the *Economist* offered this critique of the EU's failed system for tradable emission allowances:

> The principle is fine, but because governments handed out too many allowances, emissions have not fallen and the price of allowances has dropped from €34 ($42) per tonne of $CO_2$ at its peak a year ago to around €1.20 now—far too low to induce anybody to constrain their emissions.[76]

Carbon caps are likely to speed up the pace of innovation. To escape from our environmental and national security quagmire, we must take full advantage of Americans' unsurpassed aptitude for technological innovation. We strongly recommend that the states and federal governments provide regulatory incentives to speed up the commercialization of new technologies. A carbon cap would be one such incentive. As discussed in Chapter 9, vehicle fuel efficiency almost doubled after the federal government responded to the 1973 oil crisis by imposing new requirements on automakers.

Timing is critical and we are pragmatic. If cap-without-trade discussions were to drag on, and prove politically unfeasible because of well-financed industry resistance, we would support a cap and trade system with competent oversight, at least as an interim measure. We must slow and ultimately reverse the growth of carbon dioxide in the atmosphere, even if controls begin in the least ambitious way.

Of course Americans will have a national debate about the cost of a carbon cap and its impact on our economy, but there's a bigger question: "With carbon dioxide levels at their highest levels in the last 740,000 years, methane levels at their highest levels in the last 650,000 years, and the potential for more deadly releases of methane from melting permafrost in Siberia—permafrost which already has melted more than at any time since wooly mammals roamed the earth—can we afford *not* to cap carbon?"

## CAN THERE BE A HAPPY ENDING?

Can there be a happy ending? *Absolutely!* A rapid—not a casual-over-50-years—transition to a non-fossil fuel economy would significantly mitigate our environmental, energy, economic, and civil security challenges. Our global leadership could offer this same mandate and opportunity to other nations of the world so that clean, readily available energy would be democratized. As described in detail in other chapters, the Prometheus Plan rests on three pillars to be implemented over the next 10 years:

1. Immediate massive implementation of existing energy efficiency technologies, especially in transportation;

2. Rapid transition to alternative non-nuclear, non-fossil fuels based on current technologies—biofuels, wind, solar—with a focus on transportation; and

3. Transition to the hydrogen economy, finalizing our progression to a non-fossil fuel economy.

Is any of this possible? Absolutely. It's also going to be highly profitable for those "sunrise" companies that seize this opportunity to co-create a new planetary fuel system. Converting over to this new fuel system will enhance our global economies well beyond our expectations by stimulating innovation through existing, proven technologies, and creating millions of new jobs. Many companies, states, and several nations are already moving in this direction.[77] GE and BP recently signed a joint venture to develop and deploy 15 commercial hydrogen power generation projects over the next decade.[78] Costa Rica derives 92% of its energy from renewable resources. Brazil is energy-independent because of its sugar cane-to-ethanol program. Brazil is also moving aggressively into biodiesel. Germany generates one third of the world's wind-powered electricity and has plans to triple its capacity by 2030.

Tokyo Gas launched the world's first residential hydrogen fuel cell system in February 2005. Homeowners can lease the system, which extracts hydrogen from natural gas and generates up to 60% of the energy needed by a four-person household. Each unit reduces the household's annual greenhouse gas emissions by 40%. A 10-year lease costs $9,600, although the savings from reduced energy does not completely cover the cost of the lease. There is an annual shortfall of $340 per home, but this system does not require any of the large government subsidies that, for example, the oil industry currently enjoys.

These examples are evidence of an increasing sensitivity and motivation to address climate change and our global energy security challenge.

Our motivation for proceeding post-haste with the Prometheus Plan is to help America achieve energy independence and take advantage of an unparalleled opportunity through our leadership and commitment to bring peace, security, and equality to a deeply challenged world. Nowhere is this opportunity summed up more cogently and inspiringly than by Al Gore in his book and film, *An Inconvenient Truth*:

The climate change crisis offers us the opportunity to experience what very few generations in history have had the privilege of knowing: a *generational mission*; the exhilaration of a compelling moral purpose; a shared and unifying cause; the thrill of being forced by circumstances to put aside the pettiness that so often stifles the restless human need for transcendence; the *opportunity to rise*. When we do rise, it will fill our spirits, and bind us together. Those who are now suffocating in cynicism and despair will be able to breathe freely. Those who are now suffocating from a loss of meaning in their lives will find hope.[79]

# Notes and References
# Chapter 4: Climate Change

1 Eli Kintisch, "Panel Urges Unified Action, Sets 2° Target," *Science* 307 (January 28, 2005): 496.

2 Tim Flannery, *The Weather Makers: How Man Is Changing the Climate and What It Means for Life on Earth* (New York: Atlantic Monthly Press, 2005).

3 Nikita Lopoukhine, "Have a Hot, Dry, Stormy Life, Kids," Editorial, *International Herald Tribune*, December 14, 2005.

4 Robert Newman, "It's Capitalism or a Habitable Planet—You Can't Have Both," *Guardian*, February 2, 2006.

5 Svante August Arrhenius (http://www.ucc.ie/academic/chem/dolchem/html/biog/biog001.html).

6 Al Gore, *An Inconvenient Truth—The Planetary Emergency of Global Warming and What We Can Do About It* (Emmaus, PA: Rodale, 2006), 63.

7 *Ibid.*, 66.

8 Lester R. Brown, *Plan B 2.0—Rescuing a Planet Under Stress and a Civilization in Trouble,* (Earth Policy Institute 2006), 61.

9 "The Predictions Go From Bad To Worse," Summary of 2007 IPCC report in *New Scientist* (February 10, 2007): 9.

10 Rapid Climate Change," Parliamentary Office of Science and Technology, 2 (www.alphagalileo.org/images/postpn245.pdf).

11 James P. Collman, *Naturally Dangerous* (Sausalito, CA: University Science Books, 2001), 179.

12 Flannery, *op. cit.*, 182.

13 These $CO_2$ emissions result from decomposing limestone and from burning fossil fuels to get the required high temperatures. (Limestone is calcium carbonate, which is decomposed in cement kilns to $CO_2$ and calcium oxide, a cement binding agent.) Brown, *op. cit.*, 188.

14 Nicholas D. Kristof, *International Herald Tribune*, April 19, 2006.

15 Flannery, *op. cit.*, Chapters 1 and 5; *New Scientist* (April 1, 2006): 18.

16 A term in golf for taking a second shot after the golfer has badly hit the ball on the first attempt.

17 Kristof, *op. cit.*

18 Elise Kleeman, *Discover,* January 2006, 34.

19 Kristof, *op. cit.*, 5.

20 A. H. Knoll, *Life on a Young Planet* (Princeton, NJ: Princeton University Press, 2004).

21 A. J. Ridgwell, M. J. Kennedy, and K. Caldiera, "Carbonate Deposition, Climate Stability, and Neoproterozoic Ice Ages," *Science* 302 (2003): 859-62.

22 Flannery, *op. cit.*, 52ff.

23 Gerald R Dickens, "Hydrocarbon-Driven Warming," *Nature* 429 (June 3, 2004): 513-15.

24 J. Lovelock, *Gaia: A New Look at Life on Earth* (New York: Oxford University Press, 1979).

25 Flannery, *op. cit.*

26 Elizabeth Kolbert, *Field Notes From a Catastrophe* (New York: Bloomsbury, 2005), 115.

27 L. R. Kump, "Reducing Uncertainty about Carbon Dioxide as a Climate Driver," *Nature* 419 (September 12, 2002): 188-90.

28 R. A. Feely et al., "Impact of Anthropogenic $CO_2$ on $CaCO_3$ System in the Oceans," *Science* 305 (July 16, 2004): 362-6.

29 Christopher L. Sabine et al., "The Oceanic Sink for Anthropogenic $CO_2$," *Science* 305 (July 16, 2004): 367-71.

30 S. R. Weart, *The Discovery of Global Warming: New Histories of Science, Technology and Medicine* (Cambridge: Harvard University Press, 2003).

31 Flannery, *op. cit.*, 6.

32 Jerry F. McManus, "A Great Grand-Daddy of Ice Cores," *Nature* 429 (June 10, 2004): 611-12.

33 Quirin Schiermeier, "A Rising Tide," *Nature* 428 (March 11, 2004): 114-15.

34 University of Colorado at Boulder, "Global Sea Levels Likely to Rise Higher in 21st Century than Previous Predictions," Press Release, February 2002.

35 Myrna H. P. Hall and Daniel B. Fagre, "Modeled Climate-Induced Glacier Change in Glacier National Park, 1850-2100, *BioScience* (February 2003): 131-40.

36 Gore, *op. cit.*, 48.

37 "The Peak of Mt. Kilimanjaro As It Has Not Been for 11,000 Years," *Guardian*, March 14, 2005.

38 ACIA, www.acia.uaf.edu; "Rapid Arctic Warming Brings Sea Level Rise, Extinctions," *Environment News Service*, September 16, 2004.

39 Erik Stokstad, "Defrosting the Carbon Freezer of the North," *Science* 304 (June 11, 2004): 1618-20.

40 S. Perkins, *Science News* 168 (December 17, 2005): 387.

41 Juliet Eilperin, *Washington Post*, March 3, 2006.

42 U.S. Geological Survey, http://pubs.usgs.gov/fs/fs2-00/.

43 Robert Lee Hotz, "As Climate Shifts, Antarctic Ice Sheet Is Growing," *Los Angeles Times*, May 20, 2005.

44 *Ibid.*

45 *New Scientist* (February 18, 2006): 8.

46 Gore, *op. cit.*, 58.

47 *New Scientist, op. cit.*, 10.

48 "Climate Collapse: The Pentagon's Weather Nightmare," *Fortune*, February 9, 2004.

49 Harry L. Bryden *et al.*, "Slowing of the Atlantic Meridional Overturning Circulation at 25° N," *Nature* 438 (December 1, 2005): 655-57.

50 Lester R. Brown, *Earth Policy Institute*, Eco-Economy Updates, November 15, 2001-2002.

51 Donald Kennedy and Brooks Hanson, "Ice and History," *Science* 311 (March 24, 2006): 1673.

52 *Wall Street Journal,* March 3-5, 2006.

53 Gore, *op. cit.,* 102.

54 Fred Pearce, "The Gathering Storm," *New Scientist* (December 3, 2005): 36-41.

55 *Ibid.,* 38.

56 Naila Moreira, *Science News* (September 17, 2005): 184-86.

57 Kerry Emanuel, "Increasing Destructiveness of Tropical Cyclones Over the Past 30 Years," *Nature* 436 (August 4, 2005): 686-8.

58 J. Madeleine Nash, *Smithsonian,* September 2006, 96.

59 Moreira, *op. cit.,* 184-86.

60 Scott C. Doney, "The Dangers of Ocean Acidification," *Scientific American,* March 2006, 38-45.

61 Caldiera, *op. cit.,* 45.

62 The mixture of carbon monoxide and hydrogen is called "Town Gas" and was generated from coal during the late 19th and early 20th centuries, and used to fire streetlamps and gas stoves. It was eventually replaced by natural gas (methane) because the latter has a much higher heating value, and also is significantly less toxic.

63 Katie Benner, *CNN,* "Clean Coal—A Good Investment?" http://money.cnn.com/2004/10/18/news/economy/coal/.

64 Gerald A. Meehl and Claudia Tebaldi, "More Intense, More Frequent, and Longer Lasting Heat Waves in the 21st Century, *Science* 305 (August 13, 2004): 994-97.

65 http://www.worldwatercouncil.org/

66 "Climate Killing Africa's Crops," *New Scientist* (February 25, 2006): 7.

67 http://archive.greenpeace.org/climate/impacts/erwin/3erwin.html.

68 Juliet Eilperin, *Wall Street Journal,* November 18-20, 2005; Jonathan A. Patz, *et al.,* "Impact of Regional Climate Change on Human Health," *Nature* 438 (November 17, 2005): 310-18.

69 "Living with Global Warming," National Center for Policy Analysis, September 14, 2005, http://www.ncpa.org/pub/st/st278/.

70 AAAS, "AAAS Board Releases News Statement on Climate Change," February 18, 2007. http://www.aaas.org/news/releases/2007/0218am_statement.shtml.

71 National Commission on Energy Policy, "Summary of Recommendations," *Ending the Energy Stalemate: A Bipartisan Strategy to Meet America's Energy Challenges*, Washington, D.C., December 2004, 10.

72 For a comprehensive discussion of carbon taxes and carbon emissions, see "Pricing Carbon: An Overview," National Commission on Energy Policy, Staff Background Paper, NCEP, November 2002, www.energycommission.org.

73 For an analysis of the Regional Greenhouse Gas Initiative developed by New England and Mid-Atlantic states, see "The Regional Greenhouse Gas Initiative: An American Response," *Trends*, American Bar Association Section of Environment, Energy, and Resources Newsletter (January/February 2007, vol. 38:3): 1.

74 *Ibid.*, 5. For example, an emission tax caps the cost per ton paid to reduce emissions. So under a carbon tax of $10 per ton, companies would invest in all emission reduction projects that cost less than $10 per ton and pay the tax on their remaining emissions. Emission reduction costs are limited to $10 per ton, and total emission levels will fluctuate. Under a tradable permit system, where total emissions are capped, the price of the permits will rise or fall to whatever price is necessary to bring emissions to the level of the cap.

75 David Morris, http://www.alternet.org/story/49025 (2007).

76 "What Price Carbon?" The *Economist*, March 17, 2007, 16.

77 Maryann Jones Thompson, *Technology Review* (March 2005): 22-23.

78 *Chemical & Engineering News*, July 24, 2006, 11.

79 Gore, *op. cit.*, 11.

# PART II

# MORE OF THE SAME—
# ONLY WORSE!

# 5

## NUCLEAR POWER:
## A MISTAKE IN SEARCH OF A MISSION

*"It's a nuclear renaissance, right? Not yet. While smart money is placing multibillion dollar bets on ethanol, wind power, and solar, it's not throwing buckets of cash at nukes."*

— "NUCLEAR POWER'S MISSING FUEL,"
*BUSINESS WEEK,* JULY 10, 2006

**Is a revival of nuclear power the solution to global warming?** *No.*

- Wall Street will not fund a new generation of multi-billion-dollar nuclear plants.

- Nuclear power is not economical when you consider the fully-loaded costs.

- Radiation releases from all existing nuclear reactors are a probable cause of cancer.

- Congress should ascertain the safety of *normal* operations of nuclear power plants before appropriating another dime of public money to build new plants.

- Nuclear power technology allows rogue nations such as Iran and North Korea to build nuclear weapons.

- Nuclear power makes no environmental sense and it makes no economic sense.

## WALL STREET SKEPTICAL OF NUCLEAR POWER REVIVAL

Is the oft-promised nuclear power renaissance finally under-way in the United States? A few electric utilities and the small but powerful group of nuclear industry cheerleaders certainly think so, and they are doing everything they can to influence key politicians by throwing millions of dollars at the political process. Other major voices in the business media and on Wall Street are either not so sure or are strongly against the technology. This latter dose of prudence is noteworthy.

In July 2006, *Business Week* published a critical article on "Nuclear Power's Missing Fuel," which explained "Why Wall Street is skeptical of backing a new round of proposed nuke plants." The article observed that "memories of the delays, titanic cost overruns, and bankruptcies that ended America's love affair with nuclear power in the mid-twentieth century are the most daunting obstacle."[1]

Historically, the utilities did a horrible job controlling costs on massive nuclear power projects, leading to the "malpractice of nuclear economics." As a result, the bill for 75 first-generation nuclear power plants soared to nearly $225 billion (in current dollars), *219% more than estimated,* according to a 1986 U.S. Department of Energy study. That amounts to some $3 billion per plant. This is only construction costs, and does not include the costs for plant decontamination, decommissioning, and spent fuel treatment, storage, and reprocessing.

During the reactor market crash between 1974 and 1982, utilities cancelled orders for over 100 nuclear power plants, many of which were well under construction. Over time, many utility nuclear power programs simply collapsed under a mountain of debt, leaving behind concrete graveyards of nuclear white elephants.

*Business Week* quotes Bob Simon, the Democratic staff direc-tor of the Senate Energy and Natural Resources Committee, who notes, "The real obstacle isn't the Sierra Club but the 28-year-old analyst on Wall Street." Taking into account the massive costs for plant construction, fuel reprocessing, waste disposal, and plant decommissioning, nuclear plants are simply less profitable than their major competitors, coal and gas-fired plants. Echoing Simon, Jerry Taylor, a senior fellow at the libertarian Cato Institute says, "It's not as if Greenpeace killed the industry. Guys in pinstripe suits on Wall Street killed the industry."

Not since a February 11, 1985, *Forbes* cover story on "Nuclear Follies" has a major business journal taken such a critical view of the nuclear industry. In a scathing review, *Forbes* portrayed this nation's experience with nuclear power as "the largest managerial disaster in business history."[2]

Commenting on the billions of dollars invested in nuclear power, *Forbes* observed, "Only the blind, or the biased, can now think that most of the money has been well spent. It is a defeat for the U.S. consumer and for the competitiveness of U.S. industry, for the utilities that undertook the program, and for the private enterprise system that made it possible."

So, what's different about this year's nuclear revival, which is being promoted as the solution to global warming?

## A RESURRECTION OF NUCLEAR POWER?

With no new reactors having come online since 1996 and with the rapid collapse of new construction in the 1980s, a nuclear revival would indeed represent a return from the dead for the troubled industry. Like a cat with nine lives (and endless government subsidies), the nuclear industry is being marketed worldwide by a ubiquitous public relations campaign funded by a handful of companies who stand to gain tens of billions if they can talk an appropriately cautious public into buying this ill-fated technology.

In January 2006, the cover of *Newsweek* proclaimed "The Return of Nuclear Power." President Bush, in turn, launched a new Global Nuclear Energy Partnership with $250 million, beginning October 1, 2006. The partnership calls for U.S. and its partner countries to process spent nuclear fuel using techniques that would allegedly minimize the amount of high-grade nuclear waste that requires disposal, thereby limiting the risk of nuclear proliferation.

With President Bush's enthusiastic support, the Nuclear Energy Institute, the Washington, D.C.-based trade association, announced an ambitious goal of 50 new 1,000 MW reactors over the next 20 years. This would amount to nearly a 50% increase over the current 103 operating reactors.

> *"We must expand our nuclear power industry if we want to be competitive in the 21st century. We have got to be wise—we have got to push hard to build new plants."*
>
> — PRESIDENT GEORGE W. BUSH, NATIONAL ASSOCIATION OF MANUFACTURERS SPEECH, JULY 2006

Four companies—Dominion Resources, Entergy, Exelon, and the Southern Company—have filed applications for site permits, and 15 utilities have announced plans to apply for licenses to build and operate up to 33 new plants, representing approximately 40,000 megawatts (MW) of generating capacity. In June 2006, NRG Energy Inc. announced plans to invest $5.2 billion in two new nuclear reactors. The plants would be built by Hitachi Ltd. and General Electric Co. and be located near an existing reactor in Texas.

Internationally, atomic bomb historians Richard Rhodes and Denis Beller made a hard pitch for nuclear power to influential readers in the January/February 2006 issue of *Foreign Affairs*. With world population expanding and demanding increasing access to electricity, they argue, "Even with vigorous conservation, world energy production would have to triple by 2050 to support consumption at a mere one-third of today's U.S. per capita rate."[3]

Britain is considering plans for a major expansion of nuclear energy. At a recent OECD forum in Paris, advocates for nuclear power made a passionate plea that it is the only means for satisfying the world's insatiable appetite for energy while simultaneously curbing global warming.

While nuclear power has been virtually dormant in the U.S. and Europe (with the exception of France), a nuclear revival is already underway in Asia, where China and India have ambitious nuclear plans. Up to 30 plants may be built in each country over the next 20 years. If completed, the plants would produce less than 5% of those countries' electricity by 2020.

With a rising chorus of cheerleaders, many argue that this second coming of nuclear power will not easily be stopped because of skyrocketing oil prices and accelerating global warming.

## NUCLEAR POWER 101

The appeal of nuclear power is based on its being already a large and established source of electricity. Currently, 441 reactors produce 369,000 MW of power, or 16% of the world's electricity. In the U.S., the 104 operating reactors produce about 20% of the nation's electrical power. In contrast to natural gas and coal, which are also used as direct energy sources in the industrial and commercial sectors, 100% of U.S. nuclear energy is used to generate electric power.

One problem arises from the aging of the U.S. nuclear plant infrastructure. As Figure 1 shows, the industry is growing at less than 1% per year worldwide, and the construction pipeline is now virtually empty.[4] Only 23 reactors, with a total capacity of 16,000 MWs are under construction, while reactor capacity amounting to nearly 35,000 MWs has been shut down or permanently taken offline since the beginning of the nuclear power age. Even the relatively conservative International Energy Agency forecasts that nuclear power generation will peak within 10 years and *then begin a slow decline.*[5]

**Figure 1.** **World Electrical Generating Capacity of Nuclear Power Plants, 1960-2004**

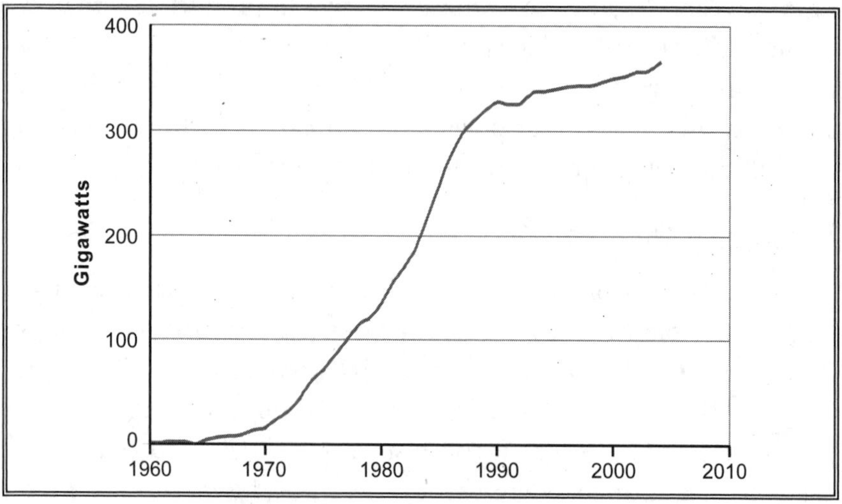

Source: Worldwatch Institute database

## BUYER BEWARE!

The bottom line question: if once burned, should the utilities and the public buy a new round of power plants from nuclear salesmen? The best way to evaluate this is to rely on the sound business principle that places high value on accurate projections and past performance. The commercial nuclear industry has been around for half a century (the first commercial plant went on line at Shippingsport, Pennsylvania, in 1957), so the prudent approach would be to look at the industry's track record.

When we do, we find a string of broken promises, product failures, massive subterranean leaks of liquid nuclear waste (at the Hanford facility), cost overruns, overly optimistic projections, stranded debts, bankruptcies, bond defaults, and a mountain of toxic waste that grows daily and cannot be removed for safe disposal. This dismal track record includes a series of catastrophic accidents and near-accidents, the most memorable of which are the 1979 near-meltdown at Three Mile Island in the U.S. and the 1986 Chernobyl disaster in the Ukraine.

When President Nixon declared Project Energy Independence in 1973 during the first Arab oil boycotts, he promised an ambitious nuclear power program that would lead to 1,000 reactors deployed across the nation by the end of the 20th century. As noted above, only 104 commercial reactors are in operation within the U.S. today. Of these, 48 have already been granted license extensions that are typically for 20 years beyond their original "useful life" cycle, and utilities have already filed or plan to request extensions for another 33 plants.

In 1954, Lewis L. Strauss, chairman of the U.S. Atomic Energy Commission (which has since become the Nuclear Regulatory Commission), issued the now infamous prediction that nuclear power would provide "electricity too cheap to meter."[6] In reality, nuclear power has turned out to be *the most expensive* form of baseload[7] electricity ever foisted off on the American public.

The Nuclear Regulatory Commission claimed that the plants were safe, and the risk of a catastrophic Class 9 accident, in which the reactor core would be breached and radioactive isotopes released, was too slim to calculate (less than 1 in 10 million). Yet as early as 1979, the Three Mile Island reactor safety systems failed, and the plant came within 30 minutes of a meltdown, leading Pennsylvania Governor Richard Thornburgh to evacuate the area around the plant. In 1986, multiple explosions at the Chernobyl reactor in the former Soviet Union blew off the reactor containment lid, spewing more than 50% of the radioactive materials thousands of feet into the air, so that the radioactive isotopes circled the Northern Hemisphere. The area around Chernobyl has been declared a "dead zone," and radioactive vegetables are still showing up in Ukrainian markets today, some 20 years after the catastrophe. While the actual death toll remains a matter of serious dispute, it is estimated to be as high as 60,000 and growing.[8] On top of this, no one has fully calculated the costs in human life of all those individuals from Scandinavia southward who came in contact with the airborne radioactivity.

Last, the government promised that there would be a long-term solution for the storage of high-level radioactive waste, primarily from spent fuel rods, which are still sitting in underwater spent fuel pools at "temporary" reactor sites around the country. As of November 2006, the Department of Energy's proposed long-term waste depository at Yucca Mountain, Nevada, is mired in scientific controversy, legal challenges, and a growing admission by all concerned that it won't prove large enough to contain the waste being created by existing reactors—let alone deal with the radioactive waste from new ones.

Based on this dismal performance, nuclear power remains a flawed technology plagued by faulty economics. From a business perspective, we must advise, *caveat emptor*! Buyer beware! This time the burden of proof must be placed squarely on the shoulders of the industry and its advocates. Before the utilities and the public rush to join the nuclear revival, they should critically examine past performance and demand experimental proof for claims that this generation of nuclear plants will be economically viable, climate-friendly, and accident-proof. The industry should also be required to publicly calculate the cost per kilowatt-hour of electricity from a new nuclear plant, including *all* subsidies; the full cost of all waste disposal for a 10,000-year period, with such waste required to be kept out of the biosphere; and the full cost of "entombing" or decommissioning the reactor. Should such a calculation be made, it would reveal the true cost of nuclear energy as *many times more expensive than existing, commercially available renewable sources.*

## $13 BILLION IN NEW NUCLEAR SUBSIDIES

Before any new plants can be built, the nuclear industry still needs to convince Wall Street to provide the capital, and state utility regulators to approve the higher electric rates needed to pay for these multi-billion dollar projects. Despite billions of dollars in new federal incentives, this won't be an easy sell, given the rapid collapse of the nuclear power market in the 1970s and 1980s.

During the 1990s, the industry's lack of credibility in the financial markets was highlighted by the World Bank, which wrote in an assessment of energy projects, "Bank lending for the energy sector requires a review of sector investments, institutions, and policies. Nuclear plants in the power sector would not be economic: they are large white elephants."[9]

Disregarding the nuclear industry's initial failure to compete in the free market, the Bush-Cheney administration plans to jumpstart it with $13 billion in new nuclear subsidies, including low-interest loan guarantees. The Energy Policy Act of 2005 includes the following incentives for nuclear power: $2.9 billion for research and development; at least $3.5 billion in construction subsidies; more than $5.7 billion in operating subsidies; and $1.3 billion to cover decommissioning of old plants. Why such largesse to an industry chronically mired in failure? An analysis by the *Boston Globe* reveals that "entities with a stated interest in energy policy" spent $387 million lobbying Capitol Hill in 2003. The nuclear industry alone spent $78 million, an amount vastly disproportionate to the industry's contribution to the overall energy supply picture.[10]

Analyzing how millions for lobbying campaigns helped fuel the nuclear industry's revival plans, MSNBC editor Mike Stuckey observed, "While the effect of the industry's campaign contributions and lobby efforts in the years before the energy bill's passage are debatable, the amount of money invested is remarkable by any measure.[11] And industry executives are obviously pleased with their investment. "As the administration's energy policy began to emerge in the spring of 2001, its support for the nuclear power industry was beyond 'my wildest dreams,' Christian H. Poindexter, chairman of the Constellation Energy Group, later told the New York Times."[12]

In effect, the federal government has acknowledged *all* of the nuclear power risks that prudent financial institutions are unwilling to take and transferred them to the taxpaying public. For example, this latest package of federal largesse includes some $2 billion for risk insurance for the builders of the first six reactors. It covers any delays in construction or licensing, including public legal challenges on safety issues, even those based on whistleblower reports of faulty construction. It provides for production tax credits of 1.7 cents per kilowatt-hour for eight years, an industry windfall estimated to be

$5.7 to $7 billion that would normally go to the U.S. Treasury. There are also provisions for taxpayer-backed loan guarantees to cover up to 80% of a reactor's cost.

Even with this federal handout to offset the high "first-of-a-kind" costs of the next-generation reactors, the jury on the nuclear revival will be out until the first new plants come in *on time and on budget*. Those are two big "ifs," given the chronic history of cost overruns. According to a 2001 Congressional Research Service Report, total construction costs for reactors started after 1974 exceeded $3,000/kilowatt (kw), and those built since the mid-1980s averaged $3,600/kw (not including waste disposal or decommissioning costs). Today, the industry promises that the new power reactors can be built for a highly optimistic $1,500-$2,000/kw.[13] Frankly, based on 50 years of history, we are skeptical.

In fact, actual costs for the Western world's only new reactor, which is being built in Finland by the French atomic energy giant, Areva, already exceed these projections. In November 2006, the French media reported that the construction schedule for this new European Pressurized Reactor has already slipped by 24 months and that the Finnish utility TVO has a fixed price for this 1,600 MW reactor of about $3.7 billion dollars, or $2,300/kw. This is already above the optimistic $2,000/kw maximum projected cost referenced above, despite highly favorable, below-market loan guarantees provided by the French government.

As quoted in a Worldwatch report on the "Brave Nuclear World," former Nuclear Regulatory Commissioner Peter Bradford observes that despite the passage of the Energy Policy Act and the

> "Utility analysts say that a power company deciding to build a nuclear plant might see its bond rating lowered to reflect the extra risk it has taken on."
>
> — CHRISTOPHER FLAVIN, WORLDWATCH INSTITUTE, 2006

accommodating Bush-Cheney administration, nothing has fundamentally changed in the nuclear world. "With $13 billion in new subsidies, if the government wants to prove that if it spends enough it can build nuclear plants, it can do that. . . . But, that's not the same as saying it makes economic sense to do it."[14]

## FREE MARKET FAILURE

Ever since President Eisenhower's "Atoms for Peace" speech at the United Nations in 1953 initiated the era of commercial nuclear power, the industry has received worldwide governmental support. While currently providing about 20% of U.S. electrical energy, between 1950 and 1993 the U.S. nuclear power industry received nearly 50% of federal funding for energy research and development, or approximately $51 billion.

At virtually every step of the nuclear fuel cycle—mining, enrichment, waste storage, and decommissioning—the industry receives favored treatment, including:

- A 22%, highest available rate depletion allowance, which allows the industry a tax write-off for the value of the uranium fuel extracted;

- The ability granted by local public utilities commissions to pass off nearly $200 billion in "stranded debt costs" of failed nuclear power plants to consumers as surcharges on electric bills;

- Regulatory permission to pass on to the public the costs of handling spent fuel—estimated at up to $100 billion for the nation's operating reactors—as well as future decommissioning costs; and

- Limited liability from the major costs of catastrophic nuclear accidents under the 1957 Price Anderson Act, which was re-authorized in 2005 for another 20 years, limiting a utility primarily responsible for an accident to only $300 million in liability.

Under the Price Anderson Act, all utilities contribute $95.8 million per reactor to an insurance pool, which for 103 operating reactors has grown to approximately $10 billion. As analyst Karen Charman points out:

> By comparison, some estimates put the cost of the Chernobyl accident at over US$350 billion, and the Union of Concerned Scientists estimates that a serious accident in New York's Indian Point plant 56 kilometers north of New York City would be in the trillions—costs mainly left to individuals because of the standard nuclear exclusion clause in home insurance policies. Without this particular liability mitigator in the United States and similar instruments in other counties, commercial nuclear power probably could not exist.[15]

After decades of subsidies, nuclear power still remains the most expensive and non-competitive way of generating electricity. Nevertheless, in attempting to promote nuclear power as one of the most economical sources of electricity, the industry's Electric Utility Cost Group focuses only on certain limited costs for fuel, labor, materials, and services that it characterizes as the "production costs" required to produce 1 kilowatt-hour of electricity. It claims that the production cost of electricity for nuclear power is 1.68 cents per kilowatt-hour, compared to the cents-per-kilowatt-hour cost of 1.90 for coal, 5.87 for natural gas, 2.48 for solar, 0.20 for wind, and 0.50 for hydroelectric.[16] The Nuclear Energy Institute, the nuclear industry's trade association which does lobbying and public relations work for the industry, relies on similarly limited definitions of nuclear "production costs" in arguing that "since 1988, nuclear power plants have achieved the lowest production costs between coal, natural gas and oil."[17] This statement is clearly false.

But these limited costs are only part of the economic picture. The real challenge facing nuclear power becomes clear when "life cycle" production costs are compared, including construction, operations, maintenance, fuel, decommissioning, and waste storage. One of the few comprehensive studies of the life cycle costs of nuclear power, including direct reactor costs, plus decommissioning, temporary waste storage, and federal subsidies, found that between 1968 and 1990 the average cost of nuclear-generated electricity was nearly twice the cost of electricity from coal, oil, or gas during that same period.[18]

One 2003 analysis reported by the Worldwatch Institute found that, *excluding external expenses such as waste disposal,* actual maximum electricity generating costs in U.S. cents per kilowatt-hour were:

- Nuclear: 14.0
- Natural gas: 5.0
- Coal: 4.8
- Wind: 5.0[19]

Recent advances in wind-power technology have now reduced its costs to 2-3 cents per kilowatt-hour. Today, nuclear power is nearly three times as expensive as coal and natural gas, *not including waste disposal and other embedded nuclear costs.*

As a result, although most existing plants are performing well, nuclear power faces tremendous risks and an uncertain future. On one hand, nuclear reactors are now operating at a 90% capacity factor, compared to around 55-60% for most of the 1980s. On the other hand, because of relatively high capital costs and numerous risks, the U.S. Energy Information Administration projects in its *Annual Energy Outlook 2006* that only a few new nuclear units will come on line between 2005 and 2020 and that no additional nuclear plants will be built after 2020, when the favorable tax credits provided by the Energy Policy Act of 2005 expire.[20]

As noted in a March 2007 MIT press release, uranium fuel shortages may limit U.S. nuclear power expansion. Worldwide uranium production meets only about 65% of current reactor fuel requirements.[21] Uranium inventories that just a few years ago were being sold at $10 per pound are now being sold at $85 and more per pound. The U.S. largely relies on overseas suppliers, and gets half its supply from Russia under a 1991 "swords to ploughshares" deal that involves converting about 20,000 Russian nuclear weapons to fuel for U.S. nuclear power plants. When that deal expires in 2013, the U.S. will have a big supply gap. In a February 2007 briefing for Wall Street, the nuclear industry, through the Nuclear Energy Institute, stated that nuclear fuel prices had gone up about 500% since 2002 as a result of many factors, and that in the medium term, prices would continue to go up.[22] We calculate the actual price increase at 850%.

From a business perspective, nuclear power has failed to fulfill its potential in the marketplace. In the early 1980s, following the financial fiasco of the Washington Public Power Supply System's $2.25 billion default (the largest default in utility history), Wall Street rated nuclear power plants as "high risk" and turned off the money machine.

Nuclear power is a financial failure in search of a new mission to justify an extravagant taxpayer-funded revival of its prospects.

## NOT A CURE FOR CLIMATE CHANGE

The new nuclear "mission" involves repackaging nuclear power as the solution to global warming. As part of a worldwide public relations campaign, a growing choir is now singing the praises of nuclear power as the "clean air energy" source.

Today's "Nuclear Now" advocates argue that nuclear power does not depend on foreign sources of fuel (despite the Russian supply dilemma noted above); does not emit conventional air pollution or contribute to smog and haze; does not burn oil, coal, or any other fossil fuel; and, therefore, does not emit carbon dioxide or other greenhouse gases.

Arguing that we can no longer afford to reject any viable energy option with the power to displace coal, which generates 40% of the world's electricity and is the largest contributor to global warming, some former opponents of nuclear energy have jumped onto the "new nuclear bandwagon." These include James Lovelock, creator of the Gaia Hypothesis; Steward Brand, founder of *The Whole Earth Catalog*; and former Greenpeace executive Patrick Moore, now a nuclear industry consultant.

The arguments that nuclear power offers the solution to global warming are dead wrong for several reasons.

First, nuclear proponents fallaciously argue that nuclear power production is "carbon-free." Certainly, fission reactors do not emit

$CO_2$ or other greenhouse gases as they generate electricity by splitting atoms. Nevertheless, considering the complete nuclear fuel life cycle, it is inaccurate to say that nuclear power, or almost any energy source for that matter, is "carbon-free."

In the case of nuclear power, significant amounts of fossil fuel are used indirectly in mining, milling, uranium fuel enrichment, construction of plants and waste storage facilities, decommissioning plants, and ultimately transportation and millennia-long storage of waste. For example, the uranium enrichment plant in Kentucky is one of the single largest users of dirty, coal-fired electricity in the United States.

A study by the Öko Institute of Germany found that when these *indirect emissions* are included, nuclear power produces significantly less greenhouse gas emissions than combined-cycle natural gas and coal plants, but more greenhouse gas emissions than wind or hydroelectric plants.[23]

> *"In a conservative estimate . . . the alternatives show $CO_2$ abatement costs which are three to four times more favorable than those of nuclear power."*
> — UWE R. FRITSCHE, ÖKO-INSTITUT, BERLIN, 1997

Second, even if we decided to replace all fossil-fuel plants with nuclear reactors—leaving cost issues aside for the moment—it would not be technically possible to build them quickly enough to meet even the modest targets of the Kyoto Protocols.

For example, in order to meet the European targets, 72 new medium-sized nuclear plants would have to be constructed for 15 European nations by 2012. In the U.S., up to 1,000 new reactors (nearly 10 times the current base) would be required at a cost of approximately $1.5 trillion to $2.0 trillion, based on *industry estimates* of $1,500-$2,000/kw for new-generation nuclear plant construction.[24] The real number, as the French are discovering in Finland, is dramatically higher.

So, just how many new nuclear power plants would it take to have a significant impact on global warming? A 2003 MIT report on "The Future of Nuclear Power" calls for the worldwide construction of 1,000-1,500 new 1,000 MW reactors by 2050, a nearly fourfold expansion of nuclear power that would potentially displace 15-25% of projected carbon emissions from generating electricity. That figure leaves Alvin M. Weinberg, former director of Oak Ridge National Laboratory, expressing skepticism. Writing on "New Life for Nuclear Power," Weinberg argues that in order to make a serious dent in carbon emissions, it would take perhaps four times as many reactors as suggested in the MIT study, or up to 6,000 reactors. This would irrevocably commit the world to a plutonium economy, with many unpleasant consequences for future generations.

Since nuclear reactors are neither economically competitive nor the solution to climate change, the serious challenges that accompany nuclear technology make it a "bad deal." These monumental challenges include public health issues, safety concerns, nuclear waste disposal, and the growing threat of terrorism and nuclear weapons proliferation in hostile nations such as Iran and North Korea.

## RADIATION RELEASES AND CANCER

We are well aware that the following information may be new, even shocking, to some readers. But no discussion of the nuclear power option would be complete without acknowledging the growing body of medical and scientific evidence linking federally-permitted radiation releases from operating nuclear power plants to cancer rates in the United States.

Today, 50% of men and 40% of women will contract some form of cancer during their lifetimes. Each year, approximately 1.5 million Americans are diagnosed with cancer and over 560,000 die of cancer.

It is probable that cancer rates have soared during the second half of the 20th century partly as a result of the radioactivity released initially from the massive Cold War atmospheric bomb testing during the 1950s and early 1960s, and more recently from nuclear power plants during the 1970s and continuing up to the present. Much consideration has been given to the health effects of a large-scale meltdown of a reactor's core (where heat is produced) and its spent fuel pools (where high-level radioactive waste is stored). The discussion about safe maintenance of spent fuel rod cooling ponds and reactor vessels themselves has been particularly serious since the terrorist attacks of September 11, 2001. What if just one airplane that day had struck a nuclear reactor vessel rather than the World Trade Center or Pentagon? Such an air strike would have created a major meltdown at the reactor. Most reactors are near large cities, and a strike would cause the worst environmental catastrophe in U.S. history, comparable to the aftermath of the Chernobyl accident in 1986 in the former Soviet Union.

Nuclear reactors, however, pose significant health concerns even in the absence of meltdowns. During normal operations *every* nuclear reactor in the world is a source of routine radioactive emissions. To produce electricity by means of nuclear fission, each reactor must periodically emit relatively low-dose amounts of airborne and liquid radioactivity. This radioactivity represents some 50 to 100 different isotopes produced in reactors and atomic bombs, including Strontium-89, Strontium-90, Cesium-137, and Iodine-131, all known carcinogens.[25] Some of these isotopes are short-lived by-products that decay in a matter of weeks, while others remain lethal for decades. The long-lived isotopes can produce internal doses of radiation in humans as a result of inhalation from air or ingestion from food or water.

Each of these isotopes interacts differently with the human body: iodine seeks out the thyroid gland; strontium, which is chemically similar to calcium, concentrates in the bone, irradiating the bone marrow where the white cells of the immune system originate; cesium is distributed throughout the soft tissues. All are highly carcinogenic. Each decays at varying rates. For example, Iodine-131 has a half-life of eight days, and remains in the body only a few weeks. Strontium-90 has a half-life of 28.7 years, and thus remains in bones and newly-forming teeth of children for more than three decades.

These *internally ingested* toxins are different from *external sources* of radioactivity such as medical x-rays, cosmic rays and gamma rays from the explosion of an atomic bomb or from radioactive uranium and radium in the soil. These highly penetrating background forms of radiation pass through the body and do not concentrate or bio-accumulate in specific organs, as do inhaled or ingested particles of Iodine-131 in the thyroid gland or Strontium-90 in bone, which result in local organ damage hundreds to thousands of times greater than the whole-body doses from external sources.

For decades, scientists have documented harm from relatively low-dose exposures to radiation previously presumed to be safe, particularly to the developing fetus in the mother's womb. In the 1950s, British physician Dr. Alice Stewart found that administering just two or three pelvic X-rays to pregnant women shortly before birth nearly doubled the risk that the child would die from cancer by age 10.[26] But not until 1997, under pressure from Congress, did the National Cancer Institute publish its estimate that "up to 212,000 Americans developed thyroid cancer after ingesting fallout from above ground nuclear weapons tests in Nevada."[27]

More recently, the U.S. Congress acknowledged that thousands of workers in atomic weapons plants developed cancer and other diseases in excess of the normally expected rate. In October 2000, Congress passed and President Clinton signed into law the Energy Employees Occupational Illness Compensation Act. This legislative package is designed to provide health care and compensation to certain groups of nuclear weapons workers who were injured from occupational exposure to radiation, beryllium, or silica. In addition to providing some 4,000 eligible workers or their survivors with a lump sum payment of $150,000, the legislation gives the benefit of the doubt to a "special exposure cohort" of workers with radiogenic cancers and presumes that their illness resulted from workplace exposure to radiation.

Elevated levels of leukemia diagnosed as early as in the first year of life have been found in children born in the U. S. in 1986 and 1987, just after the fallout from the Chernobyl disaster arrived, showing a latency period of less than two years between in-utero exposure and diagnosis. Similar increases in infant leukemia, accompanied by other childhood cancers and twice as many brain cancers, have been documented in several other nations, including Belarus, Greece, Scotland, Wales, West Germany, and other European countries which received direct fallout from Chernobyl.[28]

In 1963, the Atomic Energy Commission (predecessor to the Nuclear Regulatory Commission) hired Dr. John Gofman to establish the Biomedical Research Division at the federal Livermore Laboratory and to investigate the impact of radiation on humans. By 1969, Dr. Gofman and his colleague Dr. Arthur Tamplin had concluded that, if everyone in the United States received the official "permissible" dose of radiation from nuclear power plants, at the time 170 millirems per year, an additional 16,000 to 32,000 cancer deaths would be caused annually.[29] Writing in *Poisoned Power*, Gofman and Tamplin concluded:

> Radioactivity represents one of the worst, maybe the worst of all poisons. And it is manufactured as an inevitable by product of nuclear electricity generation. One year of operation of a single, large nuclear reactor plant generates as much long-persisting radioactive poisons as one thousand Hiroshima-type atomic bombs. There is no way the electric power can be generated in nuclear plants without generating the radioactive poisons.[30]

Cancer rates in persons living near nuclear power reactors have by now been studied in dozens of medical journal articles. For example, at least 12 studies have demonstrated high rates of childhood cancer near various nuclear plants in the United Kingdom. In the U.S., fewer studies have been done on childhood cancer near nuclear plants, but they showed a similar pattern of significant increases especially in the downwind area.[31]

But cancer increases were not confined to children. In 1996, the Radiation and Public Health Project published a study, based on National Cancer Institute data collected since 1950 on white female breast cancer mortality, which found that "women living close to reactors are at significantly greater risk of dying of breast cancer than those living further away."[32] The possibility that this increased cancer risk is the result of other factors, such as other environmental toxins, economic status, or ethnicity, is mitigated by another study which found that infant death and childhood cancer rates declined dramatically in downwind counties two years after nuclear plant closings.[33]

After demonstrating a nationwide *correlation* between proximity to nuclear power plants and breast cancer death rates, Radiation and Public Health Project scientists looked next for *physical evidence* that would show if radiation levels were increasing in the bodies of children living close to nuclear power plants. In order to gather this evidence, researchers initiated the first-ever study of in-body radioactivity near U.S. nuclear plants. Popularly known as the "baby teeth study," the research involved the collection of discarded baby teeth and independent laboratory testing for levels of radioactive Strontium-90.

The baby teeth study is not without scientific precedent. It is based on an earlier effort to measure Strontium-90 in baby teeth due to nuclear weapons testing during the Cold War. A study in St. Louis collected over 300,000 baby teeth (between 1958 and 1970) and measured them for Strontium-90. The St. Louis baby teeth study showed that, because of fall-out from atomic bomb testing in Nevada, children born in 1964 had about 50 times greater concentrations of Strontium-90 in their teeth than did children born in 1950. It also found that in-body levels of Strontium-90 *decreased* from 1964 to 1969, after the 1963 Partial Test Ban Treaty signed by President John F. Kennedy banned all above-ground testing of nuclear weapons.

However, *this decline did not continue to the present time as expected.* As shown in Figure 2 of a recent paper, "An Unexpected Rise in Strontium-90 in U.S. Deciduous Teeth in the 1990s," published in *The Science of the Total Environment*, researchers found that "Strontium-90 . . . levels rose 48.5% for persons born in the late 1990s compared to those born in the late 1980s. This trend represented the first sustained increase since the early 1960s, before atmospheric weapons test were banned." Since there was a large rise in the number of nuclear plants as well as a great increase in the percentage of time they operated per year, the paper concludes that, "It is likely that, 40 years after large-scale atmospheric atomic bomb tests ended, much of the current in-body radioactivity represents nuclear reactor emissions."[34]

**Figure 2. Average Strontium-90 Levels in U.S. Baby Teeth, 1954-97**

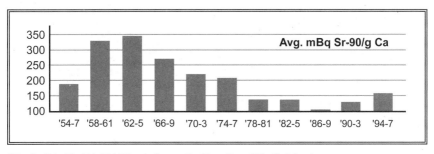

(Mostly CA, FL, NJ, NY, PA—In Avg. mBq Strontium-90/g Calcium)
Source: Radiation and Public Health Project

This recent rise of radiation levels in U.S. baby teeth thus reversed a long-term downward trend in Strontium-90 levels following the 1963 Partial Test Ban Treaty. President Kennedy negotiated the treaty with the Soviet Union and the U.K. partly due to his concerns about increasing Strontium-90 in baby teeth accompanied by rising childhood cancer and leukemia rates from fallout. Thus, Kennedy's action was based in part on precisely the same kind of technique of measuring Strontium-90 levels used in the later baby teeth study.

In evaluating the data presented in the Radiation and Public Health Project's South Florida baby teeth study, Samuel Epstein, M.D., professor emeritus of Environmental Health and Occupational Medicine at the University of Illinois, wrote:

Given prior evidence of the relationship between childhood cancer and radioactive emissions from 103 aging nuclear power plants in the U.S., and the well-established biological risks of radioactive Strontium-90, it is now critical to recognize that radioactive emissions from commercial nuclear power plants pose a grave threat to public health in southeast Florida and throughout the nation.

In its most recent assessment of *Health Risks from Exposure to Low Levels of Ionizing Radiation*, the National Academy of Science's National Research Council reported that "a preponderance of scientific evidence shows that even low doses of ionizing radiation, such as gamma rays and X-rays, are likely to pose some risk of adverse heath effects." Committee chair Dr. Richard R. Monson, Harvard School of Public Health, observed that "the scientific research base shows that there is no threshold of exposure below which low levels of ionizing radiation can be demonstrated to be harmless or beneficial."[35]

Similar concerns about the health effects of low dose ionizing radiation have been raised by the European Committee on Radiation Risk (European Committee). The European Committee used a new model for assessing cancer risks that takes into account the predominance of internal doses and the evidence of a supra-linear dose-response caused by protracted exposures to internal doses produced by low levels of fission products. Based on this assessment, the 2003 European Committee report "predicts 61,600,000 deaths from cancer, 1,600,000 infant deaths, and 1,900,000 fetal deaths" world-wide as a result of the nuclear age. The report states, "The committee concludes that the present cancer epidemic is a consequence of exposures to global atmospheric weapons fallout in the period 1959-1963 and that more recent releases of radioisotopes to the environment from the operation of the nuclear fuel cycle will result in significant increases in cancer and other types of ill health."[36]

It should be noted that these findings indicating a causal link between the low-level radiation released by the normal operations of nuclear power plants and serious health effects have not yet been acknowledged by U.S. government health agencies or any major medical and public health associations in the U.S. or the European Union. They have been vigorously denied by the nuclear utilities, the Nuclear Energy Institute, the U.S. Nuclear Regulatory Commission, and the International Commission on Radiological Protection. In fact, rather than calling for an independent assessment of the heath risks of America's aging reactors, the Nuclear Energy Institute, the trade association of the nuclear industry, prefers to shoot the messenger by labeling the baby teeth study as "junk science," despite the fact that its findings have been published in more than a dozen scientific articles in peer-reviewed journals and are supported by the 2003 European Committee report.[37]

Thus, the science behind these ominous conclusions is strong and will likely prove to be fully supported by supplemental analysis in the future. In fact, **we believe delving into these horrific cancer statistics to ascertain the safety of *normal* nuclear operations should be the first assignment Congress gives itself before appropriating another dime of public money to build new nuclear power plants.**

Since the beginning of the nuclear age over a half-century ago, human beings have been the unwitting subjects of a monumental, albeit unintended, radiation experiment initially involving atmospheric testing of nuclear weapons, and subsequently, radiation releases from nuclear power plants. It took decades before the links between other known carcinogens, such as asbestos, tobacco, and vinyl chlorine, were formally acknowledged by medical professionals and government public health officials. There seems to be a growing momentum behind a similar process of scientific peer review and validation to assess the public health impact of internally-ingested environmental radiation released by nuclear power reactors. At a time of escalating health care costs, it is only prudent for business leaders to consider increasing cancer rates as a "significant risk factor" in any discussion of a nuclear power revival; spiraling healthcare costs hit corporate balance sheets when a government committed to promotion of nuclear reactors and weapons fails to do its job.

## THE "INHERENTLY SAFE" NEXT-GENERATION REACTORS

The accidents at Three Mile Island and at Chernobyl are tragic milestones in the history of the nuclear age. Yet, since no U.S. reactor has ever experienced significant core damage after the partial meltdown at Three Mile Island, might we now conclude that nuclear power is far safer today than it was 20 years ago? While the answer may be that it is safer today, it is *clearly* not safe enough.

In a recent report, "Walking a Nuclear Tightrope: Unlearned Lessons of Year-plus Reactor Outages," the Union of Concerned Scientists suggests that, as far as nuclear safety is concerned, the Nuclear Regulatory Commission is following the script of the movie *Groundhog Day*: reliving the same bad event again and again.[38] In this case, the event—a nuclear plant outage that lasts more than a year—*has happened 51 times at 41 reactors around the U.S.* and shows no signs of stopping. These long shutdowns result from violations of federal safety regulations that require plant owners to find and ameliorate significant safety problems in a timely manner.

To extract more economic value for America's aging reactor fleet, utility operators have obtained 20-year extensions of the reactors' original licenses. They also have implemented "power uprates" that allow reactors to increase the amount of electricity they generate by up to 20%, exceeding the operating limit the plants were originally designed to handle. As a result of this pushing of the envelope, the Union of Concerned Scientists study concludes, "nuclear power is clearly not safe enough when so many reactors have to shut down for so long to restore safety to the minimum level acceptable. . . . The chronic violations of federal safety regulations must stop before the increased safety risks yield an even higher cost—human tragedy."

Nuclear advocates claim that safety concerns will be addressed by the next generation of new advanced reactor designs that are "inherently safe." This appears to be a backhand admission that the first-generation reactors were not that safe in the first place. The next-generation reactors differ dramatically from current reactors in that they replace active water cooling and multiple backup safety systems with "passive safety" designs. New reactors, including Westinghouse's AP 1000 (AP1000) pressurized water reactor, and GE's Advanced Boiling Water Reactor (ABWR) and Economic Simplified Boiling Water Reactor (ESBWR), rely on gravity rather than a huge array of pumps to push the water up into the reactor vessel and through the cooling systems. One such design is the "meltdown-proof" Pebble Bed Reactor, which uses grains of uranium encased in balls of graphite as fuel.

One of the major problems that the nuclear industry faced early on was due to financially-driven increases in reactor scale, up from 250 MWs to 1,000-plus MWs, before design and engineering problems could be fully analyzed and resolved. It appears that the same mistake is being made again in order to win speedy approval of the new reactor designs. Union of Concerned Scientists physicist Ed Lyman points out that multiple tests of the AP600, the smaller predecessor of Westinghouse's AP1000, showed that the passive system worked, and the Nuclear Regulatory Commission certified the design. However, following the trend to larger output units, the initial designs quickly morphed up to 1,000 MWs for the AP1000, 1,350 MWs for the ABWR, and 1,560 MWs for the ESBWR. Lyman's primary concern is that the regulatory agency is relying on "computer modeling," rather than on experimental field data to demonstrate that the "inherently safe" gravity-driven cooling system will work on much larger reactors.

In fact, many nuclear advocates and news reports inaccurately describe the new reactor designs, such as the pebble bed modular reactors, as "accident-proof" or "fail-safe." However, experiments conducted at the THTR-300 modular reactor in Germany led to accidental releases of radiation after one of the supposedly "accident-proof" fuel pebbles became lodged in a feeder pipe, damaging the fuel cladding. After the operators tried to conceal the malfunction and blamed the radiation release on the Chernobyl accident, the government closed the reactor.

Once again, the promises of safety are enticing, but this time around the buyer had best demand the most rigorous levels of experimental verification. As Edward Teller, father of the H-bomb, observed, "Sooner or later the fool will prove greater than the proof even in a foolproof system."

## FUSION: TECHNOLOGY OF THE FUTURE

Given the limitations of fission technology, some see nuclear fusion as the "energy of the future." While generating heat from fission chain reactions (splitting atoms) to spin electric turbines turned out to be a relatively easy technical process achieved at reasonable temperatures, fusion (joining atoms) requires stable long-lived plasma of reasonably high density with a temperature of about 1 billion degrees Kelvin, using deuterium-tritium isotopes. To date, fusion power remains "still a dream-in-waiting."

Even if a practical means of generating a sustained, net energy-producing fusion reactor were found, the remaining problems include excessive plant costs per unit of electrical output (Bechtel estimates a total plant to cost at least $15 billion); frequent reactor vessel replacement; and the need for remote maintenance to ensure vessel vacuum integrity.

Despite these challenges, several nations have joined together in the International Thermonuclear Energy Reactor project, which is described as "an experimental step between today's plasma physics and tomorrow's possible electricity-producing fusion power plants." Construction of the project, which is based on the design of a hydrogen plasma torus operating at more than 100 million degrees Centigrade to produce 500 MWs of fusion power, is expected to start soon, with first plasma operations expected by 2016.

Even if the project proves feasible and cost-effective (two very big *ifs*), it is unlikely that fusion will develop rapidly enough to address the world's pressing problems of oil dependency and climate change in a timely fashion. As a result, it appears that for practical purposes, we should consider that fusion has "always been 25 years away—and always will be." Or, as William E. Parkins recently observed in an article in *Science*, "What executive would invest in a fusion power plant if faced with any one of these obstacles. It's time to sell fusion for physics, not power."[39] We concur. In the future, society may find that it can best use fusion not as a means to generate power, but as a means to finally dispose of high-level radioactive waste created by fission.[40]

## Radioactive Waste: The Never-Ending Problem

Given the snail's pace of progress on the to-date intractable problem of high-level radioactive waste storage, it might just take another 50 years before the world comes up with a solution to this never-ending problem. Nuclear waste is produced at every stage of the nuclear fuel cycle, from uranium mining to the reprocessing of spent fuel. Some of the high-level spent fuel isotopes, such as Plutonium-239 (highly suitable for building nuclear weapons) will remain hazardous for tens of thousands of years, leaving a deadly legacy to the future. In fact, with the decline of nuclear engineering programs at major universities, there is an urgency to resolve the problem before this generation of nuclear physicists and engineers passes away and the tar baby falls "into ever less competent hands."

Because of the lack of federal disposal facilities, highly radioactive spent fuel has to be removed regularly from the reactor core and "temporarily" stored in on-site water-filled cooling pools. Experts expect the global quantity of spent fuel produced, even without a climate-propelled radical expansion of nuclear power, to increase from 160,000 tons in 1994 to 366,000 tons by 2010. A dive-bombing private plane full of fuel, let alone a fully-loaded commercial jet like the one that crashed into the Pentagon, would spray the nuclear material in any of those open-air cooling ponds and spread it downwind with a vengeance.

While a variety of disposal methods have been under study for decades, there is still no demonstrated solution for effectively isolating and storing nuclear waste from the environment for many thousands of years. In the U.S., an approach that appears to have been driven more by politics than science led the Department of Energy to designate Yucca Mountain as the long-term depository for high-level radioactive waste. Yucca Mountain sits on the edge of the U.S. Nuclear Test Site in the Nevada desert about 90 miles northwest of Las Vegas, Nevada.

According to a Worldwatch Institute report, "Aside from being located in the third most seismically active region in the country, Yucca Mountain is so porous that after just 50 years, isotopes from atmospheric atom bomb tests have already seeped down into the underlying aquifer." On the basis of the geological instability of the site, Nevada is aggressively fighting the Yucca Mountain repository, and the court challenges have been so successful that the nuclear industry is beginning to consider alternatives.

Meanwhile, the high-level radioactive waste continues to build up at 65 reactor sites in 31 states in spent fuel pools without reinforced containment buildings that are vulnerable to accidents and terrorist attacks.

## NUCLEAR TERRORISM AND PROLIFERATION

In the United States and Russia, government agencies have launched mock attacks on nuclear plants and found defenses inadequate to prevent terrorist attacks. During the 1990s, in 57 simulated attacks in the U.S., some 27 could have caused reactor core damage and deadly radiological releases. In the UK, Greenpeace activists stormed the Sizewell nuclear plant and scaled the reactor without resistance. It is chilling to observe none of the mock attacks involved a suicide bomber using a reasonably sized jet, let alone aircraft of the size that flattened the World Trade Center.

In today's world, terrorist threats are not just a theoretical possibility. The *9/11 Commission Report* disclosed that Mohammad Atta, the pilot of the first plane to hit the World Trade Center, had *considered targeting a nuclear facility he had observed during a reconnaissance flight over Manhattan.* Nevertheless, the Nuclear

Regulatory Commission has refused to require new nuclear facilities to be designed to withstand suicide airliner attacks on the reactor vessel or to require similar protection for the spent-fuel-rod water ponds. A Union of Concerned Scientists study estimates that a terrorist-caused meltdown at the Indian Point reactor, 30 miles north of New York City, could kill as many as 44,000 people from initial radiation poisoning, with more than 500,000 eventually dying from cancer and millions more requiring permanent relocations. Direct economic losses could exceed $2 trillion, and the damage to the U.S. and global economy caused by the loss of New York's international financial center would be incalculable.[41]

In addition to the significant risk of a terrorist attack on a U.S. nuclear power plant, the more certain danger is the use of civilian nuclear technology to generate the materials required to build nuclear weapons, or dirty bombs. The roots of the current conflicts between the U.S. and "axis-of-evil" nations Iran and North Korea are based on the use of commercial nuclear power facilities as key stepping stones to creating clandestine bomb factories.

On October 9, 2006, a successful atomic weapons test by North Korea increased to nine the number of nations possessing nuclear arms. If that seems frightening, one should be even more concerned about global stability because, as the *New York Times* reported after the test, "atomic officials estimate that as many as 40 more countries have the technical skill, and in some cases the required material, to build a bomb."[42]

At times, the skill has been provided inadvertently by the International Atomic Energy Agency, which has the dual—and at time contradictory—mandate of promoting nuclear power *and* serving as the world's nuclear policeman. By running technical aid programs on civilian nuclear power technology in about 100 nations, the agency has shared knowledge that can be used in weapons programs.

There are essentially two main pathways to generating weapons-grade material from civilian nuclear power technology. The first involves enriching uranium fuel from the normal level of 5% for reactor fuel rods to the 90% required for a bomb. The second is to

> "... depending on weather conditions, an attack could result in as many as 44,000 near-term deaths from acute radiation syndrome or as many as 518,000 long-term deaths from cancers among individuals within fifty miles of the plant."
>
> — EDWIN S. LYMAN, PH.D.,
> UNION OF CONCERNED SCIENTISTS, 2004

take spent reactor fuel and mine it for plutonium, the other main fuel for a nuclear weapon.

Enriching uranium is a relatively simple step that requires longer processing in centrifuges. It is the method used by Abdul Qadeer Khan in building the Pakistani bomb and in establishing the "world's largest atomic black market" for selling the centrifuges for enriching uranium to Libya, Iran, and North Korea.

The size of a revitalized global nuclear industry could be staggering, especially if the world chooses nuclear power as the preferred solution to declining oil resources and global warming. According to Dr. Hans-Holger Rogner, an economist at the International Atomic Energy Agency, "An increase to 5,000 reactors is well within the range of the longer-range studies. People are positioning themselves. There seems to be a racing coming and nobody wants to be left out."

As Iran and other developing nations assert their "inalienable right" under the Nuclear Non-Proliferation Treaty to develop their own programs for enriching uranium to make reactor fuel, the entire 40-year-old international framework for the nonproliferation of nuclear weapons seems to be coming apart. If membership in the nuclear club is seen as an essential requirement for national security in the 21st century, the risks of a second nuclear age and global arms race will grow.

Even the moral high ground once held by Nuclear Club members is rapidly eroding. President Mahmoud Ahmadinejad of Iran recently chided the U.S. by asking, "Before stopping enrichment by others, why don't you stop building the next generation of nuclear weapons?" Despite efforts by Nuclear Club members to control the nuclear fuel cycle, the reality is that nuclear power is inextricably tied to nuclear weapons proliferation.

## INVESTORS CHOOSE RENEWABLE ENERGY OVER NUCLEAR POWER

From a business perspective, private investors are the ultimate decision makers, using informed diligence and prudent criteria to determine which energy technologies can compete in the market with the best chance of generating revenues and profits.

As Amory Lovins points out, the capital markets have already spoken. Private investors and project finance lenders have flatly rejected large baseload nuclear power plants and enthusiastically embraced supply-side competitors, decentralized co-generation, and renewables. "Worldwide, by the end of 2004, these supposedly inadequate alternatives had more installed capacity than nuclear, produced 92% as much electricity, and were growing 5.9 times faster and accelerating, while nuclear was fading."[43]

The upside to nuclear power is minimal; the downside is potentially disastrous.

If a business fails, the owners face bankruptcy. If nuclear power fails, the world faces radioactive poisons, nuclear terrorism, and the specter of a dangerous future filled with bomb-rattling nations and regional nuclear arms races. We face incalculable expense and unlimited danger dealing with ever-greater quantities of highly toxic radioactive waste that remains deadly even in small quantities for millennia.

Our world needs energy sources that are safe, renewable, and non-toxic and that can supply increasing amounts of sustainable energy on a large scale. Since two-thirds of the energy demand over the next 25 years will come from developing nations, energy resources should be plentiful and available to all nations, not only to those who can afford to construct next-generation nuclear reactors at $3 billion to $4 billion per plant.

Given growing demand and limited resources, the U.S. and the nations of the world should invest in the best global energy solutions, rather than try to resurrect the failed nuclear option. Efficiency, biofuels, renewables, and hydrogen could revitalize our nation and our planet economically, environmentally, and geopolitically, while ensuring a safe future for all.

# Notes and References
# Chapter 5: Nuclear Power

1 "Nuclear Power's Missing Fuel," *Business Week Online*, July 10, 2006.

2 "Nuclear Follies," *Forbes,* February 11, 1985.

3 Richard Rhodes and Denis Beller, "The Need for Nuclear Power," *Foreign Affairs*, January/February, 2006.

4 From Christopher Flavin, "Nuclear Revival? Don't bet on it!" *World Watch* 10:4 (July/August 2006): 20.

5 *Ibid.*, 20.

6 Prepared remarks of Lewis L. Strauss, chairman, United States Atomic Energy Commission, Washington, D.C., September 16, 1954.

7 Electrical grids need a minimum threshold of power flowing through them at a steady rate. This is called the baseload.

8 *Scientific American*, October 2006, 14.

9 World Bank, *Guideline for Environmental Assessment of Energy and Industry Project*, World Bank Technical Paper No. 154, Environmental Assessment Source Book, Vol. III, 1992.

10 Susan Milligan, "Energy Bill a Special-Interests Triumph," *Boston Globe,* October 4, 2004.

11 Mike Stuckey, "New nuclear power 'wave'—or just a ripple?" MSNBC.com, January 23, 2007.

12 *Ibid.*

13 See Nuclear Energy Institute, Wall Street Briefing, "A Solid Business Platform for Future Growth," February 2, 2006, "To be conservative, the NEI financial analysis assumes a capital cost of approximately $2,000 per kilowatt for the first few plants built, declining to approximately $1,500 per kilowatt for the later plants."

14 Karen Charman, "Brave Nuclear World?" *World Watch* 19:4 (May/June 2006): 31.

15 *Ibid.*.

16  See "Nuclear Statistics, Costs" at Nuclear Energy Institute (www.nei.org).

17  *Ibid.*

18  Charles Komanoff and Cora Roelofs, *Fiscal Fission: the Economic Failure of Nuclear Power: A Report on the Historical Costs of Nuclear Power in the United States* (Washington, DC: Greenpeace, 1992), 7-8.

19  Janet Sawin, *Mainstreaming Renewable Energy in the 21st Century*, Worldwatch Paper 169, May 2004, 13. The range of low-high generating costs reported in this study is: nuclear (10.0-14.0), natural gas (3.4-5.0), coal (4.3-4.8) and wind (3.0-5.0).

20  U.S. Department of Energy, Energy Information Administration, *Annual Energy Outlook 2006*, 77. The Energy Policy Act of 2005 established a production tax credit of 1.8 cents per kilowatt-hour for up to 6,000 MWs of new nuclear capacity brought online before 2021.

21  "Lack of fuel may limit U.S. nuclear power expansion," MIT News Office, March 21, 2007, http://web.mit.edu/newsoffice/2007/fuel-supply.html.

22  Nuclear Energy Institute, "The Changing Climate for Nuclear Energy," Annual Briefing for the Financial Community, February 22, 2007, www.nei.org; "Uranium Ignites 'Gold Rush' in the West," *New York Times*, March 28, 2007, http://www.nytimes.com/2007/03/28/business/28uranium.html.

23  Uwe R. Fritsche, *Comparing Greenhouse-Gas Emissions and Abatement Costs of Nuclear and Alternative Energy Options from a Life-Cycle Perspective* (Berlin: Öko-Institut, November 1997).

24  At $1,500 per kilowatt, 1,000 kilowatts in a MW equals $1.5 million per MW. Therefore, a 1,000 MW reactor would cost $1.5 billion and 1,000 1000 MW reactors would cost $1.5 trillion.

25  For a list of the airborne and liquid effluents released by each U.S. operating reactor, see Brookhaven National Laboratory, Radioactive Materials Released from Nuclear Power Plants, Annual Report 1993, prepared for U.S. Nuclear Regulatory Commission, NUREG/CR-2907, BNL-NUREG-51581, vol.14.

26  A.M. Stewart, J. Webb and D. Hewitt, "A Survey of Childhood Malignancies," *British Medical Journal*, 1958, Vol. 1, 1495-1508.

27  S. Jablon *et al. Cancer in Populations Living near Nuclear Facilities.* NIH Pub. No. 90-847. National Cancer Institute. Washington, DC: U.S Government Printing Office, 1990.

28 Joseph J. Mangano, "A short latency between radiation exposure from nuclear plants and cancer in your children," *International Journal of Health Services*, March 2006, 36(1): 113-135.

29 This data and a discussion of Gofman's findings can be found in Jerry Brown and Rinaldo Brutoco, *Profiles in Power* (New York: Simon & Schuster Macmillan, 1997), 29-40.

30 John W. Gofman and Arthur R. Tamplin, *Poisoned Power* (Emmaus, PA.: Rodale Press, 1979), 6. These findings were first reported in a series of 20 papers to the Joint Committee on Atomic Energy of the U.S. Congress.

31 Joseph J. Mangano *et al.*, "Elevated childhood cancer incidence proximate to U.S. nuclear power plants," *Archives of Environmental Health* 2003, 58:74-82.

32 Jay M. Gould *et al.*, *The Enemy Within: The High Cost of Living Near Nuclear Reactors* (New York, Four Walls Eight Windows, 1996), 15.

33 Joseph J. Mangano *et al.*, "Infant death and childhood cancer reductions after nuclear plant closing in the U.S.," *Archives of Environmental Heath*, 2003, 58(2): 74-82.

34 Joseph J. Mangano *et al.*, "An unexpected rise in strontium-90 in U.S. deciduous teeth in the 1990s," *The Science of the Total Environment*, December 2003, 317(1-3): 37-51.

35 The National Academy report, "Low Levels of Ionizing Radiation May Cause Harm," news release, June 29, 2005.

36 C. Busby *et al.*, *2003 Recommendations of the European Committee on Radiation Risk (ECRR): Health Effects of Ionizing Radiation Exposure at Low Doses for Radiation Protection Purposes* (Green Audit Press, Castle Cottage, Aberystwyth, SY23 1DZ, UK, January 2003). See www.euradcom.org 2003.

37 For a list of the Radiation and Public Health Project's medical journals articles, see "Technical Articles" at www.radiation.org.

38 David Lochbaum, Improving Government Oversight: Unlearned Lessons from Year-plus Reactor Outages, Union of Concerned Scientists, September 2006.

39 William E. Parkins, "Fusion Power: Will It Ever Come?" Science 311 (March 10, 2006): 1380.

40 Rather than being a source of cheap energy, the "fusion torch" holds out the theoretical potential for neutralizing nuclear waste. The extremely high temperatures of the plasma state create a miniature sun which can literally change the molecular structure of radioactive waste and break it down to non-toxic elements.

41 Edwin S. Lyman, *Chernobyl on the Hudson? The Heath and Economic Impacts of a Terrorist Attack at the Indian Point Nuclear Plant,* Union of Concerned Scientists, September 2004.

42 William J. Broad and David E. Sanger, "Restraints Fray and Risks Grow as Nuclear Club Gains Members," *New York Times*, October 15, 2006.

43 Amory B. Lovins, "Competitors to Nuclear: Eat My Dust," Rocky Mountain Institute, Newsletter, Summer 2005.

# 6

## COAL, NATURAL GAS, TAR SANDS: MORE GREENHOUSE GASES AT HIGHER COST

*"Unless we free ourselves from a dependence on these fossil fuels and chart a new course on energy in this country, we are condemning future generations to global catastrophe.... So why can't we do this? Why can't we make energy security one of the great American projects of the twenty-first century? The answer is we can."*

– U. S. SENATOR BARACK OBAMA,
*THE COMING STORM*, APRIL 3, 2006

### Can the other fossil fuels save the day? *No.*

- The other fossil fuels all emit greenhouse gases and increase global warming.

- Coal and natural gas cannot replace oil for transportation.

- Coal is a major source of greenhouse gases and acid rain; natural gas supplies are limited.

- Tar sands are an eco-disaster for air, land and water.

- Oil shale is one of the most environmentally destructive processes in the world; fortunately the commercial technology is not now economical.

- Investing in obsolete or destructive technologies delays our transition to clean, sustainable energy.

## CAN THE OTHER FOSSIL FUELS FILL THE GAP?

Comedian and magician Robert Orben summed up our environmental problem in one cynical statement: "There's so much pollution in the air now that if it weren't for our lungs, there'd be no place to put it all."

There *is* more carbon and sulfur in our atmosphere than ever before. There *is* more mercury in our water than ever before. There *are* more people on the planet than ever before. And, there *are* more fossil fuels being burned than ever before.

This is no coincidence. Rather, it is the "price of progress" *within the dominant fossil-fuel paradigm.* Amazingly, all this pollution was never inevitable. We learned long ago from the Industrial Revolution that technology could advance without the sacrifice of breathable air. (For example, London banned certain uses of coal in the 20th century when it became apparent that the permanent smoke in London was too high a health price to pay for household warmth.)

In America, however, the current challenge of pollution created as a by-product of technological advancement is the outcome of a democratic system in which special-interest lobbies, such as the fossil-fuel industry, were allowed to run roughshod over the public interest.

A consequence of industrialized nations choosing to be addicted to the fossil-fuel paradigm is that we are now sitting poised at a time when global economies will deteriorate and global temperatures will gradually rise unless we finally heed the wakeup call of the energy and climate crisis.

Twenty-seven years have passed since the Iranian Revolution and the last OPEC oil shocks of the 1970s. Now, a second crisis is emerging on a global scale—a perfect storm of peak oil, geopolitical insecurity, global climate change, and China's and India's energy appetite to fuel their explosive economic growth. We have now entered the endgame of the era of cheap oil. The U.S. has one last chance to shift away from fossil fuels and to make a relatively peaceful and orderly transition to a new energy economy.

Every American business and consumer has felt the effects of high oil prices at the pump. Deep down, we all wish for one of two things: permanently lower gas prices or cheap replacements for oil that will not fundamentally change our way of life.

Frequently, the "Big Four" are touted as alternatives to oil. They are also known as the "other fossil fuels"—natural gas, coal, tar sands, and oil shale. If we want to create a sustainable energy future and reduce greenhouse gases, however, the Big Four provide *anything but* a permanent or viable solution. To solve our energy and climate crisis, government, business, and consumers must ultimately look beyond fossil fuels. In building a bridge from the end of cheap oil to a renewable, carbon-free energy future, one of the other fossil fuels—natural gas—does have a transitional role to play. Coal, tar sands, and oil shale, on the other hand, exacerbate a bad situation.

During this transition, to the extent any of the four fuels are used, it is important that they be used correctly. We cannot ever afford to see any of them as the sole permanent replacement for oil. Because they are not renewable, they will never provide long-term stability. They will neither afford protection from unpredictable market prices, nor free us from scarcity. At best, they will only defer the day and the need to construct lifeboats to escape a future *Titanic*. In sum, the other fossil fuels will never be able to completely fill the gap.

## THE "OTHER" FUELS

Close examination reveals that coal, natural gas, tar sands, and oil shale are problematic, each in its own way, in the context of creating a healthy and sustainable energy future. Each fuel has its pros and many more cons.

The U.S. has substantial reserves of two fuels, natural gas and coal. Given these reserves, it may seem logical to conclude that we have a reasonable supply of fossil fuels at our fingertips and that we should diversify our future energy use among them. The harsh realities are that natural gas and coal cannot provide solutions to our oil supply problems because they are used primarily to generate electricity. They are not liquid fuels for transportation. Worse yet, coal poses tremendous and intractable greenhouse gas and health problems that will not be resolved by the proposed panacea of "clean coal."

Furthermore, as Figure 1 shows, reliance on oil and natural gas for electrical generation will lead only to increased energy and electricity prices over time. Even the projections in Figure 1 have proved to be woefully optimistic. Energy prices have not dropped in 2007 as predicted but have risen to historical highs across the nation.

## Figure 1. History and Projections of Energy Prices, 2005

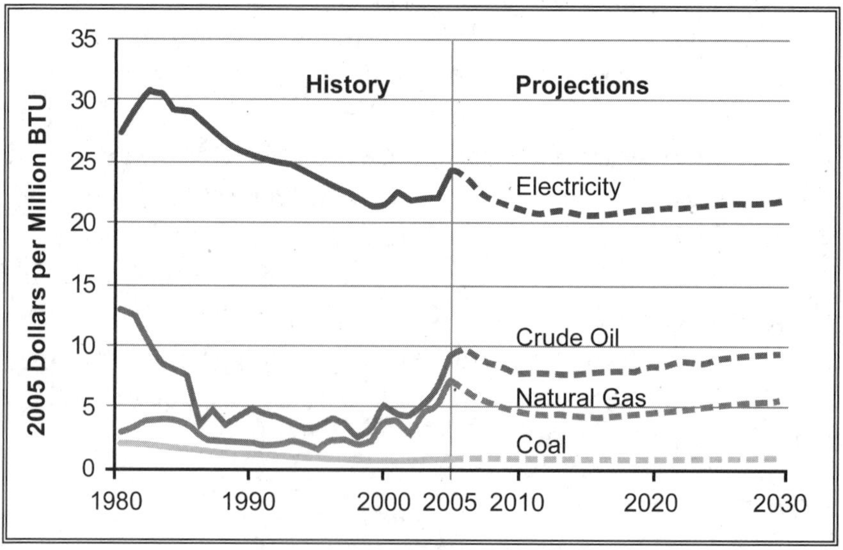

Source: U.S. Energy Information Administration, *Annual Energy Outlook*, 2007

If we continue our exclusive dependence on coal and natural gas while countries such as China and India, who have surging annual GDP growth, continue to increase their demand for energy, our national and global environment will suffer further serious harm, and global energy resource competition will increase.

It is very important, therefore, to analyze the repercussions of continuing down the "hard path" of the expanded reliance on fossil fuels. As Figure 2 and the subsequent discussion shows, in each case, the negatives of the other fossil fuels significantly outweigh the positives.

## Figure 2. Pros and Cons of Coal, Natural Gas, Tar Sands, Oil Shale and Petroleum

| FUEL | PROS | CONS | COMMENTS |
|---|---|---|---|
| Coal [2] | Low cost and plentiful; easy to transport. | Produces more $CO_2$ than any other fuel; acid rain $SO_2$; smoke, ash need disposal; mining methods are destructive. | "Clean" coal extracts only $SO_2$; $CO_2$ still produced. $SO_2$ mixed with $O_2$ becomes $SO_3$ which reacts with water, becoming acid rain. |
| Natural Gas[3] | Low cost; produces less $CO_2$ than coal, oil. | Not sustainable; limited reserves. Methane, a major greenhouse gas. | If natural gas becomes the "new oil," prices will skyrocket. However, natural gas would be ideal as a transitional fuel. Cleanest fossil alternative. |
| Tar Sands ~3.5 MBD in Canada ~0.3 to 0.6 MBD in Venezuela | One of the largest reserves is in Canada, one of America's closest allies. | One of the most greenhouse polluting and least desirable forms of fossil fuel from an environmental point of view. Generally removed by strip mining. Two tons produces one barrel of oil. It requires large amounts of water. | Oil extracted from tar sands is profitable today. Canada and Venezuela possess most of the useable tar sands. |

*Figure 2 continued . . .*

199

*Figure 2 continued*

| FUEL | PROS | CONS | COMMENTS |
|---|---|---|---|
| Oil Shale | Estimated 1.1 trillion barrel-equivalent of oil locked in U.S. shale oil reserves. | Highly inefficient (3:1 energy output/input ratio); uses vast amounts of water; produces massive rock waste; strip mining is highly destructive; Australian shale project was shut down due to air pollution; severe groundwater concerns; shale oil contains much more $CO_2$ than petroleum; carcinogenic tailings; commercial production of 1 MBD is probably 20 years into the future.[4] | Shale oil is embedded in rock. It is extracted by retorting the rock that is saturated with kerogen by heating it to about 500 degrees Celsius and refining the extracted kerogen into petroleum. Shell has been experimenting with in situ extraction, heating the oil with electricity while the rock is still in the ground, and then transporting it for refining. Another Shell subsidiary is experimenting with a super-cold freeze-barrier around the shale while the shale deposits are heated within this "envelope." |
| Oil/Gasoline[5] | Easily extracted compared to coal, tar sands, and oil shale; produces less $CO_2$ than coal | New oil reserves are becoming scarce; large reserves located in dangerous countries; rising costs; produces $CO_2$; oil spills cause major environmental damage. | |

# COAL: ONE STEP FORWARD, TWO STEPS BACK

Coal, the most abundant fossil fuel in the U.S., is also the most detrimental to our physical health and the most destructive to the environment. Only the scarcity of oil has renewed the nation's interest in coal. Unfortunately, turning to coal (again) would be taking one step forward and two steps back. Nothing would exacerbate global warming and climate change faster than relying on coal to power electric plants in order to charge electric cars or plug-in hybrids in an "all electric world" future.

When sulfur dioxide ($SO_2$) is released during coal combustion, it reacts with oxygen ($O_2$) to create sulfur trioxide ($SO_3$). When the sulfur trioxide reacts with water, sulfuric acid forms and falls back to the earth as acid rain. Coal combustion also releases small amounts of the carcinogenic radioactive elements uranium and thorium into the atmosphere. Since coal is already used to generate 51% of our electricity, using coal to generate additional electricity to meet all, or even most, of our transportation needs would result in horrific amounts of atmospheric destruction, not to mention the amount of toxic fumes that would further pollute the air.

As Figure 3 shows, coal is hands-down the most pollution-intensive fossil fuel, emitting more $CO_2$ than oil or natural gas. With some 900 million tons of the black rock burned in the U.S. for energy every year, there are risks at every step of the coal production process: mining, preparation, transportation, and usage and combustion.

## Figure 3. Fossil Fuel $CO_2$ Emission Levels, 2004

| Fossil Fuel Carbon Dioxide Emission Levels (Pounds per Billion British Thermal Units of Energy Input) | |
| --- | --- |
| Coal | 203,000 |
| Oil | 164,000 |
| Natural Gas | 117,000 |

Source: U.S. Energy Information Administration

For example, according to the Earth Policy Institute, "The largest source of mercury pollution is coal-fired power plants. Airborne mercury emitted by these facilities is deposited anywhere from within a few hundred kilometers of the smokestacks to across continents, far from its source." Forty-five states have warning advisories against fish consumption because of high levels of mercury in the water.

Even saltwater fish such as tuna and swordfish exceed the mercury limits deemed safe by the Environmental Protection Agency.

## Burying $CO_2$: What Goes Down, Must Come Up

Coal has two major advantages over other forms of energy: it is abundant in the U.S., and it is the cheapest fuel to produce. The world has an estimated trillion tons of mineable coal, and a quarter of it is in the U.S. The cost of delivered coal for electrical generation ranges from $1.00 to $2.50 per million British Thermal Units (BTUs). These advantages are far outweighed by the disadvantages of burning coal. It releases 9 billion tons of $CO_2$ per year, about 70% of which comes from power generation. This amounts to about a third of global $CO_2$ emissions. It also releases mercury and sulfur dioxide, causing major environmental damage to trees, aquifers, the ocean, and various animal species.

The coal industry is rallying around a new technology called Integrated Gasification Combined Cycle (IGCC). A Combined Cycle plant uses at least two thermodynamic processes to increase efficiency. The plant makes synthetic gas (a mixture of carbon monoxide and hydrogen) out of coal to fire its primary electrical generators and uses the waste heat to fuel steam boilers that drive a second set of generators. On the plus side, the technology (which is now commercial at eight plants around the world) does an admirable job of reducing sulfur, mercury, nitrogen oxides, and fly ash.

On other hand, IGCC does nothing to reduce $CO_2$. It is suggested that the $CO_2$ from IGCC plants can be isolated, condensed, and sunk in the ground or used to pressurize oil fields. It is a wide-open invitation to use more coal. Capital costs are immense—more than $1 billion per plant. While there is no general agreement on the IGCC premium over conventional pulverized coal plants, 10 to 30% is a frequently cited range. This translates into $1,400/kwh for IGCC plant construction. The cost of retrofitting conventional plants with IGCC technology is prohibitive, so it would be many, many years before it made even a slight dent in the world's footprint of coal-fired plants. Two coal-based IGCC plants are currently operational in the U.S.; nine more are cleared to be built in the next decade. To put this in context, the Chinese will build at least that number of dirty coal plants in the next three or four months.

Ironically, federal foot-dragging about emissions standards and the utility industry's own doubts are braking the pursuit of IGCC. John Hofmeister, head of Shell Oil's U.S. operations, believes, "If the 50 states have their own greenhouse gas framework, it will be chaotic . . . . " Speaking at the same October 2006 conference as Hofmeister,

> Randy Zwirn, chief executive officer and president of Siemens Power Generation Inc., said the energy industry is awaiting clear U.S. greenhouse policies, noting that his company recently surveyed U.S. utilities and found "a very high consensus" that $CO_2$ would be regulated within the next 10 years.
>
> But Zwirn said another key issue with IGCC was that utilities still have major concerns about the availability and long-term reliability of the [IGCC] technology. He said the industry view was partially colored by earlier IGCC plants that experienced startup and reliability problems.[6]

Given the indisputable health and environmental concerns that surround conventional coal production, the federal government has made research and development of "clean coal" a top priority, and IGCC plays only a part. In order to tap America's vast coal reserves, President Bush in 2001 announced his $2 billion Clean Coal Power Initiative as part of the Advanced Energy Initiative. Ten projects selected for government co-financing are in various stages of development. The winners of these grants, for the most part, are conspicuously silent about carbon dioxide.

The centerpiece of this program is the FutureGen Sequestration and Hydrogen Research Initiative. A $1 billion alliance between the Department of Energy, coal producers, and electrical utilities, it hopes to build by 2012 a 275 MW prototype plant that is coal-fired but almost "emission-free" insofar as smokestacks are concerned.

The plant will purportedly use the most modern approaches for the generation of electricity while attempting to capture and then store carbon dioxide in geological formations (known as "carbon sequestration"). The plant will also produce hydrogen and by-products for use by other industries.

Carbon sequestration, or "carbon capture and storage," refers to the process of compressing hot flue exhaust until it liquefies, transporting it by pipeline or tanker, and storing it underground in natural geological caverns or deep in the ocean floor below rock foundations.

Specific FutureGen optimistic goals include sequestering at least 90% of $CO_2$ emissions from the plant with the future potential to capture and sequester nearly 100%; proving the effectiveness, safety, and permanence of $CO_2$ sequestration; and establishing standardized technologies and protocols for $CO_2$ measuring, monitoring, and verification. It will also validate the engineering, economic, and environmental viability of advanced coal-based, near-zero emission technologies that by 2020 hopefully will produce electricity with less than a 10% cost increase compared to non-sequestered systems and also produce hydrogen at $4.00 per million BTUs (wholesale), equivalent to $0.48/gallon of gasoline.[7]

Carbon sequestration is a highly controversial technology. It represents Washington's efforts to satisfy the coal lobby and ensure coal's future in a greenhouse gas-filled world in which reducing $CO_2$ emissions will become national and global priorities. Just as the nuclear industry is marketing itself as the "solution to global warming," the coal industry is pitching "zero-emissions coal power."

We find carbon sequestration to be a highly questionable and risky possibility. If $CO_2$ were ever released from the earth years later, the results would be catastrophic. In the late 1990s, for example, several thousand people died of suffocation in East Africa when a volcanic lake belched up naturally occurring $CO_2$.

In order for carbon to be sequestrated, it must be separated from other atmospheric gases and captured in a concentrated form. There are several different methods for capturing the $CO_2$. Two technologies receiving attention are chemical absorption and gas separation membranes. Chemical absorption consists of the removal of $SO_2$ and $NO_X$, so the $CO_2$ can be absorbed using an acid-based neutralized reaction. The second method, shown in Figure 4, uses the installation of gas separation membranes: the $CO_2$ is dissolved into the membrane and then transported by a diffusion process.

Proponents suggest a variety of geologic and aqueous locations for storage: saline reservoirs, rock caverns, and coal seams and salt domes that we are unable to mine. The concept is to capture and store $CO_2$ much the way natural gas is stored. A third option is oceanic sequestration, which requires $CO_2$ to be injected into the ocean at depths of at least 1,000 meters, where it liquefies and is supposed to remain in place. One unresolved issue here is determining how bottom sediment will react with the $CO_2$. The volumes of liquefied $CO_2$ are so gigantic that it is likely it will have a serious effect on aquifers.

**Figure 4. Carbon Sequestration Process, Gas Separation Method**

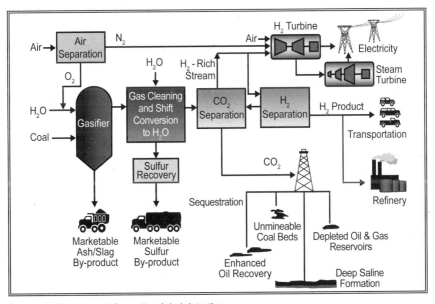

Source: U.S. Energy Information Administration

Another option is terrestrial $CO_2$ sequestration, or $CO_2$ "sinks" in which soil, vegetation, agricultural lands, pastures, tundra, forests, and wetlands increase their absorption of the gas. This requires the manipulation of ecosystems to trap and hold the $CO_2$. It includes a variety of possible storage methods, including creation of fertilizers, planting forests (because trees absorb carbon dioxide for photosynthesis), and storage in soil or biomass.

One last possibility is the separation of pure $CO_2$ for possible industrial use. Despite multiple options, a 2000 National Coal Council report found that additional research and development was still necessary for $CO_2$ sequestration technologies.

The economic viability of sequestration is also a major concern, as this carbon reduction technology may increase the cost of coal-generated electricity by 60%, undercutting the economic competitiveness of coal versus natural gas and wind. "The process of capturing and sequestering a ton of $CO_2$ currently costs approximately $150 per ton. Most sources estimate that installing current technologies at power plants would significantly increase the cost of coal-generated electricity from 2.5 to 4.0 cents per kilowatt-hour. For carbon sequestration to be economically viable, the cost would have to be reduced to about $10-$20 per ton."[8] The active commercial use of CCS (carbon capture and sequestration) still remains quite distant in the future. "A system-level analysis is needed of CCS as a carbon mitigation strategy in the energy sector—one that considers the interacting effects of sunk capital investment, the economics of plant dispatch, and coal-to-gas fuel-switching."[9]

The number of high-quality sites needed for sequestration is staggering. For every ton of anthracite burned, 3.7 tons of $CO_2$ is generated. If all of the $CO_2$ generated were to be sequestrated in liquid form, it would require a volume of 12 *cubic miles* of underground space *per day!*[10]

Today, carbon sequestration remains a future technology, not a current option. The facts are that carbon sequestration is unsafe, economically uncompetitive, environmentally unfriendly, and hazardous to our health and water supply. Just like burying high-level nuclear waste or deep-well injection of untreated human waste, pumping $CO_2$ underground into empty wells only defers the pollution problem to future generations. Even if the technology worked, it would have to be applied retroactively to the world's huge installed base of pulverized coal power plants, an even more expensive proposition.

Writing about sequestration in West Virginia's *Herald-Dispatch*, Abraham T. Mwaura and J. Scott Straight conclude, "This method is being touted as a potential source of raw material to take us into the hydrogen era. But as long as the source of the hydrogen is from fossil fuels, we are still stuck in an archaic energy era, instead of looking to the future with an eye on true alternative energy sources." The biggest problems associated with fossil fuels lie in the extraction process, where "toxic sludge ponds, worsened flooding, and blasting damage to property are ignored by these new technologies." The effects cannot be curbed by sequestration, and the untested effects of massive amounts of buried $CO_2$ could also come back to bite us.[11]

Coal is indeed a plentiful energy resource, but it is not a viable long-term option that will reduce greenhouse gas emissions. The Prometheus Plan requires solutions based on proven, available technologies that can make a major contribution within 10 years. Under the rosiest scenarios, so-called "clean" coal plants won't make a contribution until many decades into the future.

We believe that once carbon sequestering for any purpose is legally permitted, it will become very difficult to stop. It will become the basis for building more coal-fired plants.

## TAR SANDS: A "SAUDI ARABIA" NEXT DOOR?

Tar sands, or oil sands, are a mixture of clay, water, sand, and bitumen, a heavy black oil, and have the viscous consistency of thick sludge.

In order to extract the oil from tar sands (also known as heavy oil), they must be mined and heated and the residue diluted. Only then can the refiners transform the newly released bitumen into a useable, albeit heavily sulfur-laden, form of petroleum.[12] It's a

> *"Coal power is America's biggest source of heat-trapping emissions, yet new investments in coal-fired power plants will keep us burning this fossil fuel for years to come. We must not allow new coal plants to sabotage the fight against global warming."*
>
> — BARBARA FREESE AND JEFF DEYETTE,
> WORLDWATCH INSTITUTE, 2006

dirty, environmentally disastrous business. For every barrel of oil produced from Canadian tar sands, 170 pounds of greenhouse gases are released into the atmosphere.

The largest accumulations of tar sands in the world are found in the Athabasca deposit in Alberta, Canada, and in the Orinoco Province of Venezuela. Although there are meaningful qualitative differences between the two deposits, each holds a significant portion of the world's total tar sand resources.

Canada's Alberta Province holds the world's largest reserves of tar sands. With between 1.7 trillion and 2.5 trillion barrels, these oil sand reserves are considered second only to the conventional petroleum reserves of Saudi Arabia (see Figure 5). Of this total, however, only slightly more than 300 billion barrels, or 12-18%, are estimated to be recoverable. The U.S. imports about 9% of its daily crude oil supply from Canada, or an average of about 1.5 million barrels per day ("MBD"), including oil from tar sands.[13] Compared to Venezuelan deposits, extraction from Canadian tar sands is much more difficult because the bitumen-bearing sludge is generally colder, more viscous, and flows much more slowly.

Canadian deposits are highly attractive to the U.S. because they offer a large, secure supply located just across the border. Indeed, Canada currently supplies the largest fraction of U.S. oil imports. In 2006, Canadian tar sands operators were expected to produce more than 1.1 million barrels of synthetic oil per day, for the first time surpassing Canada's conventional oil production, which was forecasted at 1 MBD for the same period. This would boost Canada to fourth place in terms of the world's largest oil producers. Alberta is expected to produce 2.3 MBD by 2010, 3.4 MBD by 2015, and 5 MBD by 2035.[14] This increase in Alberta oil sand production would mean a decrease in U.S. oil imports from OPEC, which is in itself undeniably a good thing.

**Figure 5. Crude Oil including Oil Sands Reserves by Country**

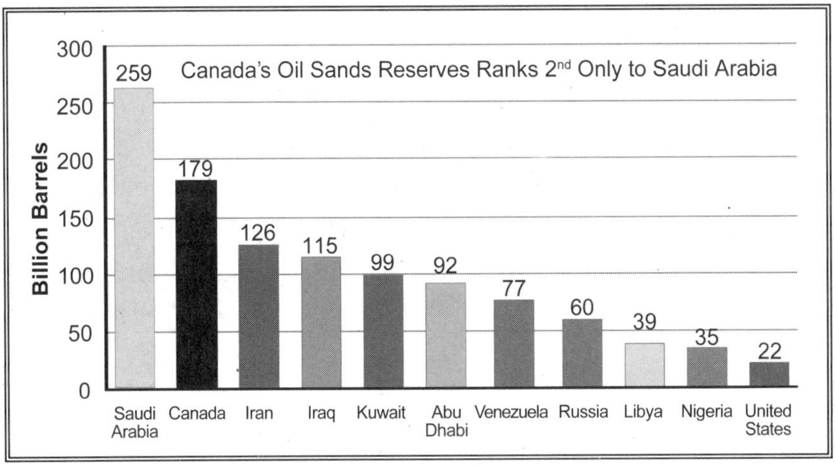

Source: *Oil & Gas Journal*, 2004

While many experts and politicians are focused exclusively on America's need to end its dependency on Middle Eastern oil, we must pause and consider the vast environmental problems that come with heavy oil.

## PRODUCING GASOLINE AND OTHER PRODUCTS FROM TAR SANDS

Once strip-mined or otherwise pumped up, tar sands and their oil are separated most often by steam that is created by burning natural gas. The process requires large amounts of both energy and water. While only a marginal amount of that water can be recycled, several barrels of water are required to process just one barrel of oil. In areas where water already is a scarce resource, this can pose a serious problem.

> *"Oil sands production is already one of the most environmentally destructive processes on this Earth. Imagine combining strip mining and a steelworks plant, and add in a 'tailings' lake the size of 20 city blocks. Now, add a nice big coal-fired electricity plant to the mix. Sounds great doesn't it?"*
>
> — MURKYVIEW.COM, CANADIAN ENVIRONMENTAL BLOG

Once this water is used to produce synthetic oil from tar sands, the biggest by-product by volume is toxic water stored in lakes. This creates a major risk of contaminating local water supplies, which would further stress an already tapped-out resource.

Strip-mining operations are used most frequently to extract oil sands. Production practices typically include clear-cutting thousands of acres of trees and digging out 200-foot-deep pits. This disturbance affects not only large populations of wildlife, but also air and water quality for local communities.

One of the biggest environmental concerns associated with tar sands is global warming and greenhouse gas emissions. Recovering and processing this heavy crude releases up to three times as much greenhouse gas as producing conventional crude.[15] Canada already is having trouble meeting its pledge to cut $CO_2$ emissions largely because of its heavy-oil production. In addition, oil sands also release significantly more sulfur dioxide and particulate matter, which is the leading cause of acid rain and which leads to a higher incidence of human respiratory problems.

Dr. John O'Connor, a Fort McMurray, Alberta, medical examiner, is in negotiations with Health Canada to start an epidemiological investigation that would track the public health in communities neighboring these Alberta tar sands operations. The small community of about 1,200 people that borders the tar sands operations has experienced a high number of illnesses, including leukemia, lymphomas, lupus, and autoimmune diseases. O'Connor says he is diagnosing unusually high numbers of immune disorders affecting the thyroid as well as less serious ones, such as rheumatoid arthritis and skin rashes. He also treated five people in the community who died recently from a rare, almost always fatal cancer that should occur only once in every 100,000 people. This increase in illness is a key indicator of the emerging public health concerns associated with oil sands production.[16]

## OIL SHALE: EXPENSIVE, ENVIRONMENTALLY DISASTROUS, AND FAR IN THE FUTURE

Oil shale generally refers to any sedimentary rock that contains kerogen, a tarry material even more challenging than bitumen to convert to oil. The kerogen is generally separated from the rock by a high temperature process called retorting. This can be done by heating the pulverized rock in a retort, or *in situ* by drilling holes in the shale and driving the oil out by hot steam injection and/or initiating a flame front to drive the kerogen to the surface. The kerogen then must be processed as in a refinery to add hydrogen and remove contaminants such as sulfur and nitrogen.

While the U.S. may not have the largest deposits, it still holds a respectable amount of oil shale—about 60-80 billion barrels, most of which are concentrated in Utah (19-32 billion barrels), Alaska (19 billion barrels), Alabama (6 billion barrels), California (5 billion barrels), and Texas (5 billion barrels). Oil shale is not by any measure the way to improve the environment because it is significantly dirtier than conventional oil and far more expensive to produce.

A study entitled, "Effects of Oil Shale Waste Disposal on Soil and Water Quality," published in the journal *Chemical Speciation and Bioavailability,* discovered that the soil and groundwater surrounding the oil shale tailings (what is left over from drilled or mined oil shale reserves) became acidified and were filled with heavy metals and sulfates, including carcinogenic substances.[18]

Those who strongly support oil shale development base their arguments primarily on the nation's need to end dependency on imports of foreign fuels. However, critics look at life cycle and

> *"Oil shale, coal gasification or coal liquefaction—the last of the fossil-fuel sources as the world's supplies of oil and natural gas are depleted—require 20 to 50 times more water to produce an equivalent amount of energy, compared to oil and gas."*
>
> — KEVIN HALL, *ENERGY REPORTER*, NOVEMBER 2005[17]

environmental impacts as well. Byron King sums up the big picture problems with oil shale as follows:

> After you retort the rock to derive the kerogen (not oil), the heating process has desiccated the shale. Sad to say, the volume of desiccated shale that you have to dispose of is now greater than that of the hole from which you dug and mined it in the first place. Any takers for trainloads of dried, dusty, gunky shale residue, rife with low levels of heavy metal residue and other toxic, but now chemically activated crap? Well, it makes for enough crap that when it rains, the toxic stuff will leach out and contaminate all of the water supplies to which gravity can reach, which is essentially all of 'em. Yeah, right. I sure want that stuff blowin' in my wind. Add up all of the capital investment to build the retorting mechanisms, cost of energy required, cost of water, costs of transport, costs of environmental compliance, costs of refining, and you have some relatively costly end product.[19]

When the price of oil spikes, interest in oil shale revives. Investors lost billions on an attempt to move mountains (literally) in western Colorado in the 1980s. While a few shale experiments are now operating around the world, scalable technology remains many decades distant. Even if the environmental problems could be overcome, oil shale would not make a meaningful contribution for at least 30 years. We need solutions much sooner than that.

## NATURAL GAS: EVERYONE'S TRANSITIONAL FUEL

Natural gas accounts for about one-fifth of total U.S. energy production, most of which is used to generate electricity. A large portion of the nation already relies on gas, but it may be possible to expand the use of gas, thereby decreasing reliance on foreign oil and reducing energy costs. However, in 2005, the U.S. had only about 204 trillion cubic feet of domestic natural gas reserves—at its 2005 annual consumption rate of about 22 trillion cubic feet, enough to last only about nine years.

Some experts claim there are sufficient reserves of natural gas to fuel the world for decades. Estimates of world natural gas reserves vary widely, from 3,000 to 9,000 trillion cubic feet. Given international concerns over declining energy resources, it is surprising that even the oil and gas companies do not have precise estimates of these reserves. According to geologists, the most commonly agreed world reserve estimate is 6,040 trillion cubic feet, which represents around 50 years' worth of natural gas at current global consumption levels.

According to *Oil and Gas Journal* data on "World Natural Gas Reserves by Country as of January 1, 2005," 10 countries control 78.9% of these reserves. The top five natural gas nations—Saudi Arabia, Iran, Venezuela, Nigeria, and Iraq—are geopolitical hot spots where supplies are subject to risks and disruptions (see Chapter 3). Completely relying on natural gas to replace oil, therefore, does not significantly enhance U.S. energy security or independence.

Furthermore, we must keep world supply trends in mind. From 1977 to 1987, 9,000 new gas fields were uncovered throughout the world. By 1997, only 2,500 additional fields had been found. In the Gulf of Mexico, the number of drilling rigs increased by 40% between April 1996 and April 2000, but production remained flat because the newly discovered fields tended to be smaller. Also, because of new technology, natural gas fields tend to be depleted faster than just five years ago, with the newer wells averaging a 56% depletion rate during the first production year.

## LNG Is Highly Explosive

Transportation of natural gas is an expensive and high-risk process, especially for natural gas vehicles that run on liquefied natural gas (LNG). Currently, there are around four million natural gas vehicles around the globe. Although popular in Western Europe, they are most commonly found in Argentina and Brazil. As of March 1, 2007, the U.S. Department of Energy calculated that the nationwide average price of natural gas was still lower than the nationwide average price of gasoline. At that time, gasoline was selling for $2.30/gallon, and natural gas was priced at $1.94/GGE (gallon of gasoline equivalent).[20]

LNG is made by refrigerating natural gas to -260°F to condense it into a liquid. This is called liquefaction. The process removes most of the water vapor, butane, propane, and other trace gases that are usually included in ordinary natural gas. The resulting LNG is usually more than 98% pure methane. When cold LNG comes in contact with warmer air, it creates a visible vapor cloud from condensed moisture in the air. As it continues to get warmer, the vapor cloud becomes lighter than air and rises. When the vapor mixes with air, it is flammable only when the mixture is between 5% and 15% natural gas. When the mixture is less than 5% natural gas, it doesn't burn. When the mixture is more than 15% natural gas, there is not enough oxygen for it to burn.

As a liquid, LNG is not explosive. LNG vapor will explode only in an enclosed space within the flammable range of 5-15%. On the plus side, LNG is produced both worldwide and domestically at a relatively low cost and burns cleaner than diesel fuel. Since LNG has a higher storage density than compressed natural gas for heavy-duty vehicle applications, it is a more viable alternative to diesel fuel. In addition, LNG in heavy-duty natural gas engines produces significantly lower emission levels than diesel.

The possibility of major accidents is of great concern. LNG undergoes a rapid transition to vapor, especially when spilled on water. When suddenly disbursed over water, the volume of the LNG instantly expands by a factor of 600, resulting in a physical explosion that poses a hazard for structures and people close to the site of the incident. The explosion may not initially involve combustion, but a subsequent inferno is almost always assured after contact with an ignition source. When LNG is spilled on water, heat is transferred from the water to the LNG. This results in a rapid transformation of liquid to gas, releasing a large amount of energy.

Compressed natural gas can also be used for transportation. It has been used to fuel taxi cabs, UPS delivery vans, postal vehicles, street sweepers, and transit and school buses. Natural gas is available outside of North America, but not via pipelines. It can be imported to the U.S. in the form of LNG, but this method of transport is highly controversial.

Because LNG occupies only a fraction (1/600) of the volume of natural gas, it is transported more economically over long distances and can be stored in larger quantities. Certainly, LNG is a price-competitive source of energy that could help meet future economic needs in the U.S. To date, there are six LNG terminals in the U.S.—in Kenai, Arkansas; Everett, Massachusetts; Cove Point, Maryland; Elba Island, Georgia; Lake Charles, Louisiana; and Penuelas, Puerto Rico.[21] To date, no catastrophic accidents have occurred at these terminals. Even operating at full capacity, however, they are capable of importing only 3% of U.S. natural gas consumption.

If natural gas vehicles are ever to have a material effect on the transportation market, we'll need to establish a national natural gas fuel infrastructure virtually from scratch. Because natural gas vehicles cannot be purchased or fueled as conveniently as gasoline-powered cars, the way to boost demand would be to significantly reduce costs. The best way to reduce costs would be to increase demand. It's a Catch-22 that can be resolved only by getting the federal, state, and local governments involved by offering short-term incentives to buyers of natural gas vehicles and by supporting U.S. Department of Energy efforts to promote "clean cities" programs based on governmental purchase and use of natural gas vehicles.[22]

Many advocates of alternative energy see natural gas as a means to shift from oil to hydrogen and renewable energy. They see it as the only viable transition fuel that can buy time as the U.S. switches from dependency on foreign crude to cheap, renewable, and clean energy sources, especially in the transportation sector. Given a choice between natural gas and oil, liquefied natural gas, obviously, would be the preferred liquid fuel.

Aside from the risks of accidents, however, the major problems with natural gas are that the U.S. has only limited domestic reserves, much of the foreign reserves are located in high-risk areas of the world, and natural gas prices tend to move with oil prices, promising future high prices for natural gas.

Any move to make natural gas the "new gasoline" would, therefore, be a colossal mistake and would simply replace one foreign addiction with another.

In sum, none of the big four other fossil fuels—coal, natural gas, tar sands, or oil shale—offers a viable long-term, economically sound, or environmentally friendly solution for generating electricity in ways that simultaneously decrease U.S. dependency on foreign energy resources *and* reduce greenhouse gas emissions. Fortunately, the penultimate resource for cheap, efficient, non-polluting, and commercially available electrical power generation is literally "blowing in the wind." The advantages of wind power along with other sustainable sources of energy are discussed in Chapter 11.

# Notes and References
## Chapter 6: Coal, Natural Gas, Tar Sands

1 "World Energy Assessment: Energy and the Challenge of Sustainability, 2000," (http://www.undp.org/energy/activities/wea/drafts-frame.html) and Paul Mobbs, *Energy Beyond Oil* (London: Matador, 2005).

2 Milken Institute, "Global Conference, An Examination of Problems and Solutions to Climate Change: A Conversation with Steven Chu," April 26, 2006, http://www.milkeninstitute.org/events/gcprogram.taf?function=detail &eventid=GC06&EvID=794 and http://www.eia.doe.gov/oiaf/ieo/pdf/coal. pdf.

3 http://www.spe.org/spe/jsp/basic/0,,1104_1008218_1109511,00.html and htpp://www.eia.doe.gov/oiaf/ieo/pdf/nat_gas.pdf.

4 James T. Bartis *et al.*, *Oil Shale Development in the United States: Prospects and Policy Issues*, Rand Corporation, 2005.

5 Oil and Gas Journal, vol. 99, December 24, 2001, 127.

6 George Lobsenz, "Reliability, Cost Recovery Issues Slow IGCC Rollout," *The Energy Daily*, October 6, 2006.

7 *FutureGen*—A Sequestration and Hydrogen Research Initiative, U.S. Department of Energy, Office of Fossil Energy, February 2003.

8 "The Northwest's rush to coal, Pt. 2: 'Clean' coal controversy," NW Energy Coalition, August 31, 2005.

9 Timothy Johnson and David Keith, "Electricity from Fossil Fuels without $CO_2$ Emissions: Assessing the Costs of Carbon Dioxide Capture and Sequestration in U.S. Electricity Markets," *Journal of the Air & Waste Management Association* 51 (October 2001): 1452-5.

10 Tim Flannery, *The Weather Makers: How Man is Changing the Climate and What It Means for Life on Earth* (Grove/Atlantic 2006).

11 Abraham T. Mwaura and J. Scott Straight, "'Clean' Coal Doesn't Do Much to Protect Environment," http://www.herald-dispatch.com/2005/March/18/ OPlist3.htm.

12 "Oil Shale/Tar Sands Guide," http://ostseis.anl.gov/guide/index.cfm.

13 "Petro-Canada Reviewing Oil Sands Strategy," May 2, 2003, http://www.fromthewilderness.com/cgi/bin/MasterPFP.cgi?doc=http://www.fromthewilderness.com/free/ww3/052703_tar_sands.html.

14 Kevin G. Hall, Knight Ridder Newspapers, "U.S. has plans for Canada oil sands," Nov. 27, 2005, http://www.azcentral.com/arizonarepublic/news/articles/1127oilsands27.html.

15 Joe Duarte, "Canadian Tar Sands: The Good, the Bad, and the Ugly," March 28 2006, http://www.rigzone.com/news/article.asp?a_id=30703.

16 CBC News, "High illness rate near oil sands worrisome, says Alberta health official," March 10, 2006, http://www.cbc.ca/story/canada/national/2006/03/10/oilsands-chipewyan060310.html.

17 Cornell University, *Science News*, January 1997, http://www.news.cornell.edu/releases/Jan97/water.hrs.html.

18 "Effects of Oil Shale Waste Disposal on Soil and Water Quality," http://www.scilet.com/Papers/csb/csb14/CSB_Ding.pdf.

19 Dan Denning, Daily Reckoning, "Oil Shale Reserves: Stinky Water, Sweet Oil," 2005, http://www.dailyreckoning.com/rpt/OilShale.html.

20 http://www.eere.energy.gov/afdc/resources/pricereport/price_report.html.

21 http://www.ferc.gov/industries/lng/indus-act/terminals/exist-term.asp.

22 http://www.ngvc.org.

# PART III

# THE CHALLENGE
# AND THE OPPORTUNITY
# —A NEW ENERGY ECONOMY

# 7

## FOREIGN OIL AND U.S. DEBT: THE FACTS

*"This is not a threat about the future; this is a crisis today. There is a direct link between our addiction to oil and our national security."*

— FORMER U.S. SENATOR JOHN EDWARDS

**What is an effective solution to the energy-climate crisis facing the U.S. and the world?**

- The Prometheus Plan can reduce U.S. oil use by 5 MBD in 10 years.

- A variety of geopolitical concerns make its adoption an absolute imperative for national security.

- The U.S. needs a national mobilization on the scale of the Manhattan and Apollo projects.

- Oil imports have been severely damaging the U.S. economy, particularly its debt levels.

- Even the most recent federally proposed "solutions" are inadequate.

- Transportation fuel efficiency offers the greatest near-term leverage.

## America's Achilles' Heel

Achilles was the greatest warrior of his time, much like America is considered today. In one of history's most epic conflicts, the Trojan War, the otherwise invincible Achilles had one fatal vulnerability: his unprotected heel. With a single arrow, Paris of Troy pierced Achilles' heel and killed him.

Today, dependence on Middle Eastern oil is America's Achilles' heel. Just like Paris, Middle Eastern potentates hold the black arrows of oil in their quivers, poised to disrupt the U.S. economy and weaken democracy. The mission of the Prometheus Plan is to make America invulnerable by placing the technological shield of energy independence over that heel. By elevating energy independence to the status of an urgent national priority—and not an empty slogan backed mostly by contradictory policies—the U.S. can protect itself, enhance national security, and lead the global transition away from oil and toward a new and sustainable energy economy.

Is there a viable solution to the unprecedented energy-climate crisis facing the U.S. and the world today? Is there a turnaround strategy for USA Inc. that dramatically reduces the role of oil imports in generating unsupportable levels of debt that threaten the dollar's decline and possible collapse?

Yes, fortunately, there is, and it uses available technology. What's sorely lacking is only the political will to mobilize the resources of this nation to the same scale as the successful Manhattan and Apollo projects. Best of all, the solution costs *far* less than the $320 billion we now pay each year for rapidly increasing foreign oil imports.

The solution is the Prometheus Plan, a turnaround strategy for USA Inc. that will achieve energy independence from all Middle Eastern oil through a rapid transition away from fossil fuels and into the next generation of fuels and vehicles *using existing, proven technologies.*

Will this program require new scientific discoveries? No. Will it require scientific development to bring existing technologies to scale? Yes, some, but nothing even close to that required in the Manhattan project or Apollo Program. And yet, just as in the space program, the technological spin-offs will likely go far beyond our expectations, creating new industries, businesses, and jobs. All we need to do is choose to deploy our technology through a collective act of will.

Adopting the Prometheus Plan will reduce U.S. oil consumption by five million barrels per day (MBD) within 10 years. Think of it—greater than all projected 2015 oil imports from Persian Gulf nations, principally Kuwait, Iran, Iraq, Qatar, Saudi Arabia, and the United Arab Emirates.

Increasing U.S. dependence on foreign oil has created unique economic, environmental, political, and security risks. These include rapidly rising oil prices, which we and others project to climb to more than $100/barrel in 2008; accelerating global warming and climate change; increasing geopolitical instability as hostile regimes hold vital oil supplies hostage; and growing competition with China and India for energy resources.

Furthermore, the projected $100/barrel oil price could occur even without any significant traumatic event—merely as a pure by-product of projected supply and demand. Such an event could be a terrorist strike on Saudi oil facilities, the sabotage or breakdown of the Alaskan oil pipelines, an Iranian oil blockade in the Strait of Hormuz, or a hurricane-caused disruption of U.S. refineries in the Gulf of Mexico. Such a calamity could generate a "Super Spike" that would lift oil prices into the $150-$250/barrel range.

For the past three decades, a succession of Democratic and Republican presidents has acted like Nero. Instead of just saying "no" to foreign oil, our leaders have fiddled as Rome burns, ignoring warnings, squandering opportunities, and allowing America to slide further and further down the slippery slope of oil dependency. Today, this habit threatens our vital interests.

The combination of a precarious balance between oil supply and demand and the simultaneous rapid economic growth of China and India have created the potential perfect storm of scarcity, instability, and soaring prices in global oil markets. Notwithstanding minor interruptions, the overall trends are clear. Demand for oil is rising inexorably, and the rate of major new discoveries has fallen precipitously. While oil prices may temporarily dip now and then, in the near future and over time they will continue their steady incline above $75/barrel by December 2007. Economic insecurity will increase throughout the world. There will be significant pressure on governments and energy companies to reassure the public by doing what they've done in the past—burn more coal, build more nuclear plants, and "drill our way out of the problem."

They will tout so-called "clean" coal, "cheaper, safer" nuclear power, and "unlimited supplies" of tar sands synthetic crude oil as solutions to our energy problems. As we have argued in the preceding chapters, it would be an economic, environmental, and political travesty of the worst kind to move in those directions.

First—an important fact which is too often overlooked—new plants for electric generation powered by oil, coal, or nuclear power will not even make a dent in America's oil imports, since nearly 70% of these imports are used for transportation (cars, trucks, and planes) and *only 2% for the generation of electricity* (see Figure 1).

**Figure 1. U.S. Oil Consumption by Sector, 2006**

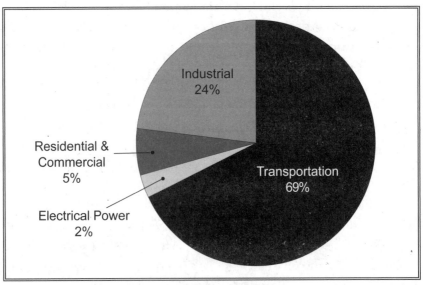

Source: U.S. Energy Information Administration, *Annual Energy Review 2006*

Second, "clean coal" is much more expensive than cleaner renewable technologies and requires the burying ("sequestering") of vast amounts of $CO_2$ greenhouse gases at huge additional costs, deep within the earth or the oceans, from which they someday may be belched up to threaten future generations.

Third, it takes about two tons of tar sands and huge investments just to produce one barrel of oil (42 gallons) from Canada's oil sands, with environmental and climate consequences far more devastating that those currently associated with petroleum. For example, Chevron expects that it will produce 155,000 barrels per day with an investment of $5 billion. Once the infrastructure is in place, it currently costs about $25/barrel to produce synthetic crude from Canada's tar sands, in comparison to $5/barrel of petroleum in the Middle East and $15/barrel in the Gulf of Mexico. In addition, oil sands require huge amounts of water (which become toxic in the process) and energy (mainly natural gas) to produce synthetic crude oil at a total recovery rate of only about 20 to 60% efficiency, depending on the recovery method.

Last, nuclear energy is an economic disaster, a public health danger, a magnet for terrorists, and the vehicle for proliferating nuclear weapons to rogue and hostile regimes around the globe and non-state terrorists. The private sector will build new reactors only if the government (i.e., *you*, the taxpaying public) bears most of the risks, including significant public subsidies, legal liability, and loan guarantees. And, even if hundreds of billions of dollars were available for the next generation of 50 new nuclear power plants, it would still take 12 to 15 years before the first ones went online, far too long to address the pending crisis. Just imagine the amount of additional nuclear waste this would create, when after a half-century of effort the U.S. still lacks a permanent solution to the high-level radioactive waste problem.

## AMERICA CAREENS TOWARD FINANCIAL RUIN

In its September 2005 *EconForecast*, the World Business Academy predicted that oil would hit $75/barrel in 2006.[1] At the beginning of the second quarter of 2006, oil prices went above $78/barrel—higher than prices after the shortages caused by Hurricane Katrina in the summer of 2005, which sent U.S. oil prices at the pump over $3/gallon nationwide. On April 21, 2006, gas was being sold for $4/gallon in Southern California.

Oil is such a large part of the American economy that one can observe a correlation between the Federal Reserve's federal funds rate, which is the interest rate at which depository institutions lend balances to each other overnight, and the price per barrel (see Figure 2).

**Figure 2. Crude Oil Prices and U.S. Federal Funds Rate**

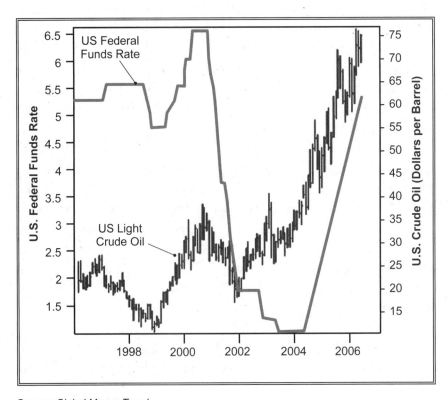

Source: *Global Money Trends*

Gary Dorsch, editor of *Global Money Trends*, has issued a stern warning to the Federal Reserve Bank, and by implication to the

Bush Administration, the Department of Energy, and anyone else "gambling on steady oil prices." As Figure 2 indicates, since 1999, crude oil has entered into uncharted territory. Prices have consistently broken psychological barriers, such as $50, $60, and $70/barrel; established new base levels of support; and then rallied to even higher ground. Dorsch observes, "Markets don't trade in a *straight* line; they usually move up and down within a trend. Crude oil has been marching higher in an orderly fashion since the U.S. conquest of Iraq, fueled by a razor-thin difference between global supply and demand."[2]

In April 2006, some analysts were already forecasting a record-breaking year in which "crude oil could hit $80 a barrel."[3] "Without question, this is the worst political-risk year we've seen for energy supplies since 1973," commented Ian Bremmer, president of the Eurasia Group, referring to the date of the first Arab oil embargo.[4]

> *"At some point in time we're going to reach a limit, and we will see a real impact of increased oil prices on our economic activity."*
> — U.S. ENERGY SECRETARY SAMUEL BODMAN, APRIL 2006

The threat of higher oil prices for extended periods of time could result in a serious economic slowdown. In fact, just as in the hurricane-plagued summer of 2005, we were "one storm away from an energy crisis," today we are "just one major supply disruption away from more serious financial consequences."

This time, however, it is not just a few "doom and gloom" analysts who are concerned. A rising chorus of energy experts and economists at major financial institutions are awakening to the risks of long-term increases in oil prices. The Academy believes that history will record that the next U.S. recession will have started somewhere between the fourth quarter of 2006 and the second quarter of 2007.

In its July 2006 *EconForecast*, the World Business Academy noted, "Evidence of mounting recessionary pressures is apparent now as higher interest rates and energy costs have contributed to reduced consumer spending and a declining housing market."

Discussing emerging recessionary trends in the U.S., the *Econ-Forecast* Committee observed:

> As we begin the second quarter earnings reporting season, at least half of the companies reporting have reported lower than expected earnings and reduced expectations for the remainder of the year. Meanwhile, higher energy prices are just beginning to work their way through the economy. In the '70s, it took almost four years for energy prices to impact consumption. To date, there is little evidence that consumers or businesses are conserving energy, especially gasoline. However, the implication from the broader economic view is that rising prices at the pump, declining disposable income, higher credit card interest, and a profusion of adjustable rate mortgages will result in a day of reckoning at some point. When the psychology changes, people will begin to conserve cash and the consumer economy will grind into a recessionary mode. The consumer economy represents over 70% of GDP and is a significant driver for global production as well.[5]

It is reasonable to ask, as does Tim McMahon, editor of the *Financial Trend Forecaster*, "Why haven't oil prices crippled the U.S. economy yet as they did back in the 1980s?"[6] As it "normally" takes higher energy prices several years to fully affect the economy, McMahon analyzes inflation-adjusted monthly crude oil prices from 1946 to the present in current dollars. He points out that the relevant statistics are not the "peak" oil prices, but rather the "average monthly" oil prices, which accurately reflect what the refineries have to pay for oil over the entire month. Back in the 1980s, monthly average oil prices peaked at $38/barrel, which, adjusted for inflation in 2005 dollars, "is the equivalent of paying $97.50 today." In 2006, oil prices increased from $60 in January to nearly $79 in July.

Obviously, the U.S. is rapidly approaching the danger zone of crippling oil prices.

# "WE WERE WARNED": TOMORROW'S OIL CRISIS

As the energy-driven economic crisis looms into view, some observers have speculated about how and when things may fall apart.

CNN produced an investigative report, "We Were Warned: Tomorrow's Oil Crisis," that described the hypothetical impact of a Category 5 hurricane slamming Houston in 2009, destroying the oil refineries, drilling platforms, and pipelines that supply a quarter of our nation's daily fuel supply. Three days later, terrorists attack key Saudi oil installations, disrupting some 8% of world oil production. Crude oil prices quickly top $150/barrel, with experts predicting that gasoline will hit $7/gallon at the pump. "In the days and weeks that follow, gasoline prices hit record highs, food prices soar as trucks cannot afford to make deliveries, and Americans begin to realize that their very way of life is in peril."[7]

James Fallows, in an article titled "Countdown to a Meltdown, America's Coming Energy Crisis: A Look Back from the Election of 2016," published in *Atlantic*, hypothesizes the CIA sponsoring a failed coup in Venezuela after Fidel Castro's death in 2009. Venezuelan President Hugo Chávez declares economic war against the U.S., effectively cutting off 15% of all U.S. oil supplies. Chávez takes this drastic step after making a secret deal to divert Venezuelan oil to the energy-hungry Chinese under favorable future oil contracts, in return for China's backing out of the Bretton Woods Agreement, two financial accords that pegged fixed currency exchange rates to the U.S. dollar. When the crisis ends, America no longer controls its economic destiny and is a shell of a former superpower (like England after World War II), an empire in decline.[8]

Unfortunately, these scenarios today resemble plausible prophecy more than far-fetched fiction.[9] Venezuela is already taking steps to break with the U.S. market and to increase oil sales to other countries. In 2006, Venezuelan exports to the U.S. dropped 8% from 2005, hitting a 12-year low. In 2007, Venezuela agreed to a series of deals with China to increase Chinese investment in Venezuelan oil fields; increase Venezuelan oil exports to China from 150,000 to 800,000 barrels a day; and create a $6 billion fund to support their joint energy projects, including three oil refineries in China. Venezuela plans to triple its tanker fleet by 2012 to reach Asian markets.

According to economist Philip Verleger, spikes in oil prices have cumulatively reduced U.S. economic growth by 15%, resulting in $1.2 trillion in direct losses.[10] This figure indicates the extraordinarily damaging impact of oil imports on the American (and hence, the world's) economy *even in the absence of any significant political, climatic, or human–induced disruption.*

*Oil plays an increasing role in the unsupportable levels of U.S. debt and in the potential dollar collapse engendered by printing money to pay for this debt.*[11]

The role of oil in U.S. debt and trade deficit levels includes not just spending on petroleum imports themselves (currently estimated at between $270 and $320 billion for 2006, depending on the reference source), but also the cost of providing military security to Middle Eastern oil producers (about $50 billion annually before the second Iraq war), and the increasing cost of that war. Counting direct Congressional appropriations alone, the war already has cost more than $450 billion. This figure does not include the cost of massive veterans' hospitalizations, medical care, and benefits triggered by the war, which a number of analysts predict will take the final figure well over $1 trillion.

In fact, spending for Iraq has risen in every year since Bush declared "Mission Accomplished." These Iraq war costs have been deliberately excluded from federal deficit compilations. The budget calculations are made on a cash basis, not an accrual basis. So pensions, VA hospital costs, and other related costs likely make the figure much, much higher.

## IT'S THE DEBT, STUPID!

In March 2006, President Bush quietly signed a bill that pushed the national public debt ceiling up to nearly $9 trillion. This debt limit increase was the fourth in the Bush administration, totaling some $3 trillion—an astonishing 58% increase during a period when prior projections suggested a federal budget surplus.[12]

The main components of the U.S. current account deficit are our imports of oil and Chinese manufactured goods. In 2007, the current account deficit reached about $850 billion, a level some economists view as unsustainable.

To educate policymakers and the public about the urgency of dealing with unsustainable debt levels, U.S. Comptroller General David Walker has been traveling the country on a fiscal wake-up tour, accompanied by economists from think tanks across the political spectrum—the Heritage Foundation, Brookings Institution, and the Concord Coalition. Walker runs the Government Accounting Office (GAO), which audits the government's fiscal condition and reports to Congress. Walker and his tour group carry the message that the U.S. has gone from being the world's largest creditor nation to the world's largest debtor nation, and warn that because of the size of the U.S. fiscal deficit, every American child now comes into the world with a "birth burden of $156,000."[13]

> *"Again and again it has always been the world's leading lending country that has been the premier country in terms of political influence, diplomatic influence, and cultural influence. Today we are no long the world's leading lending country. In fact, we are the world's biggest debtor country, and we continue to wield influence on the basis of military prowess alone."*
>
> — BENJAMIN FRIEDMAN, ECONOMIST, HARVARD UNIVERSITY

Until now, the U.S. has been able to debt-finance its economic growth because ever since World War II, the world has relied on the U.S. dollar as the standby global reserve foundation of monetary stability. The U.S. has exploited this situation by increasingly running up ever-larger trade deficits, current account deficits, and federal debt levels. About half of this debt is held by foreign nations, with most held by Asian central banks, especially in China and Japan, who show up weekly at the U.S. Treasury auction.

The dollar's "privileged" position as the global reserve currency creates a demand for dollars, as foreign nations must purchase green-backs to buy their petroleum. Petroleum has been denominated in American currency ever since 1973, as part of a deal President Nixon struck to end the OPEC oil embargo. The bottom line is that central banks need to buy dollars to buy oil, and so we have created what essentially has been a captive market.

To continue to make the dollar attractive, U.S. Treasury officials have slowly lowered the value of the dollar in relation to other currencies such as the euro. This makes all imports, including petroleum, more expensive to Americans. (Nonetheless, gasoline is often even more expensive outside the U.S. because most nations tax gas at the pump at rates hundreds of times higher than does the U.S.) We are not out of the woods, though, for if the dollar slides too much, Asian banks could demand an interest premium, which could lead to an economic downturn. Alternatively they could simply stop investing their savings in American stocks and Treasury notes, which could trigger a dollar collapse.

In April 2006, China stunned world financial markets by announcing that it may cut U.S. debt holdings as part of its foreign exchange reserves. China is a major buyer of U.S. debt. As of early 2007, it held about $354 billion in U.S. Treasury bonds, second only to Japan. Any significant reduction in China's dollar assets could hurt the U.S. economy. If China releases its dollars, the U.S. would have to make dollar investments more attractive by driving up the long-term yields it pays on U.S. bonds. This would mean higher interest rates and tighter money at home—the classic recipe for stagflation. It happened in 1979, and it can happen again.

Essentially, U.S. government expenses are out of control and significantly higher than revenues. *Private* debt levels are almost as bad. We spend much more than we earn and rely on the savings of Asian nations to prop up the U.S. economy. The authors of *Empire of Debt* wryly comment on the behavior of contemporary Americans:

> They are the richest people on the planet, but they
> have come to rely on the savings of the world's poorest
> people just to pay their bills. They routinely spend more

than they make—and think they can continue doing so indefinitely. They go deeper and deeper into debt, believing they will never have to settle up. They buy houses and then mortgage them out—room by room until they have almost nothing left. They invade foreign countries in the belief that they are spreading democracy, and depend on lending from Communist China to pay for it.[14]

America so far has been able to maintain this abnormal state of affairs primarily because of cheap foreign capital, cheaper labor in China and India for manufacturing, relatively inexpensive energy prices, and the willingness of Asian central banks to purchase U.S. debt at relatively low interest rates. But now, all of this is changing as India's and China's economies grow annually by about 8.5% to 10.5%, respectively.

Rising energy costs are bringing the U.S. economy closer to a day of reckoning resulting from profligate spending and indebtedness. In 2005, oil imports accounted for more than one-third of the U.S. trade deficit, up from one-fourth in 2004. In testimony before a U.S. Senate Committee in early 2006, Milton Copulos, president of the National Defense Council Foundation, noted, "Because the price of crude oil is expected to remain in the $60 range this year, expenditures for oil imports are expected to be at least $320 billion. This amounts to an increase of $70 billion in spending for foreign oil in just one year."[15]

In terms of energy, commodities, and currency rates, the U.S. is entering a fascinating "dance" with China. This is happening just as oil dependency is weakening America's geopolitical clout. For example, in 2005 the China National Offshore Oil Corp. made an offer of $18.5 billion for Unocal, which has oil and gas reserves that total about 1.75 billion barrels. The U.S. government, acting on behalf of Chevron Corp., essentially blocked the sale. Shortly thereafter, Chevron and Unocal announced a merger.

Most significantly, back in July 2005, China moved to decouple its currency, the yuan, from the U.S. dollar and pegged it to a "basket of currencies" valued at a secret formula (which was recently announced

> *"According to the National Defense Council Foundation, the economic penalties of America's oil dependence total $297.2 to $304.9 billion annually. If reflected at the gasoline pump, these 'hidden costs' would raise the price of a gallon of gasoline to over $5.28. A fill-up would be over $105."*
>
> — INSTITUTE FOR THE ANALYSIS OF GLOBAL SECURITY, 2006

to consist of not more than 20% U.S. dollars). If the U.S. reaches the point where it can no longer adequately service its foreign debt or needs major additional debt financing, it will have to negotiate with the Chinese. At that point, America will be under tremendous pressure to cave to Chinese demands. These could include the approval to purchase key U.S. companies with discounted dollars or guaranteed access to U.S. crops for food *and* ethanol production. China has already demonstrated a willingness to tie its demands to its dollar holdings. In mid-2007, Chinese officials stated that China's large dollar holdings contributed "a great deal to maintaining the position of the dollar as a reserve currency," and suggested that China would reduce its dollar holdings if the U.S. imposed trade sanctions to force a yuan revaluation.

## TURNAROUND STRATEGY FOR USA INC.

What do we see if we look at USA Inc. as a company instead of as a country? We see an entity divorced from financial reality, mired in debt, whose continued operations are only possible because of the "kindness of strangers." We see a company paying $1 billion a day for "security services." We see a business in distress and in desperate need of a turnaround strategy.

Oil is the vital ingredient in America's transportation and manufacturing. Prices have more than tripled since 1999, supply is tight, and supply lines are under siege.

Financially, the company has a negative net worth. It is in technical default on its debt service and continues to operate on a cash-flow basis only by repeatedly raising the debt ceiling and printing more money.

Its expenses far exceed revenues. No realistic plan exists to return it to break-even, much less profitability. It has raided its pension fund (Social Security) to pay operating expenses. In addition, it faces foreign central bankers who are increasingly skeptical about the financial stability of the enterprise, including its currency, and who have signaled that they do not want to acquire U.S. debt and dollar reserves at an increasing rate.

In addition, several countries, including Iran, Venezuela, China, and Russia, have already adopted alternatives to petrodollars and have begun denominating oil in euros.

Is it possible that Saddam wrote his own death sentence when he effectively converted sales of Iraqi oil from dollars to euros by announcing in September 2000 that he would participate in the U.N. oil-for-food exchange if his $10 billion in oil sales were denominated in euros? When the U.S. toppled him, it reverted to selling Iraqi oil in dollars.

If this collapse of petroleum-based dollar hegemony occurs on a large scale, it will eliminate the need for other nations to keep buying U.S. debt to have U.S. dollars to use for oil purchases. More significantly, if OPEC were to follow suit and sell its oil for euros rather than dollars, the U.S. would have to begin paying for oil in more expensive euros, and gas prices could climb to $8-$9 a gallon at the pump.

The transportation infrastructure is in disarray. The national passenger train system Amtrak requires permanently increasing federal bailouts just to stay in business and is continuing to reduce its services lines. Most major airlines are either bankrupt or on the verge of bankruptcy. As of June 2006, every airline except Southwest was losing money. The automobile industry is on the ropes. General Motors and Ford are barely skating the knife edge of financial disaster, from pinning their hopes in North America on increased sales of SUVs! If nothing is done soon, Germany will take an insurmountable lead in producing the super-fast maglev trains, and Asia will dominate the fast-growing market for efficient hybrid cars.

USA Inc. desperately needs new management at the top. For

> *"If this country does not change course, within 10 years the rest of the world would end up owning $15 trillion worth of the United States, equivalent to owning every share of American stock."*
> — WARREN BUFFET, CHAIRMAN, BERKSHIRE HATHAWAY, 2006

the past 20 years, no administration has been able to avoid the illusory lure of cheap oil and foreign imports. Meanwhile, the current Bush-Cheney administration is undermining the vital stability of the dollar by perpetuating the sham that we can simultaneously reduce taxes, pay for ever-more-expensive oil imports, finance an energy war in Iraq, and sustain economic growth—without ultimately sacrificing our standard of living and having to pay the piper.

This failed "strategy" assumes America can continue buying unlimited amounts of guns, butter, and oil by printing unlimited amounts of money. Pancho Villa had a similar strategy for paying off the costs of the Mexican Revolution; he precipitated disastrous hyperinflation. The Weimar Republic applied the same strategy in the 1930s to pay World War I reparations. Again, hyperinflation ensued and paved the way for fascism, Hitler, and World War II. (Hitler opened the Eastern front primarily to obtain oil supplies from Romania. Japan attacked the U.S. to gain unhampered access to British and American oil fields in Southeast Asia.) Obviously, oil is a *casus belli*, and this oil industry-inspired energy non-strategy extends beyond mere greed. It is an exercise in blatant economic irresponsibility that will produce grave social consequences.

America urgently needs visionary leadership to implement a turnaround strategy that resolves oil's supply-demand pressures. This strategy must re-engineer our energy system before climate change condemns our children and grandchildren to a horrendous future. We believe that the essence of that turnaround should be a national commitment to the Prometheus Plan. As always, in our time of national crisis, the best defense is a good offense.

The time for freedom from Middle Eastern oil is <u>NOW!</u>

## Blueprint for Energy Abundance

In his 2006 State of the Union Address, President Bush—a Texas oil man—surprised the nation by admitting, "Here we have a serious problem. America is addicted to oil, which is often imported from unstable parts of the world." President Bush argued, "The best way to break this addiction is through technology." Here we agree, but the problem demands a scale and timetable much bolder than those contemplated by the White House's energy initiatives. The good news is that all of the technologies required to achieve energy independence are currently available.

President Bush offered only one initiative, setting a "great goal: to replace more than 75% of our oil imports from the Middle East by 2025."[16] This is hardly an adequate goal, as it would be far too little and far too late to avert the economic catastrophe that is looming ahead. It is analogous to his goal to "land a man on Mars" at a similar date.

Nonetheless, while this announcement was certainly no "Nixon goes to China" moment, it was a positive step. After all, the first action in the 12-Step Alcoholics Anonymous rehabilitation program is a frank, public admission that one is an addict. Unfortunately, we read the Bush statement more as providing political rhetoric than substance because, shockingly, it lacked *any* meaningful initiatives to achieve even his woefully inadequate 2025 goal. The sad fact is that such lofty platitudes, like his 2000 campaign pledge to curb global warming by 25%, rapidly collapse under pressure from interest groups, condemning future administrations, future taxpayers, and our children to pay the bills for total inaction.

On the very next day after President Bush's address, how did Energy Secretary Samuel Bodman buttress Bush's pledge to "move beyond a petroleum-based economy and make our dependence on oil a thing of the past"? He retreated by saying, "This was purely an example." The reason he offered is that oil is fungible, which means it is interchangeable and can be replaced by the same commodity purchased elsewhere. This is a backdoor admission of a simple market reality: *you can't break oil addiction simply by switching dealers.*

Why then, one might ask, do we premise the Prometheus Plan upon eliminating all Middle Eastern oil by the year 2015 if, in fact, it just means the oil-rich countries will sell the same oil to someone else? There are several answers.

Foremost, for national security reasons, the U.S. needs to cut its umbilical cord to the Middle East. *At a moment's notice, terrorists or a belligerent Iran could sever this lifeline.*

Second, reducing U.S. oil consumption by 5 MBD from *any source* will further enhance U.S. economic competitiveness by reducing U.S. reliance on ever-more-costly oil, will put downward pressure on the price of oil by reducing global demand for an increasingly scarce resource (we're assuming that Hubbert's Peak will have passed long before 2015), and will likely lead to similar reduction of oil consumption strategies by other major consuming nations.

Third, formulating closer bilateral relationships with oil suppliers outside of the Middle East *while we are reducing our oil consumption by 5 MBD* will strengthen our negotiating position for oil supplies. The U.S. would be the world's largest oil customer with declining requirements, demanding long-term contractual protection of supplies from its non-Middle Eastern oil vendors in the event of Middle Eastern oil supply disruptions on the global market. In a phrase, reducing U.S. oil imports by 5 MBD (the amount equal to all Middle Eastern oil imports by 2015) will begin to reverse the leverage that Middle Eastern oil suppliers have over all oil-consuming nations worldwide, *regardless of which nations sell oil to any other nation.*

In addition, if the broad goal, as Secretary Bodman clarified, was really to displace foreign oil imports *from anywhere* with domestic alternatives, then the Bush initiative is terribly unambitious. As Figure 3 shows, President Bush's early-2006 "goal" at best amounts to reducing the current level of U.S. oil use by 15% in 20 years (by 2025), but by that time *total* oil use will have increased by approximately 50%. So, looking two decades down the road, Bush's goal will still leave the U.S. highly dependent on foreign sources for more than 50% of its oil (i.e., 21 MBD-4.5 MBD = 16.5 MBD, and 16.5/30 MBD = 55%).

In President Bush's 2007 State of the Union address, he announced his "Twenty in Ten" plan to reduce U.S. gasoline use by 20% in the next 10 years. The extent to which this Administration is committed to making these goals a top national priority and working with Congress to implement them remains to be seen.

**Figure 3.  Snapshot of U.S. Oil Use, 2005, 2015, 2025[17]**

With President Bush's and Prometheus Plan Goals for Middle East Oil Reductions
(In Millions of Barrels per Day, rounded)

| | 2005 | 2015 | 2025 |
|---|---|---|---|
| **U.S. Oil Use** | | | |
| - Total Oil Use (rounded nearest MBD) | 20 / 100% | 25 / 100% | 30 / 100% |
| - Transportation sector | 14 / 68% | 18 / 70% | 22 / 73% |
| - Imports—from all sources | 10 / 50% | 15 / 60% | 21 / 70% |
| - Imports—from Middle East (Persian Gulf) | 2.5 / 13% | 4.5 / 18% | 6.0 / 20% |
| President Bush's Goal, State of Union, 2006<br>- Replace > 75% Middle East oil imports by 2025 | — | — | 4.5 / 15% |
| Prometheus Plan Goals<br>- Save 5 MBD in 10 years; 15 MBD in 20 years | — | 5.0/ 20% | 15.0/50% |

Fortunately, implementing the Prometheus Plan would provide deep cuts in oil imports quickly, using currently available technology. We therefore project a major reduction of 5 MBD in U.S. oil use by 2015. This will happen not in 20 years, but in half that time.

# How Do We Get There?

*So, how do we get from here to there?*

Not through the meager funding proposed by President Bush for research into better batteries for hybrid vehicles and greater production of ethanol as an alternative fuel. As the *New York Times* commented, "His actual budget proposals were pitiful. The $150 million the White House said it would commit to making biofuels more competitive, for instance, turns out to be $50 million less than the amount authorized by last year's energy bill. And while the president talks about a new generation of vehicles, he offers virtually nothing meaningful to help Detroit get there."

Furthermore, the president shows no willingness to break the logjam in Detroit by mandating meaningful increases in automobile fuel efficiency standards. Neither will he call for higher gasoline taxes, an excess profits tax on oil companies, or other financial measures that would promote conservation and encourage development of new fuels and more fuel-efficient vehicles. Unfortunately, Congress has not done much better, but the November 2006 elections have changed the dynamics in Washington. There is a growing public call, as well as a corporate call by key members of the Business Roundtable, for the Bush Administration and Congress to take strong action to address the energy and climate change crisis.

Achieving the Prometheus goal of reducing oil use by 5 MBD in 10 years—equivalent to a saving of 500,000 MBD per year over the next decade—requires a major wartime-like mobilization to accelerate proven technologies into large-scale commercialization. The financial, environmental, and security benefits to all U.S. citizens more than justify this effort.

During the next decade, between now and 2015, the Prometheus Plan can realize oil savings of at least 5 MBD by:

- Raising the fuel efficiency of new vehicles to 40 mpg and accelerating the availability of flex-fuel vehicles that can run on either gasoline or ethanol;

- Generating additional oil savings in motor vehicles through efficiency improvements in tires, motor oil, and heavy-duty trucks;

- Realizing additional oil savings in the industrial, aviation, and residential sectors; and

- Accelerating the growth of the biofuels industry through the rapid expansion of ethanol and biodiesel production.

Looking further ahead, between 2015 and 2025, additional savings of up to 15 MBD can be achieved from the large-scale commercialization of hybrids and plug-in hybrids, along with the rapid phase-in of super-efficient, super-lightweight composite cars, trucks, and airplanes. Competitive wind power can generate off-peak electricity for dual-battery plug-in hybrids at the gas-equivalent cost of 50 cents/gallon. Eventually, we must transition completely to a climate-stabilizing and sustainable, non-fossil fuel, hydrogen economy. We can initiate this transition during the next decade and be well underway by 2020.

It is well past the time to unleash America's vast capacity for innovation and production so that we can liberate ourselves from the dire economic and environmental consequences of dependency on foreign oil and the fossil-fuel era.

Let's lay out a roadmap for implementing the Prometheus Plan.

# Notes and References
## Chapter 7: Foreign Oil and U.S. Debt

1   World Business Academy, *EconForecast*, July 14, 2006.

2   Gary Dorsch, "The Fed's Next Move and the Mid-East Powder-keg," *Global Money Trends* newsletter, July 25, 2006.

3   "Crude oil could hit $80 a barrel," *Wall Street Journal*, April 10, 2006, 3.

4   "Once Marginal, But Now Kings of the Oil World," *New York Times*, April 23, 2006.

5   World Business Academy, *EconForecast*, July 14, 2006.

6   Tim McMahon, *Financial Trend Forecaster*, July 20, 2006.

7   CNN Presents, "We Were Warned: Tomorrow's Oil Crisis," transcript of television show, March 18, 2006.

8   James Fallows, "Countdown to a Meltdown, America's Coming Energy Crisis: A Look Back from the Election of 2016," *Atlantic Monthly*, July/August 2005, 51-66. In reality, Venezuela's break with the U.S. market would be difficult in the short term because Venezuelan crude is particularly viscous and requires specialized refineries, the type found in Louisiana and Texas but not currently in China or India. The country's tanker fleet is built for transporting oil in the Gulf of Mexico and can't be re-fitted for intercontinental hauls. In addition, Venezuela sells oil in the U.S. through 14,000 Citgo stations owned by the state oil company. See Franklin Foer, "The Talented Mr. Chávez," *Atlantic Monthly*, May 2006, 104.

9   Mathew R. Simmons, "2005 Oil Outlook: Is This the Year When Demand Outstrips Supply?" *Energy Bulletin*, March 1, 2005.

10  As quoted in Paul Roberts, *The End of Oil*.

11  Other analysts who discuss the relationship among oil, debt and the dollar are Richard Heinberg, *The Party's Over: Options and Actons for a Post-Carbon World* (BC, Canada: New Society Publishers, 2005); Stephen Leeb, *The Coming Economic Collapse: How You Can Thrive When Oil COsts $200 a Barrel* (New York: Warner Business Books, 2006); William Bonner and Addison Wiggin, *Empire of Debt* (Hoboken, NJ: John Wiley & Sons, Inc., 2006); and Kevin Phillips, *American Theocracy: The Peril and Politics of Radical Religion, Oil, and Borrowed Money in the 21st Century* (New York: Penguin Group (USA) Inc. 2006).

12 The actual debt ceiling limit was $8.965 trillion. Subtracting the $5.662 trillion limit when Bush took office in January 2001 yields a $3.303 trillion increase, or an increase of 58%.

13 *"U.S. Heading for Financial Trouble?"* CBS News, July 8, 2007, http://www.cbsnews.com/stories/2007/03/01/60minutes http://www.law.virginia.edu/html/news/2006_spr/walker.htm

14 Bonner and Wiggen, *op. cit.,* 3.

15 Statement of Milton R. Copulas, Hearing before Committee on Foreign Relations, U.S. Senate, "The Hidden Cost of Oil," March 30, 2006.

16 President George W. Bush, State of the Union Address, Washington, D.C., January 31, 2006.

17 Based on Energy Information Administration, Annual Energy Outlook 2003.

# 8

# THE PROMETHEUS PLAN: THE ROADMAP

*"Live out of your imagination, not your history."*

– Stephen Covey, businessman, motivational speaker,
and Fellow of the World Business Academy

**Using *existing* technologies, can the U.S. reduce oil consumption by 5 MBD by 2015? *Yes.***

- The national Prometheus Plan for freedom from Middle Eastern oil calls for:

  - Using available technologies and policies that are tax revenue-neutral;

  - Increasing average new passenger vehicle efficiency from 24.4 to 40 miles per gallon; and

  - Dramatically accelerating the growth of the biofuels industry.

- Benefits include reduced climate change, enhanced national security, economic growth, and new jobs, which improve the likelihood of global peace and prosperity.

## REKINDLING THE HUMAN SPIRIT IN BUSINESS

The Prometheus Plan grew out of the Energy Task Force of the World Business Academy and is an ongoing program of the Academy.[1] The Academy was founded in 1987 on the principle that business is today the dominant institution in society and the one most capable of responding to rapid change. As such, business must adopt "a new tradition of responsibility for the whole." Businesses must do this by defining their own interests within the wider perspective of society in order to create a positive and sustainable future for themselves and for all. If properly executed, the Academy believes the Prometheus Plan is a win for the private enterprises who lead the transition to renewables, and because of global warming, also a win for all of the citizens of the planet.

The Academy's mission is to explore and clarify the fundamental social, economic, political, scientific, and technological trends underway globally. For 20 years, we have been commenting on the fundamental trends in human behavior, and we believe we are at an epochal transition point. We further believe a massive paradigmatic shift is underway, comparable to other major historical transformations, such as the Enlightenment and the Industrial Revolution. It is probably the largest such shift since Copernicus' observation in the 1500s that the earth revolves around the sun.

The Academy's goal is to enable its fellows, members, and subscribers to integrate knowledge about vital sociological-business trends in human behavior into their lives and business practices and to disseminate that knowledge to the world, while rekindling the human spirit in business. In the words of co-founder Willis Harmon, "The Academy is not just another association of business people to exchange information and foster collegiality. It is about investing ourselves in a task of historic proportions. Some will be called to this task and many will not. Those who are will find it to be extremely gratifying and fulfilling."

As participants in the Academy, we can conceive of no more fulfilling or critical task than mobilizing the leadership of the U.S. to fully comprehend and definitively resolve the energy and climate crisis that threatens the foundations of the global economy and, yes, of civilization itself. As historian Arnold Toynbee observed, "Civilizations die from suicide, not by murder." We Americans have allowed ourselves to be lulled by certain political and corporate leadership factions into a false sense of political, economic, environmental and social security. Such security is a dangerous illusion. Many of us are beginning to wake up to this fact and to accept the inescapable conclusion that we must replace the leaders of those corporate and political factions with courageous leaders who can set us back on the right course for current and future generations. We firmly believe that as a nation, we possess the insight, resources, and technology to prevent our own demise and revitalize the world.

In support of this goal, we cite the broad and growing consensus among energy experts at nonpartisan think tanks, public interest groups, universities, and prestigious bipartisan commissions that significant reductions in U.S. oil use on the order of 2.5 to 15 million barrels per day (MBD) are achievable within a 10 to 20-year time frame, respectively (see Figures 1 and 2 below).

Organizations that are part of this consensus include the Natural Resources Defense Council; the Rocky Mountain Institute, headed by world energy guru and World Business Academy Fellow Amory Lovins; Set America Free Coalition, spearheaded by the Apollo Alliance and the Institute for the Analysis of Global Security; the Union of Concerned Scientists; and the bipartisan National Commission on Energy Policy.[2]

Scientists and energy experts conducted these pertinent studies. They have been vetted for accuracy and in some cases have been independently peer-reviewed and Pentagon-funded. This is not to say that all of this research points to a single route out of our current predicament. In fact, while the studies share areas of agreement, they also have major differences. There is little need for incremental original research. The heavy lifting has been done. We have applied our knowledge and experience to synthesizing the best of each plan, and combining it with our own thinking, to develop a plan that is

## Figure 1. Projected Achievable Oil Savings: 2005, 2015, 2025[3]

| Baseline and Strategies | Achievable Oil Savings by Year (Millions of Barrels per Day) | | |
|---|---|---|---|
| | 2005 | 2015 | 2025 |
| **Baseline for U.S. Oil Savings—Assumes Status Quo**<br>- Total Oil Use (rounded nearest MBD)<br>- Transportation sector<br>- Imports—from all sources<br>- Imports—from Middle East (Persian Gulf) | 20 / 100%<br>14 / 68%<br>10 / 50%<br>2.5 / 13% | 25 / 100%<br>18 / 70%<br>15 / 60%<br>4.5 / 18% | 30 / 100%<br>22 / 73%<br>21 / 70%<br>6.0 / 20% |
| **A) National Commission on Energy Policy**<br>- Improve passenger vehicle fuel economy<br>- Increase contribution of alternative fuels<br>- Improve efficiency of heavy-duty truck fleet<br>- Provide fuel efficient replacement tires | — | — | 3.0 / 10%<br>5.0 / 16% |
| **B) Natural Resources Defense Council**<br>- Congress establishes minimum national mandates<br>- Raise fuel efficiency of new passenger vehicles<br>- Incentives for biofuel industry<br>- Tax credits and higher mpg standards | — | 2.5 / 10%<br>3.2 / 13% | 10.0 / 33% |
| **C) Rocky Mountain Institute**<br>- Double efficiency of oil use—advanced hybrids<br>- Speed adoption of super-efficient trucks & planes<br>- Build domestic biofuels industry—replaces ¼ oil<br>- Use saved natural gas for hydrogen generation<br>- Cost: $180 billion over 10 years | — | 2.5 / 10% | 15.0 / 50% |
| **D) Apollo Alliance/IAGS***<br>- National mandates: 10% in 10 yrs, > 20% in 20 yrs.<br>- Lightweight, plug-in, flex-fuel, hybrid vehicles<br>- Diversify fuels: additives, electricity, biofuels<br>- Supportive legislation, policies and tax incentives<br>- Cost: $300 billion over 10 years | — | 2.5 / 10% | 8.0 / 27%<br>12.0 / 40% |
| **E) Prometheus Plan**<br>- Energy Efficiency, CAFE, flex-fuel hybrid vehicles<br>- Non-fossil fuels, primarily ethanol and biodiesel<br>- Phase in hydrogen economy<br>- Supportive legislation, policies, incentives | — | 5.0 / 20% | 15.0 / 50% |

* Institute for the Analysis of Global Security
Source: Public Interest Organization Research

both technologically achievable and more ambitious than the studies cited in Figure 1.

Figure 2 presents a summary of the major oil saving strategies proposed by the Natural Resources Defense Council, the Rocky Mountain Institute, and the Apollo Alliance/Institute for the Analysis of Global Security, and of the renewable energy standard proposed by the Union of Concerned Scientists.

## Figure 2. Blueprints for Energy Abundance

• **Natural Resources Defense Council**—Proposes a firm national commitment to save at least 2.5 MBD within 10 years—or about 10% of our projected oil use by 2015—and greater amounts over time thereafter. The Defense Council estimates the U.S. could actually reduce its oil dependence 40% by 2025 by simply increasing the fuel economy of cars and trucks, producing homegrown alternative fuels and cutting wasteful oil use in residences and industries. Based on today's oil prices, these steps would save more than $30 billion in annual oil costs, while reducing smoggy skies and combating global warming.

• **Rocky Mountain Institute**—Even if "externalized" costs of oil were zero, completely displacing oil would still be profitable for the U.S. economy and other economies starting now. The solution is to save half the oil America uses and substitute cheaper alternatives for the other half through four integrated steps:

- Double the efficiency of oil use at average cost of $12 per barrel, using primarily ultra-light and ultra-strong materials for advanced hybrid gas-electric vehicles;
- Coordinate policies/business strategies to speed adoption of super-efficient, light vehicles, heavy trucks, and airplanes, yielding 52% reduction in oil use by 2025;
- Turn to modern biofuels to replace another 25% of U.S. oil needs, boosting net farm income by billions and creating 750,000 jobs; and
- Use profitable efficiency techniques to save half of projected 2025 use of natural gas, and convert saved gas into hydrogen which can displace remaining oil.

*Figure 2 (continued)*

By 2015, the early steps of this orderly 20-year transition will have saved as much oil as the U.S. now gets from the Persian Gulf, 2.5 MBD; by 2040, oil imports would be gone; by 2050, the U.S. economy would be flourishing with no oil at all.

In the process, more than 1 million high-wage automotive and related jobs can be saved and 1 million new jobs added, while American car, truck, and airplane industries can again lead the world, and the military can refocus on protecting the nation rather than trying to control foreign oil fields.

The total investment required is $180 billion in industrial capacity over the next decade, which could save $133 billion every year by 2025, *assuming $26/barrel oil (the savings per year would be $383 billion assuming $75/barrel oil)*. RMI believes this is the first strategy for displacing the black stuff not incrementally, but radically, not at a cost to the economy, but at a net gain, and in ways that will appeal to diverse business and political leaders.

• **Set America Free Coalition (Apollo Alliance)**—If by 2025, all cars on the road are hybrids and half are plug-in hybrid vehicles, U.S. oil imports would drop by 8 MBD. Today, the U.S. imports 10 MBD, and it is projected to import almost 20 MBD by 2025. If all of these cars were also flexible fuel vehicles, U.S. oil imports would drop by as much as 12 MBD.

Independently, the Apollo Alliance has a lofty goal—to garner $300 billion of investment in new energy technologies and energy conservation over 10 years to eliminate our dependence on foreign oil and add millions of new, higher paying jobs. The Apollo Alliance has a 10-point plan, with the top priority being the promotion of advanced technology and hybrid cars. Apollo estimates that this plan will create more than 3 million jobs by 2015, which will pour $95 billion into the economy through new income stimulated by good wages, resulting in $330 billion in total incremental economic output.

• **Union of Concerned Scientists**—A new Concerned Scientists analysis finds that under a national Renewable Electricity Standard (RES) of 20%, Americans would by 2020 increase their total homegrown renewable power capacity by nearly 11 times over present levels, from 17,000 megawatts (MW) in 2003 to 180,000 MW by 2020. This 20% RES would result in 157,500 net new jobs, $72.6 billion in new capital investment, $49.1 billion in consumer energy bill savings, $15 billion in biomass energy payments, $5 billion in property tax revenues, $1.2 billion in wind power land lease

*Figure 2 (continued)*

savings, 15.7 trillion cubic feet in natural gas savings, and a savings of 434 million metric tons of power plant carbon dioxide emissions.

By meeting this 20% standard, the U.S. can avoid the need for 975 new power plants (300 MW each), retire 180 old coal plants (500 MW each), retire 14 existing nuclear plants (1,000 MW each) and reduce the need for hundreds of thousands of miles of new gas pipelines and electricity transmission lines. In addition, carbon dioxide emissions will be reduced by two-thirds from business-as-usual by 2020, and harmful emissions of sulfur dioxide and nitrogen oxides by 55%.

## THE BENEFITS OF IMPLEMENTING THE PROMETHEUS PLAN

As noted, the Prometheus Plan will save more oil over a shorter period of time than the plans of any of these prestigious groups. The benefits of implementing the Prometheus Plan are enormous. In essence, it will:

- Cut U.S. oil dependence
- Increase national security
- Mitigate climate change
- Prevent economic chaos
- Diminish trade deficits
- Re-invigorate the domestic economy
- Re-establish America's global leadership

Once Americans fully understand the critical challenge that the energy and climate crisis poses to their families in the very near future and to future generations, we are confident they will rally around the leaders who will implement the Prometheus Plan.

### Our Belief—All humanity must have access to sustainable clean energy

Unless all nations of the world are free from fossil-fuel

dependency, the 21st century will be plagued by energy wars, economic chaos, social unrest, and, probably, anarchy.

## Our Vision—Global clean energy abundance through U.S. leadership

Consuming nearly 25% of global oil production as the world's sole superpower, the U.S. has the unique ability and, in truth, the responsibility to establish a credible model for transforming the planetary fuel system. It is in our vital interest to assist the emerging powers of China and India, as well as all regions of the globe, in achieving a clean and abundant energy future.

## Our Mission—Free the U.S. from Middle Eastern oil by 2015

By freeing itself from dependency on Middle Eastern oil, the U.S. will liberate itself economically, politically, and militarily from this volatile region of the world, while at the same time establishing the foundation and momentum for eventually eliminating the use of all imported oil and, ultimately, the use of all oil.

## Declaration of Energy Independence from Middle Eastern Oil—Congress should establish a national mandate to save at least 5 MBD of oil a day by 2015.

The strategies and policies needed to implement this mandate should be guided by three principles.

*First*, the strategies and policies should be implemented using only currently available technologies that can make a significant impact on oil savings within the next decade, on the order of saving at least 100,000 barrels of oil per day (i.e., 0.1 MBD) out of the total of the 5 MBD goal of the Plan.

*Second*, they should at least be neutral with respect to $CO_2$ emissions, to the extent that they will not release any additional greenhouse gases in the form of carbon dioxide into the atmosphere and preferably should lead to reductions in $CO_2$.

*Third*, over time, they should be revenue-neutral from the government expense side, in that they are expected to pay for themselves. That is, they should require no new taxes.

Guided by these principles, the U.S. could save an average of 5 MBD. Through robust efficiency gains and alternative fuels in the transportation sector, U.S. oil consumption can be reduced as broadly summarized below, by at least 20% of projected 2015 consumption of 25 MBD (see Figure 3).

### Figure 3. Prometheus Plan, Oil Use and Projected Oil Savings, 2015[4]

|  | 2005 | 2015 |
|---|---|---|
| U.S. Oil Use—Assumes Current Status Quo | | |
| - Total Oil Use (rounded to nearest MBD) | 20 / 100% | 25 / 100% |
| - Transportation sector | 14 / 68% | 18 / 70% |
| - Imports—from all sources | 10 / 50% | 15 / 60% |
| - Imports—from Middle East (Persian Gulf) | 2.5 / 13% | 4.5 / 18%* |
| Prometheus Plan Oil Savings | | 5 / 20% |

*This 4.5 MBD would be completely replaced by the Prometheus Plan oil savings

As Figure 3 shows, oil savings practices—including conservation, efficiency, and fossil-fuel replacement—will be most effective in the transportation sector, but will also have benefits in the industrial, aviation, and residential sectors of the economy.

In the transportation sector, state and federal policies should increase the fuel efficiency of new vehicles by raising the vehicle fleet or corporate average fuel ecomony (CAFE) standards, and should dramatically favor the production of flexible-fuel vehicles that can run on gasoline or ethanol, thereby increasing the number of such vehicles on the roads. Additional vehicle policies should accelerate the use of fuel-efficient replacement tires, motor oils, and heavy-duty trucks.

On the supply side, policies should encourage the rapid expansion of the domestic and international biofuels industry, especially the production of non-fossil fuels such as ethanol and biodiesel.

Figure 4 profiles each oil-saving measure to reduce oil consumption by 2015 by the quantities indicated.

**Figure 4.** Prometheus Plan Matrix: U.S. Oil Savings by 2015[5]

| Current Technology Oil Savings in Millions of Barrels of Oil Per Day (MBD) | |
|---|---|
| **Oil Savings Measures** | **MBD** |
| Raise fuel efficiency in new passenger vehicles through incentives and standards to achieve fleet average of 40 mpg by 2015 | 1.6 |
| Accelerate oil savings in motor vehicles through: | |
|    • Fuel-efficient replacement tires and motor oil | 0.5 |
|    • Efficiency improvements in heavy-duty trucks | 1.0 |
| Accelerate oil savings in industrial, aviation, and residential sectors | 0.3 |
| Accelerate growth of biofuels industry through expansion and standards for: | |
|    • Ethanol, mainly E85 from corn and sugar feedstocks | 1.4 |
|    • Biodiesel, mainly B20 from vegetable oil feedstocks | 0.2 |
| **Total oil saved by 2015:** | **5.0** |

## OIL SAVINGS AS A CONSEQUENCE OF GASOLINE SAVINGS

In the U.S. refinery system, a 42-gallon barrel of crude oil is processed to yield an average of 19.7 gallons of gasoline, among the other products into which the petroleum is converted. The other products in the average U.S. product slate are shown in Figure 5. The total number of product-gallons (44.77) is slightly more than the initial 42 barrels of crude oil because during the refining process, crude oil molecules are structurally rearranged, and hydrogen is added to some of them. As a result, the density of the final product mix is slightly lower than the initial crude oil feedstock.

## Figure 5. Petroleum Products Yielded from One Barrel of Crude, 2004

| Product | Gallons |
|---|---|
| Finished Motor Gasoline (87 Octane) | 19.65 |
| Distillate Fuel Oil | 10.03 |
| Jet Fuel | 4.07 |
| Residual Fuel Oil | 1.72 |
| Still Gas | 1.85 |
| Petroleum Coke | 2.18 |
| Liquefied Refinery Gas | 1.68 |
| Asphalt and Road Oil | 1.34 |
| Naphtha for Petrochemical Feedstock | 0.67 |
| Other Oils for Petrochemical Feedstock | 0.55 |
| Lubricants | 0.46 |
| Special Naphtha | 0.13 |
| Kerosene | 0.17 |
| Miscellaneous Products | 0.17 |
| Finished Aviation Gasoline | 0.04 |
| Waxes | 0.04 |
| **Total** | **44.77** |

Source: U.S. Energy Information Administration, Energy Information Sheets, 2005

If the U.S. were to replace 5 MBD of gasoline production with an alternate fuel such as ethanol, and assuming that the requirements for other crude-oil-derived products remain the same, U.S. refiners would be converting 5 MBD less crude oil to meet overall market demand. That is to say that for every barrel of gasoline replaced by ethanol, a barrel of crude oil would be saved. This would be accomplished by adjusting variables of the conversion process, such as temperature, pressure, reactor contact-time, and catalyst type. The primary conversion processes are cat-cracking, hydrocracking, alkylation, isomerization, hydrogenation, and reforming, and they are well-developed catalytic technologies. With proper modification of process variables and catalyst specifications, the reaction selectivity could be tuned to produce the required slate of other products and, as in our example, save 5 MBD of gasoline production.

It is worth noting that the combination of jet fuel and distillate fuel oil makes up another 14.1 gallons, or 32% of the product barrel. The largest part of this product fraction is diesel fuel. Since distillate fuel oil makes up a significant fraction of the crude oil barrel, by replacing this fraction initially with biodiesel fuels and subsequently with pure vegetable oil, there is great potential to reduce U.S. crude oil demand much further than the reduction that will come from the displacement of gasoline by ethanol. Therefore, we believe that a 5 MBD savings in crude oil is readily achievable by 2015. Most probably, we can exceed that goal. And, once the momentum has begun to swing in the favor of renewables vs. oil, in our opinion, hundreds of thousands of additional barrels will be saved daily.

## OUR PROMETHEUS PLAN GOALS

- **Reduce oil use by 5 MBD by 2015.**

  Free the U.S. from dependence on Middle Eastern oil.

- **Cut transportation sector greenhouse gas emissions by 20% by 2015.**

  Cuts will come through transportation fuel efficiency and use of nonfossil fuels.

- **Increase fuel efficiency standards, saving 1.6 MBD by 2015.**

  Significantly improve average new passenger vehicle fuel economy standards to 40 mpg.

- **Make a rapid transition to biofuels, saving 1.6 MBD by 2015.**

  Use ethanol for flex-fuel vehicles, and biodiesel or pure vegetable oil for heavy-duty trucks.

- **Produce non-fossil fuels @ $1.50 per gallon (in constant dollars) by 2015.**

  Current price of Brazilian sugar-based ethanol delivered FOB New York is only $1.00.

- **Achieve massive implementation of 20% Renewable Energy Standard.**

  Standard will change residential, commercial, and industrial energy use.

- **Stimulate agriculture and biofuels business sectors.**

  Create billions in biofuels investments and new farm revenues.

- **Save or create nearly 2 million jobs by 2015.**

  Save or create one million rural jobs and one million auto and transport jobs.

- **Produce and sell at least 1 million hybrid electric vehicles a year by 2015.**

  Ramp up to annual sales of at least 1 million hybrid and plug-in hybrid electric vehicles.

- **Produce and sell at least 100,000 hydrogen fuel cell vehicles a year by 2015.**

  Create a platform for the long-term phase-in of a hydrogen economy.

## OUR STRATEGY

Virtually everyone without a direct financial interest in the current system agrees with our beliefs, our vision, and our mission. Almost everyone—with the exception of certain hydrocarbon fuels companies and Saudi sheikhs—agrees with our goals. The big challenge in everyone's mind is *how* to achieve these goals based on beliefs, vision, and mission.

This challenge calls for the specific strategies that form the heart of the Prometheus Plan. They are not contingent upon new scientific breakthroughs such as super-efficient solar cells or nuclear fusion, or upon new energy infrastructure such as a hydrogen distribution system, or an "all-electric world." They offer a realistic roadmap for achieving major oil savings without relying on unproven assumptions about the speed of commercialization of cellulosic ethanol or about the rate of market penetration by promising technological innovations in automobile engines and designs, such as hybrids, plug-in hybrids, fuel cell cars, or super-lightweight, advanced materials vehicles (see Figure 6). We have even left out the rapidly developing (and highly economical) technologies that could be quickly deployed to decrease even further our use of fossil fuels, beyond what the Prometheus Plan stipulates. These emerging, highly economical technologies include potentially dramatic efficiency increases in solar, existing wind technology, ocean thermal energy conversion, wave energy technology, tidal energy, ocean current energy technology, and a host of other promising technologies just now emerging on the scene that are price-competitive with oil at $65 per barrel or less. The Prometheus Plan deals *only* with scalable, proven, financially positive *existing* technologies primarily in the transportation sector.

We summarize strategies for the following three areas here and discuss them in depth in Chapters 9, 10, and 11: (1) transportation fuels, which represent about 70% of U.S. oil use; (2) biofuels and a renewable energy-fed electric grid; and (3) a phased-in hydrogen economy as a carbon-free fuel system.

# Focus on Transportation Fuels— 70% of U.S. Oil Use

We must improve automobile and truck efficiency through the use of conventional technologies; increase the number of flex-fuel vehicles manufactured; accelerate the deployment of plug-in hybrid electric vehicles; and accelerate the deployment of combined flex-fuel/plug-in hybrid electric vehicles.

## Automobile and Truck Efficiency Is Key

According to most analyses, today's U.S. imports of about 10 MBD are projected to rise to about 15 MBD in 2015 and 21 MBD in 2025. As noted before, if the average combined fleet fuel efficiency of new passenger vehicles (cars and light trucks) were increased in stages from the current figure of 24.4 mpg to 40 mpg by 2015, U.S. oil imports would drop by 1.6 MBD. Likewise, a package of oil savings policies for replacement of tires, use of lower-friction motor oil, and the incorporation of alternative-fuel heavy-duty trucks (over 8,500 pounds) into the national fleet would save an additional 1.5 MBD.

As analyzed in a Natural Resources Defense Council report entitled *Securing America: Solving Our Oil Dependence by Innovation,* these auto efficiencies can be achieved through the application of conventional technologies such as flexible-fuel vehicles (FFV) and fuel-efficient vehicles (FEV) that combine vehicle load reduction, efficient engines and transmissions, and integrated starter generators beginning in the short term (2005-2010). This Defense Council study, including supporting documentation from the National Academies of Science, the Union of Concerned Scientists, and the American Council for an Energy Efficient Economy, provides key technical information for potential auto efficiencies included in the Prometheus Plan.[7]

While the goal of saving 5 MBD can be fully realized using only *conventional technologies,* the speed of reaching this goal within 10 years (while at the same time establishing the platform to go "Beyond Prometheus" and cut U.S. oil use in half by 2025) could be dramatically affected by the rapid development and commercialization of a number of *advanced technologies*. In the mid-term (2010-2015), these include hybrid electric vehicles (HEV) and advanced plug-in hybrids (PHEV), and in the long term (2015-2025), these include super-light advanced materials vehicles (AMV), fuel cell vehicles (FCV), and/or direct hydrogen-powered vehicles. See Figure 6.

## Figure 6. The Evolving Automobile

| Vehicle Type<br>• *Market penetration phase* | Vehicle Description |
|---|---|
| **Internal Combustion Vehicle (ICV)**<br>• *mass distribution* | Internal combustion engines burn gasoline with an electric spark. A series of cylinders operating in succession keep the crankshaft turning. |
| **Diesel Combustion Vehicle (DCV)**<br>• *mass distribution* | Similar to ICV, but here the compression sufficiently heats the air to ignite diesel fuel. Engines can run on diesel or biodiesel fuels without modification or pure vegetable oil with only minor modification. |
| **Fuel-Efficient Vehicle (FEV)**<br>• *initial distribution* | ICV with a number of conventional technologies for optimizing fuel efficiency: vehicle load reduction and improved engines, transmissions, and starters. |
| **Hybrid Electric Vehicle (HEV)**<br>• *initial distribution* | Uses both conventional ICV and electric motors that run on a charge drawn from engine or braking. Plug-in HEVs can be charged off regular power grid. |
| **Fuel Cell Vehicle (FCV)**<br>• *R&D phase* | FCVs combine hydrogen and oxygen on a catalyst to generate electric power to turn motor. Single fuel cells are combined into stacks to provide needed power. |
| **Advanced Materials Vehicle (AMV)/HEV**<br>• *R&D phase* | Super-lightweight, super-efficient HEV vehicles made with advanced composite materials. Designs could theoretically raise fuel efficiency to 90 mpg. |

Note: "Automobile" refers to all passenger vehicles, including cars and lightweight trucks (vans, SUVs, pickup trucks). A decrease in the percentage of SUVs and light trucks sold as a percentage of total sales will automatically increase fleet efficiency

In 2005, about 200,000 hybrid electric vehicles were sold in the U.S., and the conventional wisdom is that this sales number could reach 1 million HEVs annually by 2015, representing some 6% of new vehicles sales. We consider this assumption to be very conservative. Under the oil price increase scenarios described in this book, it is entirely conceivable that the vast majority of new vehicles sold in 10 years would be hybrid electric vehicles and plug-in hybrid electric vehicles, or some even more fuel-efficient technology.

## FLEXIBLE-FUEL VEHICLES

Flexible-fuel vehicles are designed to run on alcohol fuels (such as ethanol) or gasoline or any mixture of the two. Today, more than 5 million flexible-fuel vehicles that can run on E85 (a blend of 85% ethanol and 15% gasoline) are on the road. The E85-ready vehicles have been manufactured in the U.S. by Chevrolet, Chrysler, Dodge, Ford, GMC, Isuzu, Mazda, and Mercury. Currently, General Motors and Ford alone plan to manufacture some 800,000 new flexible-fuel vehicles in 2006, and that number should grow annually. Chrysler has announced that one-fourth of its new cars will be flexible-fuel vehicles by the 2007 model year.

The technological differentiation of flexible-fuel vehicles lies in the combination of a flexible-fuel vehicle's unique control chip plus non-corrosive fuel lines to accommodate the alcohol fuels. *The marginal cost associated with such flexible-fuel vehicle-related modifications is currently less than $200 per new vehicle.* Flexible-fuel vehicles in Brazil are currently manufactured at the same price as standard cars.

In Brazil, which revitalized its government-sponsored sugar cane-to-ethanol program some 15 years ago, flexible-fuel vehicles now account for 70% of all new car sales and 40% of the light-fuels market. Texaco, Shell, Exxon, and other oil companies are selling ethanol at their fueling stations in Brazil. They have fully hopped on the bandwagon. The transition from fossil fuels for transportation has been so successful that President Lula recently announced Brazil, the world's fifth-largest country, has achieved independence from foreign oil.

## Plug-in Hybrid Electric Vehicles

As discussed in Chapter 9, advanced technology plug-in hybrid electric vehicles will be able to get over 100 mpg of fuel. Like standard hybrids, they are powered by both liquid fuels and electricity. Because plug-in hybrid electric vehicles also have fuel tanks and internal combustion engines onboard, they can travel much further than electric-only cars that run exclusively on batteries. Given that more than half of the passenger vehicles on the road today are used for trips of only 20 miles a day or less, a plug-in with a 20-mile-range battery could reduce average fuel consumption by 85%.

## Combined Flexible-Fuel, Plug-in Hybrid Electric Vehicles

As discussed in Chapter 9, combining these two technologies produces vehicles that can be powered by any blend of alcohol fuels, gasoline, and electricity, *dramatically reducing oil consumption in the transportation sector.*

Some distinguished environmental organizations, including the Earth Policy Institute founded by World Business Academy Fellow Lester Brown, have projected:

> If we add to the gas-electric hybrid a plug-in capacity and a second battery to increase its electricity storage capacity, motorists could then do their commuting, shopping, and other short-distance travel largely with electricity, saving gasoline for the occasional long trip. This could lop another 20% off gasoline use in addition to the initial 50% cut from shifting to gas-electric hybrids, for a total reduction of 70%.[8]

Since we do not believe it practically or economically feasible to convert the *entire* U.S. fleet of some 200 million passenger vehicles to hybrids and plug-in hybrids by 2015, we have not included savings from these technologies in the Prometheus Plan strategy. However, we already are seeing surging sales of hybrids, and we expect that sales will exponentially increase over the next years. Hybrid sales will of themselves add savings of oil incremental to what the Prometheus

Plan calls for. These dramatic fuel efficiency savings indicate what is possible *Beyond Prometheus*—if we earnestly start now.

## REPLACE OIL WITH BIOFUELS AND A RENEWABLE ENERGY-FED ELECTRIC GRID.

We must create an unprecedented growth in world biofuels by increasing domestic and international production of ethanol and biodiesel; accelerate commercialization of cellulosic ethanol; and use a renewable energy-fed electric grid to provide carbon-free fuel for hybrids.

## UNPRECEDENTED GROWTH IN WORLD BIOFUELS

As Figure 4 shows, the Prometheus Plan will save an estimated 1.6 MBD by displacing oil with biofuels, primarily 1.4 MBD from ethanol for passenger vehicles and 0.2 MBD from biodiesel or pure vegetable oil for heavy-duty trucks. It is an ironic fact that when Rudolf Diesel designed the engine that bears his name, he expected it would run on vegetable oil. Things don't always work out as we plan, but they tend to come around: in 2005 the American Truckers Association endorsed the use of blended biodiesel fuel and supported federal tax incentives to boost its output. Entrepreneurs are also experimenting with pure vegetable oil in diesel motors.

At the time of a 2006 report on *Biofuels for Transportation* by the Worldwatch Institute, world biofuels production had already passed 670,000 barrels per day (or 0.7 MBD).[9] Worldwide ethanol production more than doubled between 2000 and 2005, while production of biodiesel quadrupled. Together, Brazil and the U.S. account for more than 90% of the world's fuel ethanol production. U.S. and Brazil alone will be adding more than 2 billion gallons of annual ethanol production in 2007.

## ETHANOL—CORN, SUGAR, AND CELLULOSIC FEEDSTOCKS

Ethanol (also known as grain alcohol or ethyl alcohol) is currently produced in the U.S. from corn. Corn is the least desirable feedstock for ethanol because of its relatively low net energy yield of 1.5 (that means 1.5 British Thermal Units (BTUs) out for every BTU in), compared to a higher net energy yield of 8.3 in Brazil, where ethanol is manufactured from sugar cane at the worldwide low production cost of $0.81 per gallon.[10]

According to data released by the Energy Information Administration and the Renewable Fuels Association, production of ethanol in 2006 reached 4.86 billion gallons, a 25% increase over 2005 levels. Production has been growing at that rate for several years. As of early 2007, the U.S. ethanol industry included 117 ethanol refineries nationwide with an annual production capacity of over 6.2 billion gallons. There are 78 ethanol refineries and seven expansions under construction, and dozens in the planning stage. Further dramatic increases in domestic production of corn ethanol can be achieved by 2015, while rapidly building demand for ethanol from sugar cane and sugar beets, produced in both domestic and international markets.

Advanced technology has also been developed to make ethanol from a wider variety of cellulosic feedstocks, including corn stalks and residues, grain straw, municipal wastes, and switchgrass, all of which have the potential for high fuel yields. Although most of the pieces are in place, it may take from five to 10 years to fully commercialize ethanol from cellulosic feedstocks in order to achieve production levels of at least 1 billion gallons annually. *Advanced ethanol production techniques can generate clean biofuels for a fraction of the cost of corn ethanol,* and can dramatically reduce $CO_2$ emissions because the feedstock is not burned in the cellulosic process as it is in sugar cane ethanol production. *These techniques also will end ethanol producers' competition for foodstocks* such as corn and soybeans.

The U.S. will, for political reasons, undoubtedly continue to expand corn-based ethanol production. More important, it should immediately provide major support for the rapid development of domestic and international sugar-based ethanol production and take a fast-track approach to the commercialization of cellulosic-based ethanol.

## Biodiesel from Vegetable Oils

Similarly, biodiesel fuels made from vegetable oils such as soybeans and palm oil can replace diesel fuel in heavy-duty trucks and engines, while enhancing performance and lowering fuel costs. Europe has already established a robust market for biodiesel vehicles. The U.S. should move quickly to promote the growth of domestic and international biodiesel markets.

## Electricity as Fuel

About 2% of U.S. electricity is generated from oil (although a larger amount *is* generated from natural gas), so using existing sources of electricity together with significant new renewable sources as a transportation "fuel" would greatly reduce dependence on imported petroleum. Plug-in hybrid vehicles could be charged overnight in home garages *at cheaper off-peak rates, ultimately equivalent to 50-cent-per-gallon gasoline, because all utilities have significant excess capacity during the nighttime hours.*

In order to realize the benefits of renewable sources of electricity, state utility regulators will have to provide for variable electricity pricing, reverse metering, and net metering, so that distributed power generators will be able to sell electricity back into the grid at equitable rates.

The Electric Power Research Institute estimates that up to 30% market penetration for plug-in hybrid vehicles with a 20-mile electric range could be achieved *without the need to install additional electrical generating capacity.* The accelerated adoption of a competitive wind-powered electric grid interface and of distributed-generation technologies will increase the level of zero-carbon fuels available to power hybrids.

## Phase-in Hydrogen Economy as a Carbon-Free Fuel System

The only way we can eliminate our dependence on fossil fuels is by phasing in a hydrogen economy as rapidly as possible.

The hydrogen fuel cell will be the cornerstone of a carbon-free fuel system for stationery and vehicular power. Initially, we will produce hydrogen from natural gas, but ultimately we will produce it from water. Localized generation, distribution, and use of hydrogen will reduce major capital investments.

## FUEL CELL VEHICLE

Currently, some energy experts and environmentalists are willing to accept continued burning of some fossil fuels, including "clean coal." There is no such thing! "Clean coal" technology promises that the $CO_2$ that would otherwise escape into the atmosphere will be captured in the hope that it can be sequestered indefinitely below ground. Such technology does not yet exist. Even if it were invented and proved successful, as noted in an earlier chapter, if that $CO_2$ were to "burp" into the atmosphere in subsequent generations, it would set the stage for an increasingly hot global climate.

Similarly, a very few nuclear scientists, who happen usually to enjoy lavish financing from the industry they serve, are calling for the construction of new "cheaper, safer" nuclear plants as a possible solution for the energy crisis. The mistake of building more nuclear power plants, which will enrich a tiny handful of companies at the expense of the rest of society, is more fully discussed in Chapter 5. For our purposes here, all that we need to observe is that "clean coal" and "cheap nuclear power" are expensive oxymorons with less energy potential than is generally understood. Both carry extraordinary social costs that should mark them, when those external costs are fully loaded into the equation, as unacceptable forms of energy.

Continuing down this path will create additional economic, environmental, security, and safety problems. *Every incremental MW of fossil fuel and nuclear energy will displace a cheaper and cleaner MW from efficiency savings and renewable energy.*

It is essential that we get entirely off oil as soon as possible. The only viable option for moving away from fossil fuels and toward zero-emission vehicles is to phase-in the hydrogen economy as rapidly as possible. Given our projections that about 100,000 hydrogen fuel cell vehicles will be sold by 2015, representing an oil savings of less than 0.1 MBD, we have not included hydrogen-powered vehicles in our Prometheus Plan matrix of oil savings that are technologically achievable by 2015. Our decision to exclude them does not stem from our lack of confidence in hydrogen vehicles. To the contrary, we are big believers that direct hydrogen and fuel cell hydrogen energy plants in cars and at stationary locations will be major contributors to our ability to reduce oil consumption. Our decision *not* to include them stems solely from our decision to rigorously avoid pinning our Prometheus Plan on any technology that is not commercially available *today*. BMW's recent announcement that a *direct hydrogen flex vehicle* will be available *as a production model* by late in the 2007 model year provides evidence that hydrogen-related technologies, like cellulosic biofuels, will be major contributors to our "get-off-oil-strategy" well before 2015.

## DISTRIBUTED HYDROGEN FUEL CELLS

Over the long term, the commercialization of *distributed* hydrogen fuel cells for mobile vehicles and stationary power units in homes and businesses will ultimately replace the need to build large, centralized, baseload, capital-intensive, fossil-fuel and nuclear power plants. The first mobile units will likely run on hydrogen extracted from natural gas (the process now used by Honda at its hydrogen refueling station in southern California and by other companies in other locations), which generates 70% less $CO_2$ than conventional internal combustion vehicles. By 2012, stationary fuel cells will be able to directly re-charge plug-in hybrids, further reducing carbon emissions into the atmosphere. At this point, the car will become a portable energy generator that can be driven during the day and plugged in as a power generation source for the home at night (see Chapter 12).

## TOWARD AN OIL-FREE ECONOMY

The Prometheus Plan will also accelerate the implementation timetable for the recommendations envisioned by the independent studies cited above in Figures 1 and 2, achieving an economy that is oil import-free and ultimately oil-free. For example, in *Winning the Oil Endgame*, Amory Lovins and his associates at the Rocky Mountain Institute mapped out integrated and phased goals of reducing oil imports by half by 2025; replacing all imports by 2040; and creating an oil-free economy by 2050.[11]

Similarly, in *A Strategy: Moving America Away from Oil* (2003), the Arlington Institute concludes, "In sum, it looks like the world—led by the U.S.—is moving toward the day when hydrogen will replace oil as the major source of energy for transportation. . . . What does the world of transportation look like in, say, 2050? It's our guess that it's an all-electric world."[12]

It is noteworthy that the Rocky Mountain Institute study was co-funded by the Pentagon and that the Arlington Institute project was commissioned by the Office of the Secretary of Defense-Net Assessment in the Department of Defense. This military sponsorship underscores the growing consensus that the energy crisis is a priority national security issue. It also highlights the multiple roles of the Pentagon in the energy arena: as a major consumer of petroleum products; as an early adopter and purchaser of innovative fuel systems and transport technologies; and as the agency responsible for the defense of all foreign and oil production, refining, and transportation facilities (particularly in the Middle East).

## BEYOND THE PROMETHEUS PLAN

The primary goal of the Prometheus Plan is to achieve energy independence from Middle Eastern oil in 10 years. However, it is also patently clear that ultimately the U.S. needs to move away from fossil fuels and toward a hydrogen economy—especially if increases in the price of oil and trends in climate change continue.

Obviously, significant technological and infrastructural challenges still need to be resolved before this transition can take place. Primary challenges are the large-scale production and storage of hydrogen, the high cost of fuel cells, and a national infrastructure for the hydrogen economy. While the goal of the Prometheus Plan is to use conventional technologies to replace oil in the short and

> *"By following this roadmap, the U.S. would set the stage by 2025 for the checkmate move in the Oil Endgame—the optional but advantageous displacement of oil as a direct fuel."*
> — AMORY LOVINS, *WINNING THE OIL ENDGAME*, 2005

medium term, the longer-term objective of a Beyond Prometheus Strategy is to phase-in and facilitate the transition between now and 2015 to a longer-term hydrogen future.

To reach these ambitious goals, Figure 7 outlines a three-stage *"pedal-to-the metal"* Beyond Prometheus Strategy. Within this strategy the three main objectives are the following:

- First, vast improvements in automobile efficiency through fuel-efficient and flexible-fuel vehicles in the short term, in hybrids and plug-in hybrids in the mid-term (2010-2015), and in advanced materials plug-in hybrids and fuel cell vehicles in the long term (2015-2025 and beyond).

- Second, acceleration of the domestic and international biofuels industry, initially through corn-based and sugar-based ethanol (sugar cane and sugar beets) in the short term, and ultimately through cellulosic biomass feedstocks and other biofuels, which will not compete with food or animal feed supplies, in the long term.

- Third, rapid phase-in and long-term transition to advanced materials, hydrogen fuel cell vehicles, which use as feedstocks, cellulosic ethanol and/or hydrogen, the latter generated from distributed "trickle-charge" electrolysis plants.

All of the fundamental technologies required for this strategy are available today, *and no theoretical scientific breakthroughs are needed* to eventually achieve mass distribution and commercialization. By adopting this Beyond Prometheus Strategy, America could turn the dream of an oil-free future into a reality sooner than all but the most well-informed observers realize.

## Figure 7. Beyond Prometheus Strategy:
## Short-Term, Mid-Term, and Long-Term[13]

| Time Frame | Technology | Fuel | Efficiency | Policy Steps |
|---|---|---|---|---|
| **Short -Term** **2005-2010** | All new vehicles are **FEV + Flexible-Fuel Vehicle** by 2010 | Gasoline or ethanol from mainly corn and some sugar-based feedstocks. | **ICV + Flexible-Fuel Vehicle,** **FEV + Flexible-Fuel Vehicle,** **HEV + Flexible-Fuel Vehicle** | - Major consumer tax incentives<br>- Tax penalties for non-**HEV/ Flexible-Fuel Vehicle**<br>- Excess oil company profit tax<br>- Govt. purchase of **FEV/Flexible-Fuel Vehicle/ HEV** |
| **Mid-Term** **2010-2015** | All new vehicles are **Flexible-Fuel Vehicle + HEV** or **PHEV** by 2015 | Gasoline or ethanol from corn and sugar. Cellulosic ethanol enters market. | **HEVs / PHEVs**; and **AMV** designs enter market | - R&D for cellulosic ethanol<br>- E85 infrastructure support<br>- R&D for **Flexible-Fuel Vehicle/ PHEV, AMV**, and **FCV** |
| **Long-Term** **2015-2025** **and Beyond** | **FCV** and **FCV/ PHEV** go mainstream | Ethanol, methanol, other alcohol fuels (e.g., bio-butanol) and hydro-gen for fuel cells. | **PHEV + AMV + FCV** | - Incentives for mobile and stationary distributed-fuel cell systems.<br>- Fuel cell infrastructure |

Legend: **ICV** = Internal Combustion Vehicle; Flexible-Fuel Vehicle = Flexible-Fuel Vehicle; **FEV** = Fuel-Efficient Vehicle; **HEV** = Hybrid Electric Vehicle; **PHEV** = Plug-In Hybrid Electric Vehicle; **FCV** = Fuel Cell Vehicle; and **AMV** = Advanced Materials Vehicle. (For vehicle descriptions, see Figure 6 above.)
Note: Although heavy-truck engines and other motors will burn biodiesel fuel, starting in the short term, this type of vehicle technology and fuel was not included here to enhance the simplicity and clarity of this figure.

> *"I always say to myself: What is the most important thing we can think about at this extraordinary moment?"*
>
> — R. BUCKMINSTER FULLER,
> FUTURIST AND INVENTOR OF THE 1930s DYMAXION CAR

## INVESTING IN ENERGY ABUNDANCE

Already, investors and governments around the world are putting their money behind various advanced technologies (mentioned earlier in this chapter) that are beyond the Prometheus Plan. Here are but a few examples.

- A wave-energy electric farm is about to go into service on the coast of Portugal.

- Flexible thin-film solar cells are under full-scale production in California. They could someday be incorporated into auto bodies to power cars.

- Iceland intends to obviate all fossil fuels within 30 years by producing hydrogen from water power and geothermal reserves. Sweden plans to be independent of oil by 2020.

- The Netherlands has a 50kw test plant using "blue energy," which exploits the difference in salt concentrations of fresh and salt water through a process called reverse electro-dialysis.

- China is developing a tidal power farm near the mouth of the Yalu River.

- An Israeli company is experimenting with the creation of biodiesel from algae, using $CO_2$ from factories to feed the photosynthesis. The algae also give off pure oxygen after absorbing the $CO_2$.

Hawaii is currently considering a proposal to use its excess geothermal energy during non-peak hours to create hydrogen. State Representative Mina Morita, chair of the Energy and Environmental Protection Committee, laid out a clear vision six years ago:

In the year 2020, Hawaii and her sister Pacific Islands are powerful world exporters of energy known as HOPEC, Hydrogen of Pacific Exporting Communities, controlling the hydrogen commodity trading prices as active participants in a hydrogen economy based on renewable resources such as solar, geothermal, wave, and wind. Biomass and stored hydrogen aid in making 100% uninterruptible power generation, attracting information technology firms to these Pacific islands because of their quality of life.[14]

Since that time, Hawaii has launched and is exploring a number of major hydrogen initiatives aimed at using the islands' abundant natural resources to create hydrogen to replace most petroleum imports.

Although the Prometheus Plan deals with the general cost and benefits associated with achieving freedom from Middle Eastern oil imports, the development of a *precise* projection of the costs and benefits of the Prometheus Plan over each of the next 10 years is a series of mathematical computations beyond the scope of this book. Those computations, while complex, can be made. We urge government, private industry, and well-funded private energy laboratories immediately to begin developing those figures. Completing them will take many months because of the complexity of the intertwined variables, all of which must be separately weighted. The key variables—oil prices, renewable costs, the effects of global climate change, and geopolitical tensions—have been shifting quickly even as this book was being written. Even the most simplistic and fundamental assumptions would, therefore, be subject to rapid revision. Only large-scale computing power could handle the process of fully modeling the multiple scenarios for "precise projection" of the costs and benefits.

Fortunately, several robust studies of the economics of energy independence have been conducted, primarily by the National Commission on Energy Policy, the Rocky Mountain Institute, and the Apollo Alliance.[15] All of the studies have concluded that their plans are "revenue-neutral" to the government in the long run. A combination of private investment (equity and debt financing) and government incentives will underwrite all of these initiatives, while generating huge financial benefits that are "revenue-positive" for investors, companies, consumers, and the nation.

In late 2005, Sir Nicholas Stern, former chief economist of the World Bank, was asked by the British government to calculate the economic impact of inaction on the subject of climate change. A year later, he delivered his findings in a 700-page report. Stern warned that the world must *immediately* devote 1% of global GDP—or about $350 billion—to mitigate climate change *now*, or pay a figure 5 to 20 times higher in the future as a price of inaction.[16] The upper figure of $7 trillion would exceed the combined costs of the Great Depression and both World Wars.

When one of the world's leading economists delivers such a report at the request of the Chancellor of the Exchequer, calculations of "expense" vanish as trivialities. Stern believes that the short-term survival of civilization is on the line. In this light, quibbling about the expense of taking action—based on climate change alone—is a foolish distraction from a severe crisis.

The cost of achieving energy independence varies widely depending on the assumptions, goals, and strategies used in each analysis (see Figures 1 and 2). At the low end, the Energy Policy Commission proposes a price tag of $36 billion. At the high end, total projected costs for energy conversion of the U.S. economy range from Rocky Mountain Institute's $180 billion, to the Apollo Alliance's $300 billion (less than half the cost of the War in Iraq, to date).

The U.S. now pays more than $300 billion in one year for imported oil *with zero return* when oil prices spike sharply, as they have since 2004. The oil payments enrich OPEC. They do not build infrastructure or create jobs at home, and so they impoverish us in terms of opportunity cost. For perspective, the Manhattan Project to develop an atomic bomb cost $20 billion in today's dollars, and the Apollo Project to land a man on the moon came in at more than $100 billion.

## Taxes and Incentives

There are three viable alternatives to fund our drive to independence beyond the Prometheus Plan. We must stress that gas taxes or excess profit taxes are not required to fund the Prometheus Plan itself. We bring up the discussion of taxes here solely for the purpose of demonstrating how we believe taxes could be used, if they are chosen as part of the implementation strategy to go *beyond* the Prometheus Plan to energy independence.

First, taxes could be assessed against drivers by taxing the cost of petroleum products. European drivers have for decades paid several dollars more in tax than Americans for the same fuel as part of Europe's decision to fund mass transit and disincentivize large-scale petroleum use. Second, an even more attractive tax would be one based on the excess profits of the oil companies (or any other company that achieves profits that by their very definition are excessive under a free market capitalist system and by their very existence prove that some manipulation of the market has occurred for the benefit of the company or industry achieving those excess profits). No other industry on earth generates the amount of profit that the oil industry has consistently enjoyed since 2000. Most Americans believe the level of profits the oil companies extract is egregious and reminiscent of the Robber Barons of old. Third, financial incentives to stimulate investment in the private sector could serve as an alternative or a supplement to a gas consumption or excess profits tax.

## Gas Tax

Americans use 320,500,000 gallons of gas per day, which, when multiplied by 365 days, equals approximately 117 billion gallons of gas per year. Over three years, a tax of around 50 cents per gallon would generate the $180 billion required for the transition to renewable fuels. In order to remove this burden from lower income families, this could be a sliding tax that is up to 100% recoverable as an income tax deduction, depending on income.

## Excess Profits Tax

According to a United Bank of Switzerland report on *Global OilCo 2005*, the major oil companies will have generated *more than $1 trillion in net cash flow from operations* between 2004 and 2008. These are pure profits, calculated after all other expense items. Expenses are deducted from sales, including petroleum acquisition costs, refining and transportation costs, debt service, exploration, the amortization of all capital expenses, lobbying "expenses" to influence government policies, jet aircraft for executives, lobbyists, and politicians, and excessive executive pay packages (for example, $400 million in compensation to Lee Raymond just in his last year as CEO of Exxon). Realize that the $1 trillion was *left over* after all of the costs, some of them egregiously high, were deducted from income. This spectacular increase in profits can certainly be considered excess profits. A one-time excess profits tax of approximately 20% could generate all of the capital needed for energy independence and still leave $800 billion in profits for the oil companies, which should certainly be considered more than enough!

As Chapter 3 shows, many other oil-producing countries, including Saudi Arabia and other OPEC nations, have increased their national treasuries by participating in oil company profits through a combination of increased royalties and taxes. This has resulted in their collection of up to 50% of the companies' revenue, which is far greater than the 20% excess profits tax proposed here. No single oil company has ever been shut down or forced out of business because of these fiscal policies. To the contrary, the international oil companies are cash-rich. They use this money, among other things, to buy back their own stock and buy political influence.

## Private Sector Investment

A large portion of the investment required to achieve energy independence will be needed for retooling the transportation industry to manufacture energy-efficient vehicles, trucks, and planes, as well as for expanding the capacity of the biofuels industry. Huge amounts of capital also will be required to build new wind farms, employ more photovoltaic cells, and purchase the capital plants necessary to tap the renewable energy sources outlined in this and other chapters of our book. Clearly, significant private equity will be required, which could much more easily be assembled with a package of federal incentives and loan guarantees like those used by many industries in the past, including the oil industry, the nuclear industry, the airline industry, the automotive industry, the interstate highway system, and the builders of virtually all of the transcontinental railways. These investments should provide a handsome return for investors, within reasonable time frames and with large spin-off benefits to customers, companies, and communities.

## The ROI

*How big is the return on investment?* Depending on how the Prometheus Plan strategies are implemented, the benefits will vary. From any perspective, these benefits and financial returns will be spectacular. According to the Rocky Mountain Institute's analysis, investing $180 billion over the next decade to eliminate oil dependence and revitalize strategic industries can save $130 billion gross or $70 billion net *every year* by 2025. This saving, equivalent to a large tax cut, can eliminate the approximately $300 billion that the U.S. now spends on annual oil imports and can be used for reinvestments in ourselves: $40 billion would pay farmers for biofuels, while the rest could be returned to our communities, businesses, and children.

Several million automotive and other transportation equipment jobs now at risk can be saved, and 1 million net new jobs can be added across all sectors. U.S. automotive, trucking, and aircraft production can again lead the world, underpinned by 21st century advanced materials and fuel cell industries.

A more efficient and deployable military can refocus on its core mission—protecting American citizens rather than foreign supply lines—while supporting and deploying the innovations that eliminate oil as the cause of conflict.

Carbon dioxide emissions will shrink by at least one-fifth with no additional cost or effort. The rich-poor divide can be drastically narrowed at home by increased access to affordable personal mobility which will shrink the welfare rolls, and abroad, by leapfrogging over oil-dependent development patterns. The U.S. can treat oil-rich countries the same as countries with no oil. Being no longer suspected of seeking oil in all that it does in the world would help to restore U.S. leadership and clarity of purpose.[17]

It deserves the emphasis of restatement—soundly investing $180 billion over 10 years will achieve the astronomical return of $70 billion net return *every year in perpetuity* and will go far to secure America's future. Best of all, that's based on oil priced at the U.S. Energy Information Administration's estimate of $26 per barrel! With oil already in the $75 range, nearly three times that amount (more than $200 billion) would be returned to the American public each year if the U.S. adopted the Prometheus Plan. With returns like that, the Prometheus Plan would be America's best investment since the Louisiana Purchase in 1803. Back then, President Thomas Jefferson negotiated the acquisition from France of 800,000 square miles of land, stretching from the Mississippi River to the Rocky Mountains, at a cost of $15 million, or 3 cents per acre. No one alive doubts that was a fantastic bargain. Similarly, our grandchildren will look back at funding the Prometheus Plan as an even better investment with even higher financial benefits and one that saved the planet from global climatic destruction.

*So, what's holding us back?*

## PASSION VS. FEAR[18]

Perhaps you are skeptical about the possibility that the U.S. will ever confront the energy and climate crisis and implement a Prometheus Plan. Well, let's remember that Americans have a history of pulling together in times of crisis. In fact, national crises have often brought out the best in us and created some of the defining moments in American history. A few examples:

- Detroit Arsenal Tank Plan (early 1940s)—When World War II erupted in Europe and Nazi Germany roared to early victories through its tank-led *Blitzkrieg* offensives, the U.S. did not have a tank production program. In response to President Roosevelt's mandate, the Detroit Tank Arsenal Plant sprang up seemingly overnight in the winter of 1940-41, quickly matching German tank production. This tank production was one component of Roosevelt's bold plan for the U.S. to turn its vast transportation sector around to rapidly produce 45,000 tanks, 60,000 planes, 20,000 anti-aircraft guns, and 6 million tons of merchant shipping. And we did it!

- Manhattan Project (1940s)—Born out of fear that Nazi Germany was on the verge of making an atomic bomb, the U.S developed and tested nuclear weapons within three years. These devices were instrumental to victory in World War II.

- Marshall Plan (1940s-1950s)—In order to create a bulwark against Soviet expansion, the Marshall Plan, officially known as the European Recovery Program, was established in 1947 to rebuild a war-tattered Western Europe after World War II. The plan clearly created the greatest wave of wealth for the U.S. in its entire history *and* succeeded in turning our two greatest enemies (Germany and Japan) into our two closest allies.

- Apollo Project (1960s)—In response to the Soviet launch of its Sputnik spacecraft, President Kennedy declared in 1961 that our goal was "landing a man on the moon and returning him safely to earth" before the decade was out. Project Apollo was a series of manned spaceflight missions undertaken to achieve that goal, which was accomplished with the Apollo 11 mission on July 20, 1969, when astronaut Neil Armstrong proclaimed, "That's one small step for a man, one giant leap for mankind."

In evaluating the Prometheus Plan, it is instructive to recall that reasonable skepticism about the technical possibility of manned flight to the moon surrounded the Apollo Lunar Project. When Kennedy first announced the project, America was not even capable of constructing a dependable missile system, and many of the mission-critical technologies had to be developed from scratch. No man had ever survived in space—spacesuits didn't even exist— and yet Kennedy promised to land men safely on the moon and return them safely. Technologies that no one had ever attempted to construct had to be invented and are still with us today. The technical challenges were enormous and not fully understood. In most critical areas, we were totally devoid of prior experience. In contrast, the Prometheus Plan is based on verification that it is possible to achieve energy independence from Middle Eastern oil in 10 years *using conventional technologies*, without relying on new scientific or R&D breakthroughs, and best of all, it can be done right here on earth.

Obviously, these ambitious and expensive mega-projects were inspired by the primal fear of war—World War II with Germany and Japan and the Cold War with the former Soviet Union. In our view, we are at war again, facing what some have called an "incipient national security crisis" on two fronts. On the home front, our enemies are our complaisance and the purely profit-driven motivations of overly-selfish, powerful economic forces. Together, those influences keep us addicted to oil abroad. Internationally, we are engaged in a war over access to resources, because oil, America's most vital resource, is under siege or controlled by insurgents, terrorists, and hostile producers in the Middle East. Most recently, our emerging rivals for this resource, China and India, are striking deals for oil, and the U.S. is experiencing competition for energy on a scale never before imagined.

In a major address in March 2006, British Defense Secretary John Reid warned that global climate change and dwindling natural resources are increasing the possibility of violent conflicts over land, water, and energy. Reid's speech, which was delivered at Chatham House (Britain's equivalent of the Council on Foreign Relations), echoed the warnings of an earlier report, "An Abrupt Climate Change Scenario and Its Implications for United States Security," prepared for the U.S. Department of Defense.

In preparing for the coming resource wars of the 21st century, we should follow the lead of the late Caspar Weinberger, who served as Secretary of Defense under Ronald Reagan during the 1980s. Weinberger was guided by the ancient Roman wisdom: *Igitur qui desiderat pacem, praeparet bellum.* If you wish for peace, prepare for war. The best way to "prepare for war" is to eliminate the need for scarce resource that would cause us to go to war in the first place. Apart from the wars in Afghanistan and Iraq, the U.S. spends $50 billion a year maintaining a permanent military force in the Middle East. Clearly, that military force is not there to guard the sand. It's there at least in part to guard the oil and to be ready for war should anyone threaten our oil umbilical cord. By cutting our need for this supply of oil, we can reduce the risk of war over oil. This is preferable in all ways to the current doctrine of preemptive war over oil ("defend the supply at any cost"). The Prometheus Plan provides the methodologies necessary to pre-empt future energy wars over scarce fossil fuels by making petroleum less essential.

In reality, most people have difficulty in dealing with challenging global issues such as oil depletion, avian flu, terrorism, nuclear proliferation, and climate change. Although convinced of the consequences of not addressing these complex problems, most pay only limited attention to them. Many appear to be in disbelief or denial, as though there will be no ill effects from these problems in their lifetime, if ever. Why?

The most fundamental reason is found in what we would call "The Law of Human Survival." This law asserts that human beings under the stress of rapid technological and social change ignore global challenges, especially if they are perceived to occur in the distant future. This is our "great escape clause." We can handle only so much stress-induced fear. Fear constricts the human psyche. It creates a vortex of emotional pain from which we must escape. Yes, fear has its place. It's perhaps our most ancient instinct and is found in virtually all animal species. It is time, however, for us to collectively accept that fear has no place in our consciousness when it comes to developing creative solutions to intractable problems.

> *"A range of important objectives—economic, geopolitical, environmental —would be served by our embarking on such a path. Of greatest importance, we would be substantially more secure."*
>
> — GEORGE P. SHULTZ, FORMER SECRETARY OF STATE,
> AND JAMES R. WOOLSEY, FORMER DIRECTOR OF CIA

Harvard biologist E. O. Wilson thinks that maybe human beings are hard-wired not to worry about future generations. He points out, "For hundreds of millennia, those who worked for the short-term gain within a small circle of relatives and friends lived longer and left more offspring—even when their collective striving caused their children and empires to crumble around them. The long view that might have saved their distant descendants required a vision and extended altruism instinctively difficult to marshal."[19]

Today, this long view is urgently needed, not only for the survival of distant generations, but to ensure that the world we will grow old in is one in which our children can literally survive. There is no greater indictment of any civilization than that it so abused its natural resources that it left the next generation starving or living in an increasingly hostile world.

In our opinion, there is only one force that can reverse this laissez-faire attitude toward significant global challenges: *the energy of unbridled passion.* This creative force is so powerful that it evaporates fear from the deepest level of the human spirit and can literally change the world. Recall Leonardo da Vinci, Marie Curie, Thomas Edison, Albert Einstein, Jonas Salk, and thousands of other change-makers who left their indelible passionate imprint on our planet.

Passion is also a company's most significant competitive advantage. It has been estimated that most people work at 30% efficiency. This deficit in effectiveness occurs when people feel the fear that accompanies a lack of purpose. We say they are unmotivated. Although motivation comes from within, passion can be catalyzed by creating an environment that addresses a person's need for a greater purpose. This can result in human efficiencies beyond 90%.

What will galvanize a sleeping public into action, before it's too late? With each year of accelerated change and oil reduction from implementing the Prometheus Plan, the public will reap growing rewards as positive reinforcement.

We believe that the halcyon vision of a secure and sustainable future based on energy independence and abundance for humanity can inspire unbridled passion. In his stirring documentary and book, *An Inconvenient Truth*, former Vice President Al Gore framed the spirit we'll need if we are to attain our most vital mission of preserving the planet and achieving energy independence. He said that the nature of the global climate crisis provides us the "privilege" of knowing with complete clarity that our "generational mission" is to ride from the morass of climate suffocation to a better place where we can literally and morally "breathe free." He concluded by saying, "When we rise, we will experience an epiphany as we discover that this crisis is not about politics at all. It is a moral and spiritual challenge."[20]

And we will rise. What America now needs is a Prometheus Plan that will simultaneously serve as a blueprint for energy independence and the abatement of climate change, as well as a model for the world community.

The world desperately needs a few leaders willing, out of a sense of enlightened self-interest, to stimulate the peoples of our planet with the passion necessary to move beyond the current fossil-fuel era and into a robust and sustainable alternate energy economy. We are confident that those leaders are among us, and will come forward.

# Notes and References
# Chapter 8: The Prometheus Plan

1   See www.worldbusiness.org for information about the World Business Academy.

2   For the Union of Concerned Scientists' discussion of the Renewable Energy Standard of 20% by 2020, see Steven Clemmer *et al.*, *Clean Energy Blueprint: A Smarter National Energy Policy for Today and the Future*, Union of Concerned Scientists, American Council for an Energy Efficient Economy, and Tellus Institute, October 2001.

3   The information summarized in A through D is based on the National Commission on Energy Policy, "Summary of Recommendations," *Ending the Energy Stalemate: A Bipartisan Strategy to Meet America's Energy Challenge*, December 2004; Ann Bordetsky *et al.*, *Securing America: Solving Our Oil Dependence Through Innovation* (Washington, DC: Natural Resources Defense Council and Institute for the Analysis of Global Security, February 2005); Amory Lovins *et al.*, *Winning the Oil Endgame: Innovation for Profits, Jobs and Security* (Snowmass, CO: Rocky Mountain Institute, 2005); and Apollo Alliance, *New Energy For America*. It should be noted that the Earth Policy Institute projects that 50% of gasoline use, or 6 MBD, can be saved by 2015 by converting the entire U.S. fleet to gas electric hybrid vehicles, doubling wind capacity annually over the next decade, and developing dual-battery, plug-in hybrids that would be powered by off-peak wind at the cost equivalent of 50 cents/gallon. However, since we do not believe that these objectives are achievable within the next 10 years, we have not included the otherwise excellent proposals of EPI in this summary.

4   The data in Figure 3 are based on Energy Information Administration, *Annual Energy Outlook 2003*, and on the Prometheus Plan as presented in Figure 4. However, when it comes to projecting 20 years into the future, we have rounded the data off as necessary, without sacrificing accuracy, so that comparative figures may be clearly presented and understood. Obviously, long-term projections on energy consumption may change from year to year.

5   Estimated oil savings for fuel efficiency, replacement tires and motor oil, and industrial, aviation and residential sectors are based on Bordetsky *et al.*, *op. cit.* and supporting documents cited throughout that report. Estimated oil savings for efficiency improvements in heavy-duty trucks and biofuels are based on independent analysis by the authors, as described in chapters 9 and 10.

6   Data provided by co-author James A. Cusumano, former R&D director, Exxon Research and Engineering.

7   For details, see "Methodology to Analyze Oil Savings Potential," in Bordetsky *et al., op. cit.*, 21-41.

8   Lester R. Brown, "The Short Path to Oil Independence," Earth Policy Institute, October 13, 2004.

9   Worldwatch Institute, *Biofuels for Transporation: Global Potential and Implications for Sustainable Agriculture and Energy in the 21st Century* (Washington, DC: Worldwatch Institute, June 7, 2006).

10  See U.S. Department of Agriculture, *The Economic Feasibility of Ethanol Production from Sugar in the United States* (Washington, DC: U.S. Government Printing Office, July 2006), iv.

11  Lovins, *et al., op. cit.*

12  The Arlington Institute, *A Strategy: Moving America Away From Oil,* Office of Net Assessment, Office of the Secretary of Defense, Department of Defense, 2003.

13  The format for this figure was partially derived from the Arlington Institute, *ibid.*

14  Statement by State Representative Mina Morita, California Hydrogen Business Council, Fall Meeting, October 13, 2000, Sacramento, California.

15  See the National Commission on Energy Policy, "Summary of Recommendations;" Amory Lovins *et al., Winning the Oil Endgame;* and the Apollo Alliance, *New Energy For America.*

16  "£3.68 trillion: The Price of Failing to Act on Climate Change," *Guardian,* October 31, 2006.

17  Lovins *et al., op. cit.*, xii.

18  This section is based on extensive verbatim quotations taken from an article by co-author James A. Cusumano, "The Power of Passion, the Fallacy of Fear," World Business Academy, September 1, 2005.

19  E. O. Wilson, "The Bottleneck," *Scientific American*, February 2002.

20  Al Gore, *An Inconvenient Truth—The Planetary Emergency of Global Warming and What We Can Do About It* (Emmaus, PA: Rodale, 2006), 11.

# 9

## FUEL EFFICIENCY:
## REVIVING DETROIT AT 100 MPG

*"We are putting U.S. boys in tanks that get 8 mpg to fight in the desert, because we won't increase fleet mileage by 6 miles a gallon to reduce reliance on Middle Eastern oil."*

— BRENT SCOWCROFT, NATIONAL SECURITY ADVISOR,
GULF WAR I, 1990

**Can the U.S. use readily available technology to dramatically improve fuel efficiency in cars and trucks?** *Yes.*

- We can:
  - > Raise new car and light truck average fuel efficiency from 24 to 40 mpg by 2015; and
  - > Dramatically reduce fuel consumption in heavy-duty trucks.

- We've already done it once—after the 1970s oil shocks—and we can do it again.

- Unless Detroit wakes up, Asian car makers will dominate the global auto industry.

## Down and Out in Detroit

Detroit, the sentimental heart and economic hub of the American auto industry, is in deep trouble. When gas hit $3 a gallon, Detroit's market share dropped to its lowest level in history. Meanwhile, Asian competitors who pioneered fuel-efficient and hybrid vehicles kept setting sales records and eating large chunks of Detroit's dwindling share of the market. In mid-2007, gas prices were again back up to those levels in parts of the U.S., and U.S. automakers' monthly market share dropped below 50% for the first time in history.

The good old days, when the Big Three—General Motors, Ford, and Chrysler—dominated the North American automobile industry with 90% of the market are a distant memory. By early 2007, their combined market share had fallen to less than 52% from about 55% a year earlier. In fact, the "Big Three" have evolved into the "New Six," GM, Toyota, Honda, Chrysler, Ford, and Nissan. Both Honda and Toyota are reporting record revenues, while sales are slumping at GM, Ford, and Chrysler.

At GM, a decade ago the largest industrial company in the world, market share is now fluctuating between 22 and 25%, down 50% since 1970. After an initial brush with bankruptcy in the 1990s, GM is still trying to make a come-back. In 2005, GM lost $10.6 billion on sales of $196 billion (a loss of 5 cents for every dollar in sales). To try to save itself from the bankruptcy block this time around, the company is taking drastic measures, slashing 30,000 jobs and closing 12 plants. It came as no surprise that in June 2006 GM's biggest shareholder, billionaire investor Kirk Kerkorian who owns 9.9% of the company's stock, proposed that the company's embattled CEO Rick Wagoner begin exploring a three-way alliance with Renault and Nissan.

Things are not much better at rival Ford, which reported a loss of $12 billion for 2006. In mid-2006, Ford announced it was slashing production, cutting back by one-fifth the numbers of vehicles it had planned to build in the fourth quarter. This represents the deepest production cut since the 1980s. By November 2006, 38,000 employees—44% of all North American hourly workers—had voluntarily taken early retirement. Industry analysts report that Ford's draconian rollback reflects just how urgently it must shift its model lineup to rely less on gas-guzzling SUVs and pickups. (Ford expects to hemorrhage $17 billion in the next two years alone.) Like GM, Ford's debt is already rated "below investment grade" by Standard & Poor's and Moody's. In September 2006, the Ford family reached beyond Bill Ford as CEO to recruit Alan Mulally, a senior executive with aerospace giant Boeing, to lead the troubled automaker.

As analysts had long predicted, Toyota passed Ford for the first time ever to become the No. 2 auto seller in the U.S. in July 2006, a brutal month for the Big Three. In another stunning development, Honda Motor Co. slipped past Chrysler to take the No. 3 spot. These seismic shifts prove just how difficult it will be for the Big Three to turn themselves around quickly and start producing the fuel-efficient vehicles that customers prefer in the new peak-oil world.

Without major changes, auto industry analysts predict that over the next five years GM, Ford, and Chrysler will continue to lose market share and eventually will sell only 50% of U.S. cars. Each 1% decline in U.S. market share equals more than 168,000 cars and light trucks.

## Motown's Mastodons

In July 2005, the University of Michigan Transportation Research Institute's Office for the Study of Automotive Transportation and the Natural Resources Defense Council released a report that explored the question: *what would happen if oil prices reach $80 to $100 a barrel—the equivalent then of $2.86 or $3.37 gas at the pump, respectively.*[1] The conclusion was that the Big Three would lose billions more in profits and hundreds of thousands of jobs during the next oil price spike, which—as documented in this book—has already visited us.

The report notes, "Without deeper discounts, sales volume in the North American car and light truck market will shrink between 9 and 14%, or 1.9 to 3.0 million vehicles, because of the effect of higher

287

oil prices on the economy. Detroit's Big Three automakers will absorb nearly 75% of the sales decreases." As a result, Detroit automakers will experience a $7 billion to $11 billion decline in pre-tax profits, as a result of their dependence on SUV and pickup sales.[2]

---

> *"Ford officials contended that no one in the industry could have anticipated that gasoline prices would remain so high, even though gas prices have been climbing since 2003 and spiked last year after Hurricane Katrina."*
>
> — MICHELINE MAYNARD, *NEW YORK TIMES*, AUGUST 2006

---

Roland Hwang, the Natural Resources Defense Council vehicles policy director, warned, "Given the state of the U.S. automaker finances, they simply cannot afford to make the mistake of ignoring fuel economy performance again. As a nation, we can't afford to let that happen."

If this dramatic decline in Detroit's fortunes is puzzling, *Boston Globe* columnist Derrick Z. Jackson has a simple answer: Detroit's mastodons are so deeply mired in the tar pit of denial, they have not made the changes necessary to survive.[3] Jackson suggests that everything we need to know about the Big Three's missteps can be found in newspaper clippings from August 2006:

- First clip: A *USA Today* review of the 2007 Cadillac Escalade and the GMC Yukon Denali said they had "many improvements, lavish presentations but seating and space utilization are compromised despite large overall size."

  Jackson's response: "Hit the brakes! How could it be that General Motors makes two metallic mastodons that are each over 5,600 pounds, nearly 17 feet long, 6 feet tall, and 6 feet wide, and still do not have enough space?"

- Second clip: the *Wall Street Journal* reviewed the Chevrolet Suburban and 3-ton Ford Expedition Extended Length and noted, "With their big gas tanks, a fuel stop can be jarring. It cost $97 to fill the Suburban, making it necessary to fish out a second AmEx card when we exceeded a station's $75 charge limit per credit card."

Jackson's retort: "You must be kidding. For the fourth straight Labor Day, American soldiers are dying in a botched war in an oil-rich land. What is Detroit's response? Cars that get 17 miles per gallon on the highway and cost nearly $100 to fill."

- Third clip: In a year where Toyota passed Ford in sales and was poised to pass GM globally by its end, what was the 2009 concept car that GM CEO Rick Wagoner drove, claiming it "talks profoundly about a new way of doing business at GM"?

Jackson's observations: "Surely it was a competitor to Toyota's 40-50-miles-per-gallon Prius. No, it was a muscle-bound Camaro!"

Jackson concludes rhetorically, "We all know what happened to the real mastodon."

## Autos and Oil: World's Largest Corporations

In this age of globalization, should we really care if Asian car companies, which happen to have manufacturing plants in the U.S., eat Detroit's lunch? Yes, we should be very concerned.

As Figure 1 shows, in 2005 nine of the world's 10 largest corporations were automobile and oil companies. Together, the combined revenues of these mega-corporations totaled $2.4 trillion, equal to about 5% of the world's total collective Gross Domestic Product in 2005. Only three nations had a GDP bigger than the combined auto-oil company revenues: the United States, with $13.5 trillion; Japan, with $4.6 trillion; and Germany, with $2.8 trillion.

Of the top 10 corporations, five were oil companies, and four were automobile manufacturers. Wal-Mart, which operates one of the largest private fleets of heavy-duty freight trucks, rounded out this list. Other automakers on Fortune's Top 100 list in 2005 were Volkswagon (17), Honda (31), Peugeot (60), BMW (78), Fiat (79), Hyundai (80), and Renault (100). In other words, whoever controls the oil and auto industries could possibly control the future of the global economy.

**Figure 1. World's Largest Corporations by Revenues, 2005**

| Rank 2005 | Corporation (Headquarters) | | Revenues ($ mil) | % Change vs. 2004 |
|---|---|---|---|---|
| 1 | Exxon Mobil | U.S. | 339,938.0 | 25.5 % |
| 2 | Wal-Mart Stores | U.S. | 315,654.0 | 9.6 % |
| 3 | Royal Dutch Shell | Netherlands | 306,731.0 | 14.2 % |
| 4 | BP (British Petroleum) | Britain | 267,600.0 | (6.1) % |
| 5 | General Motors | U.S. | 192,604.0 | (0.5) % |
| 6 | Chevron | U.S. | 189,481.0 | 28.1 % |
| 7 | DaimlerChrysler | Germany | 186,106.3 | 5.3 % |
| 8 | Toyota Motor | Japan | 185,805.0 | 7.6 % |
| 9 | Ford Motor | U.S. | 177,210.0 | 2.9 % |
| 10 | Conoco-Phillips | U.S. | 166,683.0 | 37.0% |

Source: *Fortune*, July 24, 2006

ExxonMobil's 2005 revenues of about $340 billion, were larger than the GDP of all but 22 nations, putting it just ahead of Saudi Arabia, the world's largest oil exporter, which had a 2005 GDP of about $315 billion. Because of two years of fast-rising crude oil prices, most of the major oil companies have realized record-breaking profits. Following soaring profits in 2004, ExxonMobil's 2005 annual profits increased over 40%, Shell's increased about 37%, and Conoco Phillips' increased about 30%.

In this context, Americans should care about the future of the U.S. automobile industry for three reasons. First, with one out of every 10 American jobs related directly or indirectly to the auto industry, Detroit's survival and well-being is central to the health of the U.S. economy.[4] Second, America's leadership in the coming global energy revolution will mainly depend on automobile manufacturers' ability to convert the U.S. fleet from fossil-fuel-burning internal combustion engines to low-emission flex fuel/hybrid vehicles and ultimately to zero-emission fuel cell vehicles. Third, if one agrees with historian Paul Kennedy's thesis in *The Rise and Fall of the Great Powers* that national economic decline is inevitably followed in time by political and military decline, then at stake here is nothing less than the long-term survival of America as a global superpower.[5]

## Auto Efficiency Is Job #1

As Figures 2 indicates, U.S. automobile and truck manufacturers hold the key to the Prometheus Plan's auto-efficiency strategy. If they alter their product strategy, by 2015 we can reduce oil consumption by 3.1 million barrels per day (MBD). Efficiencies in this one sector equate to 70% of the Prometheus Plan's savings of 5.0 MBD.

**Figure 2. Prometheus Plan Matrix: Fuel-Efficiency Strategy**

| Current Technology Oil Savings in Millions of Barrels of Oil Per Day (MBD) | |
|---|---|
| Oil Savings Measures | MBD |
| A) Fuel Efficiency—Raise average fuel efficiency in new passenger vehicles through incentives and standards from 24 mpg to 40 mpg by 2015 | 1.6 |
| Advanced Technology Vehicles—no oil savings required prior to 2015:<br>• Hybrid and Plug-in Hybrid Electric Vehicles: 1 million new vehicle sales by 2015<br>• Fuel Cell Vehicles: 100,000 new vehicle sales by 2015<br>• Super-lightweight, Advanced Materials Vehicles: sales begin in 2012 | 0.0 |
| B) Accelerate oil savings in vehicles through efficiency improvements for: | |
| • Replacement tires and motor oil | 0.5 |
| • Heavy-duty trucks - 8,500 pounds to more than 33,000 pounds | 1.0 |
| C) Accelerate oil savings in industrial, aviation, and residential sectors | 0.3 |
| Total oil saved by 2015: | 3.4 |

## U.S. Oil Savings by 2015

Of the projected 3.1 MBD in oil savings from auto efficiency, more than three-quarters comes from two measures. The first involves raising the fuel efficiency standards for new vehicles (cars and light trucks) from the base Corporate Average Fuel Economy (CAFE) figure of 24.4 mpg, to 40 mpg in 10 years (less in percentage terms than we achieved in the late 1970s and 1980s). This by itself will save 1.6 MBD. The second change requires accelerating a series of petroleum-saving measures in heavy-duty trucks. Beginning in 2008, this will save 1.0 MBD.

The good news is that as far as fuel efficiency is concerned, the U.S. has already been there and done that. In fact, America performed spectacularly during the late 1970s and early 1980s in response to OPEC-caused oil shocks. The good, good news is that similar oil savings can be achieved today, using current, off-the-shelf technologies, without having to wait for, or rely on, advanced technologies such as plug-in hybrids, advanced super-lightweight materials, or fuel cell vehicles. Indeed, these savings can be achieved even without counting on dramatic sales increases in current technology hybrid cars: we estimate that at a result of existing manufacturers' current plans, sales of conventional hybrids will increase from about 200,000 units a year in 2005 to 1,000,000 units a year by 2015.[6]

## How America Busted OPEC in the Eighties

To counteract the oil price spikes that followed the 1973 oil boycott, Congress passed the CAFE standards in 1975, forcing carmakers to design and build vehicles that achieved higher mileage per gallon of gasoline. Although the auto industry vehemently protested this legislation, in time Detroit complied and began rolling out more efficient products. In only 10 years, between 1975 and 1985, American cars were obtaining an average of 25 mpg, up from 15 mpg just 10 years earlier—a stunning increase of 66%!

Nevertheless, engineering wizards had only scratched the surface of what could be achieved by seriously tweaking car engines, transmissions, and aerodynamics. According to Paul Roberts, in *The End of Oil*, "By some estimates average fuel efficiency would, according to then-current rates, easily reach 40 miles per gallons by the end of the century."[7] This 40 mpg target is precisely where the Prometheus Plan projects that we need to be by 2015.

Efficiency in personal passenger vehicles was the capstone of America's rapid response to the two major oil shocks of the 1970s, the first being the 1973 OPEC oil embargo and the second, the 1978 Iranian Revolution. The results were speedy and spectacular. As Amory Lovins observes, "In those eight years, *the United States proved it could boost its oil efficiency faster than OPEC could cut its oil sales: the U.S. had more flexibility on the demand side than OPEC had on the supply side.*"[8]

As a result, between 1977 and 1985 the U.S. reduced overall energy demand by 14%, from 35 quads down to 30 quads.[9] While U.S. GDP *grew* by nearly 4% a year, oil consumption *fell* by 17%, and net imports from the Persian Gulf *fell* by 87%. As the world oil market shrank by one-tenth, OPEC's global market share precipitously dropped from 52% to 30%, and "its output fell by 48%, breaking its pricing power for a decade."[10]

A 2002 National Academy of Sciences report, *Effectiveness and Impact of Corporate Average Fuel Economy (CAFE) Standards*, found that fuel efficiency standards were a key factor in reducing oil use between 1975 and 1988.[11] During that period, fuel efficiency for *new* passenger cars almost doubled, from 15.8 mpg in 1975 to a peak of 28.6 in 1988—an increase of 81%. Similarly, fuel economy for *new* light trucks jumped from 17.7 mpg in 1975 to 21.6 mpg in 1987—an increase of 58%. Significantly, 96% of these new car efficiency gains occurred thanks to smarter engineering designs; only 4% came from smaller size.

*So what happened between 1988 and today?*

Simply stated, beginning in the mid-eighties, OPEC began pumping oil fast and furiously to regain market share. In current dollars, oil prices dropped back from a peak of nearly $100/barrel to $20/barrel. Under President Reagan's deregulation agenda, Congress froze the CAFE standards at 1985 levels. In order to lure back those customers it had lost to more highly efficient Japanese carmakers, Detroit did a U-turn on fuel efficiency and began building a new generation of "American muscle cars." Now, instead of using the handsome "efficiency dividend" to save even more fuel (i.e., by keeping power constant and continuing to cut fuel use per mile driven), Detroit began making bigger, heavier, more powerful cars and light trucks.

Further increasing fuel consumption was the spectacular increase in the sales of light trucks—SUVs, minivans, and pickups—which today account for one out of every two vehicles that Detroit sells. As a result, according to Lovins, "America's light-vehicle fleet today is nearly the world's most efficient per *ton-mile*, but with many more tons, it uses the most fuel per mile of any advanced country."[12]

## 40 MPG BY 2015

When it comes to increasing fuel efficiency, since we've done it before, we can do it again.

In order to get the U.S. back on the track of producing the most efficient vehicles, Congress must pass legislation to raise CAFE standards to 40 mpg by 2015. A combined fleet fuel economy of 40 mpg in 10 years can be achieved by increasing efficiency in incremental annual steps of 3 to 4% a year over the next decade.

Improving passenger vehicle fuel economy, and thereby increasing the efficiency of oil use, is the centerpiece of every major public interest organization and national commission proposal that has seriously investigated how America can quickly and reliably achieve maximum oil savings using current technologies.[13] The primary technology options for increasing fuel efficiency are outlined in Figure 3 and include vehicle load reduction, more efficient engines, integrated starter generators, and improved transmissions.

**Figure 3. Current Technology Options for Improving Fuel Economy[14]**

| | |
|---|---|
| **Vehicle Load Reduction** | - Aerodynamic improvements<br>- Rolling resistance improvements<br>- Safety-enhancing mass reduction<br>- Accessory load reduction |
| **Efficient Engines[15]** | - Variable valve control engines<br>- Stoichiometric burn direct-injection engine |
| **Integrated Starter Engines** | - Improved starter fuel efficiency |
| **Improved Transmissions** | - 5- and 6-speed automatic transmissions<br>- 5-speed motorized gear shift transmissions<br>- Optimized shift schedules<br>- Continuously variable transmissions |

Source: Natural Resources Defense Council

Multiple studies conducted by highly credible institutions all agree that automakers have the technology and ability to raise fuel economy standards for new cars and light trucks to 40 mpg by 2015, and up to 55 mpg by 2025. As background for the auto-efficiency strategy of the Prometheus Plan, we have relied extensively (with noteworthy exceptions) on the vehicle fuel efficiency findings of the Natural Resources Defense Council and the Institute for the Analysis of Global Security, as presented in their 2005 report, *Securing America: Solving Our Oil Dependence Through Innovation.* This joint Defense Council/IAGS report builds on numerous studies by the National Academy of Sciences, the Union of Concerned Scientists, the American Council for an Energy-Efficient Economy, and the Massachusetts Institute of Technology. Independently, all of the studies indicate, in the words of the report, "that cars and light trucks can achieve large additional fuel savings if fuel economy standards are increased."[16]

In order to project annual oil savings out to 2015 and 2025 from these options, the Defense Council used a vehicle stock turnover model developed by the Tellus Institute for estimated transportation and other energy demands under different technology and public policy assumptions. The Defense Council reports that "the stock model, called the Long-range Energy Alternatives Planning System, or LEAP, is calibrated to Energy Information Administration's *Annual Energy Outlook 2003* to establish a baseline of energy consumption to 2025 from the light-duty fleet."[17]

A National Academy of Sciences report suggests that even a higher standard of 47 mpg (7 mpg higher than the 40 mpg goal of the Prometheus Plan) could be achieved with additional improvements to "conventional gasoline-powered internal combustion vehicles." Furthermore, studies by both the American Council and the Union of Concerned Scientists show that by combining improvements in current vehicle technology with gasoline-electric hybrid drive systems, it would be possible to more rapidly reach a fleet average of 55 mpg.

## SMALL-CAR NATION

Given that fleetwide fuel economy has been declining for the past 15 years, it will clearly take legislation and retooling for Detroit to raise average fuel efficiency, especially when it comes to large vehicles such as SUVs, vans, pickups, and luxury cars. This has not been the case in other countries. In response to gas prices that have been rising steadily since 2000, European and Japanese carmakers are already making a new generation of small and midsize cars that combine impressive fuel economy with stylish design.

The conventional wisdom is that Americans will cling to their big cars and trucks regardless of gas prices. So, consumer acceptance of smaller cars would provide a reliable market test for the Prometheus Plan's fuel efficiency goals. Or, as *New York Times* writer Micheline Maynard asks: *"Is America ready to become a small car nation?"*[18]

As Figure 4 shows, based on automobile sales through September 2006, the answer is "yes." U.S. sales of subcompacts and compacts reached a record 2.7 million in 2006. Sales of pint-sized cars like the Honda Fit, Toyota Yaris, Chevrolet Aveo, Mini Cooper, and Nissan Versa are growing even faster in 2007 than 2006 though they still account for less than 3% of 2007 new-car sales. During the first three quarters of 2006, small car sales were stronger than any similar period since the beginning of the decade. SUV sales are well off their peak of 2.8 million vehicles in 2002, when they had 18% of the market.

**Figure 4. U.S. Vehicle Sales by Size, 2000-2006[19]**

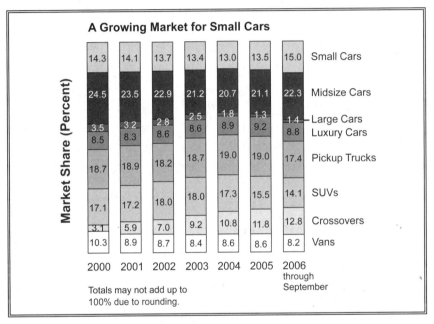

Source: MotorIntelligence.com

Today's small cars are not your father's VW Bug. When gas prices became erratic earlier in this decade, foreign automakers designed a new generation of subcompact cars that combined quality, style, and personality. Offerings include the Nissan Versa, Toyota Yaris, and Honda Fit, recently joined by the second generation of the Mini Cooper, which is made in England by BMW.

This resurgence of small cars underscores Detroit's dilemma. For nearly two decades, the Big Three's financial model has been based on building big vehicles whose profits dwarf those from small cars. For example, according to CNW Market Research, a full-sized SUV generates a gross profit of nearly $9,000—over 20 times more than Detroit earns on the sale of each subcompact.

Detroit carmakers have dabbled with, but largely failed to introduce, innovative small models comparable to strong-selling, foreign-built "personality cars" like the Mini Cooper. For example, Chrysler displayed the feisty Dodge Hornet concept car at the 2006 Geneva Motor Show. But some industry analysts, such as Karl Brauer, editor-in-chief of Edmunds.com, a Web site that offers car-buying advice, are skeptical of the Detroit-based automakers' commitment to fuel economy. Brauer argues that "they'll sit back on what they know and miss out on another market niche."[20]

So what will it take to get Detroit out of second gear when it comes to fuel efficiency? Even with the best of stated intentions by Detroit executives, during the oil crises of the 1970s, it took federal fuel efficiency standards. It will likely require similar mandates this time around to *ensure* that the Prometheus Plan succeeds.

## HIGH-TECH CARS

Beyond these small cars, which represent conventional technologies that have already gained widespread market acceptance, there are a variety of high-tech cars in development—from the next generation of hybrids to advanced hydrogen fuel cell vehicles—which, in time, could significantly increase fuel efficiency and oil savings.

According to the U.S. EPA/DOE 2005 rankings of the vehicles with the highest and lowest fuel economy, the top five fuel savers in terms of mpg rank, manufacturer/model and city/highway mpg, were:

- Honda Insight (hybrid-electric, manual) — 61/66 mpg
- Toyota Prius (hybrid-electric) — 60/51 mpg
- Honda Insight (hybrid-electric, automatic) — 57/56 mpg
- Honda Civic Hybrid (automatic, lean burn) — 48/47 mpg
- Honda Civic Hybrid (automatic) — 47/48 mpg

Conversely, the five biggest fuel burners were:

- Dodge Ram Pickup 2WD (automatic) — 9/12 mpg
- Lamborghini L-147/148 Murcielago (manual) — 9/13 mpg
- Dodge Ram Pickup 2WD (manual) — 9/15 mpg
- Bentley Arnage, Arnage LWB — 10/14 mpg
- Lamborghini L-147/148, Murcielago (automatic) — 10/15 mpg

Clearly, there is a very wide range between the 2005 top five fuel economy vehicles, which get anywhere from 48 to 66 mpg for highway driving, and the bottom five vehicles, which get only 12-15 mpg on the highway. Obviously, all of the top five gas misers are hybrid electric vehicles.

In addition to the hybrid electric vehicle, several viable advanced technology vehicles could in time contribute significantly to increasing fuel efficiency and U.S. oil savings, including the plug-in hybrid, the advanced materials vehicle (AMV), and ultimately, the hydrogen-powered fuel cell vehicle.

**Hybrid Electric Vehicles**. Combined sales of hybrid electric vehicles in 2006 were about 250,000 units and are projected to reach more than 1 million by 2015, which would represent 6% of new vehicle sales. The hybrid electric vehicle uses a conventional internal combustion engine and an electric motor, which runs on an electric charge drawn from the engine or the braking system or both.

Figure 5 shows a side view of the popular 2006 Toyota Prius Hybrid Electric Vehicle. The Prius is a four-door, five-passenger family sedan. It has a Hybrid Synergy Drive, 1.5-liter, 16-valve internal combustion engine that is front-mounted with horsepower of 76@5000 RMP, plus an electric hybrid motor with horsepower of 67@1200-1540 RMP.

**Figure 5. 2006 Toyota Prius Hybrid Electric Car**

Finally hearing the message the marketplace has been shouting for several years, GM has learned that hybrids are here to stay. GM recently showed off its newly redesigned 2008 Saturn VUE, which will arrive at some point in the future with the choice of a simplified hybrid engine (20% better fuel economy) or a standard engine. Sometime in the future, the VUE will be offered as a "full" hybrid (45% better fuel economy).

In a similar vein, Ford has improved its Ford Escape Hybrid, including a feature that will permit it to run at low speeds solely on its electrical motor, and has reduced the purchase price by $1,000 to stimulate sales.

Rick Wagoner, CEO of GM, recounted what he now sees as the inevitable competition for oil from other countries with resultant upward pressure on the per-gallon price. In remarks to the press at the opening of the Los Angeles Auto Show in late November 2006, he pledged GM to produce a plug-in hybrid as soon as it possibly could. Although it will take "several years," he called achieving greater fuel economy a "top priority program for GM given the huge potential it offers for fuel-economy improvement" and pledged to begin weaning GM vehicles off petroleum. He went on to say, "We will be in this game for the long term," because "[a]t the end of the day, the transition (from fossil fuels) will be as the conversion from horses to horsepower . . . ."

Was Wagoner sincere? Perhaps. Unfortunately, American automakers and their brethren in Big Oil have a long history of opposing innovations that would improve safety, protect the environment, improve mileage, or safeguard public health. The destruction of mass transit through an industry conspiracy, and the recent sabotage of the Zero Electric Vehicle program provide sorry bookends for this dreary tale of corporate subterfuge. In 1949, the Truman Administration won an antitrust conviction for the destruction of urban electric mass transit and its replacement with diesel buses. The guilty parties were GM, Standard Oil, Phillips Petroleum, Firestone Tire and Rubber, and Mack Truck. By then it was too late: these corporations had colluded to create a sham front organization, "National City Lines," that bought all the light rail lines it could, burned the streetcars, and paved the tracks with asphalt. Diesel buses (which they manufactured and fueled) replaced the efficient electric streetcars. Among many other cities, Los Angeles destroyed its fine mass transit system, creating environmental blight, smog, and congestion. The fine against the 25-year-old conspiracy was $5,000 per company, because the judge determined our nation's urban mass transit system was beyond salvage.[21]

The other bookend is the electric Zero Emissions Vehicle (ZEV). Jack Davis's *Taken for a Ride* describes how Big Oil and the car industries more recently conspired to outwardly support air pollution controls and the electric Zero Emissions Vehicle, while privately doing everything possible to kill them.[22] Ultimately, GM recalled every ZEV and physically crushed the highly popular cars. It also assured that the battery technology would never come to market. Former California EPA Secretary Terry Tamminen (a Republican) has detailed these and similar episodes in his recent book *Lives Per Gallon*. Through the years, the auto industry, Big Oil, or both have opposed mass transit, safety belts, padded dashboards, catalytic converters, anti-rollover designs, airbags, roof crush standards, CAFE standards, the Federal Clean Air Act, ethanol fuel, the leaded gasoline ban, and more.

In some of these cases, the industries formed "study groups" to affect the appearance of support, while destroying the initiatives behind the scenes. Is GM sincere this time? No one outside the company can know. But if we are to judge by the company's past and recent actions, we should monitor them closely and judge them by their deeds, not by their words.

The good news is that company executives are at least mouthing words that indicate they have heard the marketplace speak and that they see their future is tied to the transition from gas guzzlers to cars with mileage numbers two to three times higher than their current fleet average. If this is a conversion, it is clearly one where logic has finally triumphed over Detroit's institutional resistance.

**Plug-in Hybrid Electric Vehicles.** Like standard hybrids, plug-in hybrid electric vehicles are powered by both liquid fuels and electricity provided from a charge drawn from either the engine or captured braking energy or both. However, unlike standard hybrids, plug-ins also can be charged directly off the regular power grid from a standard electric outlet when the vehicle is parked. Since plug-in hybrid electric vehicles also have fuel tanks and internal combustion engines on board, they do not face the range limitations of electric-only cars that run exclusively on batteries.

As noted in Chapter 8, more than half of the passenger vehicles on the road today are used for trips of only 20 miles a day or less. According to the U.S. Department of Transportation and the Department of Energy's FreedomCAR & Vehicle Technologies Program, in 2001 (the most recent year for which data are available), the average trip length for American households was only 9.9 miles and their average daily travel was only 32.9 miles.

This means that a plug-in hybrid with merely a 20-mile-range battery will not need gasoline for most household trips. Because the nation's electrical grid uses petroleum for only about 2% of its fuel, plug-in hybrids will dramatically reduce oil consumption in the transportation sector. These gasoline savings will be even more striking with flexible-fuel plug-in hybrid vehicles fueled by E85 (85% ethanol and 15% gasoline) or other biofuels. Such cars' consumption of gasoline will be miniscule compared to today's Toyota Prius which gets only 55/mpg of gasoline. This potential for gasoline savings is just over the horizon in the 2010-2015 timeframe.

Detroit may be getting the message. The 2005 North

American International Auto Show in Detroit saw the introduction of both new hybrid cars and advances in automotive technology. Ford and General Motors promised to produce six different hybrid electric vehicle models by 2008. The Ford Escape Hybrid SUV also won the prize for North American Truck of the Year. Although, the production volumes of these vehicles are modest, to say the least, it appears GM and Ford finally are waking up. It can't happen too soon. Hyundai recently announced its HCD10 Helion will run on a 3.0-liter V6 diesel engine. Honda was also in Los Angeles at the auto show with its announcement of the FCX hydrogen vehicle, which is 30% lighter and 20% smaller than the last generation of its fuel cell vehicles. Honda plans to have actual consumers in the U.S. and Japan *driving* these hydrogen fuel cell cars by 2008. As noted previously, BMW has a similar objective for its hydrogen vehicles.

**Hybrid Electric Vehicles and Advanced Materials Vehicles.** The advanced materials vehicle is a super-lightweight, super-efficient hybrid electric vehicle made with advanced composite materials and designs that could, in theory, raise fuel efficiency to more than 90 mpg. Figure 6 shows a concept of one version of an advanced materials vehicle Hypercar, which is being promoted by Hypercar, Inc.'s Chairman Amory Lovins (a World Business Academy Fellow) and CEO Tom Crumm.[23]

**Figure 6. The Hypercar Concept**

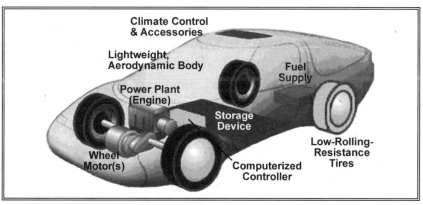

Source: www.rmi.org

According to the Rocky Mountain Institute, the Hypercar's "defining features are ultralight construction, low-drag design, hybrid-electric drive, and minimized accessory loads. Individually, none of these is economically or technically very worth doing; artfully integrated, though, they produce a whole system that's more efficient, works better, is cheaper to run, and may even be cheaper to make."

> *"Our analysis highlights an important new area of the design space— ultralight, superefficient, exceptionally safe, and cost-competitive."*
> — AMORY LOVINS, *WINNING THE OIL ENDGAME*, 2005

Unlike some ultra-efficient vehicles, Hypercar vehicles do not compromise performance, comfort, or safety. Indeed, by offering extra consumer appeal and manufacturing advantages, they may stand a better chance of getting on the road—and forcing old, polluting cars off—in sufficient numbers to make a big difference in the environment. In addition, Hypercar vehicles and their offspring could profitably reduce carbon dioxide emissions by two-thirds, in part by greatly accelerating the shift to new manufacturing materials and techniques.

**Fuel Cell Vehicles.** Fuel cell vehicles combine hydrogen and oxygen to generate electric power to operate car motors. Single fuel cells are combined into stacks to provide adequate vehicle power. In 2005, General Motors made headlines with the release of a new prototype hydrogen vehicle, the Sequel (pictured in Figure 7), which can travel 300 miles on one tank of hydrogen—roughly double what previous fuel cell cars were able to achieve.

According to Green Car Congress, "The GM Sequel combines a new fuel cell system, higher-pressure hydrogen storage, enhanced by-wire controls substituting for mechanical systems and new rear-wheel hub motors that accelerate the vehicle—slightly larger and heavier than the Cadillac SRX crossover—from 0 to 60 in less than 10 seconds and with a range of 300 miles."

**Figure 7. The GM Sequel**

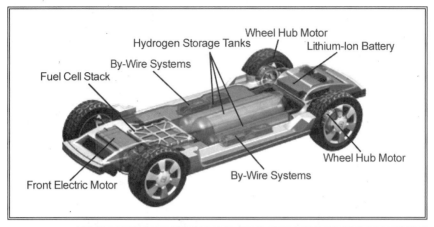

Source: Green Car Congress (www.greencarcongress.com)

The Sequel uses three traction motors—a single transverse-mounted motor in the front and two rear-wheel hub motors—that deliver a total of 110 kilowatts of power directly to the wheels. The GM 73kw fuel cell power module delivers 25% more power than its predecessor and is supplemented by a 65kw lithium-ion battery system. Advances in high-pressure hydrogen storage support Sequel's 300-mile range. Three lightweight, carbon composite tanks store hydrogen at 10,000 psi and carry 8 kg of hydrogen, more than double that of GM's HydroGen3 fuel cell vehicle.

## NEXT-GENERATION HYBRIDS

Clearly, we are in the early stages of a new era of passenger vehicle innovations. Ultimately, these not only make obsolete the old-fashioned, inefficient internal combustion engine, but will also bring forth a series of new and improved advanced technology vehicles. These will include all-electric cars, hybrids, plug-in hybrids, super-lightweight cars, and hydrogen-powered fuel cell vehicles. Prototypes of this next generation of high-tech cars, which combine efficiency, power, and comfort, are on the drawing boards or already on display at auto shows, and include:

- Tesla Motors' all-electric, two-seater roadster. This lithium-ion battery powered sports car features a 248hp (185kw) electric motor that accelerates from 0 to 60 mpg in four seconds and has a range of about 250 miles with a top speed of 130 mph.

- Aptera Concept Car, 330 mpg. This half-egg-shaped concept car, which will sell for under $20,000, combines super-high mileage efficiency with a diesel engine powered with hybrid technology. It has sophisticated aerodynamics and weighs only 850 pounds.

- DaimlerChrysler's Bionic 70 mpg Concept Car. This is a super-aerodynamic four-seater that gets 70 mpg, while exceeding the most stringent European emission regulations.

- Honda Dualnote, 400 hp and 42 mpg. Unveiled late last year, the Dualnote represents a new generation of hybrids that combines fuel efficiency with impressive horsepower. Instead of a conventional battery pack, as in the Prius and Insight, the Dualnote features a large "ultra-capacitor," a high-performance energy-storage device that charges and discharges more rapidly than batteries, providing quicker response and acceleration.

- In September 2006, German automaker BMW announced it will roll out the world's first production hydrogen-burning car, the BMW 7 Series Hydrogen Saloon, in 2008. This luxury version of the German firm's zero-emission car is powered by a 260 hp 12-cylinder engine that accelerates from 0 to 62 in 9.5 seconds with a top speed of 143 mph. BMW, which has also unveiled the world's fastest hydrogen-powered car with a top speed of 185 mph, said that its long-term goal is to offer hydrogen motors in all its cars.

This shift will also dramatically affect business models, with some possibly unforeseen positive consequences for the corporations that are involved. For example, as plug-in hybrids replace some gasoline with electricity, they could potentially pit the electric utilities against the oil industry, giving utilities the potential to sell more kilowatt-hours. Erik Straser, a general partner with Mohr Davidow Ventures, believes this also could open up a market for new technologies—such as drive trains, power-management systems, and batteries—catering to the new market. "You get a bunch of people involved in the opportunity to sell transportation, and they could be selling electrons instead of selling dead dinosaurs. This could be early signs of a shift, and that could be good for a variety of industries. Net net, I think it would be good for Silicon Valley."[24]

## FUEL-EFFICIENT REPLACEMENT TIRES AND MOTOR OIL

In order to meet even current federal fuel mileage standards, all manufacturers of new vehicles install tires that are more efficient than the replacement tires available in the market.

Overall vehicle fuel efficiency can be improved by up to 6% by legislating that replacement tires simply be as efficient as original equipment tires in terms of rolling resistance (the amount of energy required to move a tire). Some states, like California, have already initiated programs to test and rate replacement tires in the same way that home appliances such as refrigerators and dishwashers have energy efficiency and price/payback time data that are prominently displayed at point of purchase.

The technology required to make efficient replacement tires is completely current and off-the-shelf; all manufacturers use it to make original new car tires. The most common strategy for creating low rolling resistance tires is to inject silica compounds into the rubber. This can be done inexpensively and without sacrificing traction or tread life. Low-rolling resistant tires are highly economical. Consultants to the California Energy Commission estimate that an average driver would recoup in fuel savings the extra $5 to $12 spent on a set of four such tires. This could reach $50 to $150 over the life of the tires.[25] The Natural Resources Defense Council model assumes that this fuel efficiency tire technology will fully penetrate the entire vehicle market in stages by 2014, saving 0.36 MBD by 2015.

Similarly, advanced motor oil formulations can enhance the fuel efficiency of motor oil use in passenger vehicles. Research by the Society of Automotive Engineers indicates that the "fuel efficiency of mineral oils can be improved so that they qualify as ultra-low viscosity oils, which have been demonstrated to reduce fuel consumption by 3% compared to a vehicle using a 5W-rated oil."

The Defense Council has conservatively estimated that fuel-efficient motor oils reduce fuel consumption by 1% in passenger vehicles. By assuming that motor oil efficiency and labeling standards are widely available by 2011, and that all passenger vehicles are using advanced motor oils by 2012, improved alternative oils would save 0.12 MBD by 2015. In combination, fuel efficient replacement tires and motor oil can conserve a total of 0.5 MBD by 2015 (see Figure 2).

## WAL-MART CASHES IN ON HEAVY-DUTY TRUCK EFFICIENCY

In April 2006, a *Wall Street Journal* article, "Wal-Mart Exceeds Fuel-Efficiency Goals," reported that "Wal-Mart Stores, Inc.'s efforts to increase the efficiency of its trucking fleet—a key part of its plans to cut costs and portray itself as more environmentally friendly—is running ahead of schedule." Wal-Mart's efficiency improvements are discussed in Chapter 13.

Wal-Mart's achievements are indicative of the kinds of "low hanging fruit" available to enhance fuel efficiency in the nation's fleet of heavy-duty trucks, which includes all trucks with gross weight of 8,000 to 33,000 pounds or more. After light-duty passenger vehicles, heavy-duty trucks are the second largest consumers of oil in the transportation sector. They burn the equivalent of 2.84 MBD in the base case.[26] More than two-thirds of this trucking fuel is used by big-rig, long-haul tractor-trailers, while one-third is used by lighter, short-haul trucks.

A recent technology assessment by the American Council for an Energy Efficient Economy found that up to 70% of fuel efficiency improvements in all truck classes are cost-effective. Tractor-trailer and long-haul straight trucks are excellent candidates for the kind of current technology improvements so effectively used by Wal-Mart, including improved aerodynamics, rolling resistance tires, engine fuel injection, fuel management through auxiliary power units, and reductions in vehicle weight.

As Figure 8 shows, the American Council for an Energy Efficient Economy has identified a number of short- and mid-term fuel economy measures for heavy-duty trucks to light trucks for each of the following classes: long-haul tractor-trailers (Class 8: 33,000 pounds and up); long-haul straight truck (Class 7 and 8: 26,000 pounds and up); local trucks (Class 3-8: 10,000 pounds and up), and small commercial trucks and large SUVs, van and pickups (Class 2b: 8,500-10,000 pounds).

All of these technologies are cost-effective and directly contribute to improving fuel economy or reducing fuel use. Aerodynamic improvements reduce resistance created by air flowing over the cab and trailer. By pumping air streams *under* the truck, pneumatic blowing will reduce drag coefficients and lower rolling resistance.

Electric power auxiliaries for pumps, compressors, and fans replace equipment now powered by diesel engines, often while the truck is idling. Auxiliary power units obviate the need for long-haul drivers to idle a truck's diesel engine during long stops or overnight

## Figure 8. Heavy Trucks, Current Technologies to Improve Fuel Efficiency[27]

| Technology | % Fuel Efficiency Improvement |
|---|---|
| **Aerodynamics:**<br>- Cab top deflectors<br>- Cab-trailer gap closing<br>- Trailer edge curvature<br>- Pneumatic blowing | <br>1.5%<br>2.5%<br>1.3%<br>6.0% beginning in 2012 |
| **Rolling Resistance:**<br>- Low-rolling resistance, wide-based tires | <br>3.0% |
| Electrical Auxiliary Power:<br>- Starter-generator<br>- Fuel cells | <br>1.5%<br>6.0% beginning in 2012 |
| **Engine:**<br>- Friction reduction<br>- Increased peak cylinder pressure<br>- Improved fuel injection<br>- Turbo-charging and thermal management | <br>2.0%<br>4.0%<br>6.0%<br>5.0% plus additional 5.0% in 2012 |
| **Vehicle Mass Reduction:** | 7.5% beginning in 2012 |
| **Auxiliary Power Units:**<br>- Reduce heavy duty truck idling | <br>18% of heavy trucks suitable for APU |

Source: Compiled from American Council for an Energy Efficient Economy.
All technologies implemented by 2008, unless otherwise indicated.

at rest stops to heat or cool the cab and run electrical appliances. In addition to being powered by electrical generators, the auxiliaries can eventually be driven by small, on-board, stationary fuel cells. This differs substantially from using large fuel cells stacks to power the entire vehicle.

Engine efficiencies are achieved mainly through improved engineering applications. Overall truck mass reduction can be realized by replacing some steel vehicle components with lighter-weight, higher-strength metal or plastic components.

Based on projected oil savings of 0.38 MBD for fuel efficiency improvements to heavy-duty trucks, and idling reduction savings of

0.07 MBD for auxiliary power unit savings, the Natural Resources Defense Council projects a combined heavy-truck oil savings of 500,000 barrels per day (rounded from 0.45 MBD) by 2015, with the heaviest long-haul tractor trailers contributing half of the savings. Given Wal-Mart's real-world demonstration of just how quickly fleetwide energy savings can be realized, as well as the significant incentives that companies have to reduce their energy operating costs, a savings of 1.0 MBD (twice the Natural Resources Defense Council projections) is easily achievable in the trucking sector.

## INDUSTRIAL, COMMERCIAL, AND AVIATION SAVINGS

In 10 years, a variety of best practices and improved technologies can provide relatively small but important reductions of 0.3 MBD in oil consumption in the industrial, commercial, and aviation sectors, over and above oil savings relating to automobiles and trucks.[28] These efficiency measures are different from the broader applications of renewable energy technologies to electric power generation (described in Chapter 11).

In the industrial sector, manufacturing companies use a variety of petroleum fuels (heating oil, diesel fuel, and liquefied petroleum gas) for firing boilers and the heat-processing of materials. Improving boilers and furnace efficiency and substituting biomass products for petroleum feedstocks now used in chemicals and manufacturing (plastics, solvents, pharmaceuticals, and the like) produce minor but important reductions in oil consumption.

In the residential sector, the U.S. Energy Information Administration estimates that some eight million residences use petroleum-based fuels (fuel oil and liquefied petroleum gases, such as propane and kerosene) for space- and water-heating. Switching to solar-powered water heaters (ubiquitous in Israel) and substituting biofuels for home heating oil, improving the efficiency of water and space heaters, maximizing insulation, and upgrading thermostat controls can further significantly reduce the use of oil products.

Finally, the Department of Energy estimates that aviation jet fuel usage can be reduced up to 5% by streamlining flight planning and ground logistics so that airplanes fly the most direct routes and spend less time idling before takeoff and after landing. These savings can be realized through improved air traffic management and enhanced aviation communication, navigation, and surveillance systems. Since 1998, the Federal Aviation Administration has been implementing a Free Flight Program to implement these various types of system improvements. The FAA has set a goal of "improving aviation fuel efficiency per revenue-plane-mile by 1% per year through 2009, as measured by a three-year moving average, from the three-year average for calendar year 2000-2002."[29]

## PHENOMENAL POSSIBILITIES

Using current technology, the U.S. can dramatically reduce oil consumption by 3.4 MBD in 10 years through fuel efficiency measures that mainly affect petroleum fuel economy for passenger vehicles and heavy-duty trucks. Given that most American SUVs today would flunk China's 2009 vehicle efficiency standards, the Prometheus Plan goal of 40 mpg for new vehicles by 2015 is both essential to Detroit's survival and achievable with current technology. Moreover, while today's hybrids can get up to 55 mpg, tomorrow's advanced technology plug-in hybrid electric vehicles and combined plug-in hybrid/flex-fuel vehicles will deliver gasoline savings that make the achievements of today's hybrids pale in comparison.

In order to fully realize these oil savings sooner rather than later, we recommend that Congress establish tax credits for automobile manufacturers, so they can retool existing factories, and for consumers, so they have incentives to buy the next generation of fuel-efficient cars, vans, and trucks. Congress *must* raise federal fuel economy standards for all new cars and light trucks in gradual steps up to 40 mpg by 2015.[30]

We believe these measures are essential not only to revive America's automobile industry, but to safeguard jobs, stimulate the economy, reduce greenhouse gases, *and* enhance national security.

## Notes and References
## Chapter 9: Fuel Efficiency

1  Office for the Study of Automotive Transportation (OSAT), University of Michigan Transportation Research Institute (UMTRI) and Natural Resources Defense Council (NRDC), *In the Tank: How Oil Prices Threaten Automakers' Profits and Jobs*, July 2005.

2  *Ibid.*, 4.

3  Derrick Z. Jackson, "Folly of Automakers," *Boston Globe*, September 2, 2006.

4  New vehicle production, sales and other jobs related to the use of autos are responsible for one out of every 10 jobs in the U.S. economy, according to a report on "The Contribution of the Automotive Industry to the U.S. Economy," prepared by the University of Michigan and the Center for Automotive Research, 2003.

5  Paul Kennedy, *The Rise and Fall of the Great Powers* (New York: Vintage, 1987).

6  For a review of estimates of hybrid sales, see Mark Clayton, "Can Hybrids Save U.S. from Foreign Oil?," *Christian Science Monitor*, May 19, 2005.

7  Paul Roberts, *The End of Oil: On the Edge of a Perilous New World* (New York: Mariner Books, 2004), 153.

8  Amory Lovins *et al.*, *Winning the Oil Endgame: Innovation for Profits, Jobs and Security* (Snowmass, CO: Rocky Mountain Institute, 2005) 7.

9  A quad = $10^{15}$ British Thermal Units.

10  Lovins *et al.*, *op. cit.*, 7.

11  National Research Council, *Effectiveness and Impact of Corporate Average Fuel Economy (CAFE) Standards*, National Academy of Sciences (Washington, DC: National Academy Press, 2002), 2-3.

12  Lovins *et al.*, *op. cit.*, 8.

13 These organizations include the National Commission on Energy Policy, Natural Resources Defense Council, Rocky Mountain Institute, and the Apollo Alliance. For specific reports, see note 3 to Chapter 8. See for example, John DeCicco, Feng An, and Marc Ross, *Technical Options for Improving the Fuel Economy of U.S. and Light Trucks by 2010-2015* (Washington, DC: American Council for an Energy-Efficient Economy, July 2001).

14 Gasoline direct injection (GDI) is a variant of fuel injection that offers increased fuel efficiency and high power output. This is achieved by precise control over the amount of fuel and injection timings, which are varied according to load conditions. In addition, there are no throttling losses when compared to a conventional fuel-injected or carbureted engine, which greatly improves efficiency. Basically, the engine management system continuously chooses between three different modes of combustion: ultra-lean burn, stoichiometric, and high-power output. Each mode is characterized by an air-fuel ratio. For further discussion, see "Gasoline Direct Injection" at Wikepedia.

15 Ann Bordetsky *et al.*, *Securing America: Solving Our Oil Dependence Through Innovation* (Washington, DC: Natural Resources Defense Council and Institute for the Analysis of Global Security, February 2005), 24.

16 *Ibid.*, 24.

17 *Ibid.*, 25.

18 Micheline Maynard, "Small Car Nation," *New York Times*, October 25, 2006.

19 *Ibid.*

20 *Ibid.*

21 Terry Tamminen, *Lives Per Gallon: The True Cost of Our Oil Addiction* (Washington, DC: Island Press, 2006), 110-11.

22 Jack Doyle, *Taken for a Ride: Detroit's Big Three and the Politics of Air Pollution* (Emeryville, CA: Four Walls Eight Windows Press, 2000).

23 See www.rmi.org for information on the Hypercar Concept.

24 Jennifer Kho, "GM to Make Plug-in Hybrid," *Red Herring*, November 29, 2006.

25 Consultant report to the California Energy Commission, *California State Fuel-Efficient Tire Report, Volume II,* Consultant Report 600-03-001CR, January 2003.

26 For a discussion of the "base case," see Appendix, "Methodology to Analyze Oil Savings Potential," Bordetsky *et al.*, *op. cit.*, 21-41.

27 Bordetsky *et al.*, *op. cit.*, 30. See also Therese Langer, *Energy Savings Through Increased Fuel Economy for Heavy-Duty Trucks*, Report to the National Commission on Energy Policy, 2004.

28 R. Neal Elliott, Therese Langer, and Steven Nadel, *Reducing Oil Use Through Energy Efficiency: Opportunities Beyond Cars and Light Vehicles* (Washington, DC: ACEEE, January 2006).

29 See Federal Aviation Administration, *Flight Plan 2005-2009* (Washington, DC: U.S. Government Printing Office, 2004).

30 For a discussion of "feebates" incentives, see Therese Langer, *Vehicle Efficiency Incentives: An Update on Feebates for States* (Washington, DC: ACEEE, September 2005).

# 10

## BIOFUELS: GROWING ENERGY FOR $2.00 A GALLON AT THE PUMP

*"Do we want to feed our farmers or Mid-East terrorists? Do we want ANWR oil rigs or prairie grass fields? Fossil fuels or green fuels? . . . Expensive gasoline or cheaper ethanol? This appears to be nothing less than a Darwinian IQ test."*

- VINOD KHOSLA, VENTURE CAPITALIST AND BIOFUELS INVESTOR

**Can plant-based biofuels eventually replace 50% of U.S. oil use? Yes.**

- Advanced cellulosic ethanol could sell at $2.00/gallon at the pump.[1]

- In Brazil, ethanol in flexible-fuel cars now accounts for 40% of all light fuels sold.

- Replacing oil with plant fuels will dramatically increase farm income and jobs.

- In time, fuel ethanol and biodiesel can challenge petroleum fuels worldwide while increasing energy security globally, and dramatically reducing greenhouse gases.

## A WINNING BIOFUELS/BIOMASS STRATEGY

Writing in the *OECD Observer*, International Energy Agency analyst Lew Fulton notes that projections suggest ethanol could represent up to 5% of the world's transport fuel by 2010. While this may seem modest at first glance, Fulton points out that "no other alternative fuel has had the equivalent impact on the gasoline market in more than 100 years.[2]

In the big picture, biofuels are "the prize" of the fuel supply side of the Prometheus Plan. Biofuels are the only liquid, non-fossil fuels that currently have the potential to replace more than 50% of our oil use in the transportation sector by mid-century. In a comprehensive report on *Growing Energy: How Biofuels Can Help End America's Oil Dependence*, the Natural Resources Defense Council found, "If we follow an aggressive plan to develop cellulosic biofuels between now and 2015, America could produce the equivalent of nearly 7.9 million barrels of oil per day by 2050."[3]

Along the way, these fuels could generate farm profits of more than $5 billion per year. They could reduce our greenhouse gas emissions by 1.7 billion tons per year, which is equal to more than 80% of transportation-related emissions in 2002.

In the near future, biofuels could be cheaper than gasoline—with ethanol selling for $2.25/gallon or less[4] at the pump—ultimately saving the U.S. billions of dollars annually in imported fuel costs.

## BIOFUELS IN A NUTSHELL

In general, the major biofuels can be classified into three major groups: biologically produced alcohols; biologically produced gases; and biologically produced oil. A biofuel is any fuel that is derived from biomass, which originates from recently living organisms or their metabolic by-products, such as manure from cows.

The dominant biofuels are ethanol, currently produced from sugar (sugar cane, sugar beets) or starch crops (mainly corn); biodiesel produced from vegetable oils (soybeans, palm oil, rapeseed, and the like) or animal fats; and pure vegetable oil itself.

Agriculture products specifically grown for use as liquid biofuels include corn and soybeans in the U.S., sugar cane in Brazil, and flaxseed and rapeseed in Europe. A major new source of biofuel, particularly for use in diesel engines, will be oil from algae. Also, a rediscovered source, the jatropha tree in India, is now being planted at an enormous rate because it is a high-value source of vegetable oil for fuel.

Biologically produced feedstock can be collected from a wide variety of resources: agricultural and forest residues; animal waste and manure; specialized, fast growing "energy plants"; and methane capture from biodegrading organic wastes in landfills.

Just as agricultural processes can create the feedstock for ethanol plants (whether the conventional Brazilian model or using cellulosic technology now just arriving on the scene), they can also power homes and industries.[5] Generating electricity from biomass involves collecting and using organic material from America's farms, fields, forests and landfills. Next to hydropower, biomass is the nation's second largest source of renewable electricity, with more than 1.3 billion tons that could be used with "relatively modest changes" in land use and agricultural and forestry practices.[6]

To use biomass as fuel for generating electricity, it can be directly burned to produce steam to turn an electric turbine; co-fired with biofuels (ethanol and biodiesel); co-fired with fossil fuels such as coal or natural gas to "dilute" harmful greenhouse gases being released by fossil fuels; or gasified to synthesis gas (carbon monoxide + hydrogen), which is then burned in a gas turbine or furnace-boiler system to produce steam and electricity.

Today, the U.S. generates about 3% of its electricity from biomass, but the potential is much greater. More than 100 coal-fired plants are currently co-firing biomass combined with coal. Utilities can potentially substitute biomass for up to 15% of the coal used in coal plants that have been upgraded. This results in significant reductions of sulfur dioxide, carbon dioxide, nitrogen oxides, and other greenhouse gases.

## Twin pillars of the Prometheus Plan: Fuel Efficiency and Biofuels

The two pillars of the Prometheus Plan are automotive fuel efficiency (40 mpg for new passenger vehicles) and biofuels, mainly replacing gasoline with ethanol (26.4 billion gallons by 2015). Together, these two initiatives account for 60% of the targeted oil savings of 5 million barrels per day (MBD) by 2015.

In the case of biofuels, the winning ethanol strategy is clear. In the time period covered by the Prometheus Plan, the U.S. will, for political reasons, continue to aggressively increase corn-based ethanol production. It will also support the rapid expansion of sugar-based ethanol, both domestically and internationally. For the long term, starting now, we should take a fast-track approach to the commercialization of advanced, cellulosic-based ethanol, as cheaper and highly efficient cellulosic ethanol produced in the U.S. could conservatively save some 4.3 MBD of imported oil by 2025, and cut greenhouse gases by more than 80% compared to gasoline use.[7]

Several recent studies confirm this view, including the Natural Resources Defense Council's *Growing Energy* (2004); Berg and Licht, *World Fuel Ethanol Analysis and Outlook* (2004); Rocky Mountain Institute's "Substituting Biofuels and Biomaterials" (2005); and most recently the Worldwatch Institute's *Biofuels for Transportation: Global Potential and Implications for Sustainable Agriculture and Energy in the 21st Century* (2006).[8]

We are generally against corn ethanol except as an interim fuel because its production still consumes too many fossil fuels and puts undue pressure on agricultural commodity prices. However, in fairness to the corn-based ethanol industry, numerous plants are now being designed and built which use inexhaustible renewable resources like geothermal energy or methane from biodigesters of animal waste and garbage. These intelligent fuel supplies greatly enhance the desirability of corn ethanol and its energy balance ratio but still leave it lacking from our point of view because it creates unacceptable trade-offs between crops for food and fuel.

> *"Biofuels . . . offer a commercially viable alternative to gasoline that is available now; that can use existing infrastructure; and that can fuel vehicles available today at little or no additional cost."*
> — WORLDWATCH INSTITUTE, *STATE OF THE WORLD*, 2006

That having been said, we note that all too often in business and life, we let our search for "the perfect" prevent us from accepting "the good." In this context, we agree with Vinod Khosla, an engineer, a Silicon Valley venture capitalist who co-founded Sun Microsystems, a man who invested early on in Amazon and Google, and someone who now makes this case for ethanol:

- Corn ethanol is not perfect, but it is "the best alternative among realistic alternatives" available to us at the moment;

- Corn ethanol is environmentally preferable to petroleum-derived fuel;

- Corn ethanol, if managed properly, can result in lower prices for gasoline for today's automobile engines with only minor changes and without having to revolutionize the automobile industry;

- Corn ethanol primes the pump for better future options, including sugar-based ethanol, cellulosic ethanol, butanol, or other biohols (liquid alcohol fuels) from the same feedstocks, using similar technologies and the same basic automobile engines;[9] and

- Corn ethanol plants can be adapted to utilize front-end cellulosic technology when that becomes commercially available so that in the future the plants—basically distilleries—will be as economic, or more so.

As Figure 1 demonstrates, the Prometheus Plan shows that America—which has long been "the bread basket of the world"—can save 1.6 MBD of oil by 2015 by aggressively growing and developing two proven biofuels: ethanol for passenger vehicles and blends of biodiesel and pure vegetable oil for heavy trucks and diesel motors.

**Figure 1. Prometheus Plan Matrix: Biofuels Strategy— U.S. Oil Savings by 2015**[10]

| Biofuels Strategy and Current-Technology Oil Savings in Millions of Barrels of Oil Per Day | |
| --- | --- |
| **Measures** | **MBD** |
| **Accelerate growth of biofuels industry through standards for:** | |
| • **Ethanol**, mainly E85 from corn and sugar feedstocks<br>  15.0 billion gallons annually, corn— domestic<br>  +<u>11.4</u> billion gallons annually, sugar—domestic and international<br>  =26.4 billion gallons annually from corn and sugar feedstocks | 1.4 |
| • **Biodiesel**, mainly B20 from vegetable oil feedstocks<br>• 2.0 billion gallons annually from soybeans, palm kernel, and other feedstocks | 0.2 |
| • **Accelerated cellulosic ethanol development and commercialization**<br>• Estimated up to 14.6 billion gallons potential by 2015 | 0.0 |
| **Total oil saved by 2015** | **1.6** |

# THE BOOMING MARKET FOR BIODIESEL

Biodiesel is a vegetable-oil based fuel that can be burned in place of regular diesel or mixed in varying blends. A 20% biodiesel fuel (B20) is the most common mixture.

Biodiesel is coming of age, particularly in Europe, where diesel has long been a popular fuel for passenger vehicles. In the U.S., biodiesel is now used primarily for trucks and heavy equipment, but could also become the fuel of choice for ships, including ferries and cruise ships.

According to the U.S. Energy Information Administration, from 2004 to 2005, biodiesel consumption in the U.S. transportation sector increased almost fourfold to 11 trillion British Thermal Units (BTUs), up from just 1 trillion BTUs in 2001.

U.S. biodiesel sales also boomed in 2006, and sales are likely to increase exponentially for the next decade or two. Many new biodiesel facilities are under construction or in the planning stage.

For biodiesel to realize its potential, service stations will need to increase the number of pumps that can handle biodiesel. Automakers met with President Bush in March 2007 to ask for more federal financial support for pump conversions, telling him that there were only about 1,000 biodiesel pumps distributed among 170,000 gas stations. They argued that such financial support for biofuels would do more to reduce U.S. oil imports and carbon emissions than would higher fuel efficiency standards. In our opinion, there is no reason these strategies should be mutually exclusive.

The basic technology for converting vegetable oil to biodiesel is very simple. It remains to be seen what the preferred feedstock will be several years from now. Biodiesel is now being made from a variety of plant and vegetable oils, including soy, canola, rapeseed, jatropha, and palm oil, and even recycled restaurant oils. Palm oil will remain a popular feedstock for some time, but ultimately will be replaced by algae or even phytoplankton.

The simplicity of the basic biodiesel technology has not stopped displays of American ingenuity with the fuel. One chemistry professor is exploring making a "fuel-latent plastic" that is designed for conversion into a substitute diesel fuel. The plastic, made from soy oil, would be used for purposes like packaging, and later, when it would otherwise be headed for the waste pile, converted into biodiesel. The Pentagon was intrigued enough to provide $2.3 million in research funding for the project.[11]

## There's No Free Lunch

With 80 million acres of corn, U.S. farmers historically grew more corn than we were able to eat, feed to cattle, or export. We now need to convert corn into homegrown ethanol as a temporary substitute for automotive gasoline. This will especially appeal to farm state politicians concerned about rising energy prices and congressional elections.[12] Over the long haul, however, we are concerned about using a feed grain as the primary feedstock for ethanol because doing so pushes up the cost of all grain products, poultry, and beef.

When the agricultural lobby pushed through a 51-cent-a-gallon tax break on ethanol and required an ethanol additive in gasoline, it set off a "corn rush" to build new ethanol processing plants. For good measure, Congress slapped a 54-cent-a-gallon tariff on imported ethanol, aimed mainly at giving American farmers a strong competitive advantage over imports from Brazil, where ethanol from sugar cane is produced more than four times as efficiently. All this hubbub down on the farm has sparked a vigorous controversy over the role biofuels can play in replacing gasoline with competitive, renewable plant-based non-fossil fuels.

General Motors launched its corn-to-ethanol campaign with a Super Bowl ad for flexible-fuel vehicles that can burn ethanol or gasoline. The campaign urges Americans to "Live Green, Go Yellow." Although many buyers are unaware that their vehicles are flex-fuel vehicles, more than five million E85 vehicles are already on U.S. roads. New models are coming out all the time, and about one million more flex-fuel vehicles are produced each year. In March 2007, GM, Chrysler, and Ford told President Bush that half their 2012 vehicle production will be E85 flex-fuel vehicles capable of running on ethanol or biodiesel.

Ford and VeraSun Energy Corp., the leading U.S. ethanol producer, announced a new "Midwest Ethanol Corridor" along Illinois' I-55 and Missouri's I-70 to expand availability of E85 (a mixture of 85% ethanol, 15% gasoline) from Chicago to Kansas City.

As exciting as ethanol is on the world stage, not everyone has been persuaded to jump on the ethanol bandwagon just yet. In an article titled "Ethanol no 'silver bullet' for world's fuel problems," Josef Herbert points out that ethanol "would supply only 12% of the country's motor fuel—even if every hectare of corn were used."[13]

Others argue that corn is the worst feedstock crop for ethanol. This is because ethanol made from corn requires lots of petroleum-based fertilizer. And because corn must first be broken down from its natural carbohydrate structure to simple sugars before the

> "*Ethanol is not the silver bullet, but it has been tremendously good for rural communities, helping people stay on the land.*"
>
> — DAVID NELSON, PRESIDENT,
> MIDWEST GRAIN PRODUCERS CO-OP

sugars can be fermented and distilled to pure ethanol, this process, which at most ethanol plants uses *lots* of natural gas, is relatively inefficient. It generates a net energy yield of only 1.5 BTUs for every 1.0 BTU that goes in.

Brazilian ethanol made from sugar cane has a dramatically higher net energy yield of 8 BTUs for every 1.0 BTU in *and requires zero fossil fuels* to run the plant. The plants burn the sugar cane stalk to create more energy than is required to run the plant itself and can sell the excess to the electrical grid.

World Business Academy Fellow Lester Brown, a leading advocate of substituting alternative fuels for petroleum, raises the concern that "shifting food crops to fuel production could further tighten food supplies and raise prices, pitting affluent automobile owners against low-income food consumers."[14] His point is well taken and leads to the conclusion that ultimately non-food-based feedstocks will be used for ethanol production.

Obviously, when it comes to "growing energy," there is no free lunch, but the trade-off benefits dramatically outweigh the potential social costs, totally apart from the national security benefit of growing our fuel rather than importing it from Middle Eastern sheikhs. In fact, due diligence reveals that most doubts expressed about the present viability of ethanol as a fuel replacement for gasoline are based on misleading data, faulty logic, misconceptions, or even—in the case of the oil companies—hidden agendas. *Ethanol is here now!*

The bottom line is that today's ethanol producer in the Midwest can sell ethanol at "normal sustainable margins" to retailers, who will in turn re-sell it at a profit of $0.20 per gallon—twice what they make on gasoline. In July 2007, ethanol was selling for 30% less than gasoline, proving that even now the economics of corn-based ethanol works for farmers, processors, distributors, gasoline retailers, and most important, consumers.[15]

Combined with high oil prices, these ethanol economics have investors who pursue technology booms all pumped up as they search "for the Google of clean energy."[16]

No wonder that technology leaders such as Bill Gates and venture capital firms such as Nth Power have invested millions in leading ethanol producers. No wonder that former Internet investors such as Khosla have become the new techno-evangelists for biofuels, working hard toward the goal of seeing "$1.99 per gallon E85 at every Wal-Mart in America."

Notwithstanding the economics and science behind a dramatic increase in ethanol production, questions continue to arise concerning the issues of global market potential, energy balance, crop land for fuel versus food, cost versus other fuels, carbon emissions, infrastructure requirements, and technology timelines. In order to justify our claim that ethanol will be *the single most important driving force in the coming global biofuels energy revolution,* we need to address these issues head-on, one by one.

## ETHANOL HAS A 100-YEAR TRACK RECORD

Ethanol is a biologically produced alcohol biofuel with a long history and a proven production process. Rising energy prices and climate change problems have led to an increased focus on alcohol as a fuel.

Alcohol has been used as a fuel since the earliest days of the automobile industry. Otto Von Nicklous, the inventor of the combustion engine, designed his invention to run on ethanol. The early Ford Model-T cars, produced between 1903 and 1926, used ethanol. However, when relatively cheap leaded gasoline was introduced in 1924, it rapidly displaced ethanol. Hundreds of magazine articles, reports, books, and technical papers reflect that alcohol fuel was widely acknowledged as a technically feasible and economically competitive fuel if oil supplies were ever to run short.[17]

Among the alcohol fuels, also known as bioalcohols (or "biohols"), four (butanol, ethanol, methanol, and propanol) are of major interest because they can be synthesized biologically and have characteristics that allow them to be used in conventional engines. One advantage shared by all four alcohols is a high octane rating. For example, the relative Research Octane Numbers (RON) are gasoline (91-99), butanol (96), ethanol (130), and methanol (136). Octane is a measure of the ability of a hydrocarbon fuel to be burned efficiently in a high-compression internal combustion engine without inducing premature combustion in the cylinders (the cause of engine "knocking") and power loss. The higher the compression ratio[18] of the engine, the higher the octane required.

Ethanol ($C_2H_5OH$) has several advantages over other fossil fuels. For example, while ethanol has only 70% of the energy density of gasoline, it burns efficiently at a much higher compression ratio without octane-boosting additives. Ethanol's octane rating is 130 compared to 91 for regular gasoline, which explains one reason why *all the major high-compression Indy 500 race cars burn ethanol* rather than gasoline in pursuit of the checkered flag. Since ethanol burns more completely, carbon monoxide emissions can be 80-90% lower than for fossil-fueled engines.

Methanol ($CH_3OH$), which is currently produced from natural gas, can also be produced from biomass, although this is not now economically viable.

Butanol ($C_4H_{10}O$) can be produced along with acetone and ethanol by the ABE (acetone, butanol, ethanol) fermentation process, and experimental modifications of the ABE process show potentially high net energy gains, with butanol as the only product. Furthermore, butanol can be burned "straight up" in existing gasoline engines without modification. It produces more energy and is less corrosive and less water-soluble than ethanol. Butanol can be distributed via existing infrastructures. BP and DuPont have formed a joint venture in the U.K. to bring biobutanol, which has several advantages over ethanol, to market in 2007, using sugar beets as the feedstock for fermentation. Because the molecular structure of butanol much more closely resembles that of diesel and jet fuels than that of ethanol, Sir Richard Branson in October 2006 announced his intention to actively explore running butanol in Virgin Airlines' jet engines—a most intriguing concept.

While other alcohols and feedstocks will likely play a significant role as fuel substitutes, today the only practical large-scale alternative to gasoline is ethanol, with more than 4.9 billion gallons in production in the U.S. in 2006.

One of the main advantages of ethanol is that it is a renewable resource that contributes little to global warming. Like methanol, it can be blended with any amount of gasoline in the tank of a "flex-fuel vehicle," which can run on any combination of ethanol or gasoline and which many automakers are beginning to manufacturer in large numbers. In fact, some automakers are making *every one* of certain vehicle models capable of using E85 in any mixture with gasoline, at no extra charge. Thus, buyers will have nothing extra to do to enable their vehicle to use an alternative fuel such as E85.

According to the American Ethanol Coalition, ethanol can be made by a dry mill process or a wet mill process. Most of the ethanol in the U.S. is made using the dry mill process, in which the starch portion of the corn is converted into sugar and fermented, and the product ethanol is distilled from this mixture. The major steps in the dry mill process are milling, liquefaction, saccharification, fermentation, distillation, dehydration, denaturing, and the separation of certain by-products. The main by-products created in the production of ethanol are distiller's grain and carbon dioxide ($CO_2$). Distiller's grain, used wet or dry, is a highly nutritious livestock feed. Carbon dioxide is given off in great quantities during fermentation and many ethanol plants collect, compress, and sell it for use in other industries. Should the $CO_2$ be vented to the atmosphere, it would not add to greenhouse gases, as the most $CO_2$ a plant can give off is the amount it absorbed from the atmosphere during its growth cycle. In fact, the greatest quantity of the $CO_2$ is captured for other industrial purposes, thereby reducing ambient greenhouse gases in the atmosphere.

# Explosive Growth in World Biofuels Market

As Figures 2 and 3 show, worldwide production of ethanol more than doubled between 2000 and 2005, while production of biodiesel quadrupled.

**Figure 2. World Fuel Ethanol Production, 1975-2005**

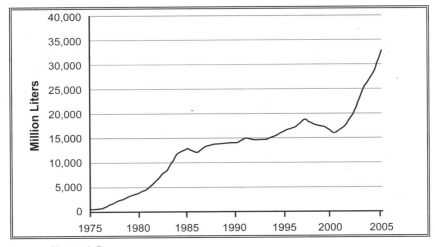

Source: Christoph Berg

**Figure 3. World Biodiesel Production, 1991-2005**

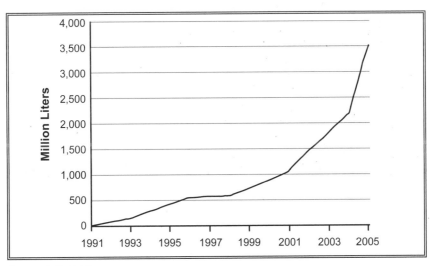

Source: F.O. Licht

By some estimates, world production of ethanol in 2005 was about 35 billion liters, or about 9.2 billion gallons (1 liter = 0.264 U.S. gallons). World production of biodiesel in 2005 was one-tenth that of ethanol, equal to about 3.5 billion liters, or almost 1 billion gallons. According to the U.S. Renewable Fuels Association, counting all grades of ethanol, world ethanol production was even higher than the above estimate. In any event, we agree with the Worldwatch Report on *Biofuels for Transportation*:

> The production and use of biofuels have entered a new era of global growth, experiencing acceleration in both the scale of the industry and the number of countries involved. Soaring investment in biofuel production is being driven by a variety of factors, including the development of more efficient conversion technologies, the introduction of strong new government policies, and, primarily, the rising price of oil. Underlying the commitment of an increasing number of governments to biofuel development is the desire to find new markets for farmers and their products and to reduce emissions of greenhouse gases.[19]

A 2004 International Energy Agency report—which predicts a post-2010 price for cellulosic ethanol at $0.72/gallon—estimates that "a third or more of road transportation fuels worldwide could be displaced by biofuels in the 2050-2100 time frame."[20]

## THE BRAZILIAN BREAKTHROUGH

Since learning about Brazil's recent declaration of independence from foreign oil, many Americans have been asking, "*If Brazil can achieve energy independence through the use of ethanol, why can't we?*" In 2005, the U.S. surpassed Brazil as the world's top ethanol producer, with 4.3 billion gallons, or 35% of world production, derived from corn. Brazil followed closely behind with 4.2 billion gallons, equal to 34% of world production, based on sugar cane. By 2006, total world ethanol production was approximately 13 billion gallons.

Back during the first oil price spikes of the 1970s, Brazil, like many other developing nations, did not have sufficient petrodollars to fund both oil imports and ambitious growth plans. Thus, the Brazilian government made reducing Brazil's dependence on oil a national priority. Through a combination of tax breaks and fuel-blending mandates that drove investment into ethanol, the industry grew rapidly. As result, by the mid-1980s, ethanol-fuel-only vehicles accounted for 96% of total car sales. Economic growth slowed dramatically in the 1990s as oil prices fell and sugar prices rose. Gasoline passed the substitution price for ethanol and by 1997, sales of ethanol vehicles had plummeted to less than 1% of total vehicle sales.

To address this, Brazil in 2003 began encouraging flexible-fuel vehicles that can run on virtually any mixture of gasoline and ethanol, which led to a stunning turnabout in the ethanol market. By 2005, flexible-fuel vehicles accounted for more than half of all new cars sold. According to the Washington Council on International Trade, "Since the 1970s, Brazil has saved almost $50 billion in imported oil costs—nearly 10 times the national investment through subsidies—while creating more than 1 million rural jobs."[21]

The current breakthrough came when Volkswagon and Ford introduced the flexible-fuel vehicle in Brazil. The engines in these cars gave consumers the choice of buying the cheapest fuel, while freeing them up from any potential shortages in ethanol supply. According to a *New York Times* report, in 2006, less than three years after the technology was introduced, more than 70% of the new automobiles sold in Brazil had flex-fuel engines. In general, such vehicles have appeared on the market without being priced higher than standard vehicles.[22] "It will be at 100% in two years," says Serge Habib, Citroën's managing director in the country. Like hybrids, flex-fuel cars retain a second-hand value greater than that of their conventional counterparts.

While ethanol can be made from the fermentation of many biological substances, the Brazilians exclusively use sugar cane as their feedstock. Sugar cane has distinct advantages over other feedstocks, including corn. For each unit of energy spent to turn cane into ethanol, up to 8.3 times as much energy is created, compared with a maximum of 1.8 times for corn ethanol produced using natural gas or other fossil fuels (see Figure 4). In addition, Brazilian sugar mills now burn the "bagasse" (green tops, attached leaves, and ground trash) to generate the electricity needed to process sugar cane into ethanol, and use other by-products to fertilize the fields where cane is planted. Some mills are producing so much electricity that they sell the excess into the national grid. A sugar cane bagasse plant on the island of Maui has operated continuously for more than 25 years and is currently a significant source of that island's electricity.

Going beyond replacing oil for ground transportation, Brazil's Embraer, the world's first manufacturer of ethanol-fueled planes, now has so many customers backlogged that there's a two-year waiting list to convert gasoline-propelled aircraft engines to alcohol. One air taxi service is now flying Embraer's latest model, a single-propeller Ipanema plane. The Ipanema flies on ethanol distilled from sugar cane, and this simple fact has dropped the plane's fuel bill by 40%, with no decrease in performance. "At this rate," says Embraer executive Acir Padilha, "the gasoline motor is headed for extinction."[23]

## POSITIVE NET ENERGY

Critics have lambasted corn-based ethanol, the most common form produced in the U.S. today, as "literally a waste of energy." They argue that it takes more energy to make corn ethanol—growing, fertilizing, transporting, and processing the corn feedstock—than would be saved by using it.

In an insightful article, "Digging into the Ethanol Debate," reporter Carl Bialik, aka "the numbers guy" at the *Wall Street Journal*, points out numerous shortcomings in this critique.[24]

The work most frequently cited in support of the negative net-energy argument is that of David Pimentel of Cornell University and Tad Patzek of the University of California at Berkeley. In a 2005 paper published in *Natural Resources Research*, Pimentel and Patzek argue, "Ethanol production using corn grain required 29% more fossil energy than the ethanol fuel produced." In contrast, they argue that the production of gasoline or diesel uses about 20% more fossil-fuel energy than the fuels produce.[25]

Far from convinced, Bialik finds their analysis biased against ethanol in several ways. First, the researchers stack a number of extraneous energy costs onto the ethanol input side of the ledger. Generally, such costs are not included in the comparable analysis of gasoline production. These include the energy required to produce the tractors used in cornfields and almost every conceivable form of energy used by agricultural workers, even their food, transportation, and police protection. Furthermore, on the output side, the research did not consider the energy value of ethanol by-products that can be used primarily as cattle feed.

Second, the analysis rests on the operation of "all technology in use at the time, including old plants." This dates the research, because it ignores the fact that the energy required to produce corn ethanol is decreasing every year, while corn yields are increasing, and ethanol from corn production techniques, such as enzymatic pre-digestion, are increasing the yields and efficiency of corn-based plants. "There are lots of new technologies," said Hossein Shapouri, an agricultural economist with the U.S. Department of Energy. "It's going to continue to improve the yield and lower the energy."[26]

Bialik points out that many of the numbers cited in the critical studies are generally based on U.S. Department of Agriculture surveys that are a few years old. Such surveys do not capture the improved performance of higher corn yields and the processing efficiencies of newer plants in the rapidly evolving ethanol industry. For example, one South Dakota processor has pioneered a method for converting corn to ethanol at 90 degrees Fahrenheit rather than the previous 230-250 degrees, improving energy efficiency by 10-12%. Ethanol investor Khosla rejects the anti-ethanol arguments that are based on operations of older plants, claiming, "It's like saying a power plant built in the '50s is very polluting, so all power plants are very polluting."

Going one step further, E3 Biofuels LLC is extracting more energy from all stages of the corn ethanol process by building plants near dairy farms, feeding cows the distillate by-products of ethanol processing, and then converting the livestock waste into biogas to help power the processing plants. These current improvements are behind Khosla's prediction: "We suspect we will see typical corn ethanol plants in just a few years ... achieve an energy balance of 3-4 [ratio of energy output to energy input] without cellulosic ethanol technologies, and many old plants will be retro-fitted with biomass gasification technologies to reduce cost and improve energy balance."[27]

Khosla's prediction that corn ethanol plants will achieve improved energy balances is already proving true due to their increased use of renewable energy rather than fossil fuels to power the production process. Increasingly, methane digesters as well as biomass gasification are being used to power such plants. Across the country, several ethanol plants are either in operation or on the drawing board which will be fueled by methane captured from animal waste or trash. A proposed new ethanol plant near Louisville, Kentucky will use wind turbines and a geothermal system. Using such renewable energy rather than natural gas significantly improves the energy balance for corn ethanol.

Third, other credible researchers contradict the Pementel-Patzek findings. For example, Michael Wang, a fuel system analyst at the Federal Argonne National Laboratories, led a study comparing the net energy value of gasoline with that of corn ethanol produced using fossil fuels. He found that it took 0.74 BTU of fossil fuel to create 1 BTU of ethanol fuel, an energy balance ratio of 1.35 (1.0/0.74 = 1.35). In contrast, it took 1.23 BTUs of fossil fuel to create 1 BTU of gasoline, an energy balance ratio of only 0.81. Many other studies corroborate Wang's general findings that ethanol is a more efficient fuel to manufacture than gasoline.

As a result, most environmental organizations, including the Natural Resources Defense Council, the Worldwatch Institute, and the Earth Policy Institute agree that the net energy of corn ethanol is indeed positive. The following table tells the story, although as discussed above and in Chapter 11, corn ethanol's energy balance is improving as production facilities convert from fossil fuels to renewable energy and use improved technology and feedstocks.

## Figure 4. Ethanol—Net Energy Yield for Selected Crops and Gasoline

| Fuel | Crop—Feedstock | Energy Output/ Fossil Energy Input |
|---|---|---|
| Ethanol | Cellulosic Switchgrass (U.S.) | 4.0 |
| | Sugar beet (France) | 1.9 |
| | Sugar cane (Brazil) | 8.0-8.3 * |
| | Cassava (Nigeria) | — |
| | Sweet Sorghum (India) | — |
| | Corn (U.S.) | 1.3-1.8 |
| | Wheat (France) | 1.2 |
| Gasoline | | 0.8 |

* Cane production and ethanol distillation burn sugar cane bagasse as heat
Sources: Lester Brown, *Plan 2.0*, 2006; Worldwatch Institute, *State of the World*, 2006

As Figure 4 suggests, the real issue here is not simply the individual net energy yield of corn ethanol. Rather, it is the net energy of corn ethanol relative to gasoline (the fuel that it replaces), as well as how corn ethanol compares to other ethanol feedstocks such as sugar cane and cellulose. In this context, Wang's analysis supports the observation that corn ethanol has approximately twice the net energy of gasoline (i.e., an average of 1.5 for corn vs. 0.8 for gasoline).

In fact, the real focus should be on how much petroleum—not fossil fuel—ethanol replaces, and here the answer is that "ethanol causes a very significant (90%) reduction in petroleum use." Given the Prometheus Plan objectives of decreasing reliance on imported oil and lowering greenhouse gas emissions, switching to available corn ethanol makes good sense in the short term. It also passes the test from a business perspective, especially since the production costs of a gallon of ethanol are substantially lower than the costs of gasoline produced from oil. More important than the efficiency of ethanol as a fuel, the corn feedstock for this type of ethanol is purchased from U.S. farmers rather than Arab sheikhs *and* is not subject to being cut off by the act of a lone terrorist or Iran's President Ahmadinejad.

## Enough Cropland for Fuel *and* Food

Both ethanol critics and environmentalists are concerned about a looming "food fight" over growing crops for energy rather than food and feedstocks. *Will there be enough land to meet our energy needs?* Currently, some 15% of the America's 80 million acres of corn are used for ethanol production. In Brazil, 50% of the nation's 13.5 million acres of sugar cane are now used for ethanol production.

If we intend to replace *all* of America's oil used in transportation with corn ethanol, then—as the critics contend—we would simply not have enough land (without dramatically expanding corn acreage). Replacing all gasoline with corn-based ethanol, however, is not going to happen for many reasons, including the tremendously high yields of sugar cane ethanol, which requires a fraction of the acreage required for corn; the availability of vast tracts of land for growing sugar beets, which also are superior in yield to corn; the dramatic technical breakthroughs that are occurring in cellulosic ethanol; and the world market developing in tropical countries for sugar cane ethanol exports. Corn-based ethanol will not be the dominant feedstock player of the future, as the demand for corn continues to grow and its price goes up. Cellulosic ethanol will prove to be far more efficient, and will use feedstocks that in the long term are far less expensive and more abundant than corn.

Equally clear is that predictable pathways exist for the large-scale production of ethanol from cellulosic biomass feedstocks such as switchgrass or hemp. North Dakota is on the cutting edge of a national movement to legalize growing hemp, a crop that would restore the state's agricultural industry, which has been devastated by a fungus that has wiped out thousands of acres of wheat. Unlike wheat, hemp can withstand the fungus and grow in the cool and wet soil. The state's soil is of limited value for most crops because the necessary harvesting equipment would be damaged by the rocky soil. North Dakota has started issuing state licenses to grow hemp, and state legislator David C. Monson and other farmers are pushing hard for approval by the federal Drug Enforcement Administration.

Using switchgrass as a preferred energy crop, the Natural

Resources Defense Council study estimates we would need only about 114 million acres of land. In one scenario, if we converted some 70 million acres in export crops such as soybeans, plus the additional 40 million acres in U.S. Conservation Reserve Program lands, we would have earmarked approximately 110 million acres of land for energy crops without using *any corn acreage*. In time, as noted above, improved efficiency in cellulosic ethanol production and in the use of waste biomass feedstocks, such as corn stover, rice husks, and sugar cane bagasse will further reduce land requirements.

Former Secretary of State George Schultz and former CIA Director James Woolsey have estimated that with efficiency improvements, we will need only 30 million acres of soil bank lands to meet half of our gasoline needs by 2025. That represents about one-half of the 2005 acreage planted in export corps such as wheat and soybeans. A 2005 Department of Energy study estimates that "1.3 billion tons of biomass could be generated with relative ease from existing cropland, resulting in more than 100 billion gallons of cellulosic ethanol without significantly changing agricultural patterns."[28] In comparison, it will require only 26.4 billion gallons of ethanol,[29] one-quarter of the Department of Energy's assessment of the ethanol that will be available, to meet the Prometheus Plan goals of 1.4 MBD in oil savings by 2015 (see Figure 1 above).

*So, how much ethanol can be produced from available lands?*

**Corn feedstocks.** As far as the limits of U.S. ethanol production capacity from corn feedstock are concerned, the Defense Council concludes:

> The Energy Policy Act of 2005 establishes a renewable fuel standard that requires the use of 7.5 billion gallons of ethanol in 2012. Many in the industry believe that production capacity will actually surpass this, however there is also broad agreement that there is a limit to how much corn can be devoted to ethanol production without causing significant distortions to agricultural markets. A reasonable near-term economic limit on corn-based ethanol is probably between 10 and 15 billion gallons . . .[30]

It is noteworthy how rapidly corn ethanol projections and mandates have increased in the past two years alone. As noted, the Energy Policy Act of 2005 mandated the production and use of 7.5 billion gallons of renewable fuels by 2012. In his 2007 State of the Union address, President Bush proposed to increase this mandate by nearly five-fold, calling for the establishment of mandatory renewable fuels standards of 35 billion gallons by 2017.

Partially in response to 2005 Energy Policy Act mandates, American farmers and processors have rapidly ramped up corn ethanol production. According to the U.S. Energy Information Administration and the Renewable Fuels Association, between 2005 and 2006, U.S. ethanol production increased by 25%, from 3.9 billion gallons to 4.9 billion gallons. Demand for ethanol also soared, reaching 5.4 billion gallons in 2006, a 33% increase over 2005 levels.

**Sugar cane and sugar beet feedstocks.** According to the U.S. Department of Agriculture's Economic Research Service, the U.S. currently has about one million acres of sugar cane planted in Florida (401,000 acres), Louisiana (455,000 acres), South Texas (42,000 acres), and Hawaii (24,000 acres). Additional sugar acreage for a new 50 to 100 million-gallons-per-year sugar cane ethanol plant is being put into cultivation in Southern California's Imperial Valley, even as we write.

In Hawaii, additional large tracts of land owned by the King Kamehaha Schools (formerly the Bishop Estate), Maui Land and Pineapple, and Gay & Robinson are in the process of being converted into sugar cane ethanol production. There are 1.3 million acres of sugar beets, which have a much broader growing range than sugar cane, distributed throughout the Great Lakes (154,000 acres in Michigan and Ohio), the Upper Midwest (746,000 acres in Minnesota and North Dakota), the Great Plains (175,000 acres in Colorado, Montana, Nebraska, Texas, and Wyoming), and in the Far West (225,000 acres in California, Idaho, Oregon, and Washington).

Since an acre of sugar cane on the U.S. mainland will produce approximately 600 tons of ethanol, and an acre of sugar beets will produce 720 tons of ethanol, it would take approximately 19 million acres of sugar cane and/or sugar beets to generate our 11.4 billion gallons of ethanol from domestic sources if we made no ethanol from corn, whatsoever.[31] Vast quantities of sugar beets can be grown for fuel in Minnesota on land unsuitable for wheat, corn, or other staple food crops. Such use of land presents no food vs. fuel trade-offs.

We know that Louisiana had more than $1 billion in agricultural losses because of Hurricane Katrina in 2005, of which $145 million was in the sugar cane crop, while Florida lost 12% of its sugar cane crop. In a severe energy crisis or in response to a dramatic increase in the price of corn, the U.S. could use all existing sugar lands (cane and beet sugar) for ethanol production, and could also convert other suitable crop lands, including cotton and tobacco lands, to easily grow feedstock for U.S. ethanol plants.

The biofuels strategy of the Prometheus Plan calls for the production of 15.0 billion gallons of corn ethanol, plus another 11.4 billion gallons from domestic and international sugar ethanol sources in order to generate the total 26.4 billion gallons required to save 1.4 MBD of oil by 2015.[32] From our review of the production capabilities and planned production set to come online in the U.S. and globally, it is our firm conclusion that 26.4 billion gallons of ethanol for consumption by 2015 will prove to be a conservative estimate of available supply.

Fortunately, there is yet another great solution for the U.S. to acquire the ethanol called for in the Prometheus Plan—buy it from developing nations instead of just giving them aid. According to a recent United Nations Food and Agricultural Organization (FAO) report, some 946 million acres of land around the world have "rain-fed cultivation potential at intermediate level inputs available in tropical areas for sugar cane crops" and are rated as "very suitable or suitable" for sugar production. To add perspective, Brazil currently has 13.5 million acres under sugar cane cultivation.[33]

Another study estimates that sugar cane grown in tropical areas could easily produce enough fuel to displace some 10% of world gasoline demand by 2020.[34] According to a widely cited report on

World Fuel Ethanol, by 2013 many Latin American and Caribbean nations, including Mexico, Cuba, Argentina, Colombia, Paraguay, and Peru, will join Brazil in producing ethanol from sugar cane both for domestic use and for export into the rapidly expanding international market for fuel ethanol.

Given that Brazilian sugar cane ethanol production costs are lower than U.S. corn ethanol ($0.81/gallon without subsidy vs. $1.05/gallon with subsidy), buying from impoverished countries makes good business sense, because it yields net living standard increases and, hence, greater global stability. It also endears us to countries that are either neutral or unfriendly toward the U.S.[35] Fortunately, this also makes broad geopolitical sense, since it will decrease global oil dependence, enhance economic growth, and provide a market-driven counterbalance for the oil-funded influence of the Venezuelan Chávez regime, while reducing the geopolitical power of various Middle Eastern countries. Unlike oil, sugar crops for ethanol can grow in many developing nations. Hence, no single country or region can dominate production.

**Cellulosic feedstocks.** Nearly every major researcher and organization, from the Natural Resources Defense Council to the Pentagon, agrees that U.S. corn ethanol production is an essential stepping stone in the evolving technology of ethanol production. Corn ethanol production will establish the processing plant and infrastructure platform necessary for the coming transition to advanced technology ethanol production from cellulosic feedstocks. Cellulosic feedstocks will be significantly cheaper and more efficient; they will produce significantly less greenhouse gas; and they will be compatible with biodiversity and the simultaneous multi-crop planting of both energy and feed crops.

According to ethanol advocate and investor Vinod Khosla, by 2030 it will take no more than 40-60 million acres of land to replace all U.S. gasoline demand, even assuming demand growth of 1% per year.[36] With production improvements, dry biomass yields of 20-30 tons per acre are feasible, and up to 40 tons/acre are possible on the best lands. At 120 gallons of ethanol per dry ton of biomass and 25

> *"New technologies can produce robustly competitive 3.7 million barrels per day of liquid fuels, mainly as cellulosic ethanol."*
> — AMORY LOVINS, *WINNING THE OIL ENDGAME*, 2005

tons of biomass per acre, 60 million acres of land can generate more than 150 billion gallons of ethanol gas-equivalent gallons by 2030.

Based on these projections, Khosla concludes, "At 24 tons per acre . . . we can replace all our oil needs even with demand growth." Multiple estimates point to this same conclusion. If in fact, since most of our agricultural land is used to produce grains and hay for animal feed (principally corn, oats, and wheat), the Natural Resources Defense Council believes that we will simultaneously be able to grow cellulose crops for ethanol and feed. At this point, concerns about limited land resources disappear.

## ETHANOL FOR $2.25 A GALLON OR LESS

When it comes to the economics of ethanol, critics typically raise three arguments. First, a gallon of ethanol provides higher octane but 30% less total energy, and, therefore, lower mileage than a gallon of gasoline. Second, ethanol is more expensive than gasoline. Third, for ethanol to be profitable, farmers and producers must receive subsidies. While all of these arguments to some extent were true *in the past,* they are all misleading because they are made out of context. *In the long run,* all are also immaterial to the decision about ethanol.

**Misleading Argument #1: Ethanol produces lower mileage than gasoline.** First, while there is a 20-30% mileage drop-off per gallon of ethanol compared to gasoline in *today's* cars, this will decline and eventually disappear over time as engines are adjusted to optimize flex-fuel efficiencies. For example, while Ford's flex-fuel Crown Victoria is rated to get 14 mpg on E85 and 20 mpg on gasoline, a reduction of 30%, Chevrolet has already improved on Ford's performance with its Impala, a large flexible-fuel vehicle that gets

19 mpg on E85 and 24 on gasoline, a reduction of only about 20%.

Furthermore, in Sweden, Saab already sells a 9-5 BioPower turbocharged engine that generates 175 horsepower on gasoline and up to 215 hp on E85, while getting only 18% less mileage on E85. This is because the engine adjusts to take full advantage of E85's higher octane rating (100-105 for E85 vs. 87-93 for gasoline), demonstrating that as engines are optimized for ethanol, the current "mileage penalty" will continue to decline. In fact, the current mileage drop is a result of data generated by running gasoline-optimized engines on ethanol. It remains to be seen what true "mileage penalty" will be paid with engines built specifically to burn gasoline and any blend of gasoline and ethanol.

Based on the older data from gasoline-designed engines converted to run on ethanol, however, many reports have noted (as we did above) that one gallon of ethanol provides only 70% of the energy of a gallon of gasoline on a worst-case basis. From this, one could conclude that it requires 1.43 gallons of ethanol to replace one gallon of gasoline.[37] Because of the higher octane of ethanol, however, we agree with the Rocky Mountain Institute's current assessment that one gallon of ethanol in today's cars is operationally equivalent to 0.8123 gallons of gasoline, or conversely, that it takes 1.23 gallons of ethanol to replace 1 gallon of gasoline.[38] We use this conversion ratio of 81% in our Prometheus Plan calculations to determine how many gallons of ethanol it will take to replace the predicted oil savings in the matrix (see Figure 1 above).[39] As shown below, ethanol is already coming to market more than 23% cheaper than gasoline, and this trend (i.e., ethanol prices dropping as a percentage of gasoline prices) will definitely continue.

**Misleading Argument #2: Ethanol is more expensive than gasoline.** Here it is important to distinguish between ethanol production costs and market prices, which historically have moved in sync with gasoline prices at the pump. According to a 2006 U.S. Department of Agriculture study, U.S. corn ethanol production cost is $1.05/gallon (composed of $0.53 for feedstock and $0.51 for dry mill processing). At this cost, ethanol production costs are substantially cheaper than those of gasoline, including the cheapest Saudi crude oil production costs—and the money stays in the U.S.! In comparison, the widely published cost of sugar cane ethanol production in Brazil is $0.81/gallon ($0.30 for feedstock and $0.51 for processing), making it the world's low-cost producer of bio-ethanol.

Driven by exploding demand and high profits, ethanol producers are rapidly expanding capacity. Between January 2000 and January 2007, the number of ethanol refineries in the U.S. more than doubled, from 54 to 119, while production capacity more than tripled, from 1748.4 to 6183.4 million gallons per year.[40] Ethanol production capacity will likely increase by at least 75% over 2004 levels, based on facilities now under construction or in the active planning stages and expected to be online by 2008.[41] The four largest processors are ADM, VersaSun, Demeter, and Cargill.

If corn prices remain within historical ranges, U.S. ethanol production costs will continue to decline because of improvements in economies of scale, technology, and processing. The potential for significant reductions in ethanol production costs has already been demonstrated over time in Brazil, where costs should fall even further from today's $0.81/gallon in currency and inflation-adjusted dollars. This represents an additional projected decrease of 38%.

Given the emerging large-scale commercialization of cellulosic ethanol, the Natural Resources Defense Council estimates that U.S. production costs could drop to $0.39-$0.69/gallon at the plant gate.[42] Additional developments could further reduce costs to producers. These include the receipt of tipping fees for biomass disposal and the production of compost, electrical energy, and other economic by-products from ethanol production, including protein for animal feed. In summary, ethanol production costs are low, are competitive with gasoline, and are projected to become even lower in the future.

As a gasoline extender and substitute and as an octane enhancer, the economic viability of ethanol has always depended on the price of gasoline. This will not change anytime soon. As a result, in recent years the pump price per gallon of ethanol has closely tracked the price of gasoline (adjusted for the relative energy content of ethanol to gasoline) plus the 51 cents-per-gallon federal excise tax credit. A short-term exception occurred when ethanol spot prices topped $4 per gallon in June 2006 because of a congressional mandate that U.S. refineries use ethanol to replace methyl-tertiary-butyl ether (MTBE), a toxic octane booster that contaminates groundwater.

As additional ethanol production capacity comes online in the U.S., and as ethanol imports expand from Brazil and the Caribbean Basin Initiative nations, ethanol prices are expected to hold steady or decline. For example, in early 2007, futures market prices for ethanol on the Chicago Board of Trade had gradually declined from more than $3/gallon in July 2006 to $2.19/gallon for May 2007 futures. Conversely, the price of gasoline over the next year is likely to increase by at least 25%, making gasoline *even less competitive with ethanol.* As noted earlier in this book, we believe that oil is heading into the $100+/barrel range. Therefore, ethanol prices could even increase over the long term, providing long-term incentives for ethanol producers to increase capacity, and still retain an increasingly large competitive advantage over gasoline.

Consumers would like to know why lower ethanol production prices can't lead to lower prices at the pump. Ethanol prices can have this effect, and indeed they have. In some local markets, ethanol prices already have drifted lower. For example, an Arizona report from April 2005 found E85 selling for $1.83 while regular gasoline at the adjacent pump was selling at $2.27. More significant for the long term is that Royal Dutch Shell is reportedly offering a long-term, fixed-price contract to cellulosic ethanol developers. This would allow Shell to profitably sell this biofuel for $1.99 at the pump.

An exciting potential of the Prometheus Plan is a biofuels future in which every Wal-Mart in America sells ethanol for $2.25 or less a gallon. Consumers benefit. Every business makes a profit along the way—farmers, producers, distributors, and retailers. This scenario frees the U.S. from concerns about rising crude oil costs as the factor that drives the increase in retail gasoline prices (see Figure 5).

**Figure 5. What Do We Pay For in a Gallon of Regular Grade?**

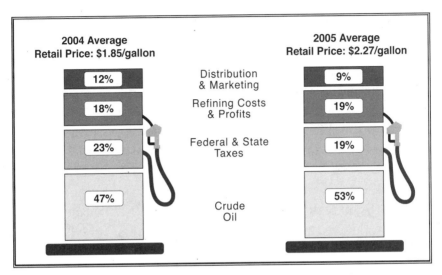

Source: U.S. Energy Information Administration

**Misleading Argument #3: Ethanol requires subsidies.** As Khosla succinctly puts it, "Wrong again. It may get subsidies, but it doesn't need them to be competitive with gasoline at any projected price of oil within the next 25 years (Energy Information Administration projections, 2006)."[43] Currently, in addition to a 51-cent-per-gallon producer tax incentive, U.S. corn ethanol is protected by a 54-cent tariff. Today, even if ethanol prices were substantially cut, corn ethanol producers would still make acceptable profit margins. And, without the import tariff, Brazilian ethanol sold in the U.S. would compete very well with oil.

Clearly, the worldwide growth of the biofuels industry has been materially supported by a broad variety of economic and political policies, including subsidies, blending mandates, and tax incentives. However, global subsidies and tax incentives since 1980 amount to a small fraction of the subsidies and incentives provided to Big Oil even in one year! As a recent study, *Biofuels in Transportation*, points out, "This support (for ethanol) must be considered in the context of the support enjoyed by the global oil industry, which—despite being a mature industry—it continues to receive. [This includes] massive subsidies to secure supply, depletion tax credits, income tax relief, and indirect subsidies from healthcare systems and international military presence."[44]

While reliable data on total subsidies to the oil industry remain elusive, based on congressional sources, we estimate that in the 32-year period between 1968 and 2000, the petroleum industry received up to $150 billion in subsidies in the U.S., or about $4.7 billion per year. In comparison, during the 21-year period between 1979 and 2000, the ethanol industry received up to $12 billion in subsidies, or about $0.5 billion per year. This does not include the indirect cost of fossil fuels, including military or health expenditures. Annual military outlays required to protect the flow of oil from the Persian Gulf to importing countries amounts to $50 billion a year, excluding the cost of the wars in Iraq and Afghanistan.

Brazil heavily subsidized its ethanol program in its earlier years. Today, Brazil is independent of foreign oil, and sugar cane ethanol *does not receive any direct government subsidies.*

At the end of the day, we can look at government support for both ethanol and oil as political realities that neither agribusiness nor the oil lobby will easily forfeit. If the essential goal is to reduce foreign oil dependence, the good news is that on a sound profit and loss basis, ethanol can stand on its own as a pillar of the Prometheus Plan—with or without subsidies. It comes down to two key questions: *"Where do we want to spend our transportation dollars, in the Middle East or in Middle America?"* and *"Do we want to take back from Big Oil the power to continually increase the egregious profits they extract through control of what we pay for gasoline at the pump?"* The answer to both questions is obvious.

## INFRASTRUCTURE IS NOT A BARRIER

Brazil has already "primed the pump" by installing simple, cheap flexible-fuel vehicle technology on 70% of all new vehicles sold, and by using, with minor modifications, existing gas stations, tanks, pumps, and tankers to distribute and sell ethanol.

> *"I can't remember the last time I saw a Marine battalion guarding a cornfield."*
>
> — DAVE BARTHMUSS,
> GM SPOKESMAN

There is no doubt that flexible-fuel vehicle technology can be implemented cheaply and rapidly. "The rate at which this technology has been adopted is remarkable, the fastest I have ever seen in the motor sector, faster than the airbag, automatic transmission or electric window," said Barry Engle, president of Ford do Brasil. "From the consumer standpoint, it's wonderful, because you get flexibility and you don't have to pay for it."[45]

Several environmental organizations have called for legislation requiring that 100% of new vehicles be flexible-fuel vehicles by 2015. We agree that this goal is both desirable and achievable. However, as Figure 6 shows, the U.S. can achieve the Prometheus Plan goal of 26 billion gallons of ethanol, saving 1.4 MBD, by 2015, through a steady ramp-up and rollout of flexible-fuel vehicles into the new vehicle fleet: from 6% in 2006 to 40% in 2011 and to 70% by 2016.

**Figure 6. Ramp-up of Flexible-Fuel Vehicles as Percentage of New Car Sales, 2006, 2011, 2016[46]**

| Year | New Cars Per Year | New Flexible-Fuel Vehicles Per Year | Cum. Flexible-Fuel Vehicle Cars | % E85 Per Flexible-Fuel Vehicle Car | E85 Demand Billion Gals. |
|---|---|---|---|---|---|
| 2006 | 15,944,000 | 1,000,000 (6% of total) | 2,000,000 | — | — |
| 2011 | 16,977,000 | 6,791,000 (40% of total) | 21,158,000 | 20% | 3 billion |
| 2016 | 17,281,000 | 12,097,000 (70% of total) | 76,069,000 | 50% | 26 billion |

Certainly, the U.S. has stricter technical and environmental regulations about gas pumps and underground gas tanks than Brazil does. Nevertheless, the funds required to achieve this flexible-fuel vehicle market penetration are miniscule compared to the size of the market.

One Natural Resources Defense Council analysis found that some existing pumps and gas station configurations can already handle ethanol, while other stations will need to install new tanks, but not new pumps, under the existing real estate; still others will need new pumps. Depending on the requirements, it would cost between $3,000 to $75,000 per station to convert existing gas stations to serve ethanol in at least one pump, or an average cost of around $50,000 per station. Another estimate found that in order to convert 10% of the nation's 121,000 gas stations to at least one E85 pump, it would take no more than a few hundred million dollars over about five years, or less than 0.1% of annual revenue. Furthermore, contrary to popular belief, E85 can be piped through most existing pipelines.

## CELLULOSIC ETHANOL READY IN FIVE YEARS

As with the rest of the biofuels industry, cellulosic ethanol is developing at a furious pace, building on decades of prior research. Most knowledgeable observers believe that the first production-scale plants will be in operation by late 2008. Full-scale production and commercialization will come online in five years, or by 2010.

The Natural Resources Defense Council argues for federal support of a pedal-to-the-metal cellulosic program that could generate one billion gallons per year by 2015. Frontline investors like Khosla foresee earlier production levels of nearly one billion gallons per year (in fact, by 2010), followed by a rapid ramp-up to 14.6 billion gallons per year by 2015, which requires adding nearly three billion gallons per year annually between 2010 and 2015.

Two major commercial cellulosic plants are already under development. Verenium, formed by a merger of Diversa and Celunol, is constructing a 1.4 million gallon-per-year demonstration-scale facility in Jennings, Louisiana that will use sugar cane bagasse and specially bred energy cane. The Iogen plant in Ottawa, Canada has now achieved an annual production capacity of about one million gallons, turning wheat, oat and barley straw into ethanol. In April 2004, Petro-Canada took delivery of Iogen's initial 1,300-gallon shipment of cellulosic ethanol, which met Canadian fuel specifications. In early 2007, the U.S. Department of Energy announced that it had selected six cellulosic ethanol plants for up to $385 million in federal funding to help bring cellulosic ethanol to market. Combined with the industry cost share, investment in the six plants will exceed $1.2 billion. One of the six selected for funding was the Iogen Biorefinery in Shelley, Idaho, which will produce 18 million gallons of ethanol annually. Partners and investors include Royal Dutch/Shell and Goldman Sachs.

Construction was planned to begin in April 2007 on a 50 million-gallons-per-year ethanol facility in the Imperial Valley of California, using the patented Swan Biomass technology. It is projected to yield 3,000 gallons of ethanol per acre of sugar cane and to have production costs of $1.10 per gallon of ethanol. Should the Swan technology prove to be commercially viable, it will dramatically increase the potential for ethanol production from sugar cane, both in the U.S. and worldwide.[47]

As reported in the Department of Energy's 2006 *Annual Energy Outlook*, "Several obstacles continue to prevent commercialization of the process, including how to accelerate the hydrolysis reaction that breaks down cellulose fibers and what to do with the lignin byproducts." Furthermore, initial investment in the first cellulosic plants is relatively high compared to operating corn ethanol plants—approximately $300 million vs. $65 million for a 50-million-gallon-per-year refinery. However, these capital costs will most definitely decline over time and with production experience.

## WHAT IS AN "EXISTING TECHNOLOGY"?

In recently granting Lockheed Martin a multibillion-dollar contract (over a Boeing-Northrop-Grumman bid) to build the nation's next spaceship for human flight, NASA said that the winning design looked more "achievable" because "it relied more heavily on known technologies than developing new ones."[48] Following the same reasoning, we have based the Prometheus Plan Matrix for saving 5 MBD on three criteria: *no new technologies, no increase in greenhouse gases, and no new taxes*. (An excess profits tax on oil companies is optional, and we think desirable. However, it is not required for the successful implementation of the Prometheus Plan).

We have rigorously interpreted (one could argue too rigorously) the Prometheus Plan's first criterion to mean that we will advocate only conventional technologies that are *currently proven and commercially available* at this time, at a scale large enough to produce oil savings by at least 0.1 MBD in 10 years. As a result, we have not included hydrogen fuel cell vehicles, because they are not commercially available today and may not be available on a broad scale for a decade or more. Thus, even if there were 100,000 fuel cell vehicles on the road by 2015, they would not make a sufficient contribution to reducing oil imports. In a similar vein, we have not focused on renewable resources for generating electricity, as such renewable resources solve many problems but do not replace petroleum products from the Middle East consumed in our transportation sector, which is where the 5 MBD can most easily be saved.

The cellulosic ethanol situation is more complex, simply because the technology is developing so rapidly that anything we say today will likely have to be revised six months from now. On the one hand, it is clear that cellulosic ethanol is not an *off-the-shelf* product that is commercially available today on the same large scale that corn- and sugar cane-based ethanol products are. On the other hand, in comparison with certain futuristic technologies, cellulosic ethanol will most likely be viable within a matter of years, not decades.

In addition, we recognize there are two kinds of "existing technologies": those that have been *proven and practiced commercially*, such as corn- and sugar cane-based ethanol; and those that *need further development and commercial demonstration*. In the second case, all of the science necessary for the process to work already has become well understood, developed, and applied at the pilot-plant stage.

Cellulosic technology still falls into the second case for several reasons. First, Iogen is operating a demonstration plant, and Verenium soon will be too. Major institutional investors have committed large sums of money to build the first commercial plant, which has a high probability of success. Second, the margins for process improvement are large. For example, in the past two years alone, the cost of catalytic hydrolysis enzymes has dropped by a factor of 30, to $0.10 per liter of ethanol.

Finally, the Natural Resources Defense Council study projects cellulosic ethanol yields will increase from 50 gallons ethanol/dry ton biomass to 117 gallons/dry ton. Similar increases in switchgrass yields from 5 to 12 dry tons/acre could ultimately result in the U.S. displacing nearly 8 MBD—nearly equal to all of the oil used by light-duty vehicles today. Based on those facts, one could certainly argue that cellulosic ethanol is a promising and "existing technology" under the second definition above and one that will become more efficient and competitive with time.

Nevertheless, in order to maintain the rigor and intellectual discipline of the Prometheus Plan, as Figure 1 shows, we have not depended on cellulosic ethanol making any contribution to oil savings by 2015. We firmly believe it is a promising technology that probably will contribute a significant portion of the 26 billion gallons of ethanol required by the Prometheus Plan to reduce oil use by 1.4 MBD by 2015.

## THAT DOG'LL HUNT

When President Lyndon B. Johnson found a political strategy that worked well and attracted broad support, he was fond of loudly proclaiming, "That dog'll hunt." The same is true for biofuels. Biofuels represent the most promising alternative to oil in the transportation sector. Furthermore, corn- and sugar cane-based ethanol reduces greenhouse gases by 20-30% in comparison to gasoline when all inputs are included. Even better, cellulosic ethanol reduces greenhouse gases by *nearly 90%*, while significantly lowering all other forms of air pollution and heath hazards.

By "growing energy" to replace oil with biofuels, we will invest billions of dollars in farms and rural communities, while decreasing our dependence on foreign oil. In addition, it will serve U.S. security interests when we support the growth of domestic and export sugar ethanol markets among friends and allies throughout the world, especially in Latin America. As a result, "energy independence" does not mean "energy autonomy" and isolationism. It means "energy abundance" for non-oil export nations.

Ethanol is a "best buy" and a road worth traveling. It creates a clear pathway to a viable future. At the end of the day, corn- and sugar-based ethanol will establish the funding, feedstock, and technological infrastructures that can lead to a worldwide revolution in biofuels. Ethanol will pose relatively little cost to consumers, industry, and government. Rather, it offers a huge upside, plus tremendous benefits for society, the environment, and national security. Ethanol, combined with automobile efficiency, is a key to transforming the fuel supply system in the U.S. and the world. As a result, ethanol producers in the U.S. are already attracting the kind of early, smart money from successful Silicon Valley entrepreneurs and venture capital firms that can lead to the major, institutional Wall Street funding necessary to fuel a new industry that in time will challenge and eventually displace oil.

# Notes and References
## Chapter 10: Biofuels

1 In July 2007, the price of ethanol was climbing toward $2.50 a gallon. The price of cellulosic ethanol should be much less than this price for less-efficient corn ethanol.

2 Lew Fulton, "Biofuels for Transport: A Viable Alternative?" *OECD Observer*, International Energy Agency, No. 249, May 2005, http://library.iea.org/dbtw-wpd/bookshop/add.aspx?id=176.

3 Nathanael Greene, *Growing Energy: How Biofuels Can Help End America's Oil Dependence* (Washington, DC: Natural Resources Defense Council, December 2004), iv ("Growing Energy").

4 To put gasoline and ethanol on an equal energy footing, it should be noted that ethanol supplies 30% less energy per gallon than gasoline.

5 Most discussions of biomass focus exclusively on biofuels production. For a concise overview of "biopower," see Worldwatch Institute, *Biofuels for Transportation: Global Potential and Implications for Sustainable Agriculture and Energy in the 21st Century (2006)*, 24.

6 U.S. Department of Energy, Oak Ridge National Laboratory, "Billion Ton Report," 2005.

7 Nathanael Greene, "How Much Ethanol, How Soon: A Q&A on Technical Limits to Growth of Ethanol," National Resources Defense Council (www.nrdc.org).

8 Nathanael Greene, *Growing Energy;* Christoph Berg and F. O. Licht, *World Fuel Ethanol Analysis and Outlook*, Ministry of Economy, Trade and Industry, Tokyo, 2004; Lovins *et al.*, "Option 2. Substituting biofuels and biomaterials," in *Winning the Oil Endgame: Innovation for Profits, Jobs and Security* (Snowmass, CO: Rocky Mountain Institute, 2005); and most recently the Worldwatch Institute's *Biofuels for Transportation.*

9 From Vinod Khosla, "Is Ethanol Controversial? Should it Be?" September 2006, and "A Near-Term Energy Solution," July 2006, which can be found on the Web site of Khosla Ventures (www.khoslaventures.com). Many of the arguments made in this chapter on behalf of ethanol draw on the materials presented in Khosla's white papers.

10 This figure cannot be calculated precisely at this time, as the technology is still under development. The authors believe, however, that when cellulosic ethanol technology is finalized, it will increase projected ethanol yields by 35% or more and vastly increase the number of feedstocks that can be economically used to make fuel.

11 "A Plastic Wrapper Today Could be Fuel Tomorrow," *New York Times*, April 9, 2007.

12 See Fred Grimm, "Oil Addiction Blinds Us to Homegrown Fix," *Miami Herald*, Op-Ed, August 15, 2006.

13 "Ethanol Is Not a Cure-all For U.S. Energy Woes," Associated Press, July 10, 2006.

14 Lester Brown, *Ethanol's Potential: Looking Beyond Corn*, Earth Policy Institute, June 29, 2005.

15 See Grimm, *op. cit.*; and Brown, *op. cit.*

16 Edward Robinson, "The Power of Green," Bloomberg Markets, August 2006.

17 William Kovarik and Matthew Hermes, Kennesaw State University http:// www.chemcases.com/fuels/fuels-11.htm.

18 Compression ratio is the ratio of the pressure in the combustion cylinder when the piston is fully retracted to that when it is fully compressed, which is the instant that combustion is designed to occur for maximum power output.

19 Worldwatch Institute, *op. cit.*, xi.

20 Fulton, *op. cit.*

21 "Can the U.S. Replicate Brazil's Success with Ethanol?" Washington Council on International Trade, Seattle, Washington, 2001 (www.wcit.org).

22 Larry Rohter, "With Big Boost from Sugar Cane, Brazil Satisfies Is Satisfying Its Fuel Needs," *New York Times*, April 10, 2006.

23 Stefan Theil, "The Next Petroleum," *Newsweek*, International Edition, August 8, 2005.

24 Carl Bailik, The Numbers Guy, "Digging Into the Ethanol Debate," *The Wall Street Journal*, June 9, 2006.

25 David Pimentel and Tad W. Patzek, "Ethanol Production Using Corn, Switchgrass, and Wood; Biodiesel Production Using Soybean and Sunflower," *Natural Resources Research* 14 (March 2005): 65-76.

26 Bialik, *op. cit.*

27 Khosla, "Is Ethanol Controversial? Should it Be?"

28 Robert Perlack, "Renewable Resources Could Provide 99% of U.S. Electricity by 2020," National Renewable Energy Laboratory Draft Paper, Energy Analysis Office, Department of Energy, January 16, 2006.

29 The 26.4 billion gallons of ethanol requirement is calculated as follows: 1,400,000 barrels/day x 365 days/year = 511,000,000 million barrels/year x 42 gallons/barrel = 21,462,000,000 gallons gasoline x .81% gasoline-to-ethanol equivalent conversion factor = 26.4 billion gallons of ethanol. The 3.3 billion gallons of biodiesel required is calculated as follows: 200,000 b/d x 365 days/year = 73,000,000 million barrel/year x 42 gallons / barrel = 3,066,000,000 x .91% gasoline-to-biodiesel conversion factor = 3.3 billion gallons of biodiesel.

30 Greene, "How Much Ethanol, How Soon?"

31 Sugar cane and sugar beet yields confirmed through personal communication with Michael Salassi, Louisiana State University.

32 Khosla, "Is Ethanol Controversial? Should it be?" 9.

33 U.N. Food and Agriculture Organization (FAO) and International Institute for Applied Systems Analysis (IIASA), *Global Agro-Ecological Zones* (Global-AEZ), Table A 27, CD-ROM, Rome and Laxenberg, Austria, 2000 (www.fao.org/landandwater/agll/gaez/index.htm). Brazil figure from Carlos Caminada and Carla Simoes, "Brazil's Sugar Cane Output Grows with Demand," *Bloomberg News*, November 2, 2006.

34 Worldwatch Institute, *op. cit.*, 31.

35 Hossein Shapouri and Michael Salassi, *The Economic Feasibility of Ethanol Production from Sugar in the United States*, U.S. Department of Agriculture and Louisiana State University, July 2006.

36 Khosla, "Is Ethanol Controversial? Should it Be?" 27.

37 1.0 / 0.7 = 1.43

38 Lovins *et al., op. cit.,* note 480, 103: "The conversion rate of 1.23 gallons of ethanol per gallon of gasoline is calculated as follows: ethanol contains only 67.7 of the heat content of gasoline 984,000 Btu/gal [Higher Heating Value] divided by 125,000 Btu/gal [also HHV]). However, Wyman *et al.* . . . . maintain that 'a 20% gain in engine efficiency can be obtained relative to gasoline in a well-designed engine. Therefore, multiplying 67.7% by 1.2 equals 0.812 gallon of gasoline pr gallon of ethanol or inversely, 1.23 gallon of ethanol per gallon of gasoline." Similarly, RMI counts 1 gallon of diesel fuel as equivalent to 1.1 gallon of biodiesel.

39 Shapouri and Salassi, *op. cit.* iv.

40 Renewable Fuels Association, *Industry Statistics, 2007:* http://www.ethanolrfa.org/industry/statistics/

41 *Ibid.,* 3.

42 Greene, "Growing Energy," v.

43 Khosla, "Is Ethanol Controversial? Should it be?" 18.

44 Worldwatch Institute, *op. cit.,* 87.

45 Rohter, *op. cit.*

46 Based on Khosla, "Is Ethanol Controversial? Should it be?" 28, with a 25% accuracy estimate. This projection does not include "other" gasoline use (lawn-mowers, boats, and such), hybrid or plug-in hybrid FFVs, lighter vehicles, or higher CAFE standards.

47 Personal communication from Gurminder Singh, advisor to the Imperial Valley project, August 29, 2006.

48 Warren E. Leary and Leslie Wayne, "Lockheed Wins Job of Building Next Spaceship," *New York Times,* September 1, 2006.

# PART IV

# THE FUTURE
# UNFOLDS

# 11

## ABUNDANT RENEWABLES: WIND, OCEAN, SOLAR, OTHER BIOFUELS, AND ENERGY SAVINGS

*"We are investing up to $8 billion over the next ten years in solar, wind, natural gas and hydrogen to provide low-carbon electricity. By 2015, we estimate that our business will eliminate $CO_2$ emissions by 24 million metric tons a year. It's a start."*

— BRITISH PETROLEUM,
BEYOND PETROLEUM CAMPAIGN, 2006

### THE TOP SCIENCE STORY OF THE YEAR

Each January *Discover* magazine publishes its list of the "Top 100 Science Stories" of the year. Looking back in its January 2007 issue over the year 2006, *Discover* concluded that the #1 story was "alternative energy." The subtitle for this piece reads: "The unnervingly high price of oil—along with the increasingly intensive drilling to get it—has suddenly pushed renewable power squarely into the mainstream."

Reflecting upon the declining availability of "cheap" petroleum products, *Discover* observed:

> In September Chevron announced the discovery of a field containing (from 2 to 15 billion barrels) of oil beneath the Gulf of Mexico, touting it as a "platform for growth for years to come." Read the fine print, though, and you get a different story. To recover the first samples of oil there in 2004, engineers floating 175 miles off the Louisiana coast had to send drill gear into 7,000-foot-deep water and penetrate four miles of rock. The company spent tens of millions of dollars on computer modeling, cutting-edge seismological tools, and exploratory drilling; just renting the drill rig cost Chevron and its partners more than $200,000 a day. *The results suggest that oil from the new reservoir, called Jack 2, could cost three to four times as much to extract as oil from traditional locations, including rigs on land* (emphasis added).

The point here is not that we are running out of oil. We are running out of cheap oil. The price per barrel for this kind of deep-sea oil is likely to be significantly higher than the equivalent energy content one could obtain from any number of commercially available renewable energy sources.

Our analysis of Hubbert's Peak in Chapter 1 was precisely validated by this late-breaking story. Of course, we won't wake up one morning to learn all the oil is gone and that the Fossil Fuel Era has ended. Rather, we will see it in the constantly rising price of purchasing a barrel of oil as each successive barrel becomes harder to find and retrieve. This trend marks the end of the Fossil Fuel Era as we know it. It also marks the beginning of the Age of Renewables, as renewables are price-competitive with fossil fuels at prices of $45-$50/barrel. Hubbert's Peak tells us that the days of purchasing oil for those prices are behind us—never to return.

Oil prices peaked at above $78/barrel in 2006 and fell back only partially to $61.50/barrel as the year ended. (The average for the full year was $66.) To make matters more complex, these higher prices resulted strictly from natural market forces rather than potential intervening traumatic events hovering on the geopolitical horizon. As discussed in Chapter 3, any one of these events could, in an instant, create a price spike or even a supply cut-off.

*Discover's* conclusions:

- Renewables are now available and price-competitive, and

- Creating sources of renewable energy that are produced and controlled entirely within American borders is a national security imperative.

There will be no turning back from the move to renewables. That really is the top news story of the year.

## THE TIPPING POINT

At this moment, renewable energy in the United States precariously balances at a tipping point. We can continue with business as usual, and bring upon ourselves the climatic, economic, and political calamities described earlier in this book. Or, we can start an energy revolution. We will take one course or the other: one road will, without overstatement, lead to disastrous consequences. As a result of global climate change, these consequences could include famine, disease, and resource wars. The other path, the one that relies increasingly on renewable technologies, will veer us away from this destructive course if we act quickly enough. This chapter describes the renewable technologies that are in advanced states of development, and their probable timelines.

Renewable technologies *will* lead us out of the fossil fuel wilderness. Ironically, the larger question is not technological. We can fairly well predict technology. The larger question is one of politics: will state and federal governments behave like leaders and provide consistent policies and incentives? If they do, we will reject new pollution-intensive centralized coal and natural gas plants, as well as the health and global security threats created by nuclear-fission energy, in favor of cleaner alternatives such as wind, geothermal, solar, and biomass. Plant-based ethanol and biodiesel will displace petroleum-based gasoline and diesel fuels. Homeowners and businesses will be able to install small, distributed stationary energy sources and use mobile or so-called "rolling" fuel cells (i.e., fuel cell cars), reducing the need for large, baseload fossil fuel and nuclear power plants. Similarly, mobile fuel cells powered by hydrogen will replace internal combustion engines, the hundred-year-old technological icon of the Hydrocarbon Age. When not in use, they may even be used to generate electricity that could be fed into the grid.

A recent assessment by the National Research Council and the National Academy of Engineering looks at technologies that can be "mainstream" in the near future—including biomass, wind, solar, on-site natural gas reformation, and on-site electrolysis—and projects that large-scale implementation of any one of them could lower the price of hydrogen at the pump to $2 to $4 per kilogram. "In this scenario, hydrogen in a fuel cell car would cost less per kilometer than gasoline in a conventional car today."[1] A kilogram of hydrogen is approximately equivalent to one gallon of gasoline on an energy basis. However, since a fuel cell is at last twice as energy efficient as an internal combustion engine, it is twice as effective on a miles-per-gallon basis. In effect, $2 to $4-per-kilogram hydrogen would be equivalent to $1 to $2 per-gallon-gasoline.

The long-term prospects are even brighter. Looking nearly 100 years ahead for just a moment, we see some futurists predicting that "ambitious new technologies could help quench the world's thirst for energy without worsening global climate change" by the late 21st century.[2] These advanced energy sources could include: hydrogen harvested from ponds of genetically engineered microbes; biodiesel harvested from saltwater algae; high altitude wind farms; computer-guided wave and tidal generators—all linked to high-efficiency, distributed generation regional grids. Indeed, today's energy science fiction may become tomorrow's reality.

Fortunately, as far as renewables are concerned, the future is now. To lay the groundwork for the hydrogen economy (described in Chapter 12), we can jumpstart the future by implementing the

Prometheus Plan, including the portfolio of abundant renewables and energy efficiency measures discussed in this chapter.

## Major Market Potential

Unlike the false starts of the 1970s and 1980s, today's renewable energy bull market is the real deal. In the last few years, capital markets have committed billions of dollars to clean energy technology. In 2006, U.S. venture capital in clean energy jumped to more than $2.4 billion, more than double the 2005 level, and more than triple the 2004 level, according to Clean Edge, a research and consulting firm.[3]

*The Economist* reports that Silicon Valley leaders recently invested $100 million in Nanosolar, a firm that hopes to dramatically reduce the cost of producing solar panels. Investors include several eBay founders along with Germany's SAP, the giant software firm. They invested in the company after Google co-founders Sergey Brin and Larry Page provided seed funds.[4]

> *"Venture capital in energy has reached a critical mass."*
> — DANIEL YERGIN,
> AUTHOR, *THE PRIZE*

The research firm New Energy Finance estimates total 2006 investment in clean energy at $63 billion, a significant increase from $49 billion in 2005 and $30 billion in 2004. In fact, according to Clean Edge and Nth Power, nearly one-tenth of all U.S. venture capital is now being invested in clean energy. Assessing this fast-paced investment activity, the Economist concludes, "After years of wondering what would be the next big thing after the dotcom boom, America's technology industry is betting on alternative energy."[5]

A recent Union of Concerned Scientists ("Concerned Scientists") study entitled *Clean Energy Blueprint* asked three key questions. First, can America develop a balanced portfolio of clean energy solutions that will increase energy security? Second, can America develop an energy system that will save consumers money, provide jobs and security, and protect the environment? Finally, can the U.S. restore international goodwill and credibility by reducing carbon dioxide (CO$_2$) emissions that threaten to destabilize the global climate? The study found that the answer to all of these questions was a resounding *yes.* "Energy efficiency and renewable energy technologies are ready to serve us. What we need now is vision, leadership, and determination to provide a clean, affordable energy future."[6]

This book makes the strong case that the "vision, leadership, and determination" will likely come from the private sector, relying on traditional approaches to profiting from new technologies, and from a few, very select courageous political leaders who understand what is at stake and the great opportunity before us. European governments, as well as those at the state and local levels in America will be the earliest supporters. The U.S. federal government will follow suit when a new and visionary administration takes office, or when the situation becomes unavoidably dire—whichever comes first. There is an overwhelming national security and economic imperative to develop renewables and reduce global climate change within the next few years. We believe these imperatives ultimately will catalyze the federal government into action as well.

A Worldwatch Institute/Center for American Progress report on *American Energy: The Renewable Path to Energy Security* draws the same conclusion that a major shift in the U.S. energy economy is now possible.[7] The report documents how three decades of pioneering research and development have produced a host of new technologies that are transforming America's abundant domestic renewable energy resources—including biofuels, solar, wind, geothermal, hydroelectric, biomass, and ocean energy—into transportation fuels and electricity.

These are not simply the views of doctrinaire environmental organizations that support renewables regardless of cost and economics. Rather, these studies are rooted in market and economic realities and are consistent with a

> *"If there was ever a time when a major shift in the U.S. energy economy was possible, it is now."*
>
> — WORLDWATCH INSTITUTE, *AMERICAN ENERGY,* 2006

growing body of findings by independent analysts: from Pentagon-funded research conducted by the Rocky Mountain Institute to a bipartisan report from the National Commission on Energy Policy, whose advisory board includes representatives from the automobile, fossil fuel, and nuclear industries.

## RENEWABLES AND ELECTRIC POWER

In November 2006 the Supreme Court of the United States heard arguments in the case of *Massachusetts v. Environmental Protection Agency*, a suit to force the EPA to classify carbon dioxide as a pollutant and to regulate its emission. In April 2007, the U.S. Supreme Court handed down its decision in the case, rejecting the EPA's argument that it had no authority to regulate carbon dioxide and other heat-trapping gases in automobile emissions. Remarkably, two electric utilities filed friend-of-the-court briefs supporting the petitioners and opposing the EPA. "This case makes for strange bedfellows," begins the brief filed by Entergy, Inc., which operates many fossil-fuel powered electrical generation plants.[8] These utilities recognize the untenability of the current situation in terms of environmental destruction, and their own inability to plan capital expenditures when they feel certain a more realistic approach in Washington will be inevitable after the Bush Administration departs. In other words, the utilities know regulation will be forthcoming, but the uncertainty they confront (due to years of deafening silence from Washington) has paralyzed their ability to plan in an environment where capacity planning requires very long lead times. A growing number of corporate and industry leaders are calling for regulatory certainty on carbon emissions to enable their companies to make strategic plans for the innovations necessary to maintain their competitiveness.

On the other side of the nation, in the same month that the utilities filed their briefs, Hawaii Electric Company (HECO), which produces 90% of the electricity in Hawaii, may have recognized it will be impossible to build any more coal or fossil-fuel fired plants in the Islands. The 110-megawatt (MW) Campbell

Industrial Park Generating Station electric plant was originally planned to run on diesel fuel. The utility reassessed the situation in late 2006, and voluntarily decided to run the plant on 100% renewable fuels (ethanol or biodiesel, or both). Renewable fuel use will actually be inserted as a condition of its operating permit. In other words, if HECO were ever to renege on this part of the agreement, the plant could be shut down. Obviously, the company is *very* serious about renewables. This is the first major electric plant in the nation that will burn only renewables.

While electric utilities use much more coal than oil, they also use a large amount of natural gas, and natural gas is in many ways a substitute for oil. After the transportation sector, the greatest potential for renewables to displace fossil fuel lies in the generation of electricity. As the "Percent of Sector" data in Figure 1 show, while petroleum alone accounts for 96% of the energy used in transportation, it accounts for only 2% of electric power generation. In contrast, other fossil fuels, mainly coal and natural gas, account for 68% of the energy used in generating electricity.

Figure 1 shows the respective percentages of total U.S. fuel provided by various sources and used by various sectors. As Figure 1 shows, of the approximately 100 Quads (quadrillion British Thermal Units [BTUs]) of energy consumed in the U.S. in 2006, nearly 40 Quads were used in the electric power sector and generated from the following sources: coal (52%), natural gas (16%), nuclear power (21%), renewable energy including hydroelectric power (10%), and petroleum (2%).

## Figure 1. U.S. Primary Energy Consumption by Source and Sector, 2006 (In Quadrillion BTU)

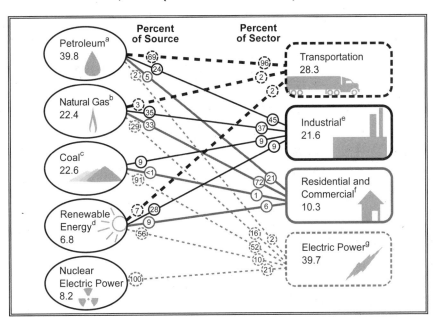

Source: U.S. Energy Information Administration, *Annual Energy Review,* 2006 [9]

The U.S. electric power industry currently relies on large, centralized power plants that burn primarily coal or natural gas, or use nuclear power to supply 89% of industry output. Renewables account for about 10% of output. Most utilities generate power through a mixture of large baseload power plants (coal and nuclear) with relatively low fuel costs (if one ignores environmental externalities and the perpetual disposal costs associated with highly toxic wastes), plus additional lower-capacity peaking plants (usually natural gas) that are used only when demand surges beyond the capacity of the baseload plants. As Figure 2 shows, several renewable sources of energy can provide constant power as needed, including geothermal, concentrated solar with storage, and biomass electricity. Other sources are irregular, meaning that they can generate electricity only when the sun is shining (photovoltaic cells and solar thermal) or when the wind is blowing (wind turbines). Nevertheless, irregular renewable resources such as solar and wind can add real value to an integrated grid by providing electricity when it is most needed, or, in the future, when stored as hydrogen for use any time and any where. In many areas of the country, such as California, peak sun days already coincide with peak demand for air conditioning. In addition, off-peak wind power can eventually provide electricity for storage in the batteries of plug-in hybrid electric vehicles to reduce petroleum demand in the transportation sector.

## Figure 2. Primary Renewable Technologies: Benefits and Issues[10]

| Technology | Benefits and Issues |
| --- | --- |
| Wind | • Is intermittent and location-specific<br>• Has spatial mismatch between demand and supply locations<br>• Faces objections based on aesthetics<br>• **Has very low long-term costs**<br>• **Has zero emissions**<br>• **Is currently competitive with fossil fuels in some areas**<br>• **Energy can be stored as hydrogen when used with an electrolyzer** |
| Geothermal[11] | • **Provides clean, reliable baseload power**<br>• **Using new technology, potentially available throughout the U.S.**<br>• **Produces no emissions**<br>• **Is very cost-effective**<br>• **Is virtually inexhaustible** |
| Biomass | • Constrained by bio-availability<br>• **Provides baseload electric power**<br>• Can generate significant conversion and/or transportation costs |
| Ethanol | • **Has lower emissions than fossil fuels and is greenhouse gas-neutral, or better** |
| Biodiesel | • **Offers domestically produced transportation fuel**<br>• **Supports agriculture industry and rural communities** |

*Figure 2 (continued)*

| Technology | Benefits and Issues |
|---|---|
| Photovoltaics | • Offers intermittent availability due to weather and time of day<br>• Generates high initial costs<br>• **Generates low long-term costs**<br>• **Emits nothing**<br>• **Has potential in all geographic regions**<br>• **Can be coincident with peak demand**<br>• **Has distributed generation benefits**<br>• **Energy can be stored as hydrogen when used with an electrolyzer** |
| Solar Thermal | • Offers irregular availability due to season, weather, time of day<br>• Imposes high initial costs<br>• **Generates low long-term costs**<br>• **Emits nothing**<br>• **Has potential in all geographic regions**<br>• **Solar thermal concentrators provide baseload electricity** |
| Ocean Energy | • Options include tides, currents, waves and ocean thermal<br>• Most options are site-specific<br>• Not yet commercially viable<br>• Undergoing first commercial tests<br>• **Provides baseload power and in the proper locations, a good substitute for air conditioning supplied by electricity** |
| Efficiency | • **Least-cost option for displacing electric demand ("negawatts")**<br>• Includes high efficiency lighting and appliances<br>• **Vast energy savings potential** |

Source: Based in part on RAND Report, 2006

As the Worldwatch report on *American Energy* points out, irregularities in renewables' electric power output can be reduced and possibly eliminated by spreading solar and wind generators across a wide geographical region. Studies show that even when wind alone supplies 20% of a regional or national electric grid, as is the case in

Denmark and some regions of Germany, backup coverage is rarely needed.[12]

Furthermore, given variations in capital costs and natural gas prices, renewable power offers utilities a simple hedge against fuel price increases in the near term. For example, while conventional coal and nuclear power plants can require five to 15 years to plan and construct, construction lead times for large renewable energy projects are typically only two to five years. According to FPL Energy, some new wind projects can become operational within three to six months after breaking ground.

Last, given the widespread discussion of a possible carbon tax or emissions trading system, renewables may also contribute to reducing a utility's regulatory and financial risk. The Worldwatch report notes that, "Since renewable power plants are emissions-free, or close to it, they also represent a hedge against future environmental regulations, including possible caps on mercury and carbon-dioxide emissions."[13]

Environmentalists claim that the terms of the private equity $45 billion buy-out of TXU, Texas' largest utility, was partly the product of such a hedge against future environmental regulation in the form of carbon taxes. TXU had taken 11 steps backward with its application in late 2006 to build 11 baseload generators using pulverized coal (an outmoded, dirty technology) for fuel. Then a proposed buy-out changed the dynamics. Before the deal was reached, the lead buyers, Kohlberg Kravis Roberts & Company and the Texas Pacific Group, contacted a group of environmentalists who had filed suit to block the new plants, to negotiate an end to the litigation. In exchange for the environmentalists dropping their suit, the new buyers agreed to drop all but three of the 11 plants and to invest more in renewable energy, including solar and wind power. Even before the deal, the TXU board had considered dropping plans for some of the proposed plants because of their impact on TXU's share price.[14]

The 11 new TXU coal plants *by themselves* would have produced more carbon dioxide than entire nations such as Denmark, Sweden, or Portugal. Texas already produces 10% of America's carbon dioxide, more than any other state. TXU's decision to construct the new plants was environmentally irresponsible on a global scale. It was also extremely unwise for the ratepayers in Texas, who would have been stuck with these dinosaur-plants for 20 to 30 years.

## Breakdown of Available Renewable Technologies

Most of the U.S. renewable energy sources shown in Figures 2 and 3 are poised for dramatic growth over the next decades. Let's look closely at each of the major renewable technologies—wind turbines, biofuels, geothermal, biomass, and solar—as well as at more complex technologies such as ocean energy and energy from brown gas and algae.

**Figure 3. Renewable Energy Consumption in the Nation's Energy Supply, 2006**

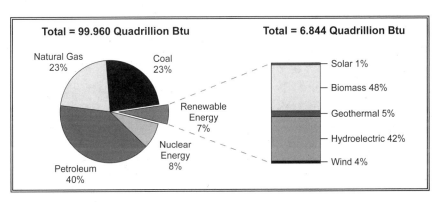

Source: U.S. Energy Information Administration, *Renewable Energy Consumption and Electricity, Preliminary 2006 Statistics*

## The Answer is Blowing in the Wind

Wind power has been expanding at an explosive pace since the mid-1990s. Between 2004 and 2006, U.S. wind power grew about 27% a year, and 2007 growth is expected to be about the same. In 2006, the U.S. wind industry invested about $4 billion to install over 2400 MW of capacity, enough to power more than 500,000 homes.

According to the U.S. Energy Information Administration, wind energy now accounts for about 4% of total U.S. renewable energy, up from 1% in 2001.

In 2006, boosted by about $22 billion in investment, global wind power capacity grew almost 26% to over 72,000 MW, up from a mere 5,000 MW in 1995. Growth was particularly strong in the European Union, where capacity grew by 23% in 2006. Not counting Germany, Spain and Denmark, which together account for 50% of the EU wind power market, there has been a six-fold increase in the annual market during the past four years. The increase is partly the result of a 2001 EU Renewable Electricity Directive and several countries' generous feed-in tariffs which require utility companies to buy electricity generated by clean energy sources at premium prices.

The U.S. has not matched Germany's and Denmark's levels of sustained growth in wind power because U.S. government incentives are shorter-term and less predictable. Since 1992, federal support for wind power has largely consisted of a tax credit for renewable energy producers for every kilowatt hour of electricity produced during a plant's first 10 years of operation. The tax credit has provided more than half the value of a typical project, and wind projects have virtually ground to a halt each of the several times that the tax credits have expired since they were first enacted in 1992. The current credit of 1.9 cents per kilowatt hour is due to expire in 2012. That uncertainty plus spiraling plant construction costs due to sharply higher prices for steel, copper, and other commodities, is causing some concern in the industry. Nevertheless, we predict continued soaring growth in the U.S. wind energy sector beyond its current capacity of about 12,000 MW.

The potential for expansion is phenomenal. Writing in a *Scientific American* special issue on "Energy's Future Beyond Carbon," Daniel Kammen notes that if the U.S. constructed sufficient wind farms to fully tap the wind resources of the Great Plains alone (especially Kansas, North Dakota, and Texas), "the turbines could generate as much as 11 trillion kilowatt-hours of electricity, *or nearly*

> *"When the U.S. Department of Energy released its first wind-resource inventory in 1991, it noted that three wind-rich states—North Dakota, Kansas, and Texas—had enough harnessable wind energy to satisfy national electricity needs."*
>
> — LESTER R. BROWN, *PLAN B 2.0*, 2006

*three times the total amount produced from all energy sources in the nation last year."* (Emphasis added.)[15]

While the Great Plains of the United States have been described as the "Persian Gulf of wind power," the U.S. Department of Energy estimates that offshore wind resources within five to 50 nautical miles of the coastline could support approximately 900,000 MWs of wind-power—a potential supply itself almost equivalent to total U.S. current electric capacity.

The past two decades have seen major advances in wind technology. Average turbine size has increased from less than 100 kilowatts to over 1,200 kilowatts today, with equipment up to 5,000 kilowatts (5 MWs) under development. Blade spans have expanded to over 300 feet, compared with 200 feet for the wing span of a typical jumbo jet. While turbine manufacturing is dominated by European companies, General Electric entered the wind business in 2002 and has rapidly become one of the world's top producers. FPL Energy has emerged as one of the largest U.S. developers and operators of wind farms.

Since the 1980s, the price of wind-generated electricity has dropped more than tenfold—from about forty cents per kilowatt-hour to about three to five cents today, making it competitive with electricity from conventional coal-fired power plants. With the recent increase in natural gas prices, wind power has become the least expensive source of new power in several regions of the country. Nearly half of the new capacity added in the U.S. during this decade has been located in Texas, largely in response to the state's Renewable Portfolio Standard. In a sign of the times, billionaire oilman

T. Boone Pickens has announced plans for a four-county, 2000 MW to 4000 MW wind energy complex in the Texas panhandle, at a cost of $3-6 billion. As planned, the complex would be four times the size of an Abilene, Texas wind facility that is now the nation's largest.

Assuming that state and federal policies provide consistent signals to the marketplace, wind power's contribution to the grid can grow dramatically.

## WIND-POWERED PLUG-IN HYBRIDS

Not only can wind be used to generate electricity for the grid, but it can also reduce oil use in transportation by providing stationary power for next generation gas/electric plug-in hybrid cars.

Toyota has announced that the 2008 Prius will be equipped with lithium-ion batteries (a battery superior to existing nickel-hydride batteries) that in future model years could be plugged into stationary wind-powered sources. Lithium-ion cells, currently found in cellular phones, portable gaming devices, and personal digital assistants, are lighter and can be built in larger sizes to power cars. When plugged into a conventional electrical outlet at home or work, passenger cars with lithium-ion batteries would have sufficient power for the short intra-urban trips that account for half of all car use. The gasoline-powered motor would never need to be used for such trips. The cost of "fuel" would only slightly increase the household electricity bill and would be insignificant on a cost-per-mile basis.

Using the lithium-ion system, projected Prius mileage estimates range from 80 to 95 miles per gallon (mpg), and as high as 500 mpg when combined with plug-in features. If government fleets and even half of American drivers begin using such extraordinarily high mileage vehicles, gasoline consumption would plummet even as wind farm demand would rise.

In addition to charging batteries, wind turbines could also be used to generate hydrogen from water via electrolysis to power the first-generation of fuel cell vehicles and other engines coming into being as part of the hydrogen economy (such as BMW's direct hydrogen-burning vehicles).

# Geothermal Heat and Power

The world has so far largely overlooked the vast potential of geothermal energy, a clean, renewable, and reliable energy resource produced by tapping the heat stored in the Earth's crust. This conclusion is bolstered by a 2007 comprehensive study led by the Massachusetts Institute of Technology which concluded that geothermal energy can produce 10% of U.S. baseload electricity by 2050 at prices competitive with electricity from fossil fuels.[16]

The MIT study found that by using enhanced, or engineered, geothermal systems (EGS), geothermal energy can be produced throughout much of the United States. To date, geothermal resources have been developed primarily where the Earth's heat is easily accessible and accompanied by ample heated fluids and permeable rock. All existing U.S. geothermal plants are in California, Utah, Nevada, and Hawaii, where molten rock and superheated water and steam are relatively close to the surface, often near hot springs, geysers, or volcanoes.

Geothermal energy is produced by drilling a well to tap superheated fluids or steam which, upon release, power a turbine and generator, producing electricity. The liquids are then re-injected into the ground and reheated. There must be sufficient connectivity within the well system to create high production rates without the rapid cooling that would reduce reservoir life.

With EGS, heat mining takes a giant step forward. Improvements in deep-drilling techniques and reservoir stimulation have created the means to enhance lower grade geothermal resources, allowing heat to be mined from greater depths and cooler and less permeable rock. The study shows that drilling several wells to reach hot rock and connecting them to a fractured rock region that has been stimulated to let water flow through creates a heat-exchanger that can produce large amounts of hot water or steam to run electric generators.

The necessary fluids can be supplied not only by geopressured and volcanic fluids, but also by heated water produced as an integral part of oil and gas production ("coproduced fluids"). Idaho's first geothermal project, being built in the Raft River Valley, is addressing the fluids challenge by using a new binary process which taps 300-degree water that heats another liquid, such as isopentane, that vaporizes at lower temperatures.

The MIT study concluded that commercializing the EGS technology in time to meet the 2050 10% target will require federal research and development funding and the right mix of government policies and incentives to reduce risk and attract private investors.

The wealth of energy resources that the EGS technology opens up is enormous. The study estimated the extractable portion of the EGS resource base "to exceed . . . about 2000 times the annual consumption of primary energy in the United States in 2005. With technology improvements, the economically extractable amount of useful energy could increase by a factor of 10 or more, thus making EGS sustainable for centuries."

Geothermal energy already provides a substantial amount of energy in California and Hawaii. The Geysers Field, about 70 miles north of San Francisco, is the largest geothermal field in the world and supplies about 60% of the electrical power from the Golden Gate Bridge to the Oregon border. California gets about 6% of its power from geothermal and 15 more projects are being developed. The Big Island of Hawaii uses geothermal energy to produce more than 15% of its electricity.

Hawaii is exploring a project to use its excess geothermal power produced during non-peak hours to create hydrogen from water, using electrolysis. Because of the promise of the project and the potential to expand the Big Island's production of geothermal energy, the state may find that geothermal is its ticket to a hydrogen economy. This is precisely the strategy adopted by Iceland, which plans to tap its vast geothermal resources to become the first fully hydrogen-based nation, and to end all its petroleum imports by 2030.

The MIT study concluded:

> EGS is one of the few renewable energy resources that can provide continuous base-load power with minimal

visual and other environmental impacts. Geothermal systems have a small footprint and virtually no emissions, including carbon dioxide. Geothermal energy has significant base-load potential, requires no storage, and thus, it complements other renewables—solar (CSP and PV), wind, hydropower—in a low-carbon energy future. In the shorter term, having a significant portion of our base-load supplied by geothermal sources would provide a buffer against the instabilities of gas price fluctuations and supply disruptions . . . .

We agree. Unlike intermittent energy sources like solar or wind, geothermal energy can be produced around the clock. Because of its 24/7 nature, geothermal energy can become the workhorse of the renewable fuels revolution and play a key role in the transition to a hydrogen economy.

## HERE COMES THE SUN

There are three main types of solar energy: solar cells, solar thermal and solar concentrators. Solar cells, also known as photo-voltaic cells or PV cells, are one of the world's fastest growing new energy technologies. PVs are typically made from crystalline silicon chips and use Einstein's photoelectric effect to generate electricity. A series of chips is wired in parallel to provide the desired power output. Since the cells have no moving parts and can be installed in a wide variety of locations, they have multiple applications and can be integrated into rooftops as building components; built into handheld electronic devices; installed in the "wings" of orbiting satellite space stations; or arrayed in large desert power plants. Some companies are even experimenting with fabricating them into automobile body parts to generate electricity for electric cars when the vehicles are parked. One application, using thin-film solar cells on the tops of golf carts at Mauna Lani Resort in Hawaii, has produced significant return on invested capital by dramatically reducing the need for supplemental electrical charges at night for the resort's golf carts.

By the end of 2006, solar cells provided a total of only 5,000 MWs, or 0.15% of total global generating capacity. However, due to the worldwide distribution of solar power, "sunlight could potentially supply 5,000 times as much energy as the world currently consumes."[17] Due to a combination of efficiency improvements, technology advances, cost declines, and favorable policies, annual global PV production has grown more than 25% a year for the past decade and has grown by an average of 41% the past three years. According to the Solar Electric Industries Association, an industry trade group, PV installations in the U.S. grew at an average rate of 52% annually the last five years.

According to the U.S. Energy Information Administration, during 2007, a 64-MW photovoltaic plant south of Las Vegas, Solar One, will become the largest photovoltaic plant to be operating anywhere in the world during the past 15 years.

Nevada Power has partnered with Sun Edison and Powered by Renewables to use the desert sun to power a $115 million-dollar solar photovoltaic facility, the largest such project in the U.S. The planned solar "farm" will produce enough electricity for 36,000 homes (18 MW), though most of the energy will be sold to nearby military bases, which would otherwise have to draw electricity from the civilian power grid. Nevada's legislated Renewable Portfolio Standard mandated that the utility draw a small percentage of power from renewable sources.

In 2006, the state of California announced its Million Solar Roof program to create 3,000 MWs of new photo-voltaic generating capacity by 2018. Governor Schwarzenegger, the Republican from California with the distinction of leading this nation's most environmentally active state government, recently signed legislation *requiring* that solar panels on all new residential construction be a standard option for all new-home buyers by 2012, *and* that all electricity generated by those panels that is returned to the grid will be "reverse metered" to provide a credit on the homeowners' monthly electricity bill. The state plans to pay $2.9 billion in rebates over 10 years to homeowners and businesses that install solar panels, and the federal government contributes a tax credit for 30% of the cost of installation.

Studies by the Renewable and Appropriate Energy Laboratory at the University of California, Berkeley indicate that annual production of solar cells in the U.S. alone could grow to 10,000 MWs by 2025 if current trends continue, provided adequate supplies of silicon are available. Sources of silicon supply have been having a difficult time keeping up with demand, creating unnecessary price increases and availability bottlenecks. Silicon is also used to produce computer chips, and the solar cell market for silicon has traditionally been a secondary market. That is changing.

Current polysilicon producers are adding capacity and new producers are entering the market, bringing an expanded use of traditional technologies as well as new technologies. The U.S. is expected to become the source of almost half of all global polysilicon production, which is now projected to reach nearly 10 GW in 2010.[18]

In comparison to wind, solar technologies are not yet competitive for most uses. Some studies indicate that PV energy may not become cost-competitive for most general applications for another decade. On the other hand, it is also clear that in some locations, rooftop and building-integrated PV power is competitive with the peak electricity prices which coincide with times of peak sunshine. The fact that PVs can serve as a building façade material (as envisioned by the Schwarzenegger new-home initiative), while producing both electricity and heat, also reduces overall project costs.

While PV costs have declined more than 60% since 1984, the National Renewable Energy Laboratory estimates that costs today are about $5 to $8 per watt, which generally translates to about 20 to 32 cents per kilowatt-hour—roughly five to six times the current kilowatt-hour cost of coal (unscrubbed) and natural gas. We believe that this downward price trend will continue from 2006 forward as silicon manufacturing catches up with demand, and as new fabrication methods, such as continuous roll fabrication or nanosolar technology for "printing" solar cells like newspapers, move from R&D into the marketplace.

The use of solar thermal and advanced-technology solar

concentrator systems, both of which are more cost-competitive than PV cells, is also growing rapidly. Solar thermal systems, typically rooftop installations used to generate direct heat mainly to provide hot water to homes and industry, are once again expanding in the market. In Israel it is difficult to see a rooftop that *doesn't* use a solar collector for water heating.

Solar thermal concentrators are most often known for their ability to produce hot water. However, they can also be used to produce electricity without the need for silicon-dependent PV cells. These concentrators are sometimes referred to as concentrating solar power, or CSP. A solar thermal concentrator array mounted in the form of a convex disk consists of thousands of dish-shaped mirrors each attached to an engine made by Stirling Energy Systems that converts heat to electricity. The numerous mirrors mounted on the concentrators are computer-guided to optimally focus reflected sunlight on the Stirling engine's receiver.[19] The high performance Stirling engine shuttles a working fluid, such as hydrogen gas, between two chambers, causing the gas to expand and move the engine's pistons, which drive a turbine that generates electricity in an alternator.

In fall 2005, Phoenix-based Stirling Energy Systems announced contracts to build two large solar-thermal power plants in California and Arizona with 20-year power purchase agreements. Under one contract, Southern California Edison will buy electricity from a 500-MW plant in the Mojave Desert, which will cover 4,500 acres with 20,000 curved dishes. Under the other, San Diego Gas & Electric will buy electricity from a 300-MW, 12,000-dish plant in the Imperial Valley. Since the concentrating mirrors are modular, both plants can be easily expanded. Pacific Gas & Electric has announced it will buy 553 MW of solar power (enough to power 400,000 homes) from Solel Solar Systems, which plans a new solar thermal plant with 1.2 million mirrors on nine square miles in the Mojave Desert in southeast California.

Current solar-thermal plants produce electricity at 5 to 13 cents per kilowatt-hour, with dish mirror systems coming in at the upper end. Daniel Kammen, distinguished professor of energy at University of California, Berkeley, reports that, because these projects "involve highly reliable technologies and mass production, however, the generation expenses are expected to ultimately drop closer to four to six cents per kilowatt-hour—that is, competitive with the current price of coal-fired power."[20]

Solar thermal concentrator plants require 2,540 acres per billion kilowatt-hours. Thus, according to the Worldwatch Institute, "A little over 4,000 square miles—equivalent to 3.4% of the land in New Mexico—would be sufficient to produce 30% of the country's electricity."[21]

Solar power still supplies only about .01% of U.S. power, despite its continuing growth. Some renewable energy investors like Vinod Khosla maintain that market forces are in themselves insufficient to move solar power into the U.S. mainstream. Government support for solar research and development is only a fraction of government R&D funding for nuclear and coal. Government solar tax credits have so far been too short-lived to encourage the necessary long-term capital investment.

In contrast, Germany and Japan became, respectively, the world's first and second largest markets for solar power largely because of government policies that favor solar power. Germany has a feed-in tariff that guarantees solar power generators 20-year, above-market rates despite the fact that the payback period for a solar panel is only 8-9 years. Japan's government incentives have taken the route of tax credits and renewable portfolio standards.

## GREEN GAS: THE CELLULOSE EXTRACTION PROCESS

In the Prometheus Plan, we outline a biofuels strategy based on ethanol and biodiesel, which can eventually replace up to 50% of U.S. oil use (see Chapter 10, Biofuels). As all thoughtful observers know, biological feedstocks can produce a wide range of fuels: bioethanol, biobutanol, biodiesel, biomass for direct combustion, biogas, hydrogen, or methane. The prior chapter discussed ethanol that can be produced by directly fermenting the sugars found in certain plants. This section discusses other important biologically-based energy technologies.

Cellulose is the building block of plant cells and the most common organic compound on earth. Cotton fibers are almost pure cellulose. Cellulose consists of hydrogen, carbon, and oxygen. However, before the parts of the polymer that are useful for energy production can be accessed, they must first be liberated from the lignin cells to which they are bound. After separation from the lignin, cellulose can be converted (hydrolyzed using a cellulase catalyst) to sugars, and the latter subsequently fermented to ethanol that, like other hydrocarbons, can be burned as fuel. An alternative cellulosic technology is to gasify a biomass feedstock at higher temperatures to a mixture of carbon monoxide, carbon dioxide and hydrogen. This gaseous mixture may then be converted to ethanol or a mixture of fuel alcohols by either reacting it over a Fischer-Tropsch catalyst, or by converting the gaseous mixture with a microorganism called *Clostridium ljungdahlii*, which catalyzes the carbon monoxide, carbon dioxide, and hydrogen mixture to ethanol and water. In both processes the ethanol is then distilled away from the water.

Producing cellulosic ethanol differs from corn-based ethanol in that the former creates almost no greenhouse gases from fossil fuels. The fermentation process for corn-based ethanol requires heat, which in the vast majority of existing plants has been supplied by natural gas. Increasingly, a more intelligent approach is being adopted and heat is supplied by methane or geothermal energy, or both. In contrast, the sugar cane ethanol production process generally gets its heat from bagasse, the residue of the sugar cane itself, and therefore has a low greenhouse gas effect, comparable to cellulosic ethanol technology.

## BROWN GAS BIODIGESTERS

At current natural gas prices, the methane captured from the decomposition of organic matter found in landfills, sewage treatment plants, and livestock facilities can produce a competitive, premium fuel while reducing greenhouse gases and waste disposal costs.

Many farms are installing anaerobic (no air) digesters to increase their profitability. Anaerobic digesters create an oxygen-free atmosphere in which bacteria digest manure and release pipeline-quality methane, equivalent to high-grade natural gas.

These so-called "brown gas" biodigesters capture methane, a harmful greenhouse gas 20-60 times more destructive than carbon dioxide over its life-cycle in the atmosphere. They generate income for the farmer by producing quality methane gas for sale, and reduce groundwater contamination, a widespread problem in the Midwest, by eliminating manure settling ponds. The biodigesters also create valuable by-products, including left-over liquids that can be used or sold as fertilizer, and fibrous solids to make bedding for cows.

Farmers are beginning to recognize the benefits of producing fuel from manure, and the potential market is huge. The biodigesters are economically viable for farms with as few as 100 cattle or pigs. According to AgStar, a federal program that promotes the conversion of manure to energy, more than 100 anaerobic digesters are operating in the U.S. today, with approximately 80 more on the drawing boards. AgStar states that "at least 70,000 dairy and swine farms are big enough to support a commercial digester and could collectively provide enough energy to power more than 560,000 homes, while keeping more than 1.4 million tons of methane out of the atmosphere."[22] In California, PG&E has already begun contracting for delivery of 100% of the fuel from the state's larger brown gas providers.

> *"We're not taking any risk, the reduction in odors is huge, and we're powering 600 homes with 900 cows. You've got to admit, that's pretty efficient."*
> — LEE JENSEN, MANAGER OF FIVE STAR DAIRY, ELK MOUND, WISCONSIN

This technology, now being fully deployed, provides a source of virtually free fuel once the cost of installation has been amortized. Payback on these units is under five years in most cases. The resulting biomass fuel can generate revenue in several ways: it can be sold to a utility, ethanol plant, or other facility; it can run a generator that powers the farm and/or returns electricity to the grid; and it can be directly burned in an internal combustion engine. In each application, one cubic centimeter of "brown gas" yields as much or more in BTUs as one cubic centimeter of natural gas.

E3 Biofuel's Nebraska plant, located next to a 28,000-head cattle feedlot, was the first plant to use a methanol closed-loop system. The 244,000 tons of manure that the cattle produce annually create more than enough methane to provide all the power for the company's 25-million-gallon ethanol plant. The cattle eat the wet distiller's grain that is a by-product of the plant's ethanol production, closing the loop between the cattle and the plant.

Compared to traditional ethanol plants powered by natural gas or other fossil fuels, ethanol plants fueled by methane have dramatically lower fuel bills and a dramatically improved energy balance (ratio of energy input to energy output). Dennis Langley, the CEO of E3 Biofuels, states that one unit of energy into his Nevada plant produces 46 units of energy from ethanol. "We blow it away," Langley said, speaking of the energy balance ratio at fossil-fuel fired ethanol plants.

As cap-and-trade systems are implemented, biodigesters and methane capture will become increasingly popular and lucrative.

## WILD CARD: ALGAE AS BIOMASS

Algae are rapidly emerging as the wild card feedstock that has the theoretical potential to replace all petroleum consumed in the U.S. for diesel engines, and to generate vast amounts of electricity with biodiesel—while at the same time consuming significant quantities of $CO_2$. Algae can be defined as "any of various chiefly aquatic, eukaryotic, photosynthetic organisms, ranging in size from single-celled forms to giant kelp." Along with soybean, rapeseed, and palm oils, algae promise to emerge soon as one of the premier virgin oil feedstocks that can be used to produce biodiesel.

Algae are by far the highest yielding feedstock for biodiesel, producing from 3,000 to 6,000 U.S. gallons per acre. These highly

> *"If the U.S. put 15 million acres of desert into algae production, we could produce enough volume of liquid fuels to get us off the Middle East oil addiction and give Iowa back to the songbirds."*
> — B. GREGORY MITCH, ALGAE RESEARCH BIOLOGIST,
> UNIVERSITY OF CALIFORNIA

efficient strains of algae can be grown in shallow ponds in the desert or near wastewater plants. Yields will vary depending on numerous factors as this new fuel begins to be available on the market a few years from now, but we know that these yield numbers will far exceed those of palm oil. At 650 gallons per acre, palm oil is currently among the most favored sources of vegetable oil for biodiesel. Still, in comparison to algae, it is far less efficient, even though it is now commercially viable, with a worldwide market demand. This is also particularly good news for consumers of soybeans, which produce only 40 gallons of oil per acre. Algae and palm oil probably will replace soybeans as a source of oil feedstocks for biodiesel, thereby proportionately reducing the upward price pressure on soybeans, and leaving that valuable crop for human and animal consumption at a lower price.

These algae-to-oil yield figures, and other figures potentially many thousands of gallons per acre higher, were verified in the Aquatic Species Program, which operated from 1978 to 1996 at the U.S. National Renewable Energy Laboratory.[23] Recently, Michael Briggs at the University of New Hampshire Biodiesel Group outlined plausible estimates for possible replacement of *all* U.S. vehicle fuel with biodiesel made from high-yield algae which have natural oil content greater than 50%.[24]

Major questions related to technology and costs of production still have to be answered before algae technology attains large scale commercialization and production as feedstock for biodiesel. As is the case with cellulosic ethanol, we believe that commercialization will happen in the short term due to high potential returns on investment.

Several companies around the globe already have algae-to-biodiesel pilot plants in the planning stage or in early production.

For example, in May 2006, Aquaflow Bionomic Corporation of New Zealand announced that it had generated initial samples of biodiesel made from algae grown in sewage settling ponds. *This represents the first time algae-for-fuel has been grown outside of a controlled laboratory environment.*

In South Africa, in November 2006, Green Star Products, Inc. signed an agreement with DeBeers Fuel Limited of South Africa to build closed bioreactors to generate 900 million gallons per year of oil from algae when operating at full capacity. This equates to four times the total 2006 U.S. output. According to the company's press release, "The final answer for biodiesel feedstock will not be oil crops—it will be algae . . . the only worldwide feedstock capable of replacing crude oil. Making use of algae also means not competing with crops for food sources that would otherwise lead to an increase in food prices.[25]

GreenFuel of Cambridge, Massachusetts, has installed algae farms at a 1040-MW fossil fuel power plant where algae are used to convert 40% of the emitted carbon dioxide into feedstock for biodiesel and ethanol. According to the company, "a large algae farm next to a 1-gigawatt plant could yield 50 million gallons a year of [fuel]."[26] Other algae farms around the U.S. range from university-affiliated projects to a small family company, LiveFuels, with a catchy company jingle, "from pond to pump."[27]

Hawaii is also about to enter the algae production-for-fuel sector. A pilot project led in part by by Barry Raleigh, former Dean of the School of Ocean and Earth Science and Technology at the University of Hawaii, will produce oil from saltwater algae that will consume an additional 5% of $CO_2$ over what is present in ambient air.

Essentially, all biofuels and biomass sources are forms of solar energy, as plants absorb $CO_2$ and use photosynthesis to convert solar energy into chemical energy feedstocks in the form of oils, carbohydrates, and proteins. Feeding fossil-fuel-produced $CO_2$ to algae has a double benefit. It increases both the rate of algae growth and the final yield, *and* simultaneously reduces $CO_2$ from the atmosphere. Algae are the most photosynthetically efficient life forms. After consuming the $CO_2$, the algae produce oil (for biodiesel manufacturing) and oxygen. Therefore, using algae creates renewable, sustainable biofuels and reduces global warming gases.

## Ocean Energy

Today, entrepreneurs and engineers are teaming to harness the seemingly perpetual motion of the ocean to deliver energy human beings can use.[28] There are several forms of ocean energy: wave, currents, tidal and ocean thermal. The last includes both ocean thermal energy conversion (OTEC) and ocean thermal air conditioning (OTAC), sometimes called saltwater air conditioning. Saltwater air conditioning has already been commercialized for two decades in Scandinavia, and wave power is undergoing its first commercial tests off the shores of Portugal.

**Energy from Waves.** Ocean Power Technologies of Scotland, the world's first publicly traded wave power company, has placed three units of its Pelamis (ocean snake) technology in a 2.25-MW wave farm located off Portugal's northeastern coast. The Pelamis is a 450-foot-long snake-shaped, dual-articulated, wave energy system that is moored to the ocean floor at both ends. As incoming waves pass down the length of the steel cylinder, hinged joints on the power conversion modules move up and down and side to side, driving pumps that push a fluid through miniature fan blades that turn generators, thus producing electricity. It will deliver energy at about 30 cents per kilowatt-hour.

If this first-phase Pelamis project, which cost U.S. $10 million to install, passes this performance test, the system will be expanded to 22.5 MWs. Its current costs compare to those of wind about 15 years ago. Knowledgeable observers expect the economics to improve steadily with wider distribution, making wave energy competitive in the near future. Ocean Power Technologies claims that total costs will be 3-4 cents/kilowatt-hour for 100-MW systems.[29]

**Energy from Currents.** Other ocean energy systems place turbines, which look like underwater windmills, in river beds or on coastlines, so that they can generate energy as the current flows in a particular direction. Current turbine projects are being built off the coasts of Tromso, Norway, and in the East River in New York City. Similar systems could use turbines placed on the floor of the Pacific Ocean, where they can capitalize on the power potential of constant fast-moving undersea currents. Energy from currents can also be taken from strong undersea water flows which occur in many places around the globe. One typically finds such conditions around headlands or between islands. These conditions produce strong and constant currents called "rips," which are common around the British Isles and the islands of Hawaii. The kinetic energy of these currents can be converted to electricity by using this rapidly developing technology.

**Energy from Tides.** Tides can be harnessed in certain very specific marine environments. Tides, which are caused by combined solar and lunar gravitational forces, are powerful forms of energy when properly tapped. Tidal forces produce powerful waves in shallow seas, especially where coastal geography causes naturally narrow constrictions that force water to move rapidly. A prime example is Captain Cook Inlet, adjacent to Anchorage, Alaska, where the tide literally comes in as a two-foot or higher wave twice each day. The world's largest tidal project is being planned for South Korea, where generators are being placed in the narrow passage between an inland bay and the ocean.

The wonderful element of tidal action as a source of energy is the predictability of tides. Their force, timing, and duration can be calculated with a very small amount of error, decades in advance because they are a function of predictable astronomical phenomena of the earth's rotation and its interaction with the moon. The drawback to tidal energy is that tides change only twice a day. Even if bi-directional turbines are used, energy can be efficiently produced only during the eight to 10 hours a day when tides are actively ebbing or flowing. Although significant in their power, tidal energy projects are less valuable when compared to geothermal and harnessed ocean currents, both of which "run" 24 hours a day.

**Ocean Thermal Energy Conversion (OTEC).** This is another "constantly on" technology that generates electricity from the differential in temperature between the tropics' warm surface water and its deep cold water. OTEC plants could be constructed on land at several hundred sites around the world and could also be built as floating installations around the earth's equatorial zones. Unlike most other renewable energy sources, OTEC also provides constant, on-demand baseload energy that is available day and night with only modest seasonal variations.

The demand for OTEC in the Pacific/Asian region has been estimated at 20 gigawatts (GW) by 2020 and up to 100 GW in 2050.[30] However, just as with large-scale hydroelectric dams, while the fuel costs are either free or very low, the front-end OTEC construction and installation costs are high. Before widespread commercialization of OTEC begins, a number of technological and economic issues need resolution, which can be accomplished with the funding and operation of a successful demonstration plant in locations where the temperature differentials are not as great. Currently, OCEES International Inc. of Honolulu is working on contracts for OTEC demonstration plants at the Natural Energy Laboratory of Hawaii and on Diego Garcia in the Indian Ocean for the U.S. Navy.

**Ocean Thermal Air Conditioning (OTAC).** This technology was long ago successfully commercialized in Scandinavia and adapted to deep, coldwater lake sites in Canada and the United States. In this application, cold water from the ocean is pumped into the centralized air conditioning systems of buildings. Honolulu Seawater Air Conditioning, LLC, is currently developing a 25,000-ton seawater air conditioning cooling system for downtown Honolulu.

Large power companies have already invested in early-stage marine energy companies. General Electric, Norsk Hydro, and German power giant Eon have made acquisitions or investments in recognition of the vast potential of ocean energy. A study by the U.K. Carbon Trust estimates that Britain could generate as much as 20% of the electricity it needs from waves and tides alone. The Electric Power Research Institute estimates that U.S. near-shore wave resources alone could generate 2.3 trillion kilowatt-hours of electricity per year, more than eight times the output of all U.S. hydropower dams.

> "It has been estimated that if less than 0.1% of the renewable energy available within the oceans could be converted into electricity it would satisfy the present world demand for energy more than five times over."
> — MARINE FORESIGHT PANEL, UNITED KINGDOM

## ENERGY EFFICIENCY: "NEGAWATTS" VS. MEGAWATTS

In every major energy study conducted since the 1970s, energy conservation and efficiency improvements are the consensus choice as the quickest and most cost-effective ways to reduce oil use and energy consumption. These conservation and efficiency "negawatts" present an enormous savings potential for the electric industry because "U.S. energy use per dollar of GNP is nearly double that of other industrial countries. More than two thirds of the fossil fuels consumed are lost as waste heat—in power plants and vehicles."[31]

Using conventional energy-efficient technologies could cut America's $200 billion annual electric bill in half. For example, under the Union of Concerned Scientists' Clean Energy Blueprint, electricity savings from energy efficiency and combined heat and power policies will result in 915 billion kilowatt-hours of savings by 2010 and 2,513 billion kilowatt-hours by 2020.[32] By the year 2020, energy efficiency measures, including advanced industrial processes and high-efficiency motors, lighting and appliances, will offset all of the growth in electricity use projected under the "business as usual" scenario.

The reduction of overall electricity demand and the addition of renewable energy to our national energy supply will diminish the risk of electricity shortages, brownouts, and blackouts. It will also avoid the kind of price spikes that allowed speculators at the now defunct Enron and other energy trading firms to drive one California utility into bankruptcy and another to the verge of bankruptcy in 2001.[33]

## AMERICA'S ELECTRIC POWER CRISIS

A good deal of ink has been spilt in warning that America has already entered a major electric power crisis, in large part a consequence of poorly executed deregulation.[34] In many regions of the country, and especially in California, peak power demands are exceeding or are about to exceed reliable generation capacity.

The North American Electric Reliability Council (the "Reliability Council") confirms the extent of this looming crisis in the U.S. electric grid. It annually forecasts the grid's ability to deliver reliable power to the United States, Mexico, and Canada over the coming decade.

*"Compared to a 1973 baseline, America now saves more energy than it produces from any single source, including oil."*

— WORLDWATCH INSTITUTE, *AMERICAN ENERGY,* **2006**

In its *2006 Long-Term Reliability Assessment,* the Reliability Council confirms a warning that "without massive investment in electric generation and transmission infrastructure, manpower and new technology, reliable electric power will become a thing of the past."[35]

For nearly a decade, the Reliability Council has been warning of the threat to reliable power created by the fact that a deregulated industry with competing utilities has displaced a regulated electric industry which placed a premium on utility cooperation to maintain the integrity of the whole system. Utilities forecast that electric demand will increase by 19% (141,000 MWs) over the next decade or so. Yet, supply is expected to increase by only 6% or (57,000 MWs) during that time. As a result, "capacity margins [that] need to be available to meet unexpected extreme weather, unscheduled maintenance of plants, and other contingencies, will fall below minimal target levels of 15% in most of the United States in the next 2-3 years."[36]

The electric utility industry is scrambling to overcome this power crisis by installing gas turbines, which can be brought online in two to three years to meet peak power demand. This is taking place just as North American natural gas reserves and worldwide natural gas prices are peaking, since natural gas prices generally track oil prices. Furthermore, it would take 5 to10 years to bring new gas supplies on line together with the liquefied natural gas terminals and port infrastructure needed to increase foreign imports.

Only one viable short term solution exists. America must greatly reduce its consumption of both electricity and natural gas with aggressive implementation of conservation and efficiency measures. As discussed in Chapters 5 and 6, building new baseload nuclear or coal-fired plants is simply not an option. Both technologies present unacceptable risks to the planet and its inhabitants. Nuclear and coal-fired plants are not even price-competitive with three rapidly growing alternative sources of energy: decentralized renewables, co-generation of heat and power, and efficient end-use of electricity.

As Lovins points out, "Per dollar of GDP, US primary energy consumption has lately been falling by about 2.5% *per annum*; electricity by 2.0% *per annum*. Only 22% of the 1996-2005 increase in delivered US energy services was fueled by increased energy supply. The balance of 78% was available because of reduced intensity [the input/output ratio of energy to produced goods]—yet the latter four-fifths of market activity remains dangerously invisible."[37] In other words, while the impact of conservation and efficiency in reducing energy demand (intensity) is highly significant, representing nearly 80% of new energy supplies, these conservation and efficiency "negawatts" are rarely included in energy projections.

The "negawatt" political and regulatory policies (saving watts through efficiency measures as opposed to building new baseload capacity) that have kept per capita energy use flat in California for 30 years are being adopted by other states. Furthermore, the purchase of cheaper carbon reduction technologies, rather than costlier options like nuclear power, produces less carbon output while costing less on a fully loaded basis. Thus, maximizing energy efficiency is the most desirable strategy for realizing the two-fold goal of simultaneously lowering energy consumption and reducing global warming.

## RENEWABLES WILL CUT CARBON EMISSIONS

In Chapter 4 on climate change, we described the potentially devastating impacts of accelerating global warming: rising sea levels with coastal area flooding; increased storm devastation; droughts and famines; intense heat waves and reduced agricultural production; rising disaster insurance payouts and premiums; ocean acidification and marine life extinction; and widespread increases of vector-born diseases such as malaria and dengue fever. Due mainly to atmospheric carbon dioxide increases, average global temperatures have risen by 1.8° Fahrenheit in the past century. More than half of this increase has occurred in the past 30 years.

The scientific evidence is irrefutable: the speed with which temperature is rising will hit a "tipping point" when enormous destabilizing forces would be unleashed with devastating potential. This conclusion is confirmed by the February 2007 report of the Intergovernmental Panel on Climate Change, and is similar to the conclusion reached by Sir Nicholas Stern in his recently released study conducted for the British government.[38] The situation is growing still worse by the day.

Carbon dioxide concentrations have been measured to be significantly higher than at any time during the past 740,000 years, thereby directly contributing to the accelerating rate of climate change. Nearly every new study reveals that global warming is progressing even faster than previously expected, possibly shifting the earth's climate into the more extreme scenarios outlined in Vice President Al Gore's essential film and book, *An Inconvenient Truth*. Since most renewable energy resources add very little or no carbon dioxide (and some such as algae even reduce ambient carbon dioxide), they can play a key role in initially slowing and ultimately reversing climate change.

It is widely understood and appreciated that fossil fuel use

in energy production causes
approximately 70% of the global
warming problem, and that the
U.S. accounts for about one-fourth
of all global emissions. In 2002,
total U.S. carbon emissions from
fossil fuel combustion totaled 1.6
billion metric tons, a 16% increase
over 1990 levels. As noted earlier,

> *"Climate change is a serious and long-term challenge that has the potential to affect every part of the globe."*
> — G-8 LEADERS STATEMENT, GLENEAGLES, SCOTLAND, JULY 2005

the electric power sector is the largest emitter, accounting for a little
over 40% of the total. Transportation is the second-largest at 33%.
Together, electric power and transportation generate nearly three-
quarters of all U.S. carbon emissions.

It is widely believed that increasing renewable energy to 25%
of current U.S. electricity production and transportation fuels would
reduce emissions of greenhouse gases and major air pollutants such
as sulfur dioxide, nitrogen oxides, and mercury. Looking at the
combined carbon dioxide reductions from the electricity and transportation sectors, the accelerated renewables future would, by some
estimates, produce about one billion tons less carbon dioxide by
2025 than the business-as-usual scenario. This is highly significant
both for the U.S. and the world.

## THE OBVIOUS CHOICE

It was only a question of time before renewables closed the
economic gap and arrived at the breakeven point with fossil fuels.
With oil having spent more time above $60/barrel than below, it
appears that time has arrived. *Without subsidies,* significant renewable energy resources are today competitive with—or even cheaper
than—traditional fossil fuels. When the costs of global warming are
internalized to the greenhouse gas emitter, *there is no competition—*
renewables are far less expensive.

What the marketplace for fuels now lacks is a level playing field.
With the entrenched financial and political power that comes from
being the dominant planetary fuel system for over a century, fossil

fuel companies demand and obtain ridiculous tax benefits, outrageous liability exemptions, and unjustly favorable financial regulations that allow them to maintain supremacy over renewables. The egregious high profits being reported quarter after quarter by "Big Oil" are symptomatic of a system of regulation that has gone badly awry. These excess profits feed politicians and lobbyists with an unending gusher of cash, which in turn buys more unequal benefits for fossil fuel.

For proof that this occurs in the U.S., one need only look at the Energy Policy Act of 2005, with all of its incentives and tax breaks for the world's worst polluting industries. It is also worth considering the backroom manner in which the bill was crafted by Vice President Cheney's industry friends. As they say in the courts, *res ipsa loquitur*—the thing speaks for itself.

When it comes to subsidies and government support, the recent openness to renewables represents the first step in leveling the playing field that has been tilted by a century of government subsidies and regulatory support for fossil fuels and a half century of the same for nuclear power. The true social and economic costs of fossil fuels and nuclear power are not reflected in the market price of energy. Nor are they incorporated into cost comparisons between fossil fuels and renewable energy. Between 1974 and 2005, fossil fuels and nuclear power received three-fourths of all federal energy R&D funding, amounting to $68 billion dollars. Today, fossil fuels and nuclear power continue to receive billions in subsidies, and many more billions of tax incentives, while the environmental, health and military costs of these energy systems are borne by taxpayers.

The way to address the energy and climate crisis is for governments to let renewables compete by closing the artificial price gap between fossil fuels and renewable energy. In the U.S. only a sustained public outcry will make this happen. A small investment that accelerates the transition to renewables is the wisest course of action any government could take to reduce the political clout and economic advantages currently enjoyed by the fossil fuel and nuclear industries. That small investment, as noted in a report by Sir Nicholas Stern below, would go a long way to putting all energy sources on an equal footing to foster the inevitable momentum toward renewables and a new planetary fuel system.[39]

We agree with the Worldwatch Institute's recommendation that, "The key to a bright American energy future and a new wave of economic activity and innovation is a robust partnership between government and the private sector—providing incentives to jumpstart the new energy industries while minimizing the cost to American taxpayers."[40] Or as Stern reported, it would cost only 1% of global GDP to protect against the 25% or greater reduction in global GDP that could result from global warming. This represents a very low cost for insurance on a risk that is now a statistical likelihood.

At this critical crossroads in American history, renewables are the right choice. In fact, together with the promotion of "negawatts" through energy efficiency, they are the only choice. The financial benefits from developing abundant renewable sources of energy and the environmental and social rewards of success far outweigh the enormous risks of ignoring our fossil fuel addiction.

Ultimately, the deep-seated concerns over the energy and climate crisis that are compelling individual cities, states, and national governments to support the development of renewables are driven by three interrelated factors: the economic impact of rising oil prices, fears over geopolitical instability, and the certainty of catastrophic climate change should we continue down our present unsustainable path.

We believe that this book makes a persuasive case that that rising oil prices, energy insecurity and climate change are long-term mega-trends that will haunt America and the world community with death, destruction, and financial chaos as we move though the 21st century unless we immediately take forceful steps to deal with them. Therefore, in addition to implementing the Prometheus Plan in the transportation sector, we strongly urge aggressive action to maximize renewables and conservation in the electric sector. These are essential steps for reducing oil use, decreasing greenhouse gas emissions, and beginning the changeover to the hydrogen economy that lies just ahead. These steps should be accompanied by caps on carbon, as discussed in Chapter 4.

Properly executed, the Prometheus Plan offers America an unprecedented opportunity for global leadership to galvanize and unify the world in creating a promising future for our children and grandchildren. Such leadership would have a profoundly positive economic, environmental and social impact on all of humanity.

# Notes and References
# Chapter 11: Abundant Renewables

1   Joan Ogden, "High Hopes for Hydrogen," *Scientific American*, Special Issue, September 2006, 99. A kilogram of hydrogen has about the same energy content as a gallon of gasoline, but it will propel a car several times as far because fuel cells are more efficient than conventional gas engines.

2   W. Wayt Gibbs, "Plan B for Energy," *Scientific American*, Special Issue, September 2006, 102

3   "Green Gold, or Just Slime?" *New York Times*, March 7, 2007.

4   See "Green Dreams," *The Economist*, November 18, 2006, 13.

5   *Ibid.*, 13.

6   "Clean Energy Blueprint," under Clean Energy, Union of Concerned Scientists, www.ucsusa.org.

7   See Worldwatch Institute, *American Energy: The Renewable Path of Energy Security*, Washington, D.C., Worldwatch Institute and Center for American Progress, September 2006.

8   Brief for Entergy Corporation as *Amicus Curiae* in Support of Petitioners, Commonwealth of Massachusetts. v. Environmental Protection Agency, Supreme Court of the United States, No. 05-1120.

.9   U.S. Energy Information Administration, *Annual Energy Review, 2006*, Tables 1.3 and 2.1b-2.1f, and 10.3. Regarding the notes in Figure 1: (a) excludes 0.5 quadrillion Btu of ethanol, which is included in "Renewable Energy"; (b) excludes supplemental gaseous fuels; (c) includes 0.1 quadrillion Btu of coal coke net imports; (d) conventional hydroelectric power, geothermal, solar/PV, wind and biomass; (e) includes industrial combined-heat-and-power and industrial electricity-only plants; (f) includes commercial combined-heat-and-power and commercial electricity-only plants; (g) electricity-only and combined-heat-and-power plants whose primary business is to sell electricity, or electricity and heat, to the public. *Note:* Sum of components may not equal 100% due to independent rounding.

10  *Ibid.*.

11 While geothermal is characterized as renewable because it is a non-fossil fuel, over long periods of time geothermal wells will see reduction in the heat available for electricity production.

12 See Worldwatch Institute, *op. cit.*, 16, for a discussion of "Powering the Electricity Grid."

13 *Ibid.*, 16.

14 "Private Equity Buyout of TXU Is Enormous in Size and in its Complexity: Regulatory Clearance Seen as Slow but Sure," *New York Times,* February 27, 2007; "A Buyout Deal That Has Many Shades of Green," *New York Times,* February 26, 2007.

15 Daniel M. Kammen, "The Rise of Renewable Energy," *Scientific American,* Special Issue on "Energy's Future Beyond Carbon," September 2006, 89.

16 Massachuetts Institute of Technology, "The Future of Geothermal Energy: Impact of Enhanced Geothermal Systems (EGS) on the United States in the 21st Century," http://web.mit.edu/newsoffice/2007/geothermal.html

17 Kammen, *op.cit.,* 86.

18 Travis Bradford, "Investment in Silicon Production Up Sharply," *Solar Today* (July/August 2007) 24. Because the transportation sector presents the greatest opportunity for cutting oil consumption, we have limited ourselves to a brief discussion of the vast potential of PV and other solar energy. The Academy will be issuing further publications on solar power. For an overview of aspects of the solar industry, see Travis Bradford, *Solar Revolution: The Economic Transformation of the Global Energy Industry* (Cambridge, MA: The MIT Press 2006); and "Solar Power Captures Imagination, Not Money," *New York Times,* July 16, 2007.

19 Kammen, *op. cit.,* 88.

20 *Ibid.*, 89.

21 Worldwatch Institute, *op. cit.,* 20.

22 Claudia H. Deutsch, "Tapping the Latent Power of What's Left Around the Barnyard," *New York Times,* July 4, 2006.

23 John Sheehan *et al., A Look Back at the U.S. Department of Energy's Aquatic Species Program—Biodiesel from Algae,* Golden, CO, National Renewable Energy Laboratory, July 1998.

24 Michael Briggs, "Widescale Biodiesel Production from Algae," University of New Hampshire Biodiesel Group, revised August 2004, www.unh.edu/p.2/biodiesel/article_alge.html.

25 "Green Star Products Signs Contract to Build 90 Biodiesel Reactors," Press Release, November 13, 2006.

26 Kammen, *op. cit.*, 114.

27 "Green Gold, or Just Slime?" *New York Times*, March 7, 2007. Colorado State University has teamed up with Solix Biofuels Inc. to mass produce algae. "Making Biofuel from Pond Scum," *New York Times*, January 26, 2007. The Biofuels Program at Utah State University plans to produce algae-biodiesel that is cost-competitive by 2009.

28 For discussion of several wave and tidal systems, see Heather Timmos, "Energy From the Restless Sea: A Renewable Source, and Clean, But Not Without Its Critics," *New York Times*, August 3, 2006.

29 Worldwatch Institute, *op. cit.*, 33.

30 Gauthier *et al.*, *Ocean Thermal Energy Conversion (OTEC) and Deep Ocean Water Applications (DOWA), Market Opportunities for European Industry*, European Union Conference, "New and Renewable Technologies for Sustainable Development," Madeira, Portugal.

31 Worldwatch Institute, *op. cit.*, 21.

32 Steve Clemmer, *Clean Energy Blueprint*, Union of Concern Scientists, October 2001.

33 To the extent utilities choose to increase MWs over and above any savings from "negawatts," they will find it is safer and economically far preferable to implement renewable technologies. Increasing renewable energy supplies protects all stakeholders: consumers will face a smaller risk of price spikes and manipulation; workers will enjoy a larger job market and higher net income than they would ever see through continued investment in fossil fuels or nuclear power; and all Americans will benefit from improved air and water quality and a decreased reliance on imported energy. A 2004 ABT Associates study estimated that fine particulate pollution from fossil fuel power plant emissions causes nearly 24,000 premature deaths annually, thousands of asthma attacks, and millions of lost workdays, resulting in more than $160 billion in medical costs due to power plant air pollution.

34 Matthew L. Wald, "Experts Assess Deregulation As Factor in '03 Blackout," *New York Times*, September 16, 2005; and Brian J. Fleay, "USA's Triple Energy Whammy in Electric Power, Natural Gas and Oil," iNet News Service, Perth, Western Australia, January 2001.

35 Marsha Freeman, "NERC Forecast; 22 Necessary Actions Required To Save U.S. Electric Grid," *Executive Intelligence Review*, October 27, 2006.

36 *Ibid.*, 1.

37 Amory B. Lovins, "Mighty Mice," *Nuclear Engineering International*, December 2005, 46.

38 Stern Review, October 30, 2006. See http://news.bbc.co.uk/1/shared/bsp/hi/pdfs/30_10_06_exec_sum.pdf.

39 "Green Dreams," *The Economist*, November 18, 2006, 13.

40 Worldwatch Institute, *op. cit.*, 34.

# 12

## HYDROGEN REVOLUTION: GROWTH, JOBS, SECURITY & SUSTAINABILITY

*"The worldwide hydrogen energy web will be the next great*
*technological, commercial, and social revolution in history."*
— JEREMY RIFKIN, *THE HYDROGEN ECONOMY*, 2003

**Will the hydrogen fuel cell replace the internal combustion engine, and is it useful beyond transportation?** *Yes.*

- The replacement could start to happen within 10 years, if we begin the transition to the new energy economy today.

- All major car manufacturers already have advanced hydrogen fuel cell programs underway.

- The hydrogen fuel cell cleanly converts $H_2 + O_2$ into electricity + $H_2O$, for vehicles, businesses, and homes.

- Critics view the challenges as hydrogen fuel cell cost, and hydrogen production, distribution, safety, and storage.

## The Hydrogen Racer

You may think that hydrogen power is some futuristic fantasy, fit only for science fiction writers like Jules Verne in his novel *Mysterious Island*. Or, at best you might consider it a viable technology that won't be ready for prime time for another 40 to 50 years. If so, think again. In a special edition on "Best Inventions 2006," *Time* magazine praises the decision by Shanghai-based Horizon Fuel Cell Technologies "to design and market the H-racer, a 6-inch-long toy car that does what Detroit still can't. It runs on hydrogen extracted from plain tap water, using the solar-power hydrogen station."[1]

Hydrogen vehicles are not mere toys. There are more than 500 now on the road. A BMW prototype with a hydrogen internal combustion engine attained a top speed of 186 mph. Mazda, Ford, Honda, and GM are developing a variety of hydrogen-powered engines: fuel cell, internal combustion, and Wankel. Perhaps most exciting, Honda is now powering vehicles with hydrogen derived from tap water in small stationary units that drivers can keep in their garages.

Honda's 80-hp experimental 2005 FCX fuel cell car is already being tested on public roads in Los Angeles, along with a second-generation hydrogen home energy station. In February 2007, Honda reported:

> With an EPA city/highway rating of 62/51 miles per kilogram (mpkg) (57mpkg combined) and an EPA-rated driving range of 190 miles, the hydrogen-powered FCX delivers nearly a 20% improvement in fuel efficiency and range versus the 2004 model . . . . In terms of energy efficiency, one mpkg of hydrogen is almost equivalent to one mile per gallon (mpg) of gasoline. The hydrogen-powered Honda FCX has been certified by CARB as a Zero Emission Vehicle and by the EPA [with] the lowest possible national emission rating.[2]

Since this announcement was made, Honda has stated its intention to sell production models of the car in 2008, with maximum ranges of 350 miles and speeds of 100 mph. Honda has also announced the development of advanced photovoltaic (PV) cells and an electrolysis unit that are mounted on the company's solar-cell powered hydrogen refueling station in Torrance, California. This technology is the primary engine for performing electrolysis, the process that separates the pure hydrogen from water. Let's remember that some 10-15 years ago, when the Japanese carmakers committed themselves to commercialize a hybrid car, Detroit was snickering that they must be joking! And now GM, Ford and others are playing catch-up hoping to someday compete with the likes of Honda and Toyota in hybrid technology that was in great part developed at Stanford University!

We believe the current rapid pace of invention, testing, and commercialization of fuel cell technologies is a sign of the early stages of the hydrogen revolution. By starting today, instead of waiting half a century as critics suggest, the large-scale commercialization of hydrogen fuel cell cars can begin very soon.

## HYDROGEN: THE NEXT ENERGY ECONOMY

We have come to a crossroads where a single, courageous decision by a few world leaders can fundamentally alter the course of history. That decision is to shift from our dependence on rapidly depleting, increasingly costly, and environmentally challenging fossil fuels to a plentiful, renewable, and clean-burning hydrogen economy.

Hydrogen is by far the most abundant energy molecule in the universe. Perhaps that fact can serve as a reminder to us of the energy source we should be tapping.

Hydrogen can be thought of as a gaseous form of electricity. Anything that electricity can do, a hydrogen fuel cell with a hydrogen supply can do as well. However, while electricity can be stored only in batteries and capacitors that have a very low energy density (energy per unit of weight), hydrogen can be stored in any container from an industrial tanker to an automobile gas tank. With advanced hydrogen storage technologies, plus water, an electrolyzer, and a renewable source of energy, in the near future cars, homes, and businesses will become independent power producers that can generate electricity and sell it to the grid. The grid will increasingly become a distribution system for many producers of electrical power. It will serve the homeowner who produces excess power just as effectively as it does a large utility plant dedicated to power production.

**False Fears:** Past American administrations, while recognizing that hydrogen may be important in the future, assumed that the orderly transition to hydrogen would require an implementation plan that spanned four or five decades. This forecast rests on two false assumptions. The first is that there will be sufficient supplies of cheap oil for the foreseeable future. The second is that even if oil prices increase significantly, new discoveries and fossil fuel technologies will fill the gap, creating at most, modest global dislocations.

Many critics and energy experts outside government believe these false assumptions about oil and think that "hydrogen won't fly" or that it will be viable only far in the future. This view is based on a series of common misconceptions about the cost, efficiency, technology, and history of hydrogen. Hydrogen is the energy source that flew the Apollo Project to the moon. It was chosen over other energy sources because of its numerous advantages, including its higher efficiency per unit of mass. When used as a power source, hydrogen produces only three things: power, pure water, and extremely small quantities of nitrogen oxides. The latter is so small that fuel cell vehicles are considered zero-emission vehicles. Thus, it is non-polluting and non-corrosive. While flammable, hydrogen burns at a low temperature and generates low radiant heat. It is more difficult to explode than most people realize because it dissipates into the atmosphere rapidly.

**Enormous Potential.** Basic scientific facts and economic realities create a compelling case for hydrogen's role as the centerpiece of the world's next energy economy for the following reasons:

- Except for hydrogen, there is no other clean, sustainable, and technologically-available energy *carrier*.

- Hydrogen does not contribute to global warming.

- While hydrogen is still expensive to create, when combined with fuel-cell technology, it generates more than twice as much energy as oil, and is therefore economically viable even at oil prices of $60/barrel.

- A hydrogen economy would allow America to achieve long-lasting energy freedom and independence from foreign oil.

- Hydrogen can be used to power any machinery in either stationary applications (homes and offices) or mobile applications (cars and trucks).

- In the long-term, the hydrogen fuel cell can replace the internal combustion engine and catalyze Detroit's economic renaissance and international economic growth.

- Hydrogen can be generated from natural gas and eventually from water via local, decentralized energy systems, removing the costs and risks of fuel distribution associated with fossil fuels and nuclear power.

- As an inexhaustible source of clean energy, hydrogen will enhance human health, protect the environment, and increase energy equality.

## THE HYDROGEN FUEL CELL: HOW IT WORKS

The hydrogen fuel cell is one of the simplest technologies for generating electricity. Electricity is essentially a stream of electrons. The hydrogen atom, comprised of one proton and one electron, is the lightest and most plentiful element in the universe. As Figure 1 shows, a hydrogen fuel cell uses an electro-chemical process, as opposed to the thermal-chemical process used in the internal combustion engine, to separate the electron from the proton; uses the electron to create electricity; and then combines the hydrogen with oxygen to make $H_2O$. Over 99% of its exhaust is ultra-pure, drinkable water. Since the hydrogen fuel cell has no moving parts, it is quiet, clean, and highly efficient.

Hydrogen can be transformed to generate electricity through five steps:

1. The hydrogen is ionized by placing a stream of hydrogen and oxygen at the anode and cathode catalytic electrodes, respectively, of the fuel cell.

2. On the anode catalyst, hydrogen is separated into protons and electrons.

3. The electrons are forced to travel an external path, thus supplying electricity.

4. The protons pass through the proton exchange membrane.

5. On the cathode catalyst, oxygen reacts with the electrons and protons to create water exhaust and some heat.

**Figure 1. How A Hydrogen Fuel Cell Works**
$$2H_2 + O_2 = \text{Electricity} + 2H_2O$$

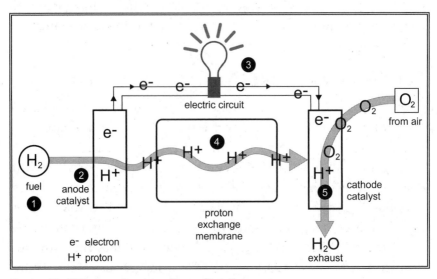

Source: World Business Academy Energy Task Force

Currently, both the anode and the cathode are coated with an ultra-thin, finely-dispersed platinum surface, which is the most expensive component in the manufacture of hydrogen fuel cells. Other types of fuel cells can use diesel, methanol, and chemical hydrides to separate electrons and create electrical power. However, on a "well-to-wheels basis," these fuels cells will generate more carbon dioxide than the "classic" hydrogen-oxygen fuel cell.

To increase the output of electricity, a series of fuel cells are linked together, creating a fuel cell stack. Since a single fuel cell produces only about one volt of electricity, fuel cells are typically layered and combined in parallel circuits. The number of cells in a fuel cell stack is typically 45, but designs and capacity vary.

The efficiency of fuel cells vastly exceeds that of the internal combustion engine due to the fuel cells' relative independence from the thermodynamic, heat transfer limitations known as the Carnot cycle. In the process of generating power, a conventional thermal engine such as the internal combustion engine loses much more energy than a hydrogen fuel cell. Therefore, hydrogen fuel cells boast very high efficiencies in their ideal state of low power density (supplied by using fuel cell stacks), when using pure hydrogen and oxygen as reactants. If a fuel cell uses the common air we breathe as its source of oxygen, its efficiency drops slightly.

**Diminishing Costs of Fuel Cell Technology.** The high cost of manufacturing hydrogen fuel cells is falling at a rate that any other technology would envy. In 2002, the average fuel cell had a price tag for its catalyst content of $1000 per kilowatt of electric power. This was projected to drop by 2007 to $30[3] per kilowatt. Here, Ballard Power Systems (NASDAQ: BLDP) one of the world's foremost major manufacturers of Proton Exchange Membrane fuel cells, is experimenting with platinum supported on carbonized silk catalysts that would reduce platinum usage by 30%, with no reduction in performance.

## HYDROGEN'S CRITICS ARE WRONG

Seventy-five percent by weight of all matter in the universe is made up of hydrogen. On earth, it is ubiquitous, most typically bound up in water, natural gas, and coal. It can be stored as a gas or a liquid and can power anything from a car to a building to an ocean liner. Hydrogen has the potential to supply the world with relatively inexpensive, clean, renewable energy, and thereby stabilize the economy and the environment.

Several standard college text books on energy either ignore hydrogen completely or give it only cursory treatment before dismissing it as a significant potential source of renewable energy.[4] Currently, the perception of hydrogen's potential is clouded by numerous myths and misconceptions voiced by naysayers, whose critiques must be addressed.

**Examples of Hydrogen Naysayers.** Some well-informed energy experts contend that hydrogen will be viable only after 20 to 30 years of development. For example, Paul Roberts, author of the widely-acclaimed, *The End of Oil*, argues that, "Hydrogen fuel cells and a ready supply of hydrogen to fuel them are still decades away from mass deployment."[5]

Similarly, Dr. Lester Brown, a world-renowned environmental scientist and a Fellow of the World Business Academy, contends that, "Unlike the widely discussed fuel cell/hydrogen transportation model, the gas-electric hybrid/wind model does not require a costly new infrastructure, since the network of gasoline service stations and the electricity grid are already in place."[6]

The Worldwatch Institute, too, holds this view, noting that "Despite recent public attention about the potential for a hydrogen economy, it could take decades to develop the infrastructure and vehicles required for a hydrogen-powered system."[7]

Richard Heinberg, author of *The Party's Over* and *Power Down*, writes that, "At this point, much of the enthusiasm about hydrogen seems to be issuing from politics rather than science."[8]

Joseph Romm, a leading hydrogen critic and author of *The*

*Hype About Hydrogen*, states that, "Hydrogen vehicles are unlikely to achieve even a 5% market share by 2030."[9]

In our view, these predictions are needlessly pessimistic, and the last is off by at least a decade. In fact, more than 250,000 recently commercialized hybrid electric vehicles were sold in 2006, and sales are expected to grow by over 226% between 2005 and 2012.[10] If America makes hydrogen a national priority, we know the first commercially available hydrogen internal combustion engines will be BMWs delivered by late 2007, and we foresee the first affordable hydrogen fuel cell cars coming to market starting in 2010-2012, together achieving 5% new car market share by 2020 or earlier.

Most of these criticisms can be reduced to a question of the timing of the economic viability of hydrogen fuel cell cars, rather than the viability, availability, or cost of the technology. They are encapsulated in Paul Roberts's assertion that "a self-sustaining fuel cell car industry is, at best, at least two decades away, and probably more—too long to wait to begin reducing our automotive emissions or energy use."[11]

Unlike the critics, we believe that, if we simultaneously implement the Prometheus Plan and the strategy for launching the U.S. hydrogen economy outlined below, then the widespread commercialization of hydrogen as a fuel source in cars, homes and businesses will be well underway by 2010. We reiterate that the oil savings that will accrue from the Prometheus Plan are *in no way dependent* on hydrogen technology. We see the freedom from Middle East oil as only a beginning. Therefore, this plan includes the outlines for a Beyond Prometheus Strategy, in which hydrogen is the core initiative.

## Eight Hydrogen Myths

Let's examine the facts about actual hydrogen usage and then analyze the critics' misconceptions about viability, availability, or cost of the technology. The most elegant and comprehensive rebuttal to these criticisms appears in World Business Academy Fellow and energy guru Amory Lovins' 2003 paper, "Twenty Hydrogen Myths."

We have consolidated his main insights below in order to address the most significant misconceptions about hydrogen.[12]

- About 75% of the known universe is comprised of hydrogen, which unlike oil, coal, wind, or sun, is not an energy source. Rather, it is an energy carrier, like electricity or gasoline.

- As an energy carrier, it needs to be freed from the chemical compounds, such as water or natural gas, into which it is bound.

- Fossil-fuel molecules are combinations of carbon, hydrogen, and other atoms. The debate centers on whether it is cheaper and more beneficial to burn the remaining carbon or simply to free and use the hydrogen.

- Using hydrogen as a fuel yields only water and traces of nitrogen oxides. This shift can significantly reduce pollution and climate change.

- Hydrogen is the lightest element in the universe. Per unit of volume, hydrogen contains only 30% as much energy as natural gas when both are at atmospheric pressure. Thus, hydrogen is most advantageous where lightness is worth more than volume, which is true for most transportation fuels.

One of the biggest challenges in addressing criticism of hydrogen is to compare hydrogen fairly and consistently with other energy carriers. For example, fuel cells, as electrochemical devices, are not subject to the same thermodynamic limits as gasoline-driven engines, which do their work by generating heat. As a result, "You can drive several times as far on a gallon-equivalent (in energy content) of hydrogen in a fuel-cell car as on a gallon of gasoline in an engine-driven car."[13]

### Myth #1: An entire hydrogen industry needs to be developed from scratch.

The production of hydrogen is already a large, mature industry, and new technology will allow the average consumer to power his or her home and car from the garage. Currently, the global hydrogen industry annually produces 50 million metric tons of hydrogen, worth about $150 billion. That's the same as 170 million tons-equivalent of oil. U.S. hydrogen production alone accounts for at least one-fifth and probably nearer one-third of the world total. To put it in perspective, the current global output of pure hydrogen has the energy-equivalence of 1.2 billion barrels of oil, or about a quarter of U.S. petroleum imports.[14]

Hydrogen production is now centralized, primarily because hydrogen usage is centralized. In the future, usage will become decentralized, leading to a demand for a distributed hydrogen production system. The growth of a distributed network of small "reformers" which extract hydrogen from natural gas or electrolyzers (which extract hydrogen from water) will easily support this demand. Initially the reformers or electrolyzers can operate on the excess power capacity of existing gas and electricity grids at off-peak hours.

Our current production is already far greater than even the above numbers indicate. If we were to funnel all current hydrogen production into advanced ultra-light vehicles as efficient as the quintupled-efficiency Revolution concept car from Hypercar, it would displace two-thirds of today's entire worldwide gasoline consumption. In contrast, one-third of all hydrogen is used in the production of gasoline. Furthermore, the world's current hydrogen production could potentially be created via direct electrolysis of water, using only cost-efficient wind power from North and South Dakota.

The hydrogen industry is growing at 6% a year and doubling every 12 years. All this is happening absent the incentive that would be provided by a growing fleet of hydrogen fuel cell vehicles in need of fuel. If the hydrogen industry can expand so quickly while "below the radar," it will have no problem expanding quickly enough to fuel any number of hydrogen fuel cell cars.

The new models of the Honda FCX are powered entirely by hydrogen, and come with a home-based hydrogen energy station that produces enough hydrogen to fuel the car and also power the owner's house by reforming hydrogen from a natural gas line. The station will soon be configured to function with 20 square yards of solar material that will make it independent from the grid. Large commercial structures can place this nano-solar material on any non-transparent surface to power both buildings and vehicles.

## Myth #2: Hydrogen is too dangerous or explosive for common use as fuel.

This myth begins with the hydrogen-filled passenger dirigible, the Hindenburg. The Hindenburg air disaster occurred at Lakehurst, New Jersey, in 1937. Recently, the event was revisited through a detailed analysis by NASA scientist Dr. Addison Bain. He found that the incident would have occurred almost identically even if the dirigible had been filled with nonflammable helium gas. It was not the hydrogen that originally combusted, it was the dirigible's outer coating, which was a highly flammable material similar to that used in rocket propellants. There was no explosion, and it was unlikely that anyone was killed by the hydrogen fire. The surviving passengers lived by riding the dirigible to the ground, since the burning hydrogen rose quickly into the air without spreading its heat to the gondola. In comparison, the explosive power of gasoline is 22 times greater by volume.

Anyone who has seen the endless replays of the September 11 disasters knows precisely how flammable our aviation fuel of choice truly is. Hydrogen is much safer. Period.

In reality, the hydrogen industry has an excellent safety record over the past half-century. Last year alone, in 40,000 shipments to 1,000 locations, it carried 100 million gallons of liquid hydrogen. Over 30 years, liquefied hydrogen shipments have logged 33 billion miles. In all this time, there have been no product losses and no fires.[15] Gasoline, our automotive fuel of choice, has a dismal safety record in comparison.

Hydrogen, though flammable, is generally more easily managed than hydrocarbon fuels, including gasoline. It is extremely light—14.4 times lighter than air and approximately seven times lighter than natural gas.

Hydrogen-air mixtures are difficult to combust, requiring a constrained volume of elongated shape. Hydrogen explosions require at least twice as rich a mixture of hydrogen as does an explosion of natural gas (i.e., they need double the density of gas to container volume). In other words, leaking hydrogen will ignite and burn, but not explode. If hydrogen is ignited, it burns with a clear flame with only one-tenth the radiant heat of a hydrocarbon fire. The heat that is produced tends to dissipate much more rapidly than does heat from gasoline or oil fires. Victims in a hydrogen fire generally are not burned unless directly in the flame, nor do they choke on smoke.

The belief that hydrogen is unusually dangerous is easy to dispel with videotapes showing modern tests of an ignited leak in a car's hydrogen fuel cell.[16] The most important comparison is between a hydrogen fire and a gasoline fire. First, a hydrogen fire was created in a test car by by-passing the triple-redundant safety interlocks. (Current industry standards for hydrogen leak detection and safety interlocks are thorough and very effective.) The leak was engineered at the highest-pressure location and discharged a full 1.54 kilograms of hydrogen in approximately 100 seconds. The resulting vertical flame plume raised the car's interior temperature by a maximum of 1-2° F (0.6-1.1° C), and its outside temperature rose by the same amount as a car sitting in direct sunlight. The passenger compartment was unharmed. In other words, a passenger wouldn't notice the heat, let alone be hurt by it.

In the second test, a 2.5-fold slower leak of *gasoline* from a 1/16 inch (1.6 mm) hole in a fuel line incinerated the car's interior and would have killed anyone trapped inside.

Bottom line: the hydrogen safety critics should turn their fire against gasoline, and agitate for the rapid adoption of hydrogen on safety grounds alone!

## Myth #3: Making hydrogen is inefficient because the energy used is greater than the energy yield.

According to physics, any conversion of energy from one form to another will use more energy than it creates. If you created more energy than you used, you would have a perpetual motion machine, which violates the laws of physics. Since it is impossible to avoid a loss of energy, the relevant question is actually, "Is the loss of energy associated with converting matter from one form to another worth the cost?"

If the answer were categorically "no," as the myth implies, then we would not make gasoline from crude oil (~73-91% efficient from wellhead-to-pump) or electricity from fossil fuel (~29-35% efficient from coal at the power plant-to-retail meter). Hydrogen converts at 72-85% efficiency in natural-gas reformers or at 70-75% efficiency in electrolyzers.

So why is it worthwhile to accept these conversion losses? It is worthwhile because hydrogen's greater and more versatile end-use efficiency can more than offset the conversion losses. This makes sense in the same manner that an air conditioner can offset fuel-to-electricity conversion losses by using one unit of electricity to deliver several units of cool air. In other words, conversion losses are acceptable if the energy produced is more versatile and can be more efficiently used than in the original form, resulting in greater economic value. Hydrogen easily meets these criteria.

It is an unfortunate fact that for today, natural gas presents the most feasible source of hydrogen. As a petrochemical feedstock that both contributes to global warming and is in questionable supply, natural gas presents many difficulties. The long run solution is obvious: use renewables to fuel the processes that will generate hydrogen from water in a decentralized system.

Another misconception commonly associated with this myth is that crude oil can be more efficiently converted into *delivered* gasoline than natural gas can be converted into *delivered* hydrogen. Any difference in the efficiency with which gasoline and hydrogen can be converted from one form of energy into another is overshadowed by hydrogen's greater efficiency over gasoline in powering a vehicle. Using hydrogen to run a fuel-cell car is two to three times more efficient than using gasoline to run an internal combustion engine. Again, this is because combustion is always limited by the thermodynamic constraints of the so-called Carnot Cycle. This is not so for electrical devices such as a fuel cell.

Using numbers from Toyota, 88% of the energy in the oil at the wellhead becomes energy in the gasoline in your tank, and 16% of gasoline's energy reaches your wheels. This well-to-wheels efficiency is therefore only 14%. On the other hand, locally reformed natural gas (with the advantage of a potentially decentralized hydrogen generation network) delivers 70% of the wellhead energy into the car's tank. The super-efficient fuel-cell drive system brings a whopping 60% of that energy to the wheels. This results in a well-to-wheels efficiency of 42%, or three times the efficiency of gasoline (i.e., 42% / 14% = 3), and even 1.5 times the efficiency of the gasoline hybrid electric car.

It is precisely because of these efficiencies that it makes sound economic and environmental sense to take the leftover natural gas which will be saved by the aggressive implementation of renewables in the electric sector, and convert it to hydrogen which will be used to power hydrogen fuel cell vehicles, thereby displacing most of the remaining oil use in the transportation sector.

Furthermore, hydrogen's efficiency is so great that it may even make good sense to use hydrogen as an electric storage medium, especially for expansion and peaking power, in the electricity market. Using hydrogen for on-site energy during peaks is a particularly interesting idea for large metropolitan areas with transmission constraints, as well as for remote off-grid locations. This would facilitate more flexible energy usage and save power plant fuel by encouraging greater use of intermittent sources like wind. And for developing countries and other remote areas where no infrastructure exists, the answer is obvious—fuel cell power is the preferred motive force, just as solar power is today.

### Myth #4: Delivery to end users consumes most of hydrogen's energy.

In 2003, two Swiss scientists analyzed the energy needed to deliver hydrogen, using a number of different methods.[17] It is only fair to note that their net-energy figures were basically correct, though not their conclusion that hydrogen's "physical properties are incompatible with the requirements of the energy market. Production, packaging, storage, transfer, and delivery of the gas . . . are so energy consuming that alternatives should be considered." There are five relevant pieces of information which invalidate this conclusion.

First, the Swiss scientists' report was published by the Methanol Institute, which promotes methanol over hydrogen, which renders their findings generally suspect.

Second, the paper presented certain hydrogen processes that have already been rejected, except in special markets, because they are too costly.

Third, the researchers focused entirely on electrolysis—the costliest method—and since the writing of their paper, the price of electrolysis has dropped from $8/kg to $3/kg, and continues to fall. Even with the high cost of electrolysis, they completely ignored any transitional hydrogen production processes such as steam reforming of natural gas.

Fourth, they admit that reforming fossil fuels such as natural gas is cheaper than electrolysis, but reject reforming because, according to their calculations, it releases more $CO_2$ than simply burning the hydrocarbon. This completely ignores hydrogen's fuel-cell efficiency advantage of 200 to 300% relative to conventional gasoline internal combustion engine cars. Using the most conservative assumptions, a car powered by hydrogen fuel cells emits 40 to 67% less carbon dioxide per mile than a gasoline-powered car of otherwise identical design. Eliminating the burning of hydrocarbons achieves a net reduction in $CO_2$ emissions.

Fifth, all of their energy transportation numbers are relevant only under a centralized hydrogen system, and not a distributed system. If the hydrogen economy were a centralized system, we would miss one of the great benefits of hydrogen—its ability to be generated in a basement or garage with a supply of water or natural gas plus an electrolysis machine or small reformer. It is the de-centralized system that will grow. The initial investment for a reformer is relatively small (as noted earlier, the Honda FCX already comes with a home hydrogen power system), eliminating the need for anything more than a natural gas line, a water line, and some electricity (off-peak grid or renewable-fueled). The reformer produces hydrogen with no transportation cost.

However, the electrolysis technology that is rapidly being developed and tested in Iceland and Hawaii to produce hydrogen with electrolyzers and water will prove to be far preferable to producing hydrogen by reforming natural gas because electrolysis does not contribute to global warming. Electrolysis will be a superior methodology for extracting hydrogen in both small and large-scale facilities. While for all the foregoing reasons, producing hydrogen from natural gas is superior to the gasoline-powered internal combustion engine, we hope the industry will rapidly switch to the far more intelligent solution of producing hydrogen with electrolyzers and water.

Furthermore, if society ever decided that the best choice is centralized hydrogen production by steam reforming of natural gas to hydrogen with carbon dioxide as a by-product, a conclusion with which we strongly disagree, this centralized production would be done near cities, not thousands of miles away. It would be easy to turn an existing oil refinery into a merchant hydrogen plant. And, if it made sense to pipe the carbon dioxide a long distance (which we doubt because it would be easier to capture the carbon dioxide and feed it to algae at the plant site), the piping of carbon dioxide is an inexpensive process and can be managed in almost any of the current types of transmission pipelines.

## Myth #5: Hydrogen cannot be distributed through existing pipelines.

The transportation of hydrogen, one of the most frequently mentioned concerns of critics, is easily accomplished through pipelines, using one of hydrogen's most beautiful advantages—simple distributed production. There is no need to create a new pipeline network to move hydrogen; we can use the one already in existence. Some existing pipelines are already hydrogen-ready. The others can easily be modified with existing technologies by adding polymer-composite liners, similar to the process used to renovate old sewer pipes. To complete the process, we could simply add a hydrogen-blocking metallic coating or liner, and convert the compressors.

Using existing pipelines creates no additional safety concerns. A 200-mile, crude-oil pipeline has already been converted to hydrogen. Because many older natural gas pipeline systems were originally created for the use of "town gas," which was 50 to 60% hydrogen by volume, they are either entirely or largely hydrogen-compatible. Any pipelines that do need to be built have the advantage of small size, making them easy to site. Furthermore, installing small reformers in buildings—which can not only power the buildings but fuel the car as well—eradicates worries about delivery of the fuel supply.

Already, hydrogen refueling stations are appearing. Governor Arnold Schwarzenegger has pledged his commitment to a California Hydrogen Highway Network initiative "to support and catalyze a rapid transition to a clean, hydrogen transportation economy."[18] Florida and British Columbia have already created similar initiatives. Other states are sure to follow.

**Myth #6: There is no practical way to run cars on hydrogen.**

Turning wheels with an electric motor has well-known and long-established advantages of torque, ruggedness, reliability, simplicity, controllability, quietness, and economy. Virtually every light rail and subway system has been doing precisely this for more than a century. So, where does 21st century technology get the electricity? A hybrid electric vehicle generates energy from braking or from an onboard engine. It provides all the advantages of an electric motor without the disadvantages of size, weight, and price associated with traditional batteries. With the addition of fuel cells, this becomes the most efficient, clean, and reliable way to make electricity from fuel, using current technology.

Hydrogen fuel cells have been used for space flights since 1965 and they were used in a passenger vehicle as early 1966 (GM's Electrovan). Fuel cells have been used for decades in aerospace and military applications. They are emerging as power sources for portable electronics and appliances. They are already competitive for buildings, as well as industrial niches, when installed in the right place and used properly.

As of today, fuel cell vehicles are undergoing rigorous testing and are far advanced. As of mid-2003, manufacturers had tens of fuel cell buses and upwards of 100 fuel cell cars on the road. There were 156 different fuel cell concept cars and 68 demonstration hydrogen filling stations (see Figure 2 below). Fuel cells are currently being tested for military vehicles on land and sea, and submarines have used them for years. Heavy trucks, which spend up to half their engine run-time idling because they have no auxiliary power source, are also beginning to utilize fuel cells. FedEx and UPS plan to introduce fuel-cell trucks by 2008.

With such a massive wave of research and trial, fuel cells will quickly advance, as each successful application benefits from its predecessors' experience. As a whole, mass production will drive down the price of fuel cells. With the 2006 sale in the U.S. of over 250,000 hybrid electric cars operating on electric motors, there is no longer any reason to perpetuate the myth that cars can not run on electricity.

## Myth #7: We lack a safe, affordable way to store hydrogen in cars.

The real issue here is mobile storage of hydrogen. The concern is that it would be necessary to equip every hydrogen fuel cell car with a steel storage tank, as opposed to the cheap plastic tanks of modern automobiles.

This concern was addressed several years ago with the creation of filament-wound, carbon-fiber tanks lined with an aluminized polyester bladder. Compared to the now-obsolete solid metal liner tanks, advanced carbon-fiber tanks reduced the weight of the fuel tank by half and cut the materials cost by a third. They have approximately 9 to 13 times the strength of their metal counterparts. They are immune to corrosion, and extremely tough, escaping undamaged in crashes that shred gasoline tanks. The pipes of a hydrogen fuel cell car are also maintained at the same low pressure as the fuel cell, thus removing the corresponding concern over the weakness of high-pressure hydrogen pipes.

The carbon-fiber tanks can be mass produced for just a few hundred dollars apiece. A 350-bar (5,000 pounds per square inch) hydrogen tank is almost 10 times the size of a comparable gasoline tank in terms of energy content. If you include the hydrogen fuel cell's greater two- or three-fold efficiency advantage over an internal combustion engine, this size differential decreases to only about four times. Furthermore, with a hydrogen fuel cell car, you can remove other car parts, such as the catalytic converter, thus compensating for the additional volume required by the hydrogen tanks.

With modern design methods and materials, cars will enjoy advanced efficiencies thanks to less aerodynamic drag, rolling resistance, and weight. Thus, they will use two-thirds less power, thereby decreasing the amount of hydrogen needed to drive over a comparable distance. The magic number that all automotive makers are targeting is a range of 300 miles on a single fueling with hydrogen. GM's Sequel, a fuel cell concept car, has achieved this range by boosting the hydrogen to 10,000 p.s.i.

**Myth #8: Hydrogen is too expensive to compete with gasoline.**[19]

Despite decades of U.S. policies favoring the use of petroleum, hydrogen technologies are already close to economic viability. When we consider system-wide life cycle costs, hydrogen *already* is a desirable alternative to fossil fuel.

The relative costs of hydrogen and gasoline-powered vehicles cannot be calculated without considering their relative wellhead-to-wheels efficiencies (i.e., the percentage of the total energy extracted that ends up powering the vehicle). As discussed above, only 14% of the total energy extracted from oil in the ground ends up powering a car. If we use natural gas as the interim source of hydrogen, the wellhead-to-wheels efficiency of hydrogen is 42%—three times greater than the efficiency of internal combustion engines which have been optimized over the past 100 years. Gasoline can't compete. These comparative efficiencies of hydrogen over gasoline also apply to cars with hydrogen internal combustion engines. This technology can play a role in a short-term hydrogen transition strategy.

The greenhouse gas emissions story is overwhelmingly favorable to hydrogen. Even when hydrogen fuel is produced from natural gas, on a per-mile-driven basis, fuel cell cars generate as little as 30% of the carbon dioxide produced by gasoline-powered cars.

Cost is the bottom line factor for many consumers contemplating the adoption of new technologies. One kilogram of hydrogen is energy-equivalent to one gallon of gasoline. Small hydrogen generators manufactured by the hundreds, installed at service stations supporting a few hundred fuel cell-powered cars that use natural gas as a raw material at a cost of $6 per million British Thermal Units, would deliver hydrogen to cars at $2.50 per kg. This is equivalent to $2.50 per gallon gasoline. As current trends continue, we believe that the days of $2.50 per gallon gasoline will be very fond memories.

In more comparable terms, namely the cost per mile driven, using modestly efficient hydrogen fuel cell cars that are two to three times more efficient than internal combustion engine cars, fully taxed gasoline at $2.25 per gallon would be equivalent to hydrogen selling at $5 per kg. In other words, hydrogen could be priced even at $5 per kg and compete with gasoline at $2.25 per gallon.

With more technological improvements certain to rapidly reduce the price of 99.99% pure hydrogen, we can rest assured that an affordable, clean energy future is not so far away. General Motors has even stated that hydrogen becomes competitive with gasoline at $2.25 per gallon.[20]

---

*"Hydrogen made in 20- or 180-nominal-car-per-day natural-gas reformers would have remained competitive with retail and wholesale gasoline, respectively, at the actual average prices of U.S. natural gas and gasoline for the past 22 years."*

— AMORY LOVINS, *TWENTY HYDROGEN MYTHS*, 2003

---

## Gentlemen, Start Your Fuel Cells

Automakers have been researching hydrogen-powered cars for over a decade, but it is only within the past five years that R&D concepts have been translated into prototypes and in some cases production-line products. As Figure 2 shows, BMW, Daimler-Chrysler, Ford Motor, General Motors, Honda, Hyundai, Mazda, Nissan, Toyota, and Volkswagon have been leading the pack and spending billions of dollars on the next frontier of automotive technology: the hydrogen fuel cell car.[21] While Honda is leading the charge with the Honda FCX and its home-based hydrogen energy station, other companies are quickly catching up with hydrogen fuel cell concept cars that push the envelope in terms of design, efficiency, and creativity.

For example, the Revolution from Hypercar, Inc. may be the most advanced hydrogen fuel cell concept car yet. Hypercar vehicles are ultralight, ultra-low-drag, hybrid electric vehicles with a highly integrated and simplified design emphasizing software-controlled functionality. While currently expensive and handmade, a new patent-pending manufacturing process is expected to make these carbon-fiber cars affordable at automotive volumes of 10,000 to 100,000 vehicles per year. This concept car will have the size, safety, comfort, and performance of a Lexus RX300, yet with a model average efficiency of 99 mpg-equivalent. Estimates are that the Revolution will have a driving range of 330 miles, with 3.4 kg of hydrogen at 350-bar (5,000 pounds per square inch) pressure. The driving range can be extended to over 500 miles with the new fuel tanks, which are being incorporated by many manufacturers.[22]

## Figure 2. Hydrogen Car Programs by Major Automobile Manufacturers

| Company | Concept Car Name | Program Description |
|---|---|---|
| BMW | 750hL, H2R | Hydrogen internal combustion engine |
| DaimlerChrysler | F-Cell | Based on Mercedes A-Class |
| Ford Motors | Ford FCV | Fuel Cell modification of Ford Focus |
| GM | Sequel, HydroGen3 | Multiple other models, listed are most important |
| Honda | Honda FCX | Current Leader, Home Hydrogen Energy Station |
| Hyundai | Tucson FCEV | Based on UTC Power fuel cell technology* |
| Mazda | RX-8 | Duel-fuel (hydrogen or gasoline) rotary engine |
| Nissan | X-TRAIL FCV | Based on UTC Power fuel cell technology* |
| Morgan Motor | LIFEcar | Performance-oriented, with other British groups |
| Toyota | Highlander FCHV | Under development and in active testing |
| Volkswagon | Bora Hy.Power | Projected to be in showrooms by 2010 |

* UTC Power is a United Technology Company (NYSE: UTX)

Research is proceeding quickly on other storage methods, including liquid hydrogen, metal hydrides, and carbon nanotubes. Each method has advantages and disadvantages; but so far none compare with the currently available high-pressure tanks in terms of weight or cost. In addition, there are no size or safety reasons that preclude using current generation tanks. While further research on storage technology is desirable, it is not essential for hydrogen car development. In the end, and analogous to natural gas as the initial source of hydrogen for automotive fuel cells, pressure tank storage can easily serve as the means to introduce fuel cell cars, while further development unfolds a host of other technologies that increase hydrogen storage density and extend driving range.

Honda is one of the few companies that are already road testing a hydrogen fuel cell car, the Honda FCX. In 2005, Honda leased its home energy station and a 2005 Honda FCX to a family in Los Angeles. It is reported to offer "every comfort and quality of a regular Honda, drove seamlessly, smoothly, and handled like the best vehicles the company makes."[23] This hydrogen fuel cell car is expected to go into production sometime between 2008 and 2009.

As GM, Ford, and Chrysler jockey for positions, foreign competitors are already announcing production dates. However, "When any of these companies roll out their production models in 2009 or 2010, those cars will not be available at showrooms, but to select commercial and government customers, such as municipalities, the military, and major corporate and government fleet owners. It will be another year or two for the production volume to bring down costs to consumer levels."[24]

> "Ironically, the American companies will not be leading the parade onto the hydrogen highway. That will be Honda, which will have to look over its shoulder continuously as it is chased by BMW, Audi, Toyota and other foreign car makers."
>
> — EDWIN BLACK, *INTERNAL COMBUSTION*, 2006

It is noteworthy that both BMW and DaimlerChrysler made significant progress with the hydrogen internal combustion engine. In fact, BMW has already announced a 2008 date for initial production of its BMW Hydrogen 7 "Eco-Luxury" cars. However, we do not believe that the hydrogen internal combustion engine will become the standard for hydrogen-powered cars. Although environmentally friendly, it uses current internal combustion technology and thus loses the fundamental advantages of the extremely efficient hydrogen fuel cell.

## Generating Hydrogen At Home

Honda R&D Co., Ltd. jointly developed its hydrogen home energy station with Plug Power Inc., Honda's strategic fuel cell partner for research and development in hydrogen energy sources. During field tests of the station's ability to generate hydrogen from natural gas for use in fuel cell vehicles while supplying electricity and hot water for the home, Honda concluded that the station can currently produce enough hydrogen to refill the tank of the Honda FCX fuel cell vehicle in a few minutes once a day. The station is made up of the following processes and components:

1. A reformer to extract hydrogen from natural gas;

2. A fuel cell unit to provide power for the overall system that uses some of the extracted hydrogen;

3. A refiner to purify the hydrogen;

4. A compressor for pressurizing the extracted hydrogen; and

5. A high pressure tank to store the pressurized hydrogen.

**Figure 3. Structural Outline for Honda Home Energy Station[25]**

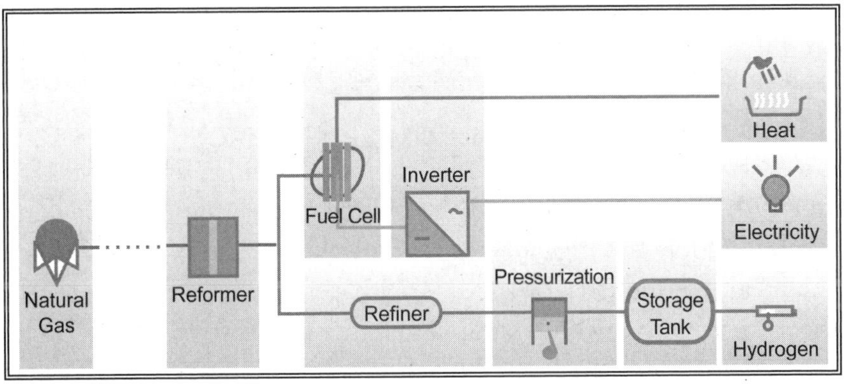

Looking ahead, Honda has also announced the development of next-generation solar cell panels made by Honda Engineering, as well as a high-efficiency electrolysis unit. Both the advanced light-absorbing solar panels and the electrolysis unit are mounted on Honda's solar cell-powered hydrogen refueling station in Torrance, California, to improve total system efficiency. As a proponent of the hydrogen future, Honda believes that "hydrogen fuel cell power has the potential to be the next-generation power plant needed to overcome problems related to the development of alternative fuels, reducing exhaust gas emissions, and reducing the effects of global warming."[26]

## HYDROGEN TECHNOLOGY AND GLOBAL ECONOMIC GROWTH

In a paper on "Hydrogen and the New Energy Economy," Julian Gresser and James A. Cusumano (one of this book's co-authors) contend that many environmental and national security arguments on behalf of hydrogen miss what is perhaps its most beneficial impact: "Hydrogen could become a strategic business sector and an engine of global economic growth within the decade and for the remainder of the 21st century."[27]

It is well known that at critical times in a nation's development, certain industries have made key technological breakthroughs and have provided dynamic engines of broader economic growth. This growth occurs when competitive advantages won through productivity gains in a strategic business sector are transferred to other industries.

Famous examples of the convergence of key technologies and rapid economic growth include: the canals and railroads of 18th and 19th century Europe and the United States; the New England machine tool factories of the early 19th century; the German chemical dye industry of the late 19th century; and most recently, the U.S. convergence of computer hardware, software, and Internet technology of the late 20th century. Japan's post-World War II industries (steel, auto, electronics, semiconductors, computers and telecommunications) show how economic innovation can trigger rapid economic growth.

Due to the tremendous public benefits realized through the

success of strategic technologies and industries, governments have usually played a critical catalytic role in accelerating their development. Notable historical examples are President Franklin D. Roosevelt's Rural Electrification Administration, President Eisenhower's interstate highway system, and President Kennedy's Apollo Project.

California has taken the national lead in implementing a "Hydrogen Highway Network Action Plan" that will build 150 to 200 hydrogen refueling stations, approximately one every 20 miles on California's major highways. Similarly, Florida has launched an innovative program to promote hydrogen as a strategic growth sector. Crafting a broad alliance among private companies, state and local government, universities, and environmental groups, the Florida Hydrogen Strategy initially focuses on fuels cells, hydrogen storage, and power-grid optimization. The strategy offers tax refunds, investment tax credits, performance incentives, and enterprise bond financing.

Japan, Germany, Canada and Iceland have major hydrogen programs underway. All of these nations understand that, in addition to laying the foundation for independence from oil and creating a key industrial sector, the rapid development of hydrogen will accelerate innovation in related sectors, such as nano-materials, biotechnology, solar photovoltaics, ultra-light materials, and even the Internet, through distributed power generation and grid interface.

## LAUNCHING THE U.S. HYDROGEN ECONOMY

Given the urgency of the energy and climate crisis, in addition to adopting the Prometheus Plan, we urge the development of a broad political consensus around a plausible strategy for the transition to a hydrogen economy. This strategy will apply regulatory, financial and other market-driven incentives, while drawing on the best available technology and talent. Under the rubric of a non-partisan National Hydrogen Task Force, the President and the Congress should convene the nation's leading hydrogen scientists, engineers and inventors, along with top environmental lawyers, finance experts, and specialists in public/private enterprises.

Their mission should be the development of a draft Strategic Hydrogen Alliance Reform and Enterprise Act (SHARE) that will create the statutory framework for accelerating the development of the hydrogen economy as quickly as possible, on a par with the urgency that accompanies a state of war or a natural disaster.

The main stages of this transition plan are outlined below and include the following milestones:

**Phase I (2007-2010)**—Deploy existing technologies and capabilities to expedite fuel cell research and development and to vigorously market smaller fuel cells to homes and businesses as local, distributed power, while the hydrogen car runs on a modified internal combustion engine that is cost-effective today. Where needed, build a national hydrogen infrastructure, including production facilities, pipelines and fueling stations in core metropolitan areas.

**Phase II (2010-2015)**—Introduce multiple varieties of fuel cell cars that run on hydrogen, generated from natural gas reformation or electrolyzed from water.

**Phase III (2015-2020)**—Achieve widespread commercialization of fuel cell vehicles that operate on hydrogen generated by renewable energy sources such as solar- and wind-powered electrolysis.

The ultimate goal is the broad transition to clean and "Green" hydrogen generated from wind, solar, geothermal and possibly biological systems, and minimum sales of 1,000,000 hydrogen fuel cell vehicles, equal to a 6% new car market penetration. The specific goals of each phase, which complement the automobile efficiency and biofuels strategies of the Prometheus Plan, are as follows. In parallel to these hydrogen milestones, the plan would require automobile engines to be developed so that they could function on a mix of plug-in technologies, renewable fuels such as ethanol or biodiesel, and hydrogen fuel cells powered by electricity from the utility grid.

## Phase I: Deploy Existing Technologies and Capabilities (~2007-2010)[28]

*Hydrogen Fuel Cell Status: Plug-in hybrid electric vehicles and internal combustion engines that run on hydrogen come into the market; hydrogen fuel cell prototypes tested*

1) Immediately implement the Prometheus Plan, which focuses primarily on oil savings through automobile efficiency and biofuels in the transportation sector.

2) Establish financial incentives through the SHARE Act to put hydrogen on an economic par with petroleum.

3) Market existing fuel cells to businesses and homes and also to the growing high-reliability niche for information technologies and commercial computer operations.

4) Conduct extensive applications research and expedite commercial development and construction of the first large-scale fuel cell plants, to bring production costs down to at least $400 per kw, competitive with most electric power.

5) Build on Ford and BMW strategies to offer current model internal combustion engines that run on hydrogen—25% more efficient and 70% less carbon dioxide emitting than conventional engines—including leased transit and business fleets with access to a central hydrogen generator unit.

6) Expand the number of hydrogen filling stations in metropolitan areas and lease prototype hydrogen fuel cell vehicles in these areas.

7) Accelerate current research into nano-materials for hydrogen storage and initiate research for hydrogen generation from solar photocatalysis and genetically modified organisms (bio-hydrogen).[29]

## Phase II: Expand Infrastructure Beyond Core Metropolitan Areas (~2010-2015)

*Hydrogen Fuel Cell Status: Initial commercialization of affordable hydrogen fuel cell and plug-in hybrid electric vehicles / hydrogen fuel cell cars*

1) Commercialize nationwide prototype fuel cell vehicles, newly affordable due to financial incentives provided to automakers, oil companies, and consumers. This should include early adoption of fuel-cell plug-in hybrid vehicles. Visionary oil companies and utilities complete the transformation into energy service companies.

2) Install new advanced wind- and solar cell-powered facilities for efficient, economic generation of "Green" hydrogen via electrolysis.

3) Expand hydrogen energy stations across the country, based on hydrogen generated from water by electrolysis, to fuel stationary fuel cells in homes and businesses.

4) Convert most large sea vessels to run on biofuels or fuel cell power.

5) Build new high-capacity hydrogen storage tanks based on breakthroughs in nanomaterials research.

6) Adapt existing pipelines to carry hydrogen, or where that is not feasible, construct new hydrogen pipelines as needed in metropolitan areas.

## Phase III: A Hydrogen Nation (~2015-2020)

*Hydrogen Fuel Cell Status: Widespread commercialization of hydrogen fuel cell cars, at least 5% of market*

1) As homes and businesses supply increasingly large amounts of hydrogen fuel cell-generated power to the grid, electric utilities increasingly become power distributors and much less power generators.

2) Consumers plug in parked fuel cell vehicles at home and work to supply electric power to the grid at peak-cost periods.

3) Businesses provide hydrogen to employees as a benefit.

4) Most services stations are converted to produce hydrogen via solar photovoltaic, wind-powered electrolysis, or by access to the national hydrogen pipeline system.

5) Dramatically reduce costs through new technologies for generating hydrogen via solar photo catalysis and bio-hydrogen and for storing hydrogen via advanced materials. This includes the early adoption of specially developed algae for farms to produce bacteria to generate hydrogen.[30]

## An International Hydrogen Prometheus Plan

The path toward the hydrogen future is already being paved by private initiatives and government support in the United States, the European Union, and Japan. Beginning with flexible-fuel hybrids and natural gas reformers, the hydrogen revolution could take place along the lines of the scenario that follows, based on *evolutionary* rather than breakthrough improvements in technology.

A viable hydrogen platform requires the development of a decentralized energy economy, beginning with the installation of natural-gas reformers or water electrolyzer units in office buildings and for use by commercial transportation fleets. Next, hydrogen fuel cell cars will be deployed in commercial fleets that return to central depots for a nightly refueling. Once there is excess hydrogen-generating capacity at fleet depots and in commercial buildings, this will be quickly followed by the leasing of mass market hydrogen fuel cell cars to people who work in or near buildings equipped with natural-gas reformers. The spare capacity of the buildings' hydrogen appliances will be sold to the leased hydrogen fuel cell cars.

As stationary hydrogen production units become cheaper, they will be deployed outside buildings. Using natural gas or electricity, these local hydrogen fuel stations will take the place of today's filling stations. Without the cost burden of transportation and distribution, hydrogen will become relatively cheap and economically viable, while reducing vehicle emissions by 50 to 82%. It is noteworthy that in addition to the fuel cell itself, many of the components have been well developed over the last decade. For example, several companies such as United Technologies Corporation in the U.S. and Haldor Topsoe in Denmark developed commercial, compact steam reformers that can generate pure hydrogen from natural gas on call. When directly interfaced with a fuel cell, they can electric-load follow, *i.e.,* they produce just the right amount of hydrogen depending on the instantaneous requirement of the fuel cell.

The hydrogen revolution will conform to the same key principles as the Prometheus Plan, including no major technological breakthroughs, just inevitable improvements on current known technologies. There will be no need for new taxes, or huge government subsides for infrastructure even though strategic federal incentives, as outlined above, will be needed to accelerate the transition.

The building of the decentralized hydrogen production economy assumes a 10% or greater per year real return. Those who participate will be able to make substantial profits even during the initial phase, and enjoy the benefits of being strategically well-positioned once the transition is complete. Major improvements in stationery hydrogen production units will be driven by a desire to either minimize the costs of improvements or maximize their durability, which criteria will respectively favor cars and buildings. It matters little which one happens to arrive first; either way the increase in production in one market will accelerate the other. Technologies will bootstrap each other as we learn from disparate applications.

As Gresser and Cusumano point out, "As hydrogen becomes a strategic economic driver for the United States and the major industrialized nations, it can serve this same function for many other countries, rich and poor."[31] Here, the size and risks of some hydrogen projects are well-suited for international collaborations that can be pursued on the same grand scale as the Apollo Project in the United States, the Marshall Plan in Europe, the worldwide International

Thermonuclear Experimental Reactor, and the Intergovernmental Panel on Climate Change projects.

As new countries enter the hydrogen consortium, each one can develop special expertise and leverage based on its unique resources and skills. Public/private hydrogen alliances can provide powerful catalysts for innovation. For example, accelerating cost breakthroughs in hydrogen generation and storage, and in fuel cell manufacturing, can produce huge commercial and governmental returns.

The financial foundation of the hydrogen Prometheus Plan could be an International Hydrogen Innovation Fund, initially capitalized with $5 billion provided by national and international entities. The fund would be managed by an international team of successful technology, business, and social entrepreneurs, with the goal of achieving superior rates of return for shareholders within five years for funding early, middle and late stage projects.

The hydrogen economy is the only reliable long-term solution to the energy and climate crises confronting civilization. There is now no other technology option that can safely produce clean energy to power transportation systems and our stationary infrastructure to sustain current levels

> *"We don't receive wisdom. We must discover it for ourselves after a journey that no one can take for us or spare us."*
> — MARCEL PROUST, AUTHOR, 1871-1922

of global prosperity, let alone increase these levels to sustain our fellow planetary citizens. If properly managed, this great transition will be profitable and beneficial for all stakeholders. The hydrogen revolution is one of the greatest legacies our generation could pass on to our children and children's children.

Horace Mann, a pioneering advocate of free, public education in the America, said, "Be ashamed to die until you've won some great victory for humanity."[32] All who join in this grand enterprise to bring about the birth of the hydrogen age will participate in one of humanity's greatest victories: the creation of a safe, clean and sustainable energy future.

## Notes and References
## Chapter 12: Hydrogen Revolution

1   "Hydrogen Bomber," *Time*, November 13, 2006.

2   http://corporate.honda.com/environment/fuel_cells.aspx?id=fuel_cells_fcx, February 6, 2007.

3   http://www.fuelcellcontrol.com/evs19.html.

4   For example, Joseph Priest, *Energy: Principles, Problems, Alternatives*, Fifth Edition (Dubuque, Iowa, Kendall, 2000), by-passes any discussion of hydrogen, while Roger A. Hinrichs and Merlin Kleinback, *Energy: Its Use in the Environment*, Fourth Edition (Belmont, California: Thompson, 2006), give it only a passing mention.

5   Paul Roberts, *The End of Oil: On the Edge of a Perilous New World* (New York: Houghton Mifflin Company, 2004), 152.

6   Lester Brown, *Plan B 2.0: Rescuing a Planet Under Stress and a Civilization in Trouble* (New York: W.W.Norton & Company, 2006), 193.

7   Worldwatch Institute, *State of the World 2006*, Chapter 4, "Cultivating Renewable Alternatives to Oil" (2006), 63.

8   Richard Heinberg, *Power Down: Options and Actions for a Post-Carbon World* (BC, Canada: New Society Publishers, 2004), 129.

9   Joseph Romm, *The Hype About Hydrogen: Fact and Fiction in the Race to Save the Climate* (Washington D.C.: Island Press, 2005), 9.

10  *"Toyota goal: 1 million Hybrids a year,"* USA Today, June 12, 2007; see John DeCicco *et al.*, *Technical Options for Improving the Fuel Economy of U.S. Cars and Light Trucks by 2010-2015*, Washington, D.C., American Council for an Energy-Efficient Economy, July 2001.

11  Roberts, *op. cit.*, 319.

12  Amory Lovins, "Twenty Hydrogen Myths," Rocky Mountain Institute, September 2003. We have adapted Myths 1-7 sequentially from the Lovins paper and incorporated Myth #9 as #8.

13  *Ibid.*, 6.

14 Hydrogen Market, Wikipedia, http://en.wikipedia.org/wiki/Hydrogen_economy#Hydrogen_market; U.S. Imports by Country of Origin, Energy Information Administration, http://tonto.eia.doe.gov/dnav/pet/pet_move_impcus_a2_nus_ep00_im0_mbbl_a.htm.

15 Dr. Addison Bain, *Introduction to Hydrogen Safety*, UNLV Hydrogen Safety Workshop, April 10, 2006.

16 See the footage taken by Dr. Michael Swain, University of Florida, Miami, at http://evworld.com/view.cfm?page=article&storyid=482.

17 B. Eliasson and U. Bossel, "The Future of the hydrogen economy: Bright or Bleak," *Proceedings, Fuel Cell World*, Luzern, Switzerland, July 1-5, 2002, 367-82.

18 Governor Schwarzenegger's Hydrogen Highway Network Action Plan, May 25, 2005, www.hydrogenhighway.ca.gov/vision/vision.html.

19 For additional information on hydrogen costs, see Julian Gresser and James A. Cusumano, "Hydrogen and the New Energy Economy: A Sensible Plan for the Next Administration," Project Earthrise, World Business Academy, 18:2, October 7, 2004.

20 Dan Lienert, "Arnold's Hydrogen Hummer," *Forbes*, January 4, 2005.

21 http://en.wikipedia.org/wiki/Hydrogen_car.

22 See www.hypercar.com. Amory Lovins, founder and CEO of the Rocky Mountain Institute, is also Chairman of the Board of Hypercar, Inc. Hypercar recently announced a change of name to Fiberforge.

23 Edwin Black, *Internal Combustion* (New York, St. Martins Press, 2006), 312.

24 *Ibid.*, 313.

25 "Honda Begins Experiments with Hydrogen Home Energy Station and Improves Solar-Cell Technology for Production of Hydrogen," Press Release, Honda Motor Company, Ltd., October 2, 2003.

26 *Ibid.*

27 Gresser and Cusumano, *op. cit.*, 11.

28 *Ibid.*, 14-15. Phase I, II and III are adapted directly and in some cases nearly verbatim from the Gresser-Cusumano strategy.

29 Black, *op. cit.*, 309, describes how scientists in Germany and the U.S. "have been able to extract hydrogen from wastewater, biomass, and even dung using a variety of common algae."

30 *Ibid.*

31 Gresser and Cusumano, *op. cit.*, 13.

32 Horace Mann, Baccalaureate Sermon, Antioch College, Antioch, Ohio, 1859.

# 13

## CORPORATE, STATE, AND LOCAL INITIATIVES LEAD THE WAY

*"My environmental agenda is not about being trendy or moral. It's about accelerating economic growth."*

-JEFF IMMELT, CEO, GENERAL ELECTRIC

**Given lack of federal leadership, who will promote the goals of the Prometheus Plan?**

- Corporate, state, and local initiatives are reducing oil use and $CO_2$ emissions.

- Major corporations, investors, and environmental groups are banding together to demand and even force change in carbon emissions laws and practices.

- Venture capitalists and investment banks are beginning to invest meaningful amounts of capital in alternative energy.

- California leads the way with its enforceable state-wide cap on carbon emissions, regulation of $CO_2$ from vehicle emissions, $3-billion solar program, hydrogen highway network, efficiency standards for consumer products, low-carbon fuel standard, and decoupling of utilities' sales and profits.

439

## Green Makes Green: A Paradigm Shift

Without doubt, the global energy system has entered the early stages of a major paradigm shift. The sun is setting on the fossil fuel era as the Age of Renewables is dawning, ultimately culminating in the Hydrogen Era. Concurrently, innovative initiatives are redefining the terms of engagement among business, energy, and the environment.

Several factors are driving a heightened awareness of the nexus between energy and profitability. First, many states, including California and New York, have adopted Renewable Portfolio Standards (RPS) and regulatory incentives to foster nascent sustainable energy industries. Other states have adopted their own climate change plans or have banded together in regional initiatives to fight climate change. State governments are also stimulating the placement of sizeable orders for efficient and environmentally friendly energy products. Such practices contribute to the creation of more stable, higher-volume markets for a new generation of renewable energy products.

Second, a growing coalition of major corporations, investment funds, and environmental groups are demanding changes in business practices, and calling for Congress to provide regulatory certainty by enacting nationwide legislation to limit carbon emissions and climate change risks. The business community has recognized its fundamental self-interest in concerted action.

Third, stricter regulations concerning energy efficiency and global warming, especially those promulgated by the European Union in response to the Kyoto Protocols, have impelled multinational corporations such as General Electric and DuPont to research, develop, and sell energy products that meet "best practices" standards and the new, higher regulatory thresholds.

Fourth, giant retailers such as Wal-Mart have come to connect their profitability to: (a) savings which can be achieved through energy efficiency policies, on-site and co-generation of electricity, and reduction of fuel bills through innovative operating practices; (b) long-term sustainable practices in the food chain, such as their push into organic foods driven by consumer demand; and (c) other initiatives to improve bottom-line profitability in the face of stagnant sales growth. Consequently, giant companies such as Wal-Mart are beginning to overhaul their sourcing and facilities policies in consideration of natural resource and environmental factors. All of these polices are attempts to shore up Wal-Mart's bottom line, at a time when increased fuel costs are taking future sales from its cash registers and bleeding disposable income out of customers at the pump.

## CORPORATIONS, INVESTORS AND ENVIRONMENTALISTS JOIN FORCES

In January 2007, 10 major companies joined several environmental groups in issuing a "Call to Action," urging Congress to swiftly set limits for reducing greenhouse gas emissions and to create market incentives for reductions. The group's unprecedented alliance, called the United States Climate Action Partnership (US-CAP), consists of prominent environmental groups and well-known companies from the energy, manufacturing, and financial services sectors. It includes Alcoa, BP America, Caterpillar, Duke Energy, DuPont, General Electric, Lehman Brothers, Pacific Gas & Electric, and Florida Power and Light. The group called for cuts in carbon dioxide emissions of 10-30% over the next 15 years, issued a detailed set of principles for new legislation, and agreed "to strongly discourage further construction of stationary sources that cannot easily capture" carbon. "This is a game-changer for action on global warming," said Environmental Defense President Fred Krupp, one of the leaders of the initiative.[1]

In February 2007, a group of leading U.S. investors announced the formation of a Climate Watch List, a list of 10 companies "identified as lagging behind their industry peers in their responses to climate change."[2] The investors did not stop there. They filed shareholder resolutions with the 10 listed companies and 26 other U.S. businesses to demand the watch-listed companies focus on the business risks and opportunities from climate change.

About a month later, dozens of institutional investors managing $4 trillion in assets joined with a dozen leading companies to call on Congress to enact strong legislation to cut greenhouse gases to meet targets that scientists say are necessary. A group statement outlined the business and economic rationale for taking climate change action and called for clear policy direction from Congress. The group was organized by the Coalition for Environmentally Responsible Economies, known as Ceres, and the Investor Network on Climate Risk. It included investors and asset managers such as Merrill Lynch, the California Public Employees Retirement System (CalPERS), as well as other companies such as Alcoa, Allianz SE, Consolidated Edison, DuPont, Sun Microsystems, and Turner Enterprises. A number of the group's members in the oil, automotive, and electric power sectors said they would face high financial risks if they were unprepared for a new carbon regulatory regime. Insurance companies and other businesses said they had financial exposure from losses related to extreme-weather events.

The group called for federal legislation that would reduce greenhouse gas emissions by 60-90% by 2050, compared to 1990 levels; a realignment of national energy and transportation policies to stimulate research and development; and clarification from the Securities and Exchange Commission about "what companies should disclose to investors on climate change" in their financial reports. "The investor and the business community are demonstrating that they are ahead of the political process. Like most responsible observers, they've seen the science and know it is real and must be responded to," said Timothy E. Wirth, president of the United Nations Foundation.[3]

## WAL-MART: FROM LOW PRICES TO LOW EMISSIONS

The summer of 2006 saw the announcement of one of the most ambitious corporate greening campaigns. Wal-Mart CEO Lee Scott revealed a "green-is-green" plan based on efficiency and sustainability designed to impact not just his own corporation, but Wal-Mart's extended value chain as well. The plan has three primary goals:

1) Run the company on 100% renewable energy sources;

2) Generate zero waste; and

3) Require suppliers to produce products through practices that sustain resources and the environment.

This announcement produced some of the first positive publicity Wal-Mart has enjoyed in years, as the press seized upon the potential impact of the changes on the company, which is the world's largest retailer and second-highest revenue-generating corporation (after ExxonMobil).

Wal-Mart is scrutinizing both external and internal operations to reduce energy consumption and waste. Another one of its initiatives, named "Zero Waste to Landfill," is seeking new packaging for cargo and freight with the goal of reducing use, composting, or recycling. Packaging redesign for one particular toy line will reduce packing and shipping costs by $240 million dollars a year, save 3,800 trees, and reduce the oil used to generate packaging materials.[4]

Wal-Mart has opened two experimental stores designed to use 30% less energy than its average stores, which will in turn dramatically improve those two stores' profitability relative to all other stores in the chain. Simple solutions, such as natural lighting during the day, better and natural insulation, small-scale solar and wind generators, and porous pavement (which greatly reduces motor oil run-off) have made these facilities models that other big-box retailers probably will seek to emulate.

Another large Wal-Mart program is the greening of its heavy-duty trucks through fuel efficiency measures, as discussed in Chapter 9. Wal-Mart owns and operates one of the largest private fleets in the world. With 7,100 trucks, even a small one-mile-a-gallon saving from their recent average of 6.5 mpg can add $50 million a year to company income.[5] Wal-Mart is refitting its entire fleet with several simple, low-cost, high-yield solutions to improve fuel efficiency, including the installation of auxiliary units that power the air conditioning when a truck is parked, eliminating the need to run the engine. In three years, this and other Wal-Mart initiatives are projected to save 25% of Wal-Mart's annual fleet fuel bill. Wal-Mart is also replacing long-haul truck tires with advanced tires that further improve efficiency and diesel mileage. Imagine the impact of these ideas when applied to every long-haul freight truck in the United States!

Wal-Mart expects to implement these fuel-saving techniques, along with others still being considered, in order to double its overall fuel efficiency in 10 years, which will in turn dramatically reduce greenhouse gas emissions. Finally, it's worth noting that Wal-Mart now owns 100 hybrid trucks and has ordered another 100 to begin improving fuel efficiency on all its local delivery routes. Lee Scott makes no pretense of being a "do-gooder." He flatly states that everything he is doing, particularly in the area of energy efficiency, is strictly about making more money; it's not about a "Green Philosophy."

Wal-Mart is also driving changes outside its own organization. As the second- largest corporation in the world, with $316 billion in 2005 revenue, it is wielding its immense purchasing power to change practices among its countless suppliers around the world, nearly 80% of which are located in China. The company is aggressively requiring that suppliers comply with certain sustainable production practices in 14 areas: facilities, internal operations, logistics, alternative fuels, packaging, chemicals, food and agriculture, electronics, textiles, forest products, jewelry, seafood, and climate change. For example, Wal-Mart already buys wild salmon from distributors who are certified by the Marine Stewardship Council. Wal-Mart is also working with scientists and fishermen to create certification standards for farmed salmon.[6] Simply by announcing its intention to buy only from certified fish farms, Wal-Mart has sent Chilean suppliers, who sell a third of their annual catch to Wal-Mart, scrambling to improve their methods.

Coffee ranchers in Brazil, corn farmers in the Midwest, and manufacturers in China already are in talks with their suppliers to find out what practices must change to continue doing business with the giant retailer.

Wal-Mart's sudden, and somewhat unexpected, adoption of

eco-friendly policies initially drew skepticism. Was this only a public relations stunt to distract the public's attention from the company's slumping profitability, its many legal battles with community zoning boards, and the frequent complaints from unions and workers? Although undeniably beneficial to Wal-Mart's image, this was not the fundamental basis for the company's decision. In 2005, Wal-Mart's financial indicators sagged badly, correlated with a sharp spike in oil prices. Research indicated that the cost of fuel was pinching its customers' disposable incomes, and also inhibiting the long drives that rural patrons customarily make to Wal-Mart. Wal-Mart realized that its traditional growth model would *not* continue to generate the returns that investors demanded. Management focused on *increasing operational efficiencies, with particular emphasis on the energy and materials components of Wal-Mart's cost structure.*

Wal-Mart has vast potential to raise the bar and influence other U.S. retailers. As amazing as it is to contemplate, Wal-Mart receives 14 cents of every U.S. retail dollar. Its massive initiative is causing a ripple effect across multiple industries. By endorsing energy-efficient practices and embracing the sale of organically certified products, Wal-Mart is taking a very long term view of the environment and the marketplace. Wal-Mart realizes that it must adopt practices that will be viable a century from now. Influencing everything from salmon fishing to electronics fabrication, this convergence of business and environmental interests is the essence of the new entrepreneurial-energy-efficiency-environmental paradigm.

## GE Brings Green Things to Life

Wal-Mart is not the only large corporation that is looking to change both its energy efficiency practices and its environmental image. General Electric is making major commitments by introducing a broad new line of Green products and by improving internal practices to maximize energy efficiency in operations and throughout its individual product lines. According to CEO Jeffrey Immelt, this innovative "Ecomagination" program represents a natural evolution for GE's durable goods products.

Ecomagination has two main goals. The first is to assess and improve the energy efficiency of GE offices, warehouses, vehicles, and laboratories. The second and more visible aspect is the creation of a new portfolio of highly efficient and environmentally sound products. For example, GE has been showcasing the GEnx jet engine that is 15% more fuel efficient and emits greenhouse gases at levels that are 95% below current regulatory limits. The GEnx is also cheaper to maintain, since it is designed with fewer parts and requires less frequent maintenance than does the class of engines against which it competes.

Other Ecomagination products include such diverse offerings as hybrid-diesel locomotives, advanced wind generators, ultra-efficient combined-cycle natural gas power plant turbines, and significantly more efficient clothes driers and light bulbs. In addition to maximizing energy efficiency, there are several products whose manufacture reduces or eliminates dependence on toxic substances. For example, GE found a way to imbed its durable LEXAN® plastics with pigments, thereby eliminating the need for toxic paints.

In the past, General Electric frequently butted heads with conservationists. Until Immelt took the helm, the company refused to accept responsibility for polluting the Hudson River, even though the EPA concluded that there was no other possible source of the nearly 1.3 million pounds of toxic waste lying in the riverbed. GE has now agreed to dredge and clean the Hudson at its own expense. What's behind this sudden corporate makeover from toxic polluter to Green advocate?

The transformation from Jack Welch's growth-for-growth's sake "corporate rules" to Jeffery Immelt's eco-friendly vision has a great deal to do with the change at the top. By no stretch of the imagination, however, does Immelt fit the stereotype of an "environmental activist." He drives an SUV, spends more time on a private jet than does any other U.S. CEO, and admits to having little interest in the outdoors. What's the true motivation for such grand initiatives? It's all about doing well by doing good, and thereby increasing profits. In the World Business Academy, we like to refer to this as "enlightened self-interest," which means that individual businesses will profit more by doing the "right thing." Sometimes referred to as the "triple bottom line," it means a true corporate focus on "People, Planet and Profits."

Immelt strongly believes that global environmental and greenhouse gas regulations will become stricter. Although the U.S. has not yet placed a cap on carbon emissions, the European Union and other individual countries already have adopted regulations imposing such caps. More than two-thirds of the total air pollution created globally is from countries that have signed the Kyoto Protocol. Among modern industrialized countries, only Australia and the U.S. have not adopted the treaty. GE recognizes that to retain its position as the durable products global leader, it needs to produce goods that meet the *highest* international standards. Remember this is the company that is the premier global practitioner of TQM (total quality management), the ISO 9000 quality standards, and the SIX SIGMA management development technology in its operations. If GE falls behind, it risks losing global market share in the two-thirds of the world which *is* addressing the global environmental crisis.

How will this strategy impact the bottom line? Immelt predicts that GE will generate an additional $15 billion in revenue, representing a 10% year-on-year improvement, and increase earnings per share by 17%. Like Wal-Mart's CEO Scott, Jeffrey Immelt is quick to point out, "My environmental agenda is not about being trendy or moral . . . . It's about accelerating economic growth."[7]

## VIRGIN AIR PLANNING TO GROW JET FUEL

When oil prices hit $70 per barrel, Virgin Atlantic Airlines added a $55 per-ticket surcharge. That was more than enough incentive to convince founder and CEO Richard Branson recently to announce plans to create a cellulosic ethanol fuel to power cars, trucks, and ultimately jets. Branson is optimistic that this alternative fuel could eventually power his entire fleet of 100 jet aircraft. He is studying the mass production of butanol from bio-feedstocks, as well as other jet fuel substitutes.

Butanol is an alcohol with four carbon atoms as compared to ethanol's two. It is often used as a solvent. Among other advantages, it is more resistant to contamination by water than is ethanol. This is critical, because it means it can be more easily transported through existing pipelines because it does not cause corrosion of the pipeline. Because butanol, unlike ethanol, does not absorb corrosion-causing water, it can be used at 85% strength in cars without any vehicle modifications, and has more energy content per gallon than ethanol. In fact, it's almost as powerful per unit mass or volume as gasoline, but has never yet been produced in mass quantities for fuel applications.

> "Butanol is 100% environmentally friendly and I believe it's the future of fuel."
> — VIRGIN ATLANTIC AIRWAYS CEO RICHARD BRANSON

The new Virgin Fuels subsidiary has tanked up with $400 million in investment capital to explore the possibility of manufacturing butanol on a large scale. BP and DuPont also announced a joint project in the summer of 2006 to produce butanol from sugar beet feedstocks with a biocatalyst, and compete with "unsubsidized petroleum production at oil prices between $30 and $40 a barrel."[8]

## BRAZILIAN AVIATION BREAKTHROUGH

There have also been major advances in the use of non-fossil fuels in propeller-driven airplanes. Embraer, the Brazilian aircraft manufacturer, has already released a crop-duster that runs on pure ethanol produced from sugar cane. In a press release, Embraer's Rosana Dias noted that they have observed "a 5% increase in power, which makes the airplane easier to take off the ground, fly higher... [and] because it is using ethanol, the engine stays cleaner much longer."[9] Cleaner burning fuels reduce maintenance costs because they leave fewer deposits on valves. Embraer's *Ipanema* plane is one of the best-selling crop-dusters on the market. The ethanol version is also selling well, with 83 filled orders in 2005 and a backlog for 2006.

> *"The function of what I call design science is to solve problems by introducing into the environment new artifacts the availability of which will induce their spontaneous employment by humans and thus, coincidentally, cause humans to abandon their previous problem-producing behaviors and devices."*
>
> — R. BUCKMINSTER FULLER, FUTURIST AND INVENTOR

## INTERFACE'S MID-COURSE CORRECTION

Ray Anderson, founder of Interface, Inc., the world's largest producer of commercial floor coverings, came to his environmental commitment the old-fashioned way. He wasn't looking to increase his profits, but to do the right thing for the environment. In that process of doing the right thing, an amazing and unexpected event occurred: his sales increased dramatically, and his profits even more. Anderson became a champion of corporate environmental innovation when he had a mid-life epiphany: "I was a plunderer of the earth, and that is not the legacy one wants to leave behind."[10] Because of the remarkable transformation that he created at Interface in 1997, Anderson was appointed Co-Chair of the President's Council on Sustainable Development.

In describing Anderson as a World Business Academy "Merchant of Vision," business writer Jeff Hutner observes that, "It's one thing to start a new visionary entrepreneurial company with great passion and commitment to things social and environmental. It's another thing to transform a half-billion-dollar-a-year carpet company that was already a major contributor to the carpet and chemical waste stream that makes up an estimated 15% of our landfills."[11]

In 1995, Anderson was shocked when he first asked for and received an analysis of Interface's impact on the planet. In order to produce $802 million worth of products, the company was extracting 1.2 billion pounds of materials and resources. Of that total, some 400 million pounds were relatively abundant inorganic materials mined from the earth, and 800 million pounds were petrochemical-based products derived from non-renewable coal, oil or natural gas. A full two-thirds of the 800 million pounds were burned to generate energy to turn the other third into products, which contributed to global warming.

By corporate standards, Anderson was a highly-successful captain of industry. He built from scratch a public company that has sales approaching one billion a year, manufactures on four continents, and does business in 100 countries. By his own new standards, his real success in life arrived at age 61, when he challenged Interface's executive team to "lead the company to sustainability." His definition of sustainability: to eventually operate the company "in such a way as to take *nothing* from the earth that is not naturally and rapidly renewable. Nor [to use] another fresh drop of oil and to do no harm to the environment."

After spending a decade doing what Anderson calls "Climbing Mt. Sustainability," Interface is doing phenomenally well. Recycling waste has generated *$263 million in cumulative savings*. Net greenhouse gas emissions have declined 52% in absolute tons

> *"I do not have a clue as to what to say, but I know 'comply' is not a vision."*
>
> — RAY ANDERSON, FOUNDER AND RETIRED CHAIRMAN, INTERFACE, INC

from the baseline year 1994, with two-thirds of this attributable to renewable energy. The non-renewable fossil fuel-derived energy in the company's carpet operations is down 43%. Water usage is down 43%. In all, the company closed 40% of its smokestacks; shut down 53% of effluent outflow pipes; and planted 52,000 trees to offset the 78 million passenger miles its employees fly around the world. As of this writing, Interface stock is approaching its five-year high, and has outperformed comparable stock indexes by 500% over that period.

One key to the Interface model for a sustainable enterprise lies in collecting billions of square yards of used carpets and textiles and supplying the company's factories with recycled "raw materials" to manufacture environmentally-friendly commercial carpets and modular carpet squares. As a result, carpet industry-generated waste to landfills is down more than 80%, and 62 million pounds of materials have been diverted from landfills and incinerators into new products. Anderson proudly proclaims, "Our customers can now buy Cool Carpet, carpet produced with no net contribution to global warming through the manufacturing cycle, including the supply chain."

In environmental circles, Anderson has been praised for being among the most advanced and progressive CEOs in the world. In business circles, he is recognized as a visionary who guided his company through multiple recessions, including one that saw its primary market shrink by 40%. As far as the bottom line is concerned, Anderson sees that "the goodwill of the marketplace has been nothing less than astounding. No amount of advertising could have generated as much, or contributed as much, to the top line, to winning business."

## GREEN CONSULTANTS GO GLOBAL

Green products and services are not only for large-cap companies. Innovative Green consulting firms, such as William McDonough & Partners, and Ove Arup & Partners, have grown rapidly by taking advantage of emerging eco-niches in the global marketplace. These niches bring into play the emerging architectural trends that emphasize design and construction efficiencies as principal objectives. With such priorities, reduced use of energy becomes an inevitable outcome. Residential and commercial architects, working with these principles, offer homes and office spaces of striking beauty with remarkably lower energy requirements. These structures take advantage of natural light, use wood cut from certified sustainable forests, and appeal to a modern aesthetic.

Green consultants are at the vanguard of rethinking the way that future eco-cities will function. For example, William McDonough & Partners has been contracted by the government of China to develop several of the country's seven experimental sustainable urbanization projects. The largest project site, Dontan, a Shanghai satellite-city, will integrate solar panels, large-scale wind, and unobtrusive hydropower. Peter Head, the project manager, says that ultimately "the goal [for Dontan] is to have a sustainable city [in terms of electricity production] online by 2025." The first phase of the city, a 600-hectare development roughly the size of Manhattan, is slated for completion by 2010.[12] The Dontan project is unique in its size and cost, but hardly unique in its focus on the merger of aesthetics, design logic, and energy efficiency.

Other projects on which Green consulting firms provide services include designing startlingly energy-efficient office buildings, such as London's new "Pickle," high-end homes, and other commercial structures. Green consulting firms are also being employed on a host of other projects, including projects to create and manage $CO_2$ "markets" for industrial emitters who want to buy and sell pollution credits.

Due to the variety of opportunities, the market for Green consulting is growing rapidly, as is the size of the contracts. There are many niche markets, such as carbon-trading, architecture, product and CSR certification, and an increasing number of Requests for Proposals from international development banks, governments, and venture capital firms. In fact, hardly any major project in any developed nation launches without employing at least one Green consultant on one or more aspects of the project. We've come a long way since the first Green consultants advised on the first "Environmental Impact Statement" some 30-plus years ago. Clearly, thinking Green has produced a great deal of "green" for an entirely new consulting industry sitting at the juncture of sustainability and the marketplace.

## STATES' RIGHTS

The absence of any meaningful leadership by the federal government on energy and climate change is best caricatured by the appointment of former Exxon CEO Lee Raymond, often criticized on energy and climate issues, to head a presidential study group on future energy policy. States have stepped into the leadership void, banding together in several regional initiatives to develop clean energy and to combat climate change.

Ten Northeastern and Mid-Atlantic states are members of the Regional Greenhouse Gas Initiative (RGGI), the nation's first cap-and-trade system for carbon dioxide emissions from regional power plants. The initiative caps emissions at 2009 levels and calls for a 10% reduction in emissions by 2019.

Western states have also joined together to develop renewable energy and reduce greenhouse gas emissions. The Western Governors' Association developed a Clean and Diversified Energy Initiative, which 18 states have joined. The Association is working with the California Energy Commission to create a system of renewable energy credits that can be traded across 11 western states to help meet state renewable portfolio standards (often referred to as "RPS").

States have long served as individual policy laboratories for social change and environmental protection. Twenty-four states and the District of Columbia have adopted timetables for the switch to renewables. Such timetables in the form of state renewable portfolio standards are becoming increasingly common.

Renewable portfolio standards require power retailers to include specified percentages of renewable energy in the mix of fuels they use to generate electricity. In their simplest form, such standards require utilities to build or buy a certain amount of renewable energy capacity each year, but the standards vary greatly state by state in the complexity of their structure. Variables include the definition of qualifying resources, the timetable for phasing renewables into the utilities' fuel mixture, the limitations on utilities' cost recovery, and the availability of renewable energy credit trading programs. In recognition of the fact that state renewable portfolio standards have helped to create a market for Green power and to foster price competition among suppliers, states continue to adopt new standards and amend their existing ones.

As an example of the kind of public sector-private sector cooperation that has become commonplace as a result of state renewable portfolio standards, Colorado's largest utility recently announced that it will achieve its 10% standard by 2007 through contracts with existing wind power producers. In addition to the Colorado, other states which have legislated a switch to renewables include: Arizona, California, Connecticut, Delaware, Hawaii, Iowa, Illinois, Massachusetts, Maryland, Maine, Minnesota, Montana, Nevada, New Jersey, New Mexico, New York, Oregon, Pennsylvania, Rhode Island, Vermont, Washington, Wisconsin, and even Texas!

Some states such as Minnesota, New Mexico, Washington, and Wisconsin have enacted "feed-in laws." In essence, the feed-in laws provide the renewable project developer with the equivalent of a Purchase Power Agreement that qualifies for long-term project financing at relatively low interest rates. In contrast to renewable portfolio standards, which mandate a specific quantity of electricity that must be generated from renewable energy, feed-in laws set a fixed price for renewable energy. This allows the market to determine the quantity provided either by utilities or qualified independent power providers. In general, prices are set above conventional power costs. Thus, the combination of a guaranteed demand and long-term minimum prices reduces the equity risks of investing in renewable energy and also makes it easier for producers to obtain debt financing.

In 2005, Washington State enacted a renewable energy production incentive similar to the national production incentive in Germany, where the approach has been astoundingly effective in making Germany a world leader in solar photovoltaic panels as well as wind energy. At the time of the Washington law's enactment, Denis Hayes, founder of Earth Day, and former director of the federal Solar Energy Research Institute, called it "the most important solar legislation ever introduced in any American state legislature."

The Pew Center for Climate Change has recently prepared a useful summary of state initiatives on climate change.[13] According to the summary, 29 states have climate action plans, and 14 have state-wide emissions targets. Forty-one states have at least one utility that allows customers to sell electricity back to the grid, an arrangement known as net-metering. About half the states have funds, sometimes known as "public benefit funds," that are used for renewable energy projects or efficiency programs. The funding is usually derived from surcharges on customers' electric bills or from utility contributions. Taken together, all these state efforts are helping make the switch to renewables.

## CALIFORNIA: A NEW GLOBAL LEADER

No state has been more aggressive than the bellwether state of California in mandating the historic switch to renewable energy. California has emerged as a global leader in combating global warming, promoting renewable energy resources, and increasing efficiency to reduce consumer demand. It is already building the infrastructure for a hydrogen economy. California's Hydrogen Highway Network initiative provides funding for roadside hydrogen fueling station demonstration projects and for the state's lease and purchase of a variety of hydrogen-fueled vehicles.

California firmly positioned itself in the vanguard in 2002 when it became the first state to regulate carbon dioxide emissions from vehicle tailpipes. The law sets stringent emissions standards for passenger vehicles sold in the state starting in 2016—requiring a cut of almost 30% in carbon dioxide emissions.

A dozen states followed California's lead, including Connecticut, New Jersey, and New York, and adopted the stricter California standard. Those three northeastern states are home to more than a third of vehicles sold in the U.S.[14] California's and the other states' laws were stayed pending legal challenges, but their position received a big boost from the April 2007 U.S. Supreme Court decision rejecting EPA's argument that it had no authority to regulate carbon dioxide and other greenhouse gases in vehicle emissions. EPA had argued that such gases were not "air pollutants" within the meaning of the Clean Air Act.[15] The Court sent the case back to the lower courts for further action, but its decision has already changed the politics of climate change and may affect other climate change litigation. The Court's ruling that California had authority to sue on behalf of its residents over climate change may strengthen suits California has filed against automakers and power companies for allegedly contributing to global warming.

In September 2006, California adopted the nation's first enforceable state-wide program to cap all greenhouse gas emissions that includes penalties for noncompliance. This landmark legislation, the Global Warming Solutions Act of 2006, is designed to reduce California's greenhouse gas emissions to 1990 levels by 2020, approximately a 25% cut. By January 1, 2008, the California Air Resources Board must adopt mandatory reporting rules for significant sources of greenhouse gases, as well as a plan for reducing those sources' emissions by means of regulations, market mechanisms, and other actions. By January 1, 2011, the Board must adopt regulations, effective a year later, imposing greenhouse gas emission limits that will impose the maximum technologically feasible and cost-effective reductions. The Board may adopt a market-based cap-and-trade system which would be operative from January 1, 2012 to December 31, 2020.

Cap-and-trade systems essentially consist of one individual, corporation, or organization paying another to reduce greenhouse gas emissions on its behalf.[16] Companies that are required or want to trim or eliminate greenhouse gas emissions—but find it too expensive or too difficult to do—can purchase the appropriate amount of emission allowances instead. Such cap-and-trade systems have the effect of bringing down the total cost of corporate compliance with carbon caps, and are discussed in Chapter 4. Two of the most remarkable features of the California Global Warming Solutions Act of 2006 are that it provides penalties for non-compliance, and is consciously designed to influence other states, the federal government, and even other nations.

In July 2006, Governor Schwarzenegger and British Prime Minister Tony Blair signed an agreement to encourage Anglo-Californian commercial development of Green technology. The agreement was also signed by Virgin CEO Richard Branson, British

*"We can now move forward with developing a market-based system that makes California a world leader in the effort to reduce carbon emissions [and] an example for other states and nations to follow as the fight against climate change continues."*

— CALIFORNIA GOVERNOR ARNOLD SCHWARZENEGGER

Petroleum chief Lord John Browne, DuPont CEO Charles Holliday, as well as representatives from two major international investment banking firms, Goldman Sachs and JP Morgan. While a state has no authority to enter into a treaty with a foreign nation, the agreement underscores California's adoption of a market-based approach to solving global environmental issues and its determination to assert itself on the world stage as a leader in renewable energy.

Another example of California's market-driven approach to energy issues is a joint initiative between the northern California utility, Pacific Gas & Electric Company (Pacific Gas) and the California Air Resources Board. Through this program, Pacific Gas is leasing 100 hybrid-electric and hydrogen fuel-cell trucks and cars from DaimlerChrysler. The lease includes a Pacific Gas hydrogen fueling station for the vehicles that the company will operate. In return for discount pricing, Pacific Gas will cooperate in collecting vehicle operating information to improve future hybrid and hydrogen vehicle design. Since these vehicles comprise only a fraction of the company's fleet, the risk of purchasing new technology is minimized and DaimlerChrysler will generate revenue while doing field testing.[17]

The California legislature has long supported renewable energy. Recently it passed a $3 billion-dollar solar initiative that enables individuals and organizations to sell excess power from their rooftop panels back to power companies. The incentives will require the state to subsidize upfront installation costs by giving tax breaks to homeowners and businesses to purchase the solar equipment, while providing inexpensive, distributed power generation for the utility at no capital cost to it. The real payback is expected to come from the reduced peak-time demand during the summer, when rolling black-outs and brown-outs have become all too common. Rather than create a direct subsidy for the solar industry, the state initiative will encourage distributed solar power production and create a healthy business environment for solar technology in California.[18]

Solar initiatives are not limited to distributed power generation. The race is also on to build bigger and better centralized solar installations. As discussed in Chapter 11, Stirling Energy and Southern California Edison are developing a California project that will use a Stirling Engine instead of photovoltaic panels to capture solar energy. It is projected to cover 4,500 acres of the southern Californian desert.[19]

Due to state-sponsored programs, investors are rapidly warming to the idea of providing large-scale funding for solar and other renewable energy technologies. In the past it was difficult for investors to commit substantial financial resources because policymakers often sent negative or mixed signals about alternative energy. After the drop in oil prices in the mid-1980s triggered lower consumer demand for efficient products, Green technologies struggled under a shadow of doubt. As a result of the new initiatives and the steady climb of oil prices over the last several years, in 2005 global solar sector merger and acquisition activity alone grew to $14 billion dollars.[20]

Another planned commercial-scale renewable energy project in Southern California is a $1 billion-dollar hydrogen power plant in Carson City. Funded by BP, the facility will provide low-carbon energy for 500,000 households. It will combine petroleum coke (a by-product of the oil refining process) and wastewater to create hydrogen, natural gas, and $CO_2$. The $CO_2$ is collected onsite and pumped into rock formations containing oil. The result is increased production of petroleum from sites which, under previous technologies, would have been tapped out. The process is considered "low-carbon" because the tonnage of carbon sequestered in the rock formations somewhat offsets the petroleum products that are extracted. It is also a test in the commercial application of hydrogen in electricity production.[21] While we believe that such carbon sequestration and/or injection projects are inherently unwise due to the ultimate increase in atmospheric $CO_2$, we included this story to show the creativity even Big Oil is demonstrating in attempting to convert "dirty" existing fossil fuels to more efficient, less polluting ones.

California's leadership on energy has resulted in the state's per capita energy consumption remaining flat for about 30 years while the rest of the nation's per capita consumption rose about 50%. This achievement is partially attributable to the state's energy efficiency standards for small consumer electronic devices, which were first adopted back in the 1970s. More stringent efficiency standards go into effect in 2007 that will apply to new electronic products sold in the state such as audio and video equipment and cell phone chargers.

California's electricity-pricing policies are another cause of the state's flat per capita energy consumption. In 1982, California cut the link between utilities' profits and their sales by allowing rate increases for utilities that helped customers reduce energy use. As the Natural Resources Defense Council said, "Every other state in the country rewards utilities for selling more energy. It's a perfectly perverse incentive." According to Hal Harvey, director of the environment program at the William and Flora Hewlett Foundation, consumers were happy because their bills went down even though rates went up. "People don't pay rates. They pay bills. You can have twice the rate and half the consumption and be just as happy."[22]

## HAWAII'S CONVERSION FROM FOSSIL FUELS TO RENEWABLES

When it comes to energy, Hawaii holds the dubious distinction of being the most dependent, most expensive, and most vulnerable state in the nation. Hawaii is almost twice as dependent on imported oil as the rest of the country—it relies on imported oil to meet almost 90% of its energy needs.

While Hawaii has two refineries that supply products to the local market, the state has no oil reserves, and no oil or gas pipelines. Partly as a result, Hawaii has the highest electric, natural gas, and gasoline prices of the 50 states. For example, in July 2006 when the average U.S. price for regular gasoline was about $2.80 per gallon, gas was selling in Hawaii for nearly $3.50 per gallon. The high cost of barging oil to and between the islands contributes to the disproportionately high cost of petroleum, which hurts the entire state economy.

This disproportionately negative influence of oil prices on the state economy is matched by Hawaii's extreme vulnerability to any petroleum disruption which could occur in the Middle East or on the U.S. mainland. Gas prices in Hawaii spiked after Hurricane Katrina hit the Gulf Coast. Another hurricane hitting Gulf refineries could cause even more severe disruptions in Hawaii if the state were left with limited tanker capacity because most oil tankers were diverted to the vulnerable East Coast.

> *"The state must take the lead to stimulate renewable energy use and research, and reduce our dependency on fossil fuels."*
>
> — HAWAII GOVERNOR
> LINDA LINGLE

Hawaii's $11.4 billion tourism industry, which accounts for almost 25% of the state's revenue, is itself vulnerable to rising energy prices, which drive up the price of airline tickets and reduce the number of tourists who can afford to fly there. One can only imagine how catastrophic even a minor supply disruption would be. Due to its relatively small population of 1.2 million people (42nd in the U.S.), Hawaii typically ranks low in gasoline, diesel and gas consumption. However, because of its remote geographical location and heavy reliance on tourism and imports, Hawaii ranks 14th in the nation in terms of jet fuel consumption. Over a quarter of the state's daily oil consumption goes for jet fuel. The state burns 1.5 million gallons of jet fuel a day, or 27% of its 5.6 million gallons per day in total petroleum consumption.

Hawaii faces a double whammy: as noted above, rising jet fuel prices translate into higher airline fares, which portend a downturn in tourism just as higher global oil prices are projected to have a negative impact on the state's tourist-dependent internal economy.[23]

To address this problem, the state has adopted several ambitious renewable energy initiatives. During the 2006 legislative session, in a striking show of bipartisanship, the overwhelmingly Democratic Hawaii legislature and Republican Governor Linda Lingle joined together to enact measures to speed the State's conversion to renewable energy. The measures adopted will:

- Increase renewable energy technologies tax credits for solar thermal, wind-powered, and photovoltaic energy systems

- Create a biofuels preference in the state procurement code

- Set an alternative fuels standard for highway fuel

- Establish a renewable hydrogen program and investment fund

- Create a solar water heating "Pay as You Save" program to allow a residential electric utility customer to purchase a solar water heating system with no up-front payments and to pay the cost of the system over time through the customer's electricity bill

- Create a pilot project to install photovoltaic systems at public schools

- Set energy efficiency and environmental standards for state facilities, motor vehicles, equipment, and products

- Create priority processing of applications for development-related permits for construction projects that incorporate energy and environmental design building standards into their project design

These measures are consistent with the State's strategic energy plan, which calls for:

- Raising transparency in gasoline markets and the energy industry

- Developing and increasing use of alternative transportation fuels
- Stimulating state and consumer energy efficiency
- Significantly increasing the use of renewable energy resources for electricity production
- Establishing Hawaii as a leader in hydrogen production

Two pillars of the plan are Alternative Fuels Standards and Renewable Portfolio Standards. The new Alternative Fuels Standards set the goal of using alternative fuels to satisfy 10% of highway fuel demand by 2010, 15% by 2015, and 20% by 2020. In practice, the standards will be achieved mainly by using ethanol, biodiesel, and pure vegetable oil (PVO).

Similarly, the Renewable Portfolio Standards for the production of electricity require each electric company to generate 10% of its electricity from renewable sources of energy by 2010, 15% by 2015, and 20% by 2020. Utilities may face penalties if the state Public Utilities Commission determines that the targets have not been met.

In response to this challenge, the Hawaiian Electric Company (HECO), which controls more than 90% of electricity generation in the state, has become a leader in the local business community in advancing a host of renewables technologies, including electricity generated from ethanol and biodiesel. HECO has made a public commitment to use only ethanol or biodiesel to fuel its upcoming new 100-MW plant at Campbell Industrial Park. In an op-ed piece which ran in the *Honolulu Advertiser* in November 2006,[24] HECO also advocated the increased use of other renewable energy sources, including the use of cold ocean water to air condition downtown Honolulu office buildings (Ocean Thermal Energy Conversion), and wave power for near-shore energy production.

Numerous other players in the Hawaii economy are helping the state achieve its renewable energy goals. Barry Raleigh, former Dean of the School of Ocean and Earth Science and Technology at the University of Hawaii, is helping lead a public-private partnership to grow saltwater algae to produce biofuels. The technology makes a unique contribution to the fight against global warming, uses no fresh water, uses less land than any other biofuels crop, and produces vastly more biofuel oil per acre than any other crop. Because the algae grow best when fed a $CO_2$-enriched air stream, the technology actually removes $CO_2$ from the atmosphere. If the pilot project demonstrates that it can be commercially successful, the plan is to locate salt water algae projects next to power plants and refineries to capture their $CO_2$ emissions. Using current technology, 4,000 to 6,000 gallons per acre of biodiesel is a realistic production target. This far surpasses the fuel yield of 1500 gallons per acre for sugar cane ethanol produced using the Brazilian method. Although the two fuels have different uses, it is interesting to note the dramatically higher yield per acre of vegetable oil from algae compared to ethanol from sugar cane, *and* the lack of fresh water required for growing algae.

In July 2006, David Cole, CEO of Maui Land and Pineapple (one of the State's largest land and agricultural interests, with AOL's Steve Case as a dominant shareholder) announced the formation of Hawaii BioEnergy LLC, a consortium that will research the production and processing of sugar cane and other potential fuel crops. The group includes other major landowners, including King Kamehameha Schools (formerly the Bishop Estate), Grove Farm on Kauai, and renowned venture capitalist Vinod Khosla. The group represents over 10% of Hawaii's total land and nearly 50% of the arable land.

Gay & Robinson, Inc. plans to partially convert its sugar cane plantation on Kauai to the production of sugar cane ethanol. Many members of the public opposed its declared intention to import coal from Australia to use as a back-up fuel despite the ready availability of more than enough biomass on the lush island of Kauai. The opposition included the argument that HECO, the state's largest utility, has foresworn coal, and other fuel and power producers should be held to the same standard. At least in the near term, Gay & Robinson appears to have circumvented the reluctance of lenders to finance projects that use coal.[25] In July 2007, it joined with Pacific West Energy, LLC to create a new company to develop facilities to produce 12 million gallons a year of ethanol and to generate electricity. Pacific West's subsidiary, Kauai Ethanol, LLC, has obtained an air permit allowing the ethanol facility to burn coal. Although the Academy whole-heartedly supports ethanol produced from sugar cane, we can find no justification whatsoever for its production using coal, with the additional harmful and unnecessary greenhouse gases that it will cause. The new company's future energy plans include a methane recovery system, solar and hydro power, and the processing of municipal solid waste.

Ethanol is just one of the biofuels to be produced in Hawaii. Biodiesel production from vegetable oil and reclaimed waste vegetable oil is about to expand, and plentiful biomass on several islands is viewed as a fuel source. There have been discussions about building a plant on the Hamakua Coast of the Big Island to produce electricity from such biomass, a prospect which is certainly worth further discussion. Enterprise Honolulu, a non-profit aggregation of business interests working to create a "New Hawaii" business framework, is working with a variety of companies in the production and distribution chain to explore biofuels and other renewable energy opportunities.

Just as "all politics are local," one could also say that "all renewable energy plans are local," since they depend on each state's unique geography, climate, and energy resource profile. The main reason Hawaii could adopt such aggressive renewable energy goals is that the island chain has an abundance of every known renewable energy source. This includes proven resources in biofuels, biomass, geothermal, hydro, solar, wind, and ocean. Hawaii can tap the energy of the ocean not only through wave power, but in an abundance of other ways. It can harness deep ocean currents (totally unlike tidal energy), tap ocean thermal differentials to create energy (both ocean thermal energy conversion and saltwater air conditioning), and develop ocean-fed algae ponds for vegetable oil as noted above.

As a result of the state's plentiful renewable energy resources and growing political will, HECO has made a public commitment to generating the next 500 MW of power exclusively from renewable energy sources (see Figure 1).

## Figure 1. Hawaii's Potential Renewable Energy Sources[26]

| | |
|---|---|
| **100 MW Wind Energy** | Wind turbines capture energy from the winds to make electricity. (Big Island, Maui, Oahu) |
| **80 MW Pumped Storage Hydro** | Water pumped uphill at night using renewable electricity is then released downhill to turn turbines. (Big Island, Maui, Oahu) |
| **50 MW Ethanol in New Plant** | Fallow fields planted with crops to make ethanol to mix with other fuels in a new plant. (Oahu) |
| **83 MW Ethanol or Biodiesel in Existing Plants** | Local ethanol and bio-diesel (from plants or waste) mixed with other fuels. (Big Island, Maui, Oahu) |
| **85 MW Solar Energy** | The sun's energy harnessed with many solar technologies. (Big Island, Maui, Oahu) |
| **40 MW Garbage to Energy** | Trash burned to make steam to turn a turbine. (Big Island, Maui, more on Oahu) |
| **30 MW Geothermal** | Volcanic heat beneath the ground creates steam to turn a turbine. (Big Island) |
| **25 MW Biomass** | Organic matter from agriculture/yard waste burned to make steam to turn a turbine. (Big Island, Maui) |
| **7 MW Landfill Gas** | Methane gas from decomposing garbage is burned for steam to turn a turbine. (Big Island, Maui, Oahu) |
| **Future Potential: Ocean Thermal Energy Conversion, Wave Power, Hydrogen, Algae** | New technologies now in research and development may enhance other sources. (All islands) |

Source: Hawaiian Electric Company

According to the Hawaii Biofuels Summit, Hawaii has more than enough land to produce the biofuels required to meet the State's goals, not only for highway fuel use, but also for the State's electric utilities and ships refueling in Hawaii. These ships consume the majority of the island's diesel fuel.[27]

Hawaii increasingly sees itself as blessed with abundant resources and as a potential global leader in biofuels, solar, wind, OTEC, and energy generated by the ocean's movements and temperature differentials. The State is beginning to recognize the urgency of addressing climate change, and in 2007 adopted a law to reduce the State's greenhouse gas emissions to 1990 levels by 2020. This will be a major challenge given the amount of emissions caused by air travel in and out of the State.

## STATE AND LOCAL GOVERNMENTS' PURCHASING POWER

States, counties and local governments are playing a key role in the research, development and commercialization of energy efficiency and renewable energy systems. By placing large orders, credit-worthy government entities can help growing companies that have innovative products establish their technical credibility and financial stability. As stewards of public lands and the environment, these governmental bodies can also purchase eco-friendly products and processes to help protect land, air, and water resources.

## CITY AND COUNTY PROGRAMS

With its 35 million citizens, California would be the 8th largest economy in the world if it were an independent nation. It's easy to see why such a large, technologically sophisticated society would be increasingly focusing on the switch to renewables. Yet government initiatives are not limited to the mega-states with vast resources or even the smaller states like Rhode Island.

Cities and counties are aggressively moving to fill the federal leadership vacuum on climate change. Lead by Seattle Mayor Greg Nickels, more than 600 U.S. mayors in all 50 states have signed the

U.S. Mayors Climate Protection Agreement, committing their cities to stop global warming by meeting or beating the U.S. emissions reduction target in the Kyoto Protocol, despite the federal government's refusal to ratify it. The Agreement, endorsed by the U.S. Conference of Mayors, commits the mayors: (1) to achieve a 7% reduction in their cities' respective 1990 emission levels by 2012; and (2) to urge their state governments and the federal government to adopt legislation to make the rest of the country do the same. The Sierra Club's Cool Cities Campaign is helping the mayors' efforts.

The mayors have also formed a Mayors' Council on Climate Protection to provide mayors with the necessary technical skills, and they have formed a new partnership with the ICLEI, called "Local Governments for Sustainability USA," to reduce greenhouse gas emissions in cities through outreach, education, and technical assistance.

The International Council for Local Environmental Initiatives (ICLEI) was formed in 1990, spearheaded by urbanologist Jeb Brugmann, and in part by a former President of the National Association of Counties, Harvey Ruvin, of Miami-Dade County. Ruvin understood the role that national and international organizations can play in advancing a local policy agenda. ICLEI's first campaign initiative, Cities for Climate Protection, started or supported greenhouse gas reduction projects in local communities around the world. Over 170 communities in 35 states and hundreds of other communities throughout the world have joined the initiative, committing themselves to meet the Kyoto Protocol standards for greenhouse gas emissions on their own. The project has already helped reduce large amounts of greenhouse gas emissions by helping communities establish, implement, and monitor greenhouse gas reduction plans.[28] Ruvin's own county, Miami-Dade, had pilot initiatives that preceded Cities for Climate Protection, and presents an excellent example of how vigorous local government efforts can be.

## Miami-Dade County Tackles Global Warming

Under the leadership of former County Commissioner Harvey Ruvin, now County Clerk, Miami-Dade established a Climate Change Adaptation Task Force to address the county's numerous severe climate change challenges. This was the first local government effort in the nation to specifically address adaptation to a renewables strategy. Ruvin hopes that "[their] experience may provide a template for other concerned local governments."[29] Miami-Dade is again in the lead, becoming a pilot for a new ICLEI campaign, Climate Resilient Communities. The goal of the campaign is to provide a template for others to make their communities as resilient to predicted climate impacts as possible.

> *"Local governments can actually have a major impact because we're the custodians of the infrastructure. This is our chance to step up and get our heads out of the sand."*
> — HARVEY RUVIN, CO-CHAIR, MIAMI-DADE COUNTY CLIMATE CHANGE ADAPTATION TASK FORCE

While Ruvin advocates local municipal action, he is extremely troubled by how bad, through federal neglect, the situation has become. "In spite of ours and other local governments' efforts to reduce emissions of greenhouse gases, and even if we were somehow able to transition immediately to renewable energy, we still have to deal with a decade of sea-level rise, extreme weather events, and a whole range of potential threats to public heath and basic infrastructure already inevitably set in motion by prior emissions."[30]

With the long-term impacts in mind, the Miami-Dade Task Force is discussing a number of ideas that could reduce $CO_2$ and other greenhouse gases, and slow the impact of global warming. These include:

- Retrofitting all county facilities with computer-based monitoring systems to ensure the county is saving energy

- Increasing ridership on Metrorail and other public transportation systems

- Capturing methane, which is a greenhouse gas, from landfills

- Pushing to raise CAFE (Corporate Average Fuel Economy) standards by using local governments to create initiatives on the issue

- Using wind power, including wind turbines anchored offshore.

In May 2006, the Task Force recommended that Miami-Dade County pass a "Resolution Supporting Development of Plug-in Hybrid Electric Vehicles." The Resolution declares that the County has joined the national Plug-in Partners Campaign and would strongly consider purchase of Plug-in Hybrid Electric Vehicles once they become commercially available. The Resolution also seeks support from local electric utilities for "potential early adoption, rebates, and other incentives for plug-in hybrid vehicles."

## AUSTIN'S PLUG-IN HYBRID MUNICIPAL PLAN

This Plug-in Partners Campaign was initiated by the city of Austin, Texas, to build a national market for "gas optional hybrids," also known as Plug-In Hybrids. The main objectives of the plan are: to establish a community campaign to demonstrate to auto manufacturers that a market exists for Plug-In Hybrids; to establish sales momentum through a program of rebates, "soft" fleet orders, petitions, and endorsements; and to build a coalition of campaign partners, encompassing local and state governments, utilities, and environmental, consumer and business organizations supportive of plug-in hybrids.

The Plug-in Hybrid Municipal Plan is based on the fact that Plug-In Hybrids use the same technology as the popular hybrids on the road today, but have a greater battery capacity that can be recharged by plugging into a standard home outlet. While a hybrid gets about twice the fuel economy of a conventional car, a plug-in hybrid gets about twice the fuel economy of a hybrid—*and possibly more*—depending on actual daily miles driven. Electricity, the supplemental fuel for plug-in hybrids, is far cheaper and less polluting than gasoline. *An "electric" gallon of gas costs about 70-80 cents at prevailing electric rates, while a comparable gallon of conventional gasoline costs $3.00 per gallon, at the national average prices prevailing in summer 2006.* Supporters of the plan, such as the Set America Free initiative, argue that, "If by 2025, all cars on the road are hybrid and half are plug-in hybrids, U.S. oil imports would drop by 8 MBD. Today the United States imports 10 MBD and is projected to import almost 20 MBD by 2025."

> *"We believe that the 50 largest cities of this country, united in purpose, can build a groundswell of demand sufficient to entice carmakers to mass produce what is the logical near term response towards the critical goal of energy independence."*
>
> — WILL WYNN, MAYOR OF AUSTIN, TEXAS

## OTHER LOCAL INITIATIVES

The number of local initiatives throughout the U.S. attests to the grass roots support for halting climate change and switching to renewable energy. In New Hampshire, towns across the state have put the climate on the agenda. Of the 234 incorporated cities and towns in New Hampshire, 180 are voting on a resolution asking the federal government to address climate change and to develop research initiatives to create "innovative energy technologies." The resolution also calls for local action and solutions. As of March 2007, 134 towns had adopted the resolution, and not all had yet voted.[31]

Woodstock, New York, a 1960s legend, put itself on the edge of social change again when it adopted a resolution in March 2007 to reduce the town's emissions to *zero* within a decade. The town has already installed enough solar panels on the town hall to supply excess energy to the grid.[32]

In 2006, Boulder, Colorado approved the first "carbon tax" in the U.S., and plans to use the revenue to fund energy efficiency improvements. Portland, Oregon reduced its emissions below the Kyoto Protocol targets with a carbon emissions-cutting campaign that included financial incentives to anyone who constructed an energy-efficient "green building."[33] In Sonoma County, California, all nine municipalities and the county government have committed to reduce greenhouse gas emissions to 25% below their 1990 levels.

Atlantic City, New Jersey, has decided to install five wind turbines with a combined energy output of 7.5 MWs, enough to power 2,500 homes. These wind turbines will power a nearby wastewater treatment facility, and the excess will be fed into the grid. The Atlantic City wind energy project is the first coastal wind farm in the United States. Atlantic City hopes to show that windmills may come to be regarded as a source of community pride instead of eyesores. Beauty is in the eye of the beholder, and to Atlantic City, gently turning offshore windmills appear as a kinetic sculpture of great beauty that also helps balance the budget!

Although the coastal mid-Atlantic region is ideal for commercial applications of wind energy, some projects have met resistance from conservation groups that claim that the windmills obscure the landscape and pose a hazard to marine birds. The truth is that environmental impact studies conducted at coastal and offshore sites have shown that there are very few fatalities. On average, 2.3 birds per year are killed at the typical U.S. wind turbine, and each new technology generation is further reducing the bird-kill.[34]

Other notable county programs to tackle the problem of high energy costs and global warming include King County's Earth Legacy Initiative in Washington State, and Multnomah County's Global Warming Action Plan in Oregon.[35]

## Investors Jump on Alternative Energy Bandwagon

When the last major technology bull market formed around the convergence of computers, telecommunications, and the Internet, the strategic placement of capital by investment firms and venture capitalists served as a driving force. Without vast infusions of institutional capital, these convergence technologies would not have grown as rapidly as they did. Today, one of the most promising indicators of the coming energy revolution is the rapid infusion of venture and growth capital into Green technologies.

Since 1999, the Cleantech Venture Network, LLC has tracked investment in the new sector of clean technologies ("cleantech," sometimes used interchangeably with "green-tech"). It reported that in 2006, North American venture investment in cleantech nearly doubled to $2.9 billion from $1.6 billion in 2005.[36] Initial public offerings of cleantech companies now attract major capital market players. The American ethanol producer VeraSun (VSE) raised $420 million in the largest Initial Public Offering of shares to date by an alternative energy firm.

> *"The industry isn't just for the Birkenstock set anymore; it's got serious capital behind it now."*
>
> — NANCY FLOYD, COFOUNDER OF NTH POWER LLC

Cleantech Venture Network joined with Environmental Entrepreneurs (E2), in reporting that investments in clean technology soared in 2006, growing by 78% over 2005 levels. In the first quarter of 2007, such investment grew almost 60% compared to the same quarter the year before. The report states that cleantech is now the third largest venture investment category, surpassing telecommunications and medical devices. Only biotech and software remain ahead of it.[37]

*Cleantech Venture Monitor* reports that, "The term 'Cleantech' is now heard in corporate boardrooms, legislative forums and broadcast news reports around the globe. It has entered into the worlds of private equity, corporate venture and public markets."[38]

For years, Hazel Henderson, a Fellow of the World Business Academy and a well-known analyst of both development policy and economics, has been advocating the incorporation of social and environmental costs into the way economists evaluate companies and countries. For example, Gross Domestic Product does not account for unpaid services, infrastructure or environmental costs. Applying these concepts, Henderson coordinated an interdisciplinary team of researchers and investment advisors that developed the first social-environmental index, the Calvert-Henderson Quality of Life Indicators. First published in 2000, these indicators make a major contribution to "the worldwide effort to develop comprehensive statistics of national well-being that go beyond traditional macroeconomic indicators."[39]

Wall Street has picked up on this trend. Goldman Sachs, a leading investment banking firm, developed the Goldman Sachs Energy Environment and Social Index. According to Goldman, companies that qualify for the index generally outperform peer companies by 24%. A company's environmental and social policies and practices, Goldman believes, "serve as a proxy for good management."[40]

Successful Internet entrepreneurs and venture capitalists are also looking to cash in on Cleantech / Green-tech opportunities. Bill Gates, Paul Allen, Steve Jobs, and Vinod Khosla have each pumped over $50 million into renewable energy firms. If these venture investments create fast-growing alternative energy companies that are profitable enough to attract major institutional investment, the industry will finally be able to fulfill its promise of challenging the currently dominant fossil fuel industry. This is a *very* tall mountain to climb, but none of the aforesaid gentleman have previously been daunted by entrenched industry forces—nor have they often failed to bring about massive change when they marshaled their formidable financial resources alongside their intellectual commitment.

## The National Political Winds Change and Congress Wakes Up

The November 2006 elections may or may not portend the end of Congress' decade-long practice of ceding all energy and environmental leadership to the states. In short order, the new Congress declared its bipartisan resolve to tackle energy and climate change issues. The results have been mixed.

In mid-January 2007, the House voted 264-163 to eliminate about $14 billion in federal subsidies and tax breaks for oil and gas companies, and to funnel the money to renewable energy projects. The legislation was the final piece in the "first 100 hours" agenda pushed by Speaker Nancy Pelosi (D-Calif.). To keep up the tempo, the Speaker asked House committees to produce global warming legislation by July 4, 2007. That deadline later slipped away.

The Speaker tried to circumvent obstacles to climate change bills by establishing a new Select Committee to prepare a package on energy independence and global warming. The genesis of the new committee was widely perceived as a desire to by-pass Congressman John Dingell (D-Mich.), an auto industry ally and chair of the House Energy and Commerce Committee, who had been expected to oppose new limits on auto emissions and other global warming initiatives. Congressman Dingell has held numerous hearings on new automibile efficiency standards and other carbon measures.[41] The auto industry opposes stricter fuel efficiency standards and wants to stay in front of any new carbon-capping legislation, insisting that any caps apply to all sectors of the economy.

The call for action on climate change was not confined to the House. Senator Barbara Boxer (D-Calif.), the new chair of the Senate Environment and Public Works Committee, has called global warming "the greatest challenge of our generation." She succeeded James Inhofe (R-Okla.) as chair, who famously called global warming "the greatest hoax ever perpetrated on mankind" and the scientists who warned of it "Chicken Little types." Senator Inhofe, now the top Republican on the committee, has vowed to block any bills that require mandatory cuts in greenhouse gas emissions. The 60 votes necessary to dislodge any bill he blocked would require nine Republican votes. Despite his vow, bipartisan coalitions continued to form around energy and global warming bills.

By the time Congress departed for its August 2007 recess, the Senate and House had adopted sharply differing energy bills which were each as notable for what was omitted as for what was included.

The Senate, but not the House, approved the first significant increase in automobile efficiency standards in 30 years. In the face of opposition to tighter automobile fuel efficiency standards from automakers and a group led by Congressman Dingell, the Speaker beat a tactical retreat and postponed a vote on the issue.

The Senate had its own difficulty standing up to automakers. It could not muster the political will to include a provision requiring a 4% annual increase in mileage standards—about 1 mile per gallon per year. A bill introduced by a bipartisan group of senators would have required such an increase.[42]

The Senate's new Corporate Average Fuel Economy standards are laced with loopholes. The Senate bill would require the Administration to study replacing the present standards with a flex-ible, fleetwide average target of 35 mpg by 2020. The new stan-dards' attribute-based approach would create different targets for different size vehicles. The Administration could lower the new standards if it determined that they were not "cost effective"—essen-tially, too expensive for American auto manufacturers who too often would rather lose market share than invest in the innovation neces-sary to compete with foreign automakers. This loophole must be eliminated in conference committee. As Thomas L. Friedman says, there should be "no more assisted suicide of the U.S. auto industry by the U.S. Congress."[43]

> *"We can't keep buying oil from countries that use the profits to shoot bullets back at us."*
> — SENATOR GORDON SMITH, R.-ORE

The House and Senate also differed on a renewable electricity mandate. The House, but not the Senate, adopted a new renewable energy standard requiring utilities to obtain or produce at least 15% of their power from a combination of energy efficiency measures and renewable resources such as wind, solar, and biomass.

A host of contentious issues must be resolved in conference committee: continued financial support for the mature fossil fuel and nuclear industries, including tax breaks, incentives for oil and

gas drilling, and loan guarantees for new nuclear plants;
protection of the Arctic
National Wildlife Refuge
from drilling; incentives for
producers and distributors of
biofuels; increased ethanol
fuel-blending requirements;
and other incentives for

> *"It's now going to be a multi-dimensional chess game with the planet's future in the balance."*
> — REP. EDWARD MARKEY, CHAIR, HOUSE SELECT COMMITTEE ON ENERGY INDEPENDENCE AND GLOBAL WARMING

producers and consumers of renewable energy. There will have
to be some heavy lifting in conference committee if Congress is
going to be a force in meeting the nation's intertwined energy and
climate change challenges. The House and Senate have yet to tackle
the need to limit carbon dioxide emissions by adopting either a
cap-and-trade system or a carbon tax.

In light of the number of global warming and energy bills
pending in Congress, we do not make any attempt here to summarize all the relevant ones. As a Clean Air Watch representative wrote
in January 2007, "It is becoming nearly a full-time job just tracking
various global warming plans in our nation's capitol."[44] The same
could be said for energy bills.

Whether Congress succeeds in enacting meaningful energy
and global warming legislation remains to be seen. Time will tell
whether Congress will be ready any time soon to grab the energy
leadership mantle that state and local leaders have long assumed.
One thing seems certain: a growing public demand for change and an
unprecedented alliance of concerned stakeholders—U.S. businesses,
environmental organizations, and faith-based organizations—will
stiffen Congressional resolve.

We strongly urge, as a matter of economic sanity and national
security, that the Prometheus Plan be immediately debated and
adopted as a roadmap for achieving energy independence in less than
10 years. By fully implementing the Prometheus Plan, the United
States would take a major stride toward reducing oil consumption
and dependence on foreign oil, and would start to slow the rate

of increased global warming. The Prometheus Plan would lay the foundation for the sustainable and climate-friendly energy system of the future while simultaneously protecting our economy, our environment, and our national security throughout the 21st century.

In essence the Prometheus Plan is about switching *profitably* from scarcity-driven fossil fuel consumption that is destroying our home planet, to a future of renewable abundant energy that powers the rest of the universe. It will propel our global economy indefinitely into the future, and it will do so by providing a means for all nations, rich and poor alike, to access the energy they so vitally need for growth and development. When you look at it that way, moving ahead with the Prometheus Plan presents the opportunity to end our current self-destructive behavior, and instead generate untold riches as we co-create an abundant global energy economy. By embracing the inexhaustible and renewable gifts Mother Nature offers us, we can restore the Garden of Eden that pervaded this beautiful planet when we first began our human journey.

## Notes and References
## Chapter 13: Corporate, State, and Local Initiatives Lead the Way

1  http://environmentaldefense.org/article.cfm?contentID=5828.

2  http://www.ceres.org/news/pf.php?nid=267.

3  http://www.ceres.org/news/pf.php?nid=276.

4  Gunther, Mark, "The Green Machine," *Fortune Magazine*, July 26, 2006.

5  James Covert, "Wal-Mart Exceeds Fuel-Efficiency Goals," *Wall Street Journal*, April 20, 2006.

6  Gunther, Mark, "Can Wal-Mart Save Seafood?" CNNMoney.com, July, 31st, 2006.

7  Amanda Griscomm Little, "G.E.'s Green Gamble," *Vanity Fair*, August 2006.

8  "DuPont, BP join to make butanol; they say it outperforms ethanol as a fuel additive," *USA Today*, June 23, 2006.

9  http://www.embraer.com.br/institucional/download/2_015-Com-VPI-1000th_Ipanema_Delivery-I-05.pdf

10 See "Interface's Ray Anderson: Mid-Course Correction," *Global Reconstruction*, World Business Academy, June 2, 2005. This section on Interface is in part adapted from the information in this article.

11 Jeff Hutner, "Ray Anderson: A Passion for Sustainability," *Perspectives*, World Business Academy, 14:3, 2000. Hutner's profile is adapted from Ray Anderson's book *Mid-Course Correction: Toward a Sustainable Enterprise—The Interface Model*, (White River Jct., VT, Chelsea Green, 1998).

12 Sudjic, Dusan. (06/21/2006) "Making Cities Work: China" *BBC News*, http://news.bbc.co.uk/2/hi/asia-pacific/5084852.stm.

13 Pew Center on Global Climate Change, "Learning from State Action on Climate Change," March 2007 update, www.pewclimate.org.

14 "Ruling Undermines Lawsuits Opposing Emissions Controls," New York Times, April 3, 2007.

15 Massachusetts v. Environmental Protection Agency, No. 05-1120, April 2, 2007.

16 A similar cap-and-trade system was put into place by the United States Congress in response to concerns about acid rain in the late 1980s. The Clean Air Act of 1990 established a cap-and-trade system which has been a bipartisan success story. It is projected that sulfur dioxide emission levels will be reduced by 50% from 1980 to 2010. (http://www.epa.gov/air/urbanair/so2/effrt1.html).

17 "PG & E Add Fuel-Cell Vehicles to Fleet," http://www.greencarcongress.com/2006/02/pge_adds_three_.html#more.

18 "About the California Initiative," http://www.cpuc.ca.gov/static/energy/solar/aboutsolar.htm.

19 A Stirling Engine, mounted at the focal point of a parabolic dish, converts heat into mechanical energy, by way of expanding hydrogen gas which pushes a piston which generates electricity. One advantage of this form of solar energy is that silicon, an expensive and necessary material for photovoltaic cells, is not needed.

20 Catherine Lacoursiere, InvestorIdeas.com, "Silicon Shortage Drives Global Solar M&A," February 16, 2006, http://www.renewableenergystocks.com/CL/News/Silicon_Shortage.asp.

21 "Hydrogen Power: Carson Hydrogen Power Plant," http://www.bpalternativenergy.com/liveassets/bp_internet/alternativenergy/next_generation_hydrogen_carson.html.

22 "California, Taking Big Gamble, Tries to Curb Greenhouse Gases," *New York Times,* September 15, 2006.

23 For data on Hawaii's petroleum supply, see U.S. Energy Information Administration, Petroleum Profile, Hawaii, released October 2006.

24 "Hawai'i has fuel to power energy revolution," *Honolulu Advertiser,* November 14, 2006.

25 "Banks are Urged Not to Finance Coal Power,"*Boston Globe,* January 16, 2007, www.boston.com/news/nation/washington/articles/2007/01/16/.

26 Hawaiian Electric Company, "Renewable Energy Sources," www.hawaiisenergyfuture.com. With a total installed generating capacity of approximately 1,700 MW, this projection of 500 MW of future renewable energy represents a significant commitment.

27 State of Hawaii, "Hawaii Biofuels Summit: Briefing Book," August 8, 2006.

28 For information on ICLEI's Cities for Climate Protection projects, see www. iclei.org.

29 Paul Mackie, "Global warming gets a closer look in Miami-Dade County," County News, National Association of Counties, March 1, 2004, http:// www.naco.org/CountyNewsTemplate.cfm?template=/ContentManagement/ ContentDisplay.cfm&ContentID=11405.

30 Paul Mackie, *op. cit.*

31 "In New Hampshire, Towns Put Climate on the Agenda," *New York Times*, March 19, 2007.

32 "A '60s Legend Points the Way, Again," *New York Times*, March 18, 2007.

33 *Ibid.*

34 "The Environmental Case for Wind Power in New Jersey," http://www.njpirg. org/NJ.asp?id2=16596&id3=NJ&

35 For additional information on the King County plan see www.metrokc.gov/ earthlegacy and for Multnomah County, see www.newrules.org/electricity/ climateportland.html.

36 "Biodiesel Powers Up on Financing," *Wall Street Journal*, February 21, 2007.

37 http://arstechnica.com/news.ars/post/20070606-clean-tech-investments-pull-in-10-percent-of-us-venture-capital.html

38 *Ibid.*, 3.

39 See Calvert-Henderson Quality of Life Indicators, www.calvert-henderson. com.

40 *Goldman Sachs Environmental Policy*, http://www2.goldmansachs.com/our_ firm/our_culture/corporate_citizenship/environmental_policy_framework/ index.html.

41 "Changing Mood on Carbon Caps," *Council on Foreign Relations*, Daily Analysis, March 21, 2007; "Congress Tackles Global Warming," *The Washington Times*, February 12, 2007; "Taming Fossil Fuels," *New York Times*, March 17, 2007.

42  The co-sponsors of the bill for the Fuel Economy Reform Act of 2007 were Senators Barack Obama (D-Ill.), Richard Lugar (R-Ind.), Joseph Biden (D-Del.), Gordon Smith (R-Ore.), Arlen Specter (R-Pa.), Jeff Bingaman (D-N. Mex.), and Norm Coleman (R-Minn.). Despite opposition from Detroit auto-makers, the bill's supporters said that there was no reason—technological, economic or otherwise—that these new regulations could not be enforced. Press release, "Senators Reintroduce Initiative to Reduce Gasoline Consumption by Half a Trillion Gallons," March 5, 2007, http://obama.senate.gov/press/070305.

43  Thomas L. Friedman, "Capitol creates its own energy crisis," *New York Times,* June 24, 2007.

44  Jessica Holzer, "Global warming becomes hot topic on Capitol Hill," January 18, 2007, http://thehill.com/index2php?option=com_contents&task=view&id=61668&pop.

# 14

## Epilogue: An Urgent Appeal to a Few Courageous Leaders and to the Public At Large

*"America is great because she is good. If America ever stops being good, she will stop being great."*

- Alexis de Tocqueville

Ladies and Gentlemen:

America needs your leadership now, more than ever before. The energy-security and climate-change challenges before us are both national and global issues. We could rightfully say they are *crises*, and you can be absolutely sure that time is of the essence to save us from the bitter consequences. The Chinese taught us ages ago that the word *"crisis"* embodies the simultaneous elements of *challenge* and *opportunity*. So *what is this challenge, and what is the opportunity?*

Our words at times may seem harsh and harrowing, but they are a measure of the challenge before us, and they are meant to get your undivided and serious attention, as now is not a time to equivocate. The issues we have analyzed and presented within the pages of this text are crises which have been building for a long time. Unfortunately, the time necessary to rectify and reverse what is now quietly unfolding is very short. We must begin at once.

Please understand that America and the rest of the world face the greatest challenge that has confronted our civilization. Ironically, we also face the greatest opportunity to build a better world—a world blessed with more peace and prosperity than we have ever known. We can build this world with American leadership, but not without it. It is absolutely necessary for America to show the way. It will not be easy, and it will require your highest levels of courage and leadership, but then again, when has any magnificent opportunity materialized without immense challenge and diligent, hard work? So how serious is our challenge?

Confronting the threat to its national security posed by the inescapable energy and climate crisis of the 21st century, America stands at a pivotal crossroads in world history. Apart from the possibility of a "nuclear winter" or an asteroid impact, human civilization has never before faced the possible outcomes now predicted by an overwhelming majority of the world's 2,000 top climate scientists. Catastrophic global climate change scenarios, unlike an asteroid impact, are not remote possibilities. If we do not act now, some or all of these scenarios will be inevitable. Unless we begin to function in a sustainable manner *now*, hundreds of millions of us are at serious risk—a hurricane named Katrina hitting New Orleans will be but a trivial footnote in such a future.

Climate change is occurring every second of every day. It is simply a matter of how significant we allow it to become. Scientists now know with certainty that left unchanged, our current trajectory will immensely diminish our way of life. If we continue with "business as usual," that trajectory will not change. We will pass a so-called "tipping point," a point of no return, beyond which global warming will irreversibly spiral and accelerate in ways not seen on this planet for more than 55 million years. We then will face the incredibly difficult task of rebuilding civilization essentially without the great coastal cities of New York, London, Washington, and many others.

We face a bleak future in a perilous world unless we liberate ourselves from our fossil fuel addiction. Price shocks and supply disruptions will strike our Achilles heel of oil dependency, leaving our society progressively weaker and deeply vulnerable.

Without hyperbole or exaggeration, our continued dependence on oil and other fossil fuels will burden us and future generations with economic chaos and global unrest. The price for doing the wrong thing, or nothing—as we have until now—by far exceeds the cost of changing our course *today*.

Faced with record high oil prices, terrorism, Middle East instability, melting ice caps, and rising sea levels, we have a once-in-a-lifetime opportunity to set this great nation—and by our example and leadership, the rest of the international community—on a firm path towards an affordable, clean and sustainable energy future. If we do this correctly, we can enhance our global economy, increase the number of quality jobs, and make significant progress in eliminating global poverty. Make no mistake; there will be some economic discontinuities, just as there were when we progressed to the telephone, to the automobile, to television, and to computers. But just as with those earlier technological jumps, the transformation from fossil fuels to renewables, properly executed, will yield a stronger, more robust global economy with many more opportunities for many more people.

Several times in the past century, each time led by a handful of visionary men and women, America marshaled its vast resources and indefatigable political will in responding to Herculean challenges such as the Great Depression, World War II, the creation and implementation of the Marshall Plan, and the stresses of the Cold War. To move the U.S. away from an oil economy, we must recognize that we face an even more significant challenge, and once again we must marshal our vast resources and political will to this common purpose. It will require monumental national, and ultimately, global commitment.

In this book, we have asked one of the central questions of our generation: *Can the U.S. save five million barrels of oil by 2015, the equivalent of all projected Middle Eastern oil imports, with (i) current technology, (ii) no new taxes, and (iii) significantly decreased greenhouse gas emissions?* Our answer is a resounding *"yes."* The Prometheus

Plan offers a specific realistic strategy for dramatically reducing U.S. oil consumption in 10 years, while establishing the basis for even deeper savings by 2025, and ultimately a global transition to a fossil-fuel-free hydrogen economy. We are convinced that hydrogen will ultimately power planet Earth just as it has powered the entire universe almost since the beginning of time. The outline of how this will happen has already become clear.

Equally clear, however, is that conversion to hydrogen will take time, perhaps a couple of decades—precious time that we cannot lose because of the speed with which we are approaching a "tipping point." To arrive safely on the shores of an energy-abundant hydrogen economy two decades from now, we must set off in life boats powered by clean, sustainable and renewable energy, *today*. There truly is no time to waste.

Climate change momentum is like a heavily loaded freight train. It starts slowly, but once moving, even at a modest pace, it is very difficult to stop and reverse. And, this train is barreling downhill with no brakes! Indeed, because of the damage we have already done to our biosphere, some scientists fear that hundreds of millions of us may perish, and 25% *or more* of our total global wealth may be lost before environmental stability can be restored—even if we start today.

The amount of pain humanity will suffer in this transition is directly related to: (a) the wisdom of our energy choices from this moment forward, (b) the speed with which we implement new energy solutions, and (c) the comprehensive nature of the various interrelated steps we take to unravel the impact of global warming while building our global renewable energy economy. All of these steps must occur against the backdrop of a deteriorating global economy, and the unfortunate impact of increasing climate change, such as the savage storms served up by Mother Nature that increasingly wrack the surface of our planet.

And we best not be lulled by false signs of peace and tranquility such as a year of only modest energy-intensive hurricanes in the Caribbean and the Gulf of Mexico, or a temporary drop in oil prices. These fluctuations are false prophets, the product of complex systems that inevitably experience variations on their way to their next stage. You will recall the significant progress that the U.S. made in energy conservation after the 1973 and 1978 Arab oil embargoes, only to be lost a decade later as we built less energy-efficient automobiles, factories and buildings. We can not afford a replay of that scenario. There will be no second chance this time.

On behalf of the Energy Task Force of the World Business Academy, we offer the Prometheus Plan to those of you who are willing to exercise your courageous leadership and political will, for which this extraordinary nation and the world so deeply yearn. We appeal to you to implement this plan, a thoroughly researched white paper, as the capstone of America's energy policy and to educate the public about the merits of this plan.

Our strategy requires no new technology to completely eliminate America's need to import Middle Eastern oil by 2015. Based on technical and economic analyses, we conclude that renewable energy, combined with high levels of energy efficiency, is a practical and economically viable alternative to fossil fuels. And in the long run—beginning during the next two decades—we see our great nation and the rest of the world moving to a hydrogen economy, an economy that is clean, safe, and sustainable into the indefinite future.

In fact, there are no physical or practical limits that would prevent renewable energy and hydrogen from providing most of the world's energy. The critical element that will make or break this achievement is our political will as embodied in corporate and governmental policies—which is why the world needs you now.

A summary of the key policy recommendations essential to implementing the Prometheus Plan follows:

## 1.  Protect Energy Security

- Establish a national bipartisan commitment to save five million barrels of oil a day by 2015 and 15 million barrels of oil a day by 2025, and to initiate the rapid transition, through the interim use of renewables and new electricity storage technologies, to a hydrogen economy.

- Build a broad consensus in support of this commitment, including business and consumers, automakers and unions, farmers and environmentalists, military and scientists—and all Americans who understand that the transition to renewable energy is essential to the national security of our country and the security of our world.

- Set up an independent national commission, chaired by the World Business Academy or some other respected, non-partisan, competent institution, to review the implications of the Prometheus Plan and to determine the best technologies, policies, and financial mechanisms for implementing it.

- Establish the Office of the Director of Energy and Climate Security charged with the task of rapidly converting U.S. energy consumption to domestically produced renewable energy resources—specifically excluding coal and nuclear. This office must have the authority to coordinate all programs related to energy security, including those impacting agriculture, commerce, transportation, treasury, and national defense.

## 2. Increase Automobile and Energy Efficiency

The transportation sector can have the most significant and immediate impact on energy efficiency.

- In stages over the next 10 years, raise federal fuel economy (CAFE) standards for new cars and light trucks to 40 miles per gallon.

- Evaluate and implement the best incentives for increasing fleet efficiency, including consumer feebates, low income scrap-and-replacement programs, smart government fleet procurement, and rewards for major technological advances.

- Accelerate oil savings in motor vehicles by requiring replacement tires and motor oil to be at least as efficient as original equipment tires and motor oil.

- Require state-of-the-art efficiency improvements for heavy-duty trucks.

- Implement cost-effective oil savings in the industrial, residential and aviation sectors, including the replacement of petrochemical products with bio-products, e.g., biopolymers.

### 3. Accelerate the Development of Biofuels

- Increase the supply of renewable fuels by expanding the current federal Renewable Fuels Standard (RFS) to require 28.4 billion gallons annually of ethanol and biodiesel by 2015, and require policies that protect air, soil and water quality.

- Allocate *at least* $3 billion or more of existing research funds each year to the development and deployment of commercially viable renewable fuels, including biodiesel from algae, ocean current technology, energy storage improvements by way of batteries or other means, demonstration of commercially economical hydrogen production by water electrolysis from renewable energy sources, and the development of advanced materials and nanotechnology to accelerate the switch from fossil fuels.

- Allocate *at least* $1 billion or more of existing research funds each year to R&D, demonstration and deployment of the first 5 billion gallons of cellulosic ethanol plant capacity.[1]

- Require that all new cars and trucks be "flex-fuel" vehicles, capable of operating on either gasoline or biofuels such as ethanol.

- Use the Environmental Protection Agency's authority over air quality to ban the licensing of any new power plant that will cause an increase in greenhouse gases.

### 4. Initiate Transition to the Hydrogen Economy

- Convene a National Hydrogen Task Force to design the Strategic Hydrogen Alliance Reform and Enterprise Act

(SHARE), creating the statutory framework for accelerating the transition to a hydrogen economy as quickly as possible.[2]

- Deploy existing hydrogen technologies to achieve initial commercialization of direct burn hydrogen internal combustion engines, hydrogen fuel cell cars and plug-in hybrid/ hydrogen fuel cell cars by 2010 to 2015.

- Provide an incentive to automotive companies to manufacture light-weight cars made from strong fiber-reinforced advanced materials. This not only enhances mileage, but provides a more effective vehicle for hydrogen fuel-cell power.

- Following California's example, develop a local and national hydrogen infrastructure to achieve widespread commercialization of stationary and mobile hydrogen fuel cells by 2015 to 2020, including minimum sales of one million hydrogen fuel cell vehicles.

- Provide U.S. leadership for an International Hydrogen Innovation Fund, initially capitalized with $5 billion from multinational private and public sources to underwrite innovative early, middle, and late-stage hydrogen projects.

## 5.  Ensure Reliable Energy Supplies

- Adopt a national Renewable Energy Standard of 20% by 2020.

- Move away from existing tax incentives for oil and other fossil fuel production (including production and depletion tax credits), and move toward renewable energy incentives for all environmentally acceptable alternative energy sources.

- Reduce barriers to siting and operating necessary energy infrastructure, especially for the generation and transmission of distributed and/or renewable resources used in powering plug-in hybrid vehicles and hydrogen-generating natural gas reformers.

- Adopt policies which favor and encourage the development and commercialization of distributed power generation, using fuel cells, micro-turbines, solar and wind systems, etc.

- Require utilities to develop a plan to upgrade the national power grid so it can be operated on a "distributed generation, distributed use" basis which can provide a means of accessing excess consumer-generated power and moving distributed power when necessary.

6. **Prometheus Plan Funding and the Reduction of Global Warming**

- Have the United States become a signatory to the Kyoto Protocol and engage in upcoming discussions under the United Nations Framework Convention on Climate Change to agree on post-Kyoto Protocol cuts in greenhouse gases, including carbon dioxide ($CO_2$).

- At a minimum, establish a mandatory, nationwide cap and trade program to limit greenhouse gases, based on economically viable initial costs per metric-ton of $CO_2$-equivalent reductions—or even better, establish a "cap and no trade" program.

- To achieve revenue neutrality, adopt a strategy proposed by the bipartisan National Commission on Energy Policy, and fund the implementation of the Prometheus Plan recommendations over the next decade through the sale of a portion of emission allowance permits, along with re-allocation of existing government R&D funds.[3]

The Prometheus Plan recommendations require no new taxes and are revenue-positive; they will take dollars now spent in wasteful and environmentally destructive ways and redirect a tiny fraction of those funds to create our future energy infrastructure. The transition from fossil fuels to a renewable energy economy is a massive and already highly-profitable undertaking that private enterprise should continue to lead.

Unfortunately, as many studies have documented, including one funded by the Pentagon, too often the current federal energy policy framework is "indifferent, inconsistent, rife with distortions and scarcely focused on accelerating fundamental innovations."[4] Since the Prometheus Plan provides significant benefits to all Americans, the appropriate role of government is to facilitate this long-term energy transition, something that individual companies focused on short-term financial gains are ill-suited to do.

In this capacity, government can accelerate the transition, reduce economic risks, and ensure success by:

- Reducing the risk of retooling and retraining in the auto industry and other selected industries.

- Supporting R&D in efficiency, biofuels, battery storage technology, renewables and the hydrogen economy.

- Creating incentives for consumer purchases of high quality, high performance *and* high efficiency vehicles within a framework of freedom of choice.

- Supporting private investment in domestic and international renewable energy supplies and infrastructure.

By fully implementing the Prometheus Plan, the United States can significantly reduce oil consumption, slow and eventually reverse global warming, and lay the foundation for a sustainable and climate-friendly energy system that will stimulate our economy, protect our environment and begin rebuilding our national security throughout the 21st century and beyond.

## Yes We Can

Some who read these words will bemoan the possibility that America cannot change its "fuelish" ways in time. The World Business Academy, whose desire to help America equals its sincere concern for all nations, is ever mindful of the enormous productive capacity America has shown when it sets its mind to accomplish an objective that it knows, deep within its soul, it must achieve.

Solving the energy and climate challenge is such an objective. It must be, and will be, accomplished. During the darkest days of the Battle of Britain, when that island-nation lay in ruins from constant Nazi bombardment, Winston Churchill was asked if England and its allies could possibly triumph. He responded, "The opposite conclusion is unthinkable."

So too it is with the energy and climate change challenge. We will triumph simply because we must. We have only one planet, Mother Earth, so we must ensure that it is here as a safe nest as we grow older, depart, and leave a legacy of hope and prosperity for our children and our children's children. Think about your response to your children and grandchildren when a decade or so from now they ask you, "What did you do to help save our civilization from itself?"

Quite frankly, there is no alternative. On behalf of a nation hungry for values-based leadership, it is your opportunity and your duty to use your fullest efforts to minimize the pain inherent in the transition we must make. We are passing, ever so swiftly, from the Fossil Fuel Era to the Age of Abundant Renewables that can restore our biosphere. Our great nation is struggling with a violent addiction. Please demonstrate for our country and as stewards for the planet, that you have sworn off fossil fuel dependency and that you have the courage and political will to change the things that you must.

The future of humanity rests in your hands.

Sincerely yours,


Jerry B. Brown, Ph.D.
Rinaldo S. Brutoco, J.D.
James A. Cusumano, Ph.D.

# Notes and References
## Chapter 14: Epilogue

1. For program details, see Nathanael Greene, *Growing Energy: How Biofuels Can Help End America's Oil Dependence* (Washington, D.C.: Natural Resources Defense Council, December 2004).

2  Julian Gresser, and James A. Cusumano, "Hydrogen and the New Energy Economy: A Sensible Plan for the Next Administration," Project Earthrise— Energy Task Force, World Business Academy, Volume 18, No. 2, October 7, 2004.

3  The National Commission on Energy Policy, "Summary of Recommendations," *Ending the Energy Stalemate: A Bipartisan Strategy to Meet America's Energy Challenges*, Washington, D.C., December 2004, 8.

4  Amory Lovins *et al.*, *Winning the Oil Endgame* (Snow Mass, CO: Rocky Mountain Institute, 2005) 169.

# INDEX

demand. *See* supply/demand issues

deMenocal, Peter, 120

Demeter, 343

dengue fever, 139–140

Denmark, 372

Detroit. *See* automobile industry

Detroit Arsenal Tank Plan, 277–278

deuterium-tritium isotopes, 184

Diamond, Jared, *Collapse,* 120

Dias, Rosana, 448

dichlorotrifluoroethane, 121, 122

Diesel, Rudolf, 263

diesel-combustion vehicles (DCVs), 260

diesel engines, 301, 303, 306, 309, 384

diesel fuel, 214, 256, 323, 409. *See also* trucks/truck fuels

Dingell, John, 474, 475

dipole moment, 111

dirty bombs, 187

*Discover,* 359–361

distillate fuel oil, 256

Diversa, 348–349

dollar (USD), 231–232, 233–234

Dominion Resources, 162

Dorgan, Bryon, 29

Dorsch, Gary, 226–227

Drake, Edwin L., 50

drilling. *See* oil drilling

droughts, 137–138

DuPont, 327, 448

**E**

Earth Day, 454

Earth Legacy Initiative (King County, Washington), 471

Earth Policy Institute, 11, 201

E3 Biofuels LLC, 332–333, 384

eco-cities, 451–452

Ecomagination program (GE), 442–447

*Econ-Forecast,* 225–226, 227–228

economic implications of oil dependency, 34–36, 47, 62

economic security, 56–57

E85 pumps, 347, 348

E2 (Environmental Entrepreneurs), 472

*Effectiveness and Impact of Corporate Average Fuel Economy (CAFE) Standards,* 293. *See also* CAFE (Corporate Average Fuel Economy) standards

"Effects of Oil Shale Waste Disposal on Soil and Water Quality," 211

efficiency dividends, 294

efficiency measures/issues

  aerodynamics for fuel efficiency, 309

  American Council for an Energy-Efficient Economy, 295

  automobile and truck efficiency, 15, 22, 23, 259–261, 269, 488

  comparisons, 415–417, 418, 422–424

  energy efficiency (generally), 28, 369, 390–391, 488

  fuel efficiency (*See* fuel efficiency)

  fuel-efficient tires, 307–308

  hydrogen power, 409, 415–417, 418, 422–424

  renewable energy, 390–391

  standards (*See* standards)

  studies, 259, 308

  Toyota's well-to-wheels efficiency, 417

  Wal-Mart's, 308–311, 442–444

EGS (enhanced geothermal systems), 375–377

Egypt, 79–80, 128

EIA (Energy Information Administration), 47, 296

electricity
from biomass, 319
Brazilian sugar mills, 332
California pricing policies, 459
generation of, 164, 165, 170, 197–198, 377, 408–409
irregular power sources, 367–368
price of wind-powered, 373
reduction of demand in U.S., 390–391
renewable energy-fed electric grids, 263
U.S. power crisis, 391–393
Electric Power Research Institute, 265
electric utilities, 366
Electric Utility Cost Group, 170
electrolysis technology, 405, 418–419
Emanuel, Kerry, 134
embargoes
Arab, 58–59, 63, 227
OPEC, 58, 79–80, 232, 293
threatened, 83
Venezuelan, 16
by Yamani, 76
Embraer, 332, 448
emissions. *See also by name of specific gas or toxin, e.g.,* carbon dioxide; carbon sequestration (capture)
baseline, 146
California emissions regulations, 439
capping, 143–148
carcinogenic, 201, 211
from coal-fired plants, 319
indirect, 173
market-based mechanisms for reduction, 143–145
opposition to lowering fuel emissions, 301
permits for, 143

radioactive, 175–182
reducing, 146–148, 166–169, 318, 393–394
regulatory issues, 147–148, 365, 439
safety valve mechanisms, 143
studies, 173, 174, 393
taxes, 143–145, 370
tradable emissions permits, 143–145
zero-emissions coal power, 204
Zero Emissions Vehicles (ZEVs), 301
emissions trading systems, 143–145, 370. *See also* cap-and-trade
emission-trading scheme (ETS), 147
*Empire of Debt*, 232–233
*End of Oil, The*, 9–10, 293, 410
energy abundance
blueprints for, 249–251
investing in, 271–273, 276–277
energy as weapon, 53
energy bills, Senate and House, 474–475
energy consumption, 15, 41, 366–367, 371, 390. *See also* oil consumption
Energy Crisis Simulation games, 72, 74–75
energy efficiency, 28, 369, 390–391, 488
Energy employees Occupational Illness Compensation Act, 176
energy futures studies, 11
energy independence
cost of achieving, 273
declaring, 252
future of, 3
meaning of, 352
Project Energy Independence, 165
Energy Information Administration (EIA), 47, 296

504

hypothetical crisis scenarios, 229
liquefied natural gas (LNG), 392
nuclear power, 174
odds of near-future terror attacks, 70–71
oil prices, 17, 48

# G

Gadaffi, Muammar al-, 79
GAO (Government Accounting Office), 231
garbage to energy plan, 465
Gardner, Gary, 94
gas composition analysis, 105
gasoline
    ethanol compared to, 341–345
    oil savings as consequence of saving, 254–256
    prices, 46, 57, 83, 214, 232, 293–294, 345, 470
    safety of, 414
    service stations, 323, 348
gas turbines, 392
Gates, Bill, 473
Gay & Robinson, 463–464
Gazprom, 82
GDP
    automobile and oil company revenues, 289–290
    China's, 49, 55, 198
    consumer economy and, 228
    global, 273, 289–290, 293
    India's, 49, 55, 198
    U.S., 13, 15, 63, 94, 103, 293
GE (Ecomagination program), 442–447
General Electric (GE), 149, 162, 373, 389
General Motors (GM)

corn to ethanol campaign, 324, 425, 426
Electrovan, 420
financial problems of, 235, 286
fuel cell cars, 422
fuel cell models, 304
statement on hydrogen versus gasoline, 423
genetically modified organisms, 431
geology
    coastlines, 131–132
    oil fields, 59–60
    volcanic eruptions, 135
geopolitical issues
    "Geopolitics of Energy in 2015" conference, 9
    hot spots, 82, 213, 396
    recessions, 81
    security, 57–59
geopolitics
    of oil, 75–76
    of scarcity, 75, 96
geothermal energy, 271, 368, 375–377, 465
Germany, 372, 381
Geysers Field, 376
Ghawar oil field, 59
glaciers, 124–125, 128. *See also* ice sheets
Global OilCo, 25, 275
global warming. *See also* climate change
    carbon dioxide concentrations, 24
    climate change as issue of, 99
    effects of, 393
    ExxonMobil's view on, 48
    global temperature patterns, 106, 107
    greenhouse gases, 31
    melting of permafrost, 5

industrial sector, 22

infectious diseases, 99, 110, 139–140, 361, 393

infrared radiation, 111

Inhofe, James, 474

initiatives

Atlantic City, New Jersey initiative, 471

Boulder, Colorado initiative, 471

Caribbean Basin Initiative nations, 344

Clean Coal Power Initiative, 203

Earth Legacy Initiative (King County, Washington), 471

energy initiatives, 33, 237–239

FutureGen Sequestration and Hydrogen Research Initiative, 203–204

government initiatives, 466–467

Hydrogen Highway Network initiative (California), 455–459

International Council for Local Environmental Initiatives (ICLEI), 467, 468

local, 466–471

New Hampshire initiatives, 470

opposition to initiatives against global warming, 474

Portland, Oregon initiative, 471

Regional Greenhouse Gas Initiative (RGGI), 453

Sonoma County, California initiative, 471

state initiatives, 420, 452–455

U.S. Mayors Climate Protection Agreement, 466–467

Woodstock, New York initiative, 470

Zero Waste to Landfill initiative (Wal-Mart), 443

Institute for the Analysis of Global Security, 11, 248, 249

Integrated Gasification Combined Cycle (IGCC), 202–204

Interface, Inc., 449–451

Intergovernmental Panel on Climate Change (IPCC), 53–54, 55, 108, 115, 123–124, 393

internal combustion engines, 260, 270, 327, 403, 425

internal combustion vehicles (ICVs), 260, 270

International Atomic Energy Agency, 187

International Commission on Radiological Protection, 181

International Council for Local Environmental Initiatives (ICLEI), 467, 468

International Energy Agency, 14, 52, 330

International Thermonuclear Energy Reactor Project, 184

investment banking firms, 46

Investor Network on Climate Risk, 442

investors

in advanced technologies, 271–273

in energy market, 189–190, 212, 344, 348

environmentally responsible, 442

renewable energy technologies market, 275–276, 363, 471–473

returns on investment (ROI), 276–277

iodine isotopes, 175

Iogen, 349, 351

IPCC (Intergovernmental Panel on Climate Change), 53–54, 55, 108, 115, 123–124, 393

Iran

control of oil reserves, 8

current U.S. conflict with, 187, 188

Strategic Hydrogen Alliance Reform and Enterprise Act (SHARE), 430, 431
Supreme Court decisions, 76, 365, 455–456
leukemia, 176–177
Libya, 79, 188
Licht, F. O., 320
life cycle production costs (nuclear power), 170–171
Lingle, Linda, 461
lithium-ion batteries, 374
Livermore Laboratory, 177
*Lives Per Gallon*, 301
LNG (liquefied natural gas)
  explosions, 214–215
  future demand, 392
  origin of global, 63
  preference for, 216
  storing, 214
lobbying campaigns
  fossil fuels, 30
  for nuclear power, 167
local government purchasing power, 466
local initiatives, 470–471. *See also* initiatives
Lockheed Martin, 349–350
Long-range Energy Alternatives Planning System (LEAP), 296
*2006 Long-Term Reliability Assessment*, 391
Lopoukhine, Nikita, 102
Lovins, Amory, 189, 268, 293, 303, 392
  *Twenty Hydrogen Myths*, 411–412
  *Winning the Oil Endgame*, 25
Lula da Silva, Luis Inacio, 261
Lyman, Ed, 183

# M

Maass, Peter, 61–62
Mahdi (Imam), 86
malaria, 139, 140
Manhattan Project, 19, 273, 278
Mann, Horace, 435
manure, 318, 319, 383–384. *See also* methane
Marine Stewardship Council, 444
Mars, 111–112
Marshall Plan, 278
Massachusetts Institute of Technology (MIT), 10, 375–376
*Massachusetts v. Environmental Protection Agency*, 365
mass transit system, U.S., 301
Maui Land and Pineapple, 463
Mauna Loa, Mt., 118–119
Maynard, Micheline, 296
Mayors Climate Protection Agreement, 466–467
Mazda, 425
McCormack, Sean, 84
McGill, Stuart, 47–48
McMahon, Tim, 227–228
megawatts and negawatts, 390–391, 392
mercury, 201–202
methane. *See also* manure
  capture of, 319
  role in climate change, 5, 113–115, 121–122
  current levels, 5, 113–115, 121, 148
  digesters, 320, 334 (*See also* biodigesters)
  heat supplied by, 382–383
  from landfills, 465
  from melting permafrost, 113–114, 126
  problems caused by, 54

# S

solar tax credits, 381
windfall profits tax, 32
Taylor, Jerry, 161
Teller, Edward, 184
Tellus Institute, 295
temperature patterns. *See also* climate
change
changing oceans, 110
global, 106, 107–108, 124, 393
history of, 116
oceans, 110, 134
terrorism/terrorist attacks
in Iraq, 91
nations sponsoring, 57–58
nuclear reactor vulnerability, 174,
186–189
odds of near-future attacks, 70–71
on oil supplies, 16–17, 75
projected global attacks, 70
targets of terrorist groups, 62–64
U.S. policies and, 96
Tesla Motors, 306
Texas Pacific Group, 370
*The Economist,* 363
thermohaline circulation, 129
thorium, 185
Thornburgh, Richard, 165
Three Mile Island, 164, 182
Tibet, 129
tidal power, 271, 388–389
*Time* magazine, 404
*Titanic* analogy, 3–4, 197
Tokyo Gas, 149
tornadoes, 110
Toynbee, Arnold, 247
Toyota, 286, 287, 374, 417, 425
tradable emissions permits, 143–145.
*See also* cap-and-trade

transportation fuels. *See* automobile
industry; aviation industry; gasoline;
trucks/truck fuels
transportation of fuels. *See also*
pipelines
butanol, 448
costs of, 460
hydrogen, 419–420
LNG, 214
percent of U.S. oil use in, 259
transportation sector policies, 253, 256
treaties
Nuclear Non-Proliferation Treaty,
87, 188
Partial Test Ban Treaty, 178
trickle-charge electrolysis plants, 269
*Trimtab Factor, The,* 37
trucks/truck fuels
American Truckers Association,
263
biodiesel fuels, 21
efficiency measures/issues, 15, 22,
23, 259–261, 269, 488, 489
hydrogen fuel cells, 421
vegetable oil fuels, 263, 265
Wal-Mart fleet's efficiency
measures, 443–444
Turner, Ted, 17–18
Tuvalu, 132
TVO (Finland utility company), 168
Twenty in Ten plan, 239
*Twilight in the Desert,* 13–14
TXU buy-out, 370

# U

*UBS Global OilCo 2005* report, 32
UBS (United Bank of Switzerland),
25
"Unexpected Rise in Strontium-90 in
U.S. Deciduous Teeth in the 1990s,"
178–179

# About the Authors

## Jerry B. Brown, Ph.D., Founding Professor, Florida International University

Jerry Brown is a futurist, energy expert, writer and business advisor. As an inspiring communicator and consultant, he has facilitated leading-edge innovations in companies and public interest organizations.

In the 1960s, he coordinated César Chávez's Grape Boycott on behalf of California farm workers. In the 1980s, he worked with Business Executives for National Security, an organization of Fortune 1000 executives that lobbied to prevent nuclear war and end the Cold War. From 1998-2003, Dr. Brown served as a Research Associate with the Radiation and Public Health Project, a national research organization investigating the links between environmental radiation from nuclear power plants and America's cancer crisis.

Dr. Brown is co-author of *Profiles in Power: The Antinuclear Movement and the Dawn of the Solar Age* (1997), which predicted the emerging global shift to renewable energy, and of numerous articles on energy policy and social change. He is a Fellow of the World Business Academy, and a Founding Professor at Florida International University in Miami, where he teaches courses on anthropology, energy policy, social movements, and the impact of technology on society.

Dr. Brown is president of Jerald Brown & Associates, Inc., an international business consulting company, specializing in energy and environmental projects.

A researcher, award-winning teacher and outstanding public speaker for over twenty-five years, Dr. Brown received his undergraduate degree in Philosophy from Antioch College and his doctorate in Anthropology from Cornell University.

On a personal note, Dr. Brown enjoys travel, hiking and song-writing. He and his wife, Julie, have two sons and live in Miami Beach.

## RINALDO S. BRUTOCO, J.D., FOUNDER & PRESIDENT, WORLD BUSINESS ACADEMY

A leading international executive, writer, and keynote speaker for over twenty-five years, Mr. Brutoco is widely recognized as a practical visionary, change agent and futurist. He uniquely combines theory and practice to assist executives and organizations in adapting to change through the analysis and application of "breakthrough" ideas.

An expert in emerging technologies and industries, Mr. Brutoco was co-founder and Chief Operating Officer of the nation's first pay cable television operation, Optical Systems Corporation, as well as founder and Chief Executive Officer of one of the first companies to offer over-the-air television transmissions of major motion pictures, Universal Subscription Television. For 13 years, Mr. Brutoco also served as the Chairman of Logical Data Management, which pioneered distributed data processing transfers.

For sixteen years, from its initial IPO to the present, Mr. Brutoco has served on the board of The Men's Wearhouse, a $2 billion-dollar, New York Stock Exchange company. During that same time period, Mr. Brutoco was founder, CEO and Chairman of the Red Rose Collection, which was named for three consecutive years to INC Magazine's 500 fastest growing privately held companies. Among many other distinctions garnered by the company and its commonly controlled merchant bank, Dorason Corporation, the Red Rose Collection served for the last twelve years of Mother Teresa's life as the sole distributor of her personally endorsed biographical motion picture.

In 1986 Mr. Brutoco founded and currently serves as President and CEO of the World Business Academy, a collaborative network of mindful individuals collectively exploring the leading edge of business, and a pre-eminent publisher of new paradigm business literature. He has also served on numerous non-profit boards, including The Gorbachev Foundation, Institute of Transpersonal Psychology, State of the World Forum, the Center for Earth Concerns, Omega Point Institute and the Brutoco Family Foundation, adding to his ability to transform companies through a multi-disciplinary approach.

In 1999 he formed the ShangriLa Group, a consulting firm and commercial group of companies with numerous investments in various enterprises and commercial real estate. He continues to serve as the Principal and CEO of the ShangriLa Group.

He is the co-author of a book on nuclear energy, *Profiles in Power: The Antinuclear Movement and the Dawn of the Solar Age*, published by Simon & Schuster in 1997, and has been the contributor to, or principal author resource for, several other books including *Winning the Innovation Game* and *New Paradigms in Business*. He has also been the author of numerous articles and a featured speaker at senior-level executive meetings throughout the world for more than two decades.

Mr. Brutoco graduated with majors in both Economics and Philosophy from Santa Clara University, and received a Juris Doctorate, Order of the Coif, from UCLA School of Law in 1971.

Mr. Brutoco enjoys sailing, swimming, scuba diving, organic farming, walking, the simple pleasures of a great conversation, and reading as much as time allows on an extremely broad range of subjects. He and his wife, Lalla Shanna, share three daughters, one son, and two grandchildren as they shuttle between their homes on the Big Island of Hawaii and in Ojai, California.

## JAMES A. CUSUMANO, PH.D.,
### FOUNDER, CATALYTICA, INC.,
### FORMER R&D DIRECTOR, EXXON

James A. Cusumano obtained a B.A. in chemistry and a Ph.D. in physical chemistry from Rutgers University. He studied business at Harvard and Stanford Universities, and is a Fellow of Churchill College at Cambridge University. Following his studies, he joined Exxon Research & Engineering Company where he became Director of Catalytic Research and Development. He and his team worked on fundamental and applied  research projects in petroleum and petrochemical processing, fuel cells, synthetic fuels, and emissions control, which resulted in several $100 million per year in revenues for Exxon.

He left Exxon to found Catalytica, Inc., a public company, which consisted of two business units, Catalytica Energy Systems, Inc. (CESI—NASDAQ), which develops clean energy systems, and Catalytica Pharmaceuticals, Inc., which developed pharmaceutical technologies and manufactured prescription drugs such as AZT, Lanoxin, Wellbutrin, and Zyban, and OTC medications such as Sudafed and Neosporin. Catalytica Pharmaceuticals, Inc. became one of the foremost catalytic technology and manufacturing companies in the world, and was later sold to DSM Pharmaceuticals in Holland, at which time Dr. Cusumano retired as Executive Chairman.

Dr. Cusumano has authored more than 50 papers and holds 20 patents in the areas of energy and environmental sustainability, and has lectured extensively throughout the United States, Europe and Japan. He is an advisor to the Fulbright Scholar Program, and is a founding editor of Applied Catalysis. He serves as President of Cotrugli Business Academy in Zagreb, Croatia (www.CBA. Com.hr).

In June of 2000, he founded a feature film production company, Chateau Wally Films (www.ChateauWallyFilms.Com). As President, CEO and Executive Producer, he produced and marketed his first feature film entitled "What Matters Most," which won numerous awards at international film festivals and is currently distributed in more than 35 countries.

With his wife, Inez, Dr. Cusumano is currently engaged in the operation of Chateau Mcely, a castle located just outside Prague in the Czech Republic (www.ChateauMcely.Com), where it functions as an executive education and retreat center, a 5-STAR luxury hotel, and is home to the School of NeoAlchemy, a not-for-profit foundation. The foundation explores the creation of productive linkages among technology, business and the critical needs of humanity.

On the personal front, Dr. Cusumano enjoys high-altitude mountaineering and the history of alchemy. He is a former recording artist and was a member of a group that sold several million records. He has three daughters and three grandchildren and has homes in Prague and Annapolis.

# ABOUT THE WORLD BUSINESS ACADEMY

The World Business Academy was founded in 1987 as a result of discussions conducted at the Stanford Research Institute (SRI) International in Menlo Park, California, USA. These talks centered upon the role and responsibility of business in relation to the critical moral, environmental and social dilemmas of the day. A small group of senior business executives and academics emerged from these meetings to create a research and education institution, the World Business Academy, to help the global business community understand and participate in the new constructive role of business in society.

Core areas of the Academy's research and work include sustainable business strategies, global reconstruction, the challenge of values-driven leadership, development of the human potential at work, and understanding "best practices" within new business paradigms. All of these concepts, linked together and applied, represent the ongoing work of the Academy in its dialogues, research, publications, meetings, and networking. The Academy provides a collaborative network for cutting-edge business leaders, entrepreneurs, and scholars who are aware of business' seminal role in society. The Academy hosts world-class forums, dialogues, and retreats. It also publishes over 850 pages of content a year on topics of concern to business today and tomorrow. The Academy forms alliances with like-minded businesses and non-profit organizations and periodically delivers research and disseminates knowledge from the world's top thinkers, many of them Academy Fellows.

Throughout the year, the Academy delivers self-learning and educational resources to its sponsors and members, and conducts world research projects and forums in the areas of business consciousness, corporate responsibility, global reconstruction, human potential, and innovative and values-driven leadership. The Academy has extensive archives of published materials on the "new business paradigm" and innovative business practices. It maintains an extensive electronic publications program that regularly distributes timely information under titles that include *Currents in Commerce, Connections, Continuum, EconForecast, Global Reconstruction, Perspectives, Signposts, Common ¢ents* and *Viewpoint.*

In addition to this extensive publications program the Academy has a unique resource in its 100 Academy Fellows who comprise a veritable Who's Who of world-class thinkers. These include Warren Bennis (leadership and management), Lester Brown (global environment), Deepak Chopra (healing and wellness), Steven Covey (author, *The 7 Habits of Highly Effective People*), Hazel Henderson (economic futures), Amory Lovins (energy policy), Michael Ray (creativity in business), John Raisian (Hoover Institution), Peter Senge (business theory), and Margaret Wheatley (business leadership).

For information on the Academy, please see:
**www.worldbusiness.org.**

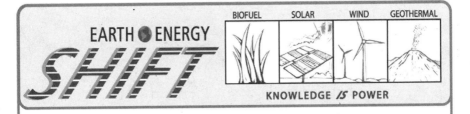

EARTH ● ENERGY
SHIFT

BIOFUEL  SOLAR  WIND  GEOTHERMAL

KNOWLEDGE *IS* POWER

## ABOUT *Earth Energy SHIFT*
*Tomorrow's Energy Solutions Today*

The primary systems that fuel our planet are rapidly shifting. *Earth Energy SHIFT* is a monthly electronic publication that delivers timely news updates and analyses on all the essential economic, technical, energy, national security, climatic, and geopolitical topics originally presented in *Freedom from Mid-East Oil*. Prepared by the World Business Academy editorial staff, *Earth Energy SHIFT* provides the tools for global business to become more competitive in a world where the primary fossil fuel system is literally changing before our eyes.

More than ever, *knowledge is power*. Thoughtful people want an easy way to stay abreast of the fast-paced changes that now occur daily in traditional fossil fuel systems, as well as nuclear power, coal sequestration, sunset and sunrise industries, energy efficiency, plug-in hybrid cars, biofuels, photovoltaics, wind turbines, ocean energy, carbon caps, and the transition to a hydrogen economy.

*Earth Energy SHIFT* will cover all this, and more. It is written in a straightforward way, designed to give busy executives and public policy makers efficient and powerful information to address the critical energy and climate topics of our times.

To subscribe or learn more, please visit:
**www.earthenergyshift.org.**